shut up and
give me the mic

DEE SNIDER

shut up and
give me the mic

⊰ A TWISTED MEMOIR ⊱

GALLERY BOOKS

NEW YORK   LONDON   TORONTO   SYDNEY   NEW DELHI

G

Gallery Books
A Division of Simon & Schuster, Inc.
1230 Avenue of the Americas
New York, NY 10020

First Gallery Books hardcover edition May 2012

GALLERY BOOKS and colophon are registered trademarks of Simon & Schuster, Inc.

For information about special discounts for bulk purchases, please contact Simon & Schuster Special Sales at 1-866-506-1949 or business@simonandschuster.com.

The Simon & Schuster Speakers Bureau can bring authors to your live event. For more information or to book an event, contact the Simon & Schuster Speakers Bureau at 1-866-248-3049 or visit our website at www.simonspeakers.com.

Designed by Jaime Putorti

Manufactured in the United States of America

10 9 8 7 6 5 4 3 2 1

Library of Congress Cataloging-in-Publication Data
Snider, Dee
    Shut up and give me the mic : a twisted memoir / Dee Snider. —1st hardcover ed.
        p.   cm.
    1. Snider, Dee.   2. Rock musicians—United States—Biography.   I. Title.
    ML420.S6728A3 2012
    782.42166092—dc23
    [B]   2012000597

ISBN 978-1-4516-3739-7
ISBN 978-1-4516-3741-0 (ebook)

For Suzette

Your undying and selfless love, support, and devotion helped all my dreams come true. I could never have done it without you . . . and I wouldn't have wanted to.

I love you, forever. . . .

⇥ Forewarned ⇤

ex, drugs, and rock 'n' roll.
People never seem to get tired of hearing about it. I guess that's the great promise (or failure) of rock 'n' roll. Not for me, but for most people. If that's the only thing you're interested in, this ain't the book for you. *Anger, violence, love, and rock 'n' roll is more like it.*

If the only things that float your boat are journals from drug-addled, ex-junkie, sex-addicted rockers, forget it. Those books are bullshit anyway. Have you ever known a junkie? They can't remember what they did thirty minutes ago, let alone thirty years ago. They kept a journal? And you believe them? Real heroin addicts can't hold their own dicks; forget about a pen or pencil. And who isn't addicted to sex? What a scam.

I'm the guy that gave it all to beat the odds, left everything he had on the stage each night, didn't screw around on his woman, took care of his kids, and was sober enough to remember it all and write about it . . . *himself.* The only things clouding my memory are the years and a storyteller's natural tendency to embellish for the better enjoyment of the reader. But no lies.

This is a true story of childish dreams, great struggle, Job-like perseverance, ascension to dazzling heights, megalomaniacal obsession, and a mind-numbing, brutal fall from grace. It's also about an undying love and dedication between a man and a woman that—

though sorely tried—withstood it all. It's *Rocky I, II, III, IV,* and the first half of *V* all rolled into one.

From the vantage point of reinvention and reclamation of my former status, it's almost hard to believe I was ever that far down. *Almost.* The physical and emotional scars of my life-wreck remind me just how truly catastrophic my epic failure was . . . and how I never want to do that again. Hell, if a video of my fall were available on YouTube, it would have like a billion hits. My story should inspire and be a cautionary tale at the same time. I hope.

Though I am best known for being the front man for the seminal eighties hair band Twisted Sister, since my return to grace I have done movies, television, radio, and Broadway, been the national spokesperson for a major charitable organization, and even had a town named after me. No mean feat for a *two*-hit wonder (sorry to disagree with you, VH1) who had been written off as dead and buried by 1987. I know some people out there are *still* scratching their heads at my even being around. And writing a book? Ha! Trust me, I'm self-aware. I'm not sitting here all puffed up on my "amazing" achievements. I don't put much importance in what I've done, but hopefully something is to be learned from *how* I did it or didn't do it. And I do know there are *three sides* to every story. That's right, three. Yours, theirs . . . and the truth.

This story is mine.

The one thing that has surprised and confused me though is my unlikely transformation into a "beloved public figure." How did the unpopular kid who grew up to be the angry young man, who became the eighties poster boy for the evils of rock 'n' roll, arrested for profanity and assault, and boycotted by parents and religious groups, become the likable mensch he is today? Alice Cooper—a man who has experienced this same strange phenomenon—says that people just got used to us. "If you stay around long enough, you become a part of Americana," he once told me. "People just expect us to be there." Kind of like Norm from *Cheers,* I guess. (Everyone in the bar yells, "Dee!") Any way you explain it, after years of rejection, final acceptance, then wholesale abandonment, it did take a bit of getting used to. But I have.

i just kept hoping i'd wake up

It's raining. Great. Way to make a bad situation even worse. It's 1993 and as I sit inside my beat-up, over-135,000-mile 1984 Toyota minivan (anything but "rock star"), I read the flyers one last time: HAIR & MAKEUP FOR WEDDINGS. CALL SUZETTE, then our phone number. Simple, to the point, and a way for Suzette to make a hundred bucks for a couple of hours' work on a weekend. Nothing like pimping out your wife's talents.

Loser.

I pull the hood of my sweatshirt tightly over my head, not just to protect me better from the rain, but to keep people from recognizing me. Almost ten years after my heyday, and even with a hat and glasses on, people are still coming up to me every day and saying "Hey, aren't you . . . ?" *Damn this face!* I remember working with Billy Joel and him saying, "Being rich and famous is tough; being poor and famous must *really* suck." He was right. *Think Billy's putting flyers on cars tonight?*

But that was a decade ago, and I was sitting on top of the world with my band Twisted Sister. We were chart toppers, worldwide media darlings, with a multiplatinum-selling album and international tours. I was the poster boy for heavy metal. I had nice cars, boats, and an expensive house in an upscale neighborhood. We had a housekeeper and a nanny, landscapers, maintenance men, and accountants who paid my bills. I had charge accounts in every store, bodyguards, and first-class everything.

Now it was the '90s, and I had lost it all. Everything. Except for the truly most important things in life—my wife and kids . . . and I had to provide for them.

Enough stalling, it's time to get it over with. Spring weddings mean late-winter wedding expos at local catering halls. I step out of the minivan into the night and the bone-chilling rain. Slipping into the secured parking area, I begin to put flyers on windshields. I move fast, not because it's cold or to finish the job quickly . . . I just don't want anybody to see me.

Along the way I run into another guy putting flyers on cars . . . *and he offers me a job!* He's impressed how fast I work. If only he knew.

Suddenly, I'm spotted by a security guard and I run. Not because of what he will do—throw me off the property?—but because I'm afraid he'll recognize me and say, "Hey, you're Dee Snider. What happened to you?"

As I run, I think for the millionth time, *How the hell did I come to this?*

1

i'm gonna be a beatle

id you see 'em last night?! Did you see 'em?!"

Russell Neiderman, the kid I despised most in our neighborhood, was brimming with uncharacteristic, nonconfrontational excitement. It was 8:00 a.m. Monday morning, and all the kids waiting at the bus stop in Freeport, Long Island, were abuzz.

"Did I see who?" I responded, confused by the neighborhood bully's unusual enthusiasm.

"The Beatles!"

On February 9, 1964, four guys from Liverpool, England, lit up the country with their groundbreaking appearance on the original "Must See TV," *The Ed Sullivan Show*. More than 70 million people tuned in to see the show that Sunday night, but I was apparently the only person who didn't see it. Why? Because my father had banned television in our house. Earlier that year, my father proclaimed (conveniently after our television had broken) that we had all become obsessed with TV and were going to get back to basics: reading, playing board games, building models, etc.

On the upside, I was introduced to comic books and learned to build balsa planes from scratch. On the downside . . . *while rock 'n' roll history was being made, I was building a fucking puzzle!*

At the bus stop, I was more than a little confused by the fuss. *"The Whatles?"* I asked.

"The *Beat*les," Neiderman emphatically corrected me. "They're a rock 'n' roll group. Everyone was screaming!"

That was all I needed to hear.

BORN ON MARCH 15, 1955, in Astoria, Queens, New York (Not Austria! *Astoria*), I was the oldest of six children and the firstborn grandchild on my mother's side of the family. From the day of my birth, and for a little more than a year afterward, I was the golden child. The center of attention and adoration, I could not have been more doted upon by my mother, father, grandparents, aunts and uncles ... until the deluge began. My mother (and her siblings) started dropping babies as if it were a contest. My mom delivered six babies in eight years. I was not only quickly shoved aside for my more adorable and needy brothers and sister, but more and more expected to fend for myself.

At times, growing up in the Snider household was like living in a madhouse—especially when my father wasn't around. I clearly remember one rainy day, looking at my mother holding a crying baby in each arm (Mark and Doug), my devilish, five-year-old brother, Frank, chasing my screaming, four-year-old brother, Matt, around her in circles, and my seven-year-old sister, Sue, complaining loudly about *something*. My mom looked as if she were about to lose her mind. That woman has earned every twitch and neurosis she has!

I went from being the center of attention to being "the oldest" before I was even aware of what had happened, but I still had a desperate need to be the epicenter. So when, at the ripe old age of almost nine, I heard the words "Everyone was screaming" spill from Russell Neiderman's ofttimes foul mouth, I knew what I had to do. I announced to everyone at the bus stop, who I'm sure didn't even listen, "I'm going to be a Beatle." My die had been cast and I didn't even have the slightest idea what a Beatle actually was!

I quickly found out the Beatles were a really cool-looking rock band who sang incredible songs. I couldn't be an actual Beatle, but I could be in my own rock band and hopefully cause that same hysteria. I didn't care about any of the trappings of rock stardom other than the chance for me to once again be the golden child, the center of the universe. I was that desperate for attention. As it turned out, rock 'n' roll stardom would be the only way I would get it.

My road to becoming a "rich, famous rock 'n' roll star" was long and arduous. The childish ideas I had on what it took, compounded by my natural procrastinating tendencies, didn't have me actually sinking my teeth into the real process of becoming a star until I was fifteen or sixteen. My elementary-school wannabe rock star buddies and I figured we would literally be discovered by some music impresario, à la Sonny Fox,* then whisked away to record an album and be on TV. We didn't play instruments, rehearse, have original songs, or anything! We were friggin' idiots.

Along the way I did take some "baby steps." I formed a number of "bands" in third and fourth grade, built solely around a kid I went to school with named Scott, who not only played guitar, but had an electric one and an amp. Our band was initially called Snider's Spiders, playing off the Beatles' "bug thing" and that my last name rhymes with *spider*. Great, right? It also foreshadowed the "spotlight hog" I was to become.

The name lasted all of a day or so, before the other guys in the "band" got hip and started wondering why *their* names weren't being used.

Because your name didn't rhyme with anything cool, Conway!

The extent of our band experience was hanging out in Scott's room, singing Beatles songs, and acting cool while he played guitar. Hey, we were nine.

Occasionally, a bunch of us would get together and put on lip-synch shows for the neighborhood kids. We'd don our Sunday church clothes (contrary to popular belief, I'm not Jewish), put on readily available Beatles wigs (they were all the rage), use tennis rackets for guitars and overturned garbage cans for drums, stand atop a picnic table, and mouth Beatles songs played on a portable record player.

We were good, too. We'd charge two cents per kid (it was the sixties) to watch us do our thing. I remember one show we made

---

* He was the host of a Saturday-morning kids' show that had up-and-coming rock bands on from time to time.

twenty-eight cents! That means fourteen neighborhood kids *paid* to see us. Not too shabby. I guess even then I could rock!

IN 1965, FACED WITH the choice of putting an extension on our house to better fit our growing family or moving, my family opted for the latter, primarily because my parents hated the Neiderman family as much as I hated Russell. For the record, we weren't the only ones. When the Neidermans finally moved out of the neighborhood years later, the entire block threw a going-away party . . . and didn't invite the Neidermans. Oh, snap!

The Snider family made the big move to the next town over, Baldwin, Long Island. A definite step up for us, but still very much middle/lower-middle-class suburbia . . . and we didn't really do much to class the place up. Besides that eight of us were bursting out of a four-bedroom house, my father had a unique view on suburban living.

An insurance salesman/state trooper, Dad once pulled over a guy illegally towing a car on the parkway and did him the favor of not giving him a ticket. Instead, he took the junker off the guy's hands, promptly towed it to our house (illegally), and put it in the backyard "for the kids to play on." The neighbors must have loved us ("Look, honey, we can see the Sniders' junk car from our screen room").

In my old elementary school, Bayview Avenue, I was a fairly cool, fairly popular, and fairly smart kid. *Fairly.* Unbeknownst to me, the Freeport school district was easy, and I effortlessly achieved good grades. When I was in fourth grade, my parents received a letter from the school stating, grade-wise, I was in the top 10 percent. My mom and dad were so proud, they took me to IHOP (a Snider-family favorite, then and now) for dinner *without* my brothers and sister (center of attention! center of attention!), then bought me the thing I wanted more than anything else in the world . . . a pair of Beatle boots. The shoes the Beatles wore had pointed toes with a Cuban heel (a style of shoe I still wear to this day). They were a bit pricey and "tough," but I had earned them with my effortlessly achieved good grades.

My having those boots totally elevated my cool status. When I combined them with a black turtleneck shirt, relatively tight pants, and my faux-silver ID bracelet, I was really stylin'. What a tool.

Our move "up" to Baldwin was a rude awakening for me, yet another baby step toward the dysfunctional rocker I was to become. You see, being cool and popular as a kid works directly against the drive and motivation you need to become a rock star. You can't be out partying, dating, and having a great time after school and on weekends. You need to be locked in your room, miserable and working on your craft.

The very first day of fifth grade in my new school, I fixed that.

I was dressed to impress. My mom always got us some new clothes for the start of the school year, and I was wearing the best I had. Resplendent in dark green pants, green button-down shirt (what was I, a leprechaun?) with a black turtleneck dickey underneath, and my Beatle boots, I was ready to take Shubert Elementary School by storm.

⚜ DEE LIFE LESSON ⚜

Never walk into a completely new environment as if you own the place. Take the time to get to know the lay of the land before you throw your weight around.

I walked into Mrs. Saltzman's class with all the cool and attitude a new kid could muster. I knew I was really making points with my classmates, especially when I got in the face of this big, dumb guy who thought he was tough. Things quickly escalated, and the stage was set for a classic, after-school showdown: 3:00 p.m. at the flag-pole!

For the rest of the day, I was the talk of the school. I was the cool (crazy?) new kid who had the guts to call out "Hammy."

Unbeknownst to me, Robert "Hammy" Hemburger (what a horrible name) was the toughest kid in the school. Besides having kicked the asses of all comers over the years, his claim to fame was that when he was only eight years old, he picked up a cast-iron man-hole cover to gain sewer access to retrieve a lost ball. This is the kid physical equivalent of a grown man lifting a car! Unfortunately for Hammy, he crushed the tips of all his fingers while putting the man-hole cover back in place. His fingers eventually healed, but they—and his fingernails—seemed to have a pronounced "smooshed" look to them.

The school day finally ended, and I strode out to the flagpole in my "Irish pride" outfit (no, I'm not Irish) to set this moron straight and cement my reputation in my new school. I cemented a reputation all right. Hammy *literally* picked me up and threw me against a brick wall. I'm sure some other things happened between my strid-ing and being thrown, but for the life of me I can't remember. I probably had a minor concussion.

The entire school was there to witness it (as is the case any-time the toughest guy in the school fights someone, especially an unknown new kid), and the only thing I earned that day was my reputation as the moron who called out Hammy.

Shortly after that, Hammy decided my last name, Snider, rhymed with *snot*(?!), and that became his nickname for me: Snots. Nobody else called me that, but since I wasn't prepared to get back in the ring with Hammy, Snots I remained. Having him call me Snots for all of fifth and sixth grade, and occasionally when he ran into me over the years until he dropped out of school, didn't do wonders for my coolness factor or popularity.

But ponder this: If I had beat Hammy that day, I would have become popular. If I had been popular, my road to becoming a rock 'n' roll star would have been cut short.

⊰ DEE LIFE LESSON ⊱

Popularity = attention.

Attention = socializing.

Socializing = *the end of motivation.*

It's a fact: popularity kills creativity and drive. Why sit in your room working on your craft if you can be out getting laid? Show me truly great-looking entertainers and I guarantee that for some reason they weren't popular and partying and were, instead, holed up in their bedrooms and practicing their craft.

My favorite example of this is the time I met an eighties Canadian pop/rock sensation on *The Howard Stern Show*. I used to spend a lot of time in the mid to late eighties hanging out on Howard's show, and this guy came in one morning to promote his new record. He had striking, James Dean good looks, so, during an extended commercial break, I asked him what had happened in his youth that kept him from using his "handsomeness" to hang out, party, and get laid. His face dropped and he looked at me as if I had psychic powers.

"How did you know?" the heartthrob asked, truly unnerved by my query. I quickly explained my theory to him, and he spilled his guts.

When he was just six years old, dead in the middle of a brutal winter, he was invited to the birthday party of a girl in his class; all of his classmates were invited.

He was excited about going, especially because his mom had bought the girl a cool gift: a live, baby painted turtle, completely set up in a bowl with gravel, a rock, and a fake plastic palm tree. Though illegal to sell in many places now, back in the sixties this was pretty much the ultimate gift you could get a kid. His mom wrapped the bowl—turtle safely ensconced inside—and dropped him off at the party. When he entered the house, the little girl's mom took the gift and put it with the others, *on top of the radiator.*

The party was going great, and when it finally came time for the birthday girl to open her gifts, all of her classmates gathered around to ooh and aah. His classmate finally got to his unopened gift, and he pushed through the crowd to the front, proudly exclaiming, "That one's from me! That one's from me!"

The excitement in the room was palpable as the little girl excitedly tore off the wrapping paper, revealing the turtle bowl . . . with a dead baby turtle hanging out of its shell inside. The blazing-hot radiator had cooked the poor thing alive.

Well, the birthday girl screamed, children cried, and from that moment on, he was known to all as Turtle Boy. He grew up an outcast and the brunt of jokes, and no matter how handsome he got, no matter how talented he was or what he did, he was always just a loser to the kids in his town. So, he sat in his room alone and . . . you know the rest. Lack of popularity = creative development and ambition.

Meanwhile, back at my personal humiliating, life-defining moment, my popularity was crushed like Hammy's fingers, and I sank further into my dreamworld of becoming a rich, famous rock 'n' roll star.

Funny how things work out.

2

"this boy can sing!"

With the options of being the tough kid, the cool kid, or the popular kid removed from my class-hierarchy choices, I opted for another position . . . class clown. Mildly disruptive and at times entertaining, this job gave me some needed attention (albeit often negative), and the girls kind of liked it. Plus, it beat the hell out of being a nothing.

To add insult to my new school injury, the Baldwin school district was at that time one of the top-rated school districts in the country. My effortless A's in Freeport turned into effortless C's in Baldwin. *My parents were less than pleased.* One of the few ways I could get special attention from them had dried up. I had to struggle to get decent grades pretty much the rest of my time in school. It wasn't that I wasn't smart, I just didn't want to "apply myself" (as just about every one of my report cards stated).

Early in my sixth-grade year, auditions were held for a solo in the glee club. I had always sung in music class, but so did everyone else. This was the first time I had to audition for something. Like all the others, I went down to sing for the glee club conductor, Mrs. Sarullo, who was also my teacher. A dark, mothering Italian woman, Mrs. Sarullo was easy to like and knew how to handle her class. She was a lot of fun, but nobody's fool. She nicknamed me "Hood" because of my pointy shoes and obvious desire to look like a dirtbag. It was a hell of a lot better than "Snots."

I walked into the "cafe-gym-itorium" for my audition, Beatle boots clacking loudly on the floor. Mrs. Sarullo sat at the piano, awaiting her next victim. I don't remember if I was nervous or not (I probably was. Who isn't?), and I don't remember what song I sang. All I remember is Mrs. Sarullo stopped the song halfway through and exclaimed, "This boy can sing like a bird!" *I can?* "Hood, you've got a beautiful voice!"

And just like that, my life was changed.

I not only got the glee club solo, but Mrs. Sarullo smiled her big, toothy smile down upon me, and I was the center of attention . . . *in choir.* Which is where I remained for all my school years. It was the one place where people thought I was special. Add to that, I now knew I brought something to any rock band: *I was a singer!*

CLICK. (Sound of a tumbler in a combination lock falling in place.)

Each year the school had a Spring Concert, and of course the sixth-grade glee club's was the featured performance. The plan was for the choir to sing first, then I would enter for my solo on cue. The glee club headed down to the stage and I had a bit of time to kill. I made my way to the side of the stage for my entrance. When I heard my cue, I walked out onto the stage to unusually wild applause and cheering. I was blown away! I hadn't even sung yet.

It turned out I was late, and the choir had for several minutes been repeating my musical cue over and over, waiting for me. Be that as it may, the audience reaction when I walked out on the stage changed me forever. This was what I wanted. This is what I needed. I had to experience that rush of audience reaction again and I wouldn't stop until I did.

WHEN I MOVED TO seventh grade the following year, Mrs. Sarullo—for reasons unbeknownst to me—moved up to the junior high school as well. Unfortunately, due to scheduling conflicts, and a lack of room in the class, I was unable to get into Concert Choir, a daily class for singers. Bummer.

A few days into the school year, I ran into Mrs. Sarullo in the hall and she asked me how choir was going. While she handled both general education *and* glee club as a teacher in elementary school, as a junior-high-school teacher she was solely relegated to teaching social studies. I told my "choral fairy godmother" I wasn't in the choir, and she became enraged. "We'll see about that!" she said as she stormed off down the hall.

The next day I got a note from the office saying my schedule had been changed and I was now in Concert Choir. As I said before, there I remained until the end of my school days. There I was special. There I was somebody. I don't have fond memories of school—no glory days for me—but I loved singing in choir. It was my only solace. Thank you for that, Dolores Sarullo, wherever you are. Thank you for recognizing and championing my talent. Thank you for making me feel special when I needed to feel special. I couldn't have done it without you. You were a great teacher.

AS I REFLECT ON these pivotal moments in my life, the realization sets in that relatively few life experiences make us who we are, define us as individuals, and set the course by which our lives will be guided. *It's terrifying.* Not that I wasn't aware of this before, but setting it down in words makes me painfully aware of the arbitrariness of it all and how the slightest change in any of these events could have had me careening down some other path, in a completely different direction. Then again, I can't help but feel when you want something badly and life events occur that continually push you toward your goal . . . exactly how arbitrary were they? Was it fate? Is a higher power guiding us? Are we subconsciously causing our own experiences, thus guiding ourselves? Take the CPO debacle, for example.

When I was in sixth grade, a fashion trend swept my school: CPOs. Standing for "chief petty officer," they were shirtlike light jackets that absolutely everybody was wearing. They came in navy blue or maroon and I desperately wanted to get one. I had to fit in.

Now, *fashionable* and *clothes* were mutually exclusive words in the Snider household. With eight mouths to feed, clothe, and take care of, my dad was working two, sometimes three jobs to make ends meet. Thanks for that, Dad. We always had three meals a day, though we didn't have meat on the table every night (and when we did, organ meats such as liver, kidney, and tongue were not uncommon; yikes!) . . . and we didn't have fashionable clothes. It was not unusual for my family to shop at the Salvation Army. There's no shame in that, but for a young boy desperately trying to fit in, it wasn't really cutting it.

Christmas was coming, and traditionally my siblings and I could expect one "frivolous" gift—something that we really wanted—and a bunch of other practical things we needed, such as socks and such. *Party.* I decided I would campaign for my one gift to be a CPO.

Because I was the oldest of six, my parents worked extrahard to keep me in the dark regarding "the truth" about Santa, for fear that once I knew, I would either deliberately or unintentionally spill the beans to my younger brothers and sister and ruin Christmas for everyone. The smarter and more suspicious I became, the more intense my parents' machinations got to keep me a believer. When I noticed the wrapping paper on all the gifts was the same, they asked in disbelief, "You didn't actually think Santa wrapped every gift in the world himself, did you?" *What an idiot!* Of course parents needed to help. When I stumbled on all the gifts under my parents' bed, weeks before Christmas, I was mocked, "You really thought St. Nick delivered all the gifts in the world in one night?" *I guess I'm a moron!* Obviously he would have to spread his deliveries out. On and on it went, my parents capitalizing on a child's insecurities inherent to not believing. Of course, if all else failed, they had their fail-safe: "Well, children who don't believe don't get presents." *I believe! I believe!* That is, until one Sunday at church when I was twelve . . . and the news was broken to me in an awkward way.

My mother taught the sixth-grade Sunday-school class at my church. A devout Christian woman, born and raised Roman Catholic by her Swiss parents, she went to church every Sunday of her life . . . until the day she married my formerly Jewish dad. I say *formerly* because my baseball-playing cop father, upon being bar mitzvahed at fourteen . . . quit. Hey, they did say "Today you are a man." A man can quit his faith if he wants to, right?

Proclaiming that Judaism is a belief, not a nationality (He would say, "Show me 'Jewland' on a map!"), my father became an agnostic and set his sights on gentile girls. Well, I'm not sure he actually set his sights, but he met my *goy* mother in high school, fell head over heels in love, and eventually proposed.

Since the Catholic Church doesn't accept love as an excuse for blasphemy, the priests refused to marry my parents and told my mother she was no longer welcome in the Church and was going to "burn in hell." (Good title for a song, don'tcha think?) So my parents had a civil ceremony and were married at town hall by a judge. For the record, they've been married ever since.

One Sunday, a short time after I was born, my mother missed the bus to her Catholic church (where she was still going despite their pronouncement) and literally wandered into an Episcopal church. They welcomed her with open arms, and I (and all my brothers and sister) was baptized, confirmed, and raised (and sang in the church choir) in the Episcopal Church. Thank ya, Jesus!

Now, one Sunday, in class, my mother was imparting some Christian teaching or another *unto us* when the subject of Santa Claus came up. Staring directly at me from the front of the room, she said, "Of course you all know there is no Santa Claus." *I did now!*

When Christmas finally arrived, I was beyond excited. I knew that as long as you only asked for one thing (a CPO), and it wasn't too expensive (it wasn't), you would get your wish. Sure it was a little cold out for a light jacket, but I didn't care. I was going to wear my CPO until the sleeves rotted off!

As was tradition, we got to open our "filler" gifts first, building up to our big one. Socks, chocolate, a shirt or two; whatever—it was all good. *Come on, CPO!*

Finally, they handed me *the box*. I knew by the shape, weight, and size, it was CPO "go time." I tore off the wrapping paper and ripped open the box to find . . . *a military-style coat*. What!? *No CPO?!* I burst into tears (hey, I was twelve) as my mother desperately tried to explain how they looked everywhere, but the stores were all sold out. I wouldn't even look at the coat they got me. I cried, screamed I hated the coat, and told my mom that my Christmas was ruined. To this day I can remember the hurt look on her face. She genuinely felt terrible. *Sorry about that, Mom.*

True to my word, I wouldn't even look at the stupid coat she got me. When spring finally rolled around (and I'd calmed down), I needed a lighter jacket and for some reason pulled out my Christmas present and put it on. It was nothing like a CPO . . . but it was kind of cool. Military collar, gold buttons down the front . . . but, no, I hated it. Until I went to school . . .

Everyone flipped! They all wanted to know what kind of jacket it was and where I got it . . . and I was the only person who had one! (Center of attention! Center of attention!)

I loved the response I was getting from being different from everyone else. I loved the notice it brought me and the admiration, too. From that day on I did everything I could to look different and be different. Like a junkie, I had to have that reaction as much as possible and whenever I could. It didn't even have to be positive, I just had to be noticed. *I had to be an individual.*

To this day I tell my mother it's all her fault. If she'd only got me the jacket that everyone else had, the one I asked for, things would be completely different. I wouldn't be so dead set on being different.

Course set for rock stardom? Aye, aye, Captain!

3

no, no, a hundred times no

Over the next few years, I continued to "play in bands," which consisted of me and a couple of guys talking a lot about what our band was going to do (and drawing the various band names on our notebooks) and practicing little. In elementary school my bandmates were Rich Squillacioti (a constant until around my senior year in high school) on drums and David Lepiscopo on guitar. We never had a bass player (nobody wanted to do that), and at first I don't think we even had a microphone for me to sing in. But we were still "a band" and talked a great game. I remember one day we piled all of our equipment into a *shopping cart* and pushed it around the neighborhood to show off. We were going to be huge!

One constant in my life was the full-length mirror in my bedroom. Every day, the moment I got home from school, I would go to my room (actually my and one or two of my brothers' room), lock the door, put on music, and lip-synch intensely in front of that mirror for the imaginary audience on the other side. I would rock out until I was either dripping with sweat or my parents screamed for me to "turn down the damn music/let your brothers in their room." Now, I'm known for being a great stage performer—it's probably the thing I do best. People always ask me how I got so good, and I answer, "By jumping around in front of my bedroom mirror." Oh, sure, all my years of live performing helped, but performing in the mirror gave me the confidence to get out there in the first place, knowing how what I was doing looked to the audience. I still can't resist making faces or throwing shapes in any available mirror. For years it was my only audience.

Musically, in late 1965, '66, and '67 everybody was into the Beatles, Stones, and the whole British Invasion/British Invasion Impersonation thing going on. But in the summer of 1965 and the fall of 1966, two new television shows, featuring definitively "American" bands, hit the airwaves. *Where the Action Is* and *The Monkees* introduced two pop/rock bands to the masses, Paul Revere and the Raiders and the Monkees, respectively.* These two bands not only had tremendous appeal to young people, but we got to watch their antics daily or weekly, further fueling my, and many other kids', desire to be a rock star.

While the majority of kids in my school and house were Monkees fans, I was drawn to the subtle danger of singer Mark Lindsay from Paul Revere and the Raiders. I know, I know, *danger* and *the Raiders* may seem, to those of you aware of those "happy rock" bands, to be a bit of an oxymoron,† but unlike the Monkees, whose every song was pure pop pablum, Paul Revere and the Raiders songs were innuendo-filled. Hits such as "Hungry" and "Kicks" were barely veiled songs about sex, drugs, and alcohol. Mark Lindsay's slight rasp along with the generally "heavier" tone of the band's music are recognized precursors to what would become "hard rock" . . . and eventually "heavy metal." I am an original headbanger and I credit Paul Revere and the Raiders for starting me down that path. *Thank you, boys!*

My father didn't want to know about my passion for rock 'n' roll. His dream as a kid was to be a professional baseball player (no, I'm not related to Duke Snider), a dream that he could never pursue or realize. He was convinced that his oldest son was a natural and wanted me to be the ballplayer he couldn't be. Now, I liked playing

---

*   For those wondering, after a television-less year, my father finally had enough "puzzle making" and one night stormed out of the house with a simple "That's it!" He came home a short time later carrying two new televisions. We were reconnected!

†   Paul Revere and the Raiders are one of the original "garage rock" bands out of Portland, Oregon, and the first to record the federal-government-investigated "Louie, Louie."

baseball, but not as much as I wanted to rock. I think my dad saw my love of rock 'n' roll as a potential threat to his plans for me.

To my mother's credit, she was positive and encouraging about my "silly" obsession. Herself an artist and singer in various choirs, she saw the value of anything creative and paid for me out of her own hard-earned money (she taught seniors art classes) to take "group guitar lessons" the summer of seventh grade. We didn't have a lot of money, and it went directly against the wishes of my perpetually angry dad (personified by Mark Metcalf in the Twisted Sister videos), so this was a big deal. Every morning for a few weeks my mother drove me to the lessons and I learned to play basic guitar. *Thank you for that, Mom.* Armed with my newfound ability to play some basic chords and an acoustic guitar, I felt I was finally on my way.

My siblings often talked of forming a "family rock band" like the Osmonds or the Cowsills. My sister, Sue, younger than me by a year, shared a passion for a lot of the same music* and enjoyed listening to me sing songs or singing them with me, but to actually get any of my much younger brothers to learn an instrument was yet another rock 'n' roll fantasy. We did however all sing in the church choir and one time performed "Lo, How a Rose E'er Blooming" as a family for the congregation. To this day I dread when someone at a family gathering starts singing that song (usually in jest), my mother enthusiastically joins in, and we're all forced to repeat our 1971 Sunday command performance. Once was definitely enough.

In 1968, a band called the Human Beinz released a cover of an Isley Brothers song called "Nobody but Me." This two-chord, catchy little ditty, repeats the word *no* a hundred times during the song and *nobody* forty-six, making it "mildly" repetitive. It reached the Top 10 of the *Billboard* charts, and its "hit" status, and simple lyrical and chord structure, made it perfect fodder for two-fifths of "The Snider Family" singing group. I played guitar and sang lead, while the enthusiastic Sue played tambourine and shouted out the backing chants of "Shing-a-ling! Skate! Boogaloo! Philly!" It was the best song we had ever done and we practiced it all day long.

---

* Sue turned me on to Deep Purple's *Machine Head*—an early metal album—and was into Alice Cooper before I was.

Just to be sure we weren't kidding ourselves about how great it was, we performed it for all of our brothers and my mom, and they loved it. I couldn't wait for my cynical, nonbeliever dad to get home. I was going to blow him away!

When my father finally arrived, Sue and I could not contain our excitement. We ran into the living room to greet him, armed with guitar, tambourine, and sheet music.

"Daddy! Daddy! Wait'll you hear! We learned a song! We've been practicing all day!"

With all the genuine rock energy we could muster, Sue and I performed our song for him, "no, no, noing" and "boogalooing" our hearts out. When we finished, awaiting his highest praise for the great job we had done . . . *he mocked us mercilessly.*

"You call that a song? It's a joke! 'No, no, no, no, no'? What kind of stupid song is that?!"

We were devastated. To make matters worse, for weeks after, anytime one of my parents' friends came over, my dad would tell the story of his idiot son (my younger sister was clearly duped into singing it with me) and his asinine "No-No" song. I was completely humiliated, but inside me was building a righteous anger. The old man had lit the pilot light to a flame that eventually evolved into the towering inferno of rage that would drive me all the way to the top.

Years later, my dad tried to take credit for my success, suggesting that his being so hard on me as a boy is what drove me on. "It's like that Johnny Cash song 'A Boy Named Sue,' " he proclaimed. "If I wasn't so tough on you, you never would have made it."

To this stupidity I responded, "How do you know I wouldn't be happier as a well-adjusted accountant?" *Dick.*

IN EIGHTH GRADE, THE kids in my church choir were approached to record one hundred children's songs for a series of albums designed to provide elementary schools without a formal music program something for the children to sing along with. We were all super-excited. Not only were we going to get to record in a real recording studio, but we were going to be paid with "a color television" each.

Now, in 1968, color TV was still a relatively new thing. You couldn't find a set cheaper than $350. So for giving up an afternoon a week to rehearse, and every Saturday for five months to record, we twelve- and thirteen-year-old kids would be rich! My sister and I (Sue also sang in the church choir)—still smarting from our television-less year—fantasized about lying in our own beds, watching our own *color television*! It was incredible.

When we finally finished the Herculean task (during which time a couple of us boys in the choir went through puberty and our voices awkwardly changed), we were informed that unbeknownst to anybody, including our parents and the church choir directors, some Japanese company had come out with a cheap, portable color television valued at $150. In the sixties *Made in Japan* was a sign of inferiority. Funny how things have changed, huh? For all of our hard months of work, we were offered a piece-of-crap TV or $150 in cash. My first involvement with the recording industry and I was already being taken advantage of . . . foreshadowing things to come. My sister and I both took the cash (still a chunk of change for a couple of kids), and I learned a serious life lesson.

Somewhere out there in the school closets of America, I'm sure some dusty Strawberry Wristwatch LPs still exist. That's what our choir directors named us; it was the psychedelic era. Were *they* on psychedelics? That would explain our shitty deal. I wonder if anyone knows (or cares) that they are Dee Snider's first recordings.

Oh yeah; I took my 150 bucks and with an additional $15 kicked in from my dad (thanks) bought my first, real electric guitar: a Gibson SG Special. Now I was starting to rock.

THE PINNACLE OF MY "all talk, no action" band experience came toward the tail end of junior high. I now had a band called Brighton Rock, consisting of myself on guitar and vocals, Rich Squillacioti on drums, Phil Knourzer on bass (finally a bass player!), and Timmy Smith on lead guitar. Rich and I had an interesting life experience with Timmy before he joined the band.

Timmy was our only cool friend, who, at fourteen, smoked so many nonfiltered cigarettes, he had yellow, nicotine-stained fingers. When Rich and I decided that the only way we were going to get girls was to smoke (yeah, that was the problem), Tim took us out one day to teach us how, starting us on filtered Tareyton cigarettes to ease us into that harsh world. After an afternoon filled with chain-smoking, acting cool, and dealing with the bad taste, breath, and cigarette smell on our bodies, Rich and I decided if we had to smoke to get girls, we would be celibate. Life lesson learned.

Like many of my bands before, Brighton Rock *never* rehearsed, but we talked a good game. We sat together every day at lunch, discussing how we would rock, and acting like the Beatles and the Monkees. One day Phil came in with amazing news. They were having a dance at his church and he got us the gig! While church dances were a typical venue for young bands, Phil went to the Unitarian Church, which was the hippest of the churches, making this booking that much cooler. This would be my first gig ever. *I had finally arrived!* Sure we had never rehearsed, but the show was six months away, plenty of time to put a set together.

As the weeks and months rolled by, we promised each other we would rehearse, but something always kept us from getting together. For some reason or another, over six months we could not find even *one* day for a rehearsal. I don't know about the other guys, but I was a full-of-shit, chronic procrastinator who always put everything off until the last minute. Up until that time, I viewed being in a band as effortless, as something that just somehow "happened." Boy, was I wrong.

The week of the show, the reality that time had run out hit us, and the undeniable fact that we couldn't do a whole show on our own set in. We still figured we could rehearse a short set at the church the *day of the show*, but we knew we needed someone to headline.

Some of our best friends, and a true inspiration to Brighton Rock, were an actual performing band called Armadillo. The same age as us, these guys were advanced; read, *they weren't full of shit and actually took lessons and rehearsed.* They were such an early inspiration, I want to make sure I recognize them individually: Doug Steigerwald on guitar (more on him later), Denny McNerney on drums (still a dear friend of mine), Mike Graziano on bass, and the much older (he was in high school!) Don Koenig on vocals. These guys could play, and their performance of Black Sabbath's "Black

Sabbath" was not only my introduction to heavy metal, but scared the living crap out of me. Amazing.

My band approached the guys in Armadillo (sitting at *their* band table during lunch) and asked if they would headline the Unitarian-church show that weekend, and they accepted. Joy of joys, we were saved! Now all we had to do was rehearse a short set the day of the show. *Ha!*

Saturday arrived and we loaded in nice and early so we could get maximum rehearsal time before the dance. Timmy brought his older (equally nicotine-stained) brother with him to play harmonica. We hadn't even worked out a set list! For the first time we attempted to run through songs we all mutually knew and—surprise, surprise—we all only knew *three* songs. We rehearsed our "set" for a while (a couple of hours, tops) and were stunned to discover—*we sucked!* I couldn't believe it. How was that possible? We *talked* about our band all the time.

We were such garbage that we instantaneously renamed our band just that, Garbage (predating the much more popular band Garbage by about three decades). I remember Phil literally throwing his bass on the floor in anger, and instead of continuing to rehearse and work on the songs (why do that?), we did what any all-talk, no-action band would do: we went around to all the posters in the building, crossed out the name *Brighton Rock*, and wrote in *Garbage*. Talk about a self-fulfilling prophecy.

Our time to perform came all too soon, and we headed out onto the stage (the floor of the church gathering room) to face a full house of kids sitting on the floor, waiting to be rocked. Somebody introduced the band to the confused crowd ("Ladies and gentlemen, we are Garbage!"), and we launched into the funeral dirge that is Donovan's "Atlantis." *What a shitty opener!* We made it through the song, to a tepid response from the crowd, at which point Phil and I decided that we had had enough. *What the hell were we thinking?!* Being closest to the exit, without a word to the other band members, Phil and I walked off. Not realizing his bass guitarist and rhythm guitarist/lead vocalist had left the stage, Rich counted off the next song, and he, Timmy, and Timmy's brother (let's just call him Stainy) started playing the next song without us. Stunned by what was going on, Phil and I watched as this catastrophe continued to unfold. Heaven forbid we go back out onstage.

The audience was more than a little confused, and as the remaining band members slowly realized Phil and I were no longer onstage (what was in those cigarettes they were smoking!?), they stopped playing and, one by one, walked off. What a debacle.

Backstage, we stood in stunned silence, too overwhelmed by the harsh reality that had just hit us. And then it got even worse. The door to the backstage area opened and in walked *my father*. Unbeknownst to me, after years of listening to me prattle on about my bands and music, he had decided to come, unannounced, and check out my first show. I looked at him, he looked at me, he shook his head in disappointment and disgust, then walked out without saying a word. To this day, that show has never been mentioned or discussed.

I could not have been more humiliated or embarrassed. That experience scarred and changed me for life. I vowed to never, *ever* perform again unless I was completely and thoroughly rehearsed and ready. Only in recent years have I even considered getting up and "jamming" with another band. I had fucked up big-time. My bluff had been called and I had no one to blame but myself. I now knew that if I wanted to be a rock star, it would take hard work and perseverance. Nobody was going to hand me fame and fortune.

FROM THAT POINT ON, all of my many bands rehearsed, a lot. Along the way I discovered a new axiom:

⇥ DEE LIFE LESSON ⇝
A band is only as good as its weakest link.

How? When I realized I could get into a lot better bands if I just sang rather than insisting on playing sucky guitar as well. While being able to play a little guitar has over the years served me well (I would always translate my vocally composed Twisted Sister songs to guitar and show them to the band), the time had come to free myself and become the wild-man performer I knew I was meant to be. Hell, one of the reasons I sucked on guitar was because I moved around too much to play well, but I looked good doing it!

My father fought my pursuing a career in music more than ever. After what he had witnessed, why wouldn't he? He couldn't have been more disappointed in the path his oldest son was taking. Once I had given up playing baseball completely and started growing my hair out (after an ugly, forced-haircut incident in the beginning of tenth grade), my dad pretty much gave up on me. He barely talked to or even acknowledged me for years. Things didn't get better until my younger brother Mark showed an intense interest in baseball and my father could once again focus his fatherly pride and support on something he understood.

In fairness to my dad, he was raised during the Great Depression, a time when dreams were shattered, not achieved. He was raised to believe that the only way you get anything in life is by fighting and clawing every inch of the way, and that dreams don't come true. Well, he was right about the first part. Add that to rock 'n' roll being alien entertainment to his generation, and I can understand his resistance. I don't think my father was truly proud of me until only recently, when I did my run on Broadway in 2010. A Broadway star was a concept he could understand. My going after a pipe dream of a career in rock 'n' roll was, from his point of view, watching his child heading for massive disappointment and self-destruction. *Man, was he wrong!*

The man did pretty much everything he could to stop and discourage me. Though outward displays of rebellion were met with swift, forceful punishment, he could not stop the growing fire inside me. I remember one time my father banned me from rehearsing with my then band, The Quivering Thigh. So I took up jogging. Each night, dressed in running clothes, I would leave the house, jog several miles to rehearsal, rehearse with the band for a bit, then jog home. Where there's a will, there's a way.

By my junior year in high school, I was playing dances and parties occasionally, while most of my buddies in Armadillo had moved on to a new band, Harvest, and were already out playing clubs at night—even though they weren't even old enough to drink. Harvest's lead guitarist extraordinaire, Doug Steigerwald, was a long-time friend, altar boy at my church, and a true inspiration to me. I was always in awe of him. Both having *S* last names, we sat next to each other each morning in homeroom. One day he was recovering from a late night of rocking and I was blathering on (as usual) about my band, his band, rock music, and anything else that remotely related to our common passion. Finally Doug, who was on the quiet side, said, almost as a revelation to himself, "You're really serious about making it, aren't you?"

"Yeah!" I responded in disbelief. I'd been annoying him about it for years. He was just realizing this? Doug's next, Yoda-like words to me affected me like few others. I've reflected on them, followed them, and repeated them often over the last four decades. "Don't let anybody stop you from moving toward your dream. Not family, not friends, not girlfriends . . . *nobody*. The minute you let *anyone* stop you from moving forward, you are *finished*. Try not to be shitty about it, but whatever you do, do not let anyone stop you."

I sat there dumbfounded by Doug's profound statement, the words etching into my psyche. A couple of years later I would watch my dear friend Rich Squillacioti literally cry when we replaced him in our band because he just wasn't good enough to take us to the next level. If I'd allowed our friendship to prevent what was right for my career and the band, that would have been the end of me, too.

To this day, I don't know what was going on in Doug's life to have him make such a pronouncement, but it must have been heavy. A few years later, Doug would abandon his dreams of rock stardom and join the US Air Force after being seriously ripped off and lied to by some music-industry asshole. Doug loved music, but like many, he couldn't take the ugliness of the business. They call it the music *business* for a reason.

Armed with this newfound knowledge, I headed off into the unknown, knowing where I was going, but not how I was going to get there.

4

to be or not to be

While music was a constant in my life, my place, in the complex system of cliques and social circles in high school, was anything but constant. I was always struggling to fit in with some crowd. I wanted to be accepted. Since I wanted to look like a badass, and I had a connection through my nicotine-stained friend Timmy Smith, at first I tried to hang with the troublemakers. We called them dirtbags or greasers. While I liked their vibe, I just couldn't get into picking on people for the hell of it (a prerequisite), and my solid C average was off-putting to the other guys. Report-card day would come, and we'd all stand around comparing grades. "I got three F's and two D's," one lowlife would brag. "Oh, yeah, I got four F's and one attendance failure," another piece of shit would boast. "What did you get, Snider?" "Straight C's," I would mumble, hoping they wouldn't notice. "Whoa . . . get a load of the big brain on Snider!" I just didn't fit.

Needless to say, my 2.0 grade point average and lack of interest in Mathletes and Chess Club wasn't making any inroads for me with the intellectuals in school either. I did have an A average in gym, but I had to work every day after school (no weekly allowances in the Snider household), so I couldn't go out for after-school sports and I didn't think the world was shaped like a football. That meant being a jock was out. You would think, since I was in bands, that hanging with the "freaks" (rockers, stoners, artsy kids) would have been a natural fit, but it wasn't. I didn't drink or get high. They just looked at me as if I were weird.

That I didn't drink or party was a deal breaker with a lot of the cliques. Partyers just aren't comfortable with people who are sober. They don't trust them. So, when I wasn't at school, working, or rehearsing with my bands, I pretty much kept to myself or hung with my few outcast buddies.

Why don't I party? Ah, the million-dollar question. Well, I don't drink because I had a bad experience when I was fourteen. I got so smashed I couldn't get off the floor and swore that if the good Lord above ever let me walk again, I would never touch demon alcohol. I kept that promise until a few years ago, after reading so many good things about the health value of having a glass of red wine with dinner (Jesus drank wine). You should have seen the faces of my family and friends the first time they saw me pick up a glass. They thought it was a sign of the Apocalypse!

As for drugs, I've always known I have an obsessive personality, and if I started doing drugs, I wouldn't be able to control myself. Besides, I've never really had a problem "letting myself go." I was always a crazy kid, and at first the people I knew who partied would say "Snider, we want to see what you're like high." Then after spending a bit more time with me, they would say "On second thought, *we don't.*"

Am I anti-drugs-and-alcohol? Not really. I'm just anti-asshole. If you can party and remain who you are or become a looser, more fun version of who you are, God bless you. But if when you party, you become some shape-shifting, obnoxious asshole who doesn't know when to quit . . . you, I can live without.

The unfortunate thing is, society has created an environment where people don't feel comfortable letting themselves go unless they're high or have a few in them. How many times have you been somewhere and asked someone, or been asked by someone, to do something such as dance or sing and heard, or said, "Just let me have a couple of drinks." Why? Because society dictates that it's okay to get crazy, silly, or act foolish if you're high. It gives you an excuse to embarrass yourself. "Oh, I was soooo wasted." If I climb on top of a bar, pull out my dick, and piss on the floor and I'm drunk, they put me in a cab and send me home. If I do the same thing and I'm sober, they say I'm crazy and I get my ass kicked, arrested, or both. That double standard creates a dangerous environment.

I've been clean and sober my whole career. People see the way I dress, act, and perform and assume I'm wasted. "Dude, you must be so high," people say to me, admiring my crazed state. When I tell them I'm stone-cold sober, they look at me as if I am insane. What a fucked-up world! If you want people to stop getting drunk and high (especially kids), you need to change the way society perceives it. Stop making it an acceptable excuse for poor behavior. Stop portraying it as cool. And stop viewing outgoing behavior when you're not high as weird. Then you'll see some changes.

Add my nonpartying attitude to my already confused persona and you had a complete outcast. By my junior year in high school I had tried to fit in and fell out of, or was kicked out of, every group or clique. Yes, I had my other outcast friends, but I wanted to be popular, or at least a part of some character-defining group.*

I felt as if I were fading away, becoming just a part of the background to the beautiful people living exciting lives. Then I decided I wasn't going to take it. One day I just realized that if I didn't resist— if I didn't refuse to go quietly into the night—I would become just another nameless, faceless person in the world. I made a conscious decision that day that I would no longer give a shit what other people thought. I didn't need their approval or acceptance, and I'd rather be alone and happy than just another follower in some lame-ass clique. I decided that I was going to be me, and—I know this sounds corny—that's the day my life began.

From that day on, I was me—or at least the me I was going to become. It didn't happen that instantly. It was a self-fulfilling prophecy. The more I forced myself to be whom I wanted to be and not give a shit what others thought, the more of a reality it became.

About that same time, I came up with a new, personal motivation

---

* Oddly, I believe it's that undefinable quality that has allowed me to appeal to so many different types of people over the years. Even my religion and politics are blurred. Go online and you will find I'm Jewish, Christian, a satanist, a Republican, Democrat, Liberal, Conservative, and Independent, heralded and reviled at the same time by supporting and opposing groups! I love it!

concept: PMA, or positive mental attitude. I kid you not. I believed that if I thought and acted positively, positive things would happen for me, and my positive thoughts would become reality. I still do. I now know that's just another form of self-fulfilling prophecy, but when I was sixteen, it was more my becoming aware of the power of positive thinking. From that time on (and to this day), when people asked me how I was doing, I didn't say "Okay," or even "Good," I said "Excellent!" Even when I wasn't. This mind-set has taken me everywhere, and when things were bad, it kept me from wallowing in self-pity and negativity and focused on the promise of what lay ahead. And it kept people wondering what the hell I had going on that they didn't know about. Besides, it sure beat the hell out of such mantras as "It's just one of those days," "It's just my luck," and "Murphy's Law." To hear kids reinforcing these negative thoughts in their young, fertile minds is simply maddening to me. Thinking like that sets you up for a lifetime of accepting failure. Screw that!

⮜   DEE LIFE LESSON   ⮞

PMA: positive mental attitude. Life will be great because I say it will!

"PMA" became my daily mantra and a source of great amusement to my father. Whenever things weren't working out for me, he was quick to throw PMA in my face or beat me to the positive punch and say with disdain, "I know, I know, PMA," before I could. He never deterred me. From time to time, he still mentions PMA, but it's more in amazement and recognition that my approach to living has paid off and I was right. Even if I hadn't been right . . . what's the advantage of living life with a negative attitude?

With newfound self-confidence, my mission was clear: move forward. I was living the "Doug Steigerwald success axiom." Each band I formed or joined was a step in the direction *to the top*—and nobody, *no thing*, was going to stop me.

In my senior year of high school, I was in a band called Dusk, along with my perennial drummer, Rich Squillacioti (this is the band where I bid him farewell), and my best friend and fellow outcast, guitarist Don Mannello.* Joined by keyboardist Mark Williamson and bass player James "Dino" Dionisio, we had the distinction of being the most popular *new rock* band in the school. I make that distinction because there was a fifties tribute band (the fifties were all the rage in the seventies) called The Dukes, who were also popular. More about them later.

Because Dino Dionisio was the toughest guy in the school (he had once thrown a guy *over* the roof of a car), I was able to take my newly discovered I-don't-give-a-shit-what-you-think attitude to a new level. For the first time I explored what some would pejoratively call "fag" things such as wearing sparkles, women's jewelry, pink clothes, and dancing around onstage. This was all a part of the popular "glitter rock" movement of the time, but for a kid in a suburban high school, to wear stuff and perform like that at a dance was pretty risqué. Thanks to Dino, I not only got away with it, but all the cool kids danced furiously to my band, cheering, requesting songs, and a lot of the hot girls looked at me for the first time as if I wasn't a total loser. I had a steady girlfriend by then, but it was nice anyway. Oh, yeah . . . fuck you all.

I graduated from high school in 1973, on the honor roll (I finally applied myself), and headed off into my future without ever looking back. Other than for my time in the concert choir† and maybe drama club, I had absolutely no "glory days." I didn't go to the prom or even buy a yearbook.

With my buddy Don Mannello (this time on bass) we formed a new band called Harlequin, but I also enrolled at the New York Institute of Technology, majoring in communications. Due to pressure from my parents and a girlfriend, I went to school as a "safety net" in case I didn't make it in rock 'n' roll. I figured if I couldn't make records, I would play them, so I went to school to learn to be a disc jockey. I know . . . foreshadowing.

---

* Don Mannello went on to become Don Fury, legendary New York City hardcore-music producer. I'm proud of you, Don!

† I ultimately finished high school a classically trained countertenor, making All County, All State, and All Eastern Seaboard Choirs (making me one of the three hundred top high school voices on the East Coast), and received a 6A rating, the highest rating from the New York State School Music Association (NYSSMA). The only negative on my rating card was the comment "Moves too much."

Harlequin was a classic, self-indulgent seventies power trio with a vocalist (me) that was very impressed with itself. Roger Peterson (guitar), Joe Moro (drums), Don, and I homed in on being loud and heavy for the sake of being loud and heavy. In my first true metal band, I was finally playing music I totally loved.

Until the early metal bands arrived, tremendous unity existed among rock fans. Just look at the bands on the bill at the original Woodstock: The Who, Richie Havens, Crosby, Stills & Nash, Mountain, Country Joe and the Fish, Jimi Hendrix, Sha Na Na, Ten Years After, Sly and the Family Stone, Santana—what a confused mishmash of genres! And the audience cheered equally for all of them.

Not me. I liked the heavy bands and hated the light ones. I was into Mountain, Cream, and Hendrix, bought the first Led Zeppelin and Black Sabbath records when they were released, and purchased Grand Funk Railroad's *On Time* the very day it came out. Hell, in ninth grade I was in a band that *only* played Black Sabbath. For me it was "Helter Skelter" not "Blackbird," "Jumpin' Jack Flash" not "Angie," and I didn't want to "mellow out," I wanted to rock!

In 1972 I remember being at a high school party and Don Mannello and I nearly coming to blows with Phil Knourzer (yes, my ex–bass player) and his hippie friends over negative comments they made about Jimi Hendrix and Deep Purple. The Woodstock Nation was crumbling and I was swinging a heavy-metal sledgehammer!

Harlequin played out more than my other bands and rehearsed more, too. I improved my vocal and performing chops. We were locally popular, and for the first time I felt I might be in the band that would take me to the top.

Then I received the phone call from Peacock.

I DON'T REMEMBER HOW they heard of or found me, but a working cover band called Peacock approached me about singing for them. They had just canned their vocalist and needed a replacement. I went to see them perform and was less than impressed. They had the worst introduction I'd ever heard. "We're Peacock! *P* as in *pea;*

C as in *cock*! Those of you on the left can see the *pea*, those of you on the right can see the *cock*!" Yikes!

They were a human jukebox, playing "the rock hits and nothing but the rock hits, so help me God" adequately enough, but I was in a badass heavy-metal band with virtuoso musicians; this was definitely a step down. As I stood there watching, the memory of Doug Steigerwald's voice rang in my ears: "The minute you stop moving forward, you are done."

Harlequin was struggling to get into the club scene, getting only an occasional lousy booking and playing outdoor shows in county parks. Peacock was working five nights a week, every week. This was an opportunity not only to make my living playing music, but also to develop my chops and be seen. Peacock wasn't *the* band, but *that* band might be out there watching.

I knew it was going to take everything I had to make it in music, but I also knew this about myself: if I had a safety net (going to college) . . . I would use it.

⇥ DEE LIFE LESSON ⇤

It's too easy to allow yourself to fail when failure "isn't that bad." When failing means complete and total self-destruction, you work much harder to succeed.

At least that's how it is for me. The choice for me needed to be succeed or die . . . so away the net went. Once again, being the least asshole I could, I left my friends in Harlequin (including my long-time best friend and bandmate Don Mannello), broke the news of my leaving school to my parents, and joined Peacock.

PLAYING FIVE NIGHTS A week did help me get my act together. I moved out of my house (and into my grandfather's basement apartment in Flushing, Queens) and became a professional musician. I clearly remember riding home in the band truck (they had their own equipment truck!) before sunrise my first night with the band, hanging out the truck window, and screaming, "I love this!" Playing in a working band, being a rock 'n' roll vampire, is all I wanted to do. And I did.

During my time with Peacock I learned a few things. The biggest being "always bring your A game." Doing five sets a night (forty minutes on, twenty minutes off) meant starting early with a sparsely filled club and ending late with a near-empty club. The middle set was the most crowded, and the second and fourth were the build up and the build down. The guys in Peacock wore stage clothes and such, but only really put on a show for the middle sets. They adjusted their dress and performance to the number of people in the club. Weekday nights were slower, so they did less (if it was really slow, we didn't dress or put on a show at all), while weekends were packed, so they kicked it up. What a stupid concept.

The fewer people there are, the *harder* you have to work. You want those people to stay, tell their friends, and come back next time to see that incredible band that kicked ass to four people! When I joined Twisted Sister (the next working band I was in), I made sure that every set, no matter how empty the place was, got 110 percent of what I had to offer. I firmly believe that *that* is the attitude that helped Twisted become a tristate club phenomenon and to this day one of the greatest live performing bands ever. Ask anyone who has seen us in concert.* And, no, none of the other members of Peacock ever did anything significant with their music careers.

The other major thing I learned was more lifestyle-related. I lived in the basement apartment alone and kept traditional musician hours: go to bed at sunrise, get up in the afternoon. Well, one winter night I got back to my apartment around 4:00 a.m. It was still dark out. I was exhausted, so I hit the sack immediately. When I woke up, it was still dark out, so I checked the clock and saw it was a little after five. At first I thought, *Oh, I've only been asleep for an*

---

* Randy Jackson, guitarist/lead singer of Zebra, told Atlantic record company mogul Jason in 1982, "Twisted Sister is the best live performing band in the world. We can't touch 'em and neither can anyone else." After seeing the band that night, Jason said, "The band (Twisted Sister) . . . put on one of the best concerts I've ever seen (and I've pretty much seen them all)."

hour, but I didn't feel tired at all. Confused, I finally realized that it was after 5:00 *p.m. . . . and I wasn't even sure what day it was!*

This may not seem like a big deal to you, but I was freaked. I turned on the TV and figured out that I'd been asleep for over thirteen hours. The concept boggled my mind. I sat there realizing how an entire day had gone by. People had gone to school or work and come home, the stock exchange had opened and closed, major events had been held, etc. I didn't know if it had been sunny or cloudy because I had slept a whole day! I vowed that, even though my profession of choice was a night job, from that day on I would never sleep the day away again, and I would wake up early on my days off and get the hell out of my apartment. There was more to life than just playing in the band. (Did I just say that?) Maybe not the most stunning revelation, but it was the start of an understanding of balance that would affect my life and career.

I had a few other epiphanies while I was in Peacock. The first was with my grandfather. Moving into the basement apartment at my mom's dad's house served two purposes. First, it got me out of my parents' house and closer to Peacock's home base in Queens. I couldn't stand living at home anymore. My life choices were a constant source of friction between my father and me, I had no privacy, and I couldn't stand suburbia. I shared my room with my two younger brothers, Mark and Doug (then thirteen and eleven years old), with only a Peg-Board divider to section off my cell-like space and give any kind of privacy. We were living on top of one another, and when I'd blast my heavy music, my little brothers would beg for mercy.* I guess it wasn't easy on them either.

At times, life in the Snider household got to be so maddening, I'd get in my car, drive somewhere, park, and just sit there, blasting my music, with the heat on high (Dad kept the thermostat at home set to a chilly sixty-eight degrees Fahrenheit to save money), and read comics. It felt great to have my own little space.

To make matters worse, I found suburbia to be absolutely suffocating. The congestion of Baldwin, the monotony of tract housing,

---

* As much as they used to beg, they eventually grew to love metal. My brother Mark became the producer and writer of the legendary, hugely popular eighties syndicated-radio metal show *Metal Shop.* I was so proud.

and the cookie-cutter existence of everyone there drove me nuts. I knew there had to be more to life than this out there somewhere. Early in the morning, before the cacophony of sound that was suburbia kicked in, I could actually hear a waterfall somewhere in the distance. In all my years of living and wandering around my neighborhood, I had never seen one, but I could clearly hear it. Just knowing of something nearby as beautiful as a waterfall brought me joy and inner peace. I used to sit on the front porch early in the morning, drinking coffee, and just listen. It made me smile.

One morning, I was outside so content, just listening and smiling, when my dad came out. "What are you doing?"

"Listening to the waterfall." Even he couldn't ruin that.

Dad stopped, listened for a moment, then laughed. "That's not a waterfall. That's the sound of the cars on the parkway, stupid!" With that, he walked off. He had other dreams and fantasies to destroy. I was devastated.

The other reason for moving in with my grandfather was to keep him company. My grandmother had recently passed away, leaving him alone for the first time since he was a young man. My parents figured just having another person's energy in the house would be good for him during the transition.

I really liked my grandfather, and from time to time he would cook and we'd have dinner together. One night he opened up to me and changed my life forever. Grandpa was a tool-and-die man in his day, making specialty, precision mechanical pieces for machinery. He actually made parts used on the first lunar landing. Grandpa had worked extremely hard his whole life and provided well for his family, but he told me how he had allowed himself to be taken advantage of by his fellow workers, often doing their work without getting the credit, accolades, and advancement. Frank Schenker (my grandfather) was a great guy and a good worker, but he was a sucker and a pushover. His next words to me fell hard on a nineteen-year-old whose life lay ahead of him, like so many blank pages waiting to be written. "Danny, don't be wishy-washy like I was," my eightysomething-year-old grandfather warned. "Don't let people walk all over you." I understood what my grandfather was saying to me. Thank you for that advice, Grandpa. *I never did.*

The life lessons were mounting during my less than one-year

stint in Peacock. But the biggest—about relationships—I came to on my own.

Being single in a working rock band meant there was no shortage of girls. It doesn't matter if you are in a good band or bad, unknown or famous, rich or poor (of course the better and more famous the band, and the more money you have, the hotter the girls you will get), there will always be girls out there who want to be with guys in bands. It's without a doubt the most common reason you will hear for guys joining bands in the first place: to meet chicks. A different club every night meant a different girl every night, and while that certainly has its appeal, for me something was lacking.

One miserable winter day, I had a bad cold and was alone in my apartment. It was rainy and I was staring out of the little basement window at the grayness outside, the cold radiating through the glass. I felt terrible and badly wanted someone to be with, but what "rock chick" would want to hang with a sick rocker with a runny nose, a fever, and a cough? And what rock chick would I want to be with when I felt like this? At the ripe old age of nineteen, I clearly remember thinking to myself, *Will I ever meet someone who will be with me all the time?* I already knew that the traditional rock-star life would not be for me.

Less than two years later, my prayer would be answered.

❧ 5 ❧

crash and burn #1

My time in Peacock ended with my first of many crash-and-burns. You'd think I would learn. Growing issues with the disgusting bass player (who shall remain nameless because he is a douche) finally peaked with a physical confrontation, and I quit. I had tolerated his hygiene, cigarette smoking, difficult personality, and naked jumping jacks. I could deal with all that (well, maybe not the jumping jacks), but the minute things turned violent, I was out. I know you've heard a myriad of stories of great rock bands having physical altercations among themselves (sometimes even onstage), but with what sometimes seemed like the whole world against me, the one place I would not and will not tolerate fistfights is within my band. No doubt at times you want to kill each other, but this is your art and your passion. Save that hostility for the haters.

Within weeks of leaving the band I was broke. I've always been terrible with money and had mismanaged what I made with the band. My rent was months overdue and I had no cash for food; I was living on peanut-butter-and-jelly sandwiches. My parents, seeing how I had fallen flat on my independent face, "ordered" me to move back home. They knew they couldn't actually command me, but they saw I was too proud to ask, so they *told me* I was coming back, whether I liked it or not, until I got back on my feet. *Thanks for that, Mom and Dad.*

Within weeks of moving back in, I'd hit real rock bottom: my car broke down and I couldn't afford to get it fixed. In suburbia, not having a car is worse than not having a place to live. You can always live in your car. No money, no job, no girlfriend, in debt, living with my parents, no band *and* no car? Yeah, that's about as low as you can go. My only choice was to set aside my dream of being a rock star and do what I had to do to get back on my feet. I swallowed what was left of my pride and got a job on the loading dock of a new department store, Korvettes, about to open.

Now, I've never had a problem with manual labor; I'd been working since I was twelve. My family didn't have a lot of money, so if you wanted something, you had to earn the money to buy it, and what kid doesn't want things? Especially when you get to junior high and high school and start wanting clothes and records and money to go out. As a result, starting with a paper route when I was twelve (and various odd jobs such as housepainting, mowing lawns, and snow shoveling), I always worked. I was a busboy, bathroom attendant, landscaper, grillman, taxi driver, garbage collector, baby-sitter, and more. You do what you have to do.

The job on the loading dock seemed like a fair enough way to get out of the hole I was in, but at the orientation I discovered not everyone saw the work the way I did. At the end of the job orientation, the managers opened the floor to questions. I had none. I'd work, get paid, and when I was back on my feet, I'd be gone. Not my coworkers. They wanted to know about benefits, retirement plans, workmen's comp, maternity leave, and more. All these nineteen- and twentysomethings were talking as if they were going to be there forever.

Later, on the loading dock, I asked the guys about their long-term goals. They unanimously responded, "It's a good company. There's a future here. Why? You're not looking to stay?" Without giving a thought to the consequences, I blurted, "Hell no! I'm gonna be a rock star!" Big mistake.

"Rock star." That was my new nickname, and it wasn't meant as a compliment. I was mercilessly goofed on for my ambition and it was used against me.

"Hey, Rock star, pick up that garbage." "Rock star, scrape that gum off the floor." "Hey, Rock star, one of the toilets over-flowed." If there was a humiliating job to be done, it was given to me, always announced loudly for all to hear and prefaced with "Hey, Rock star . . ." Sometimes they would even say it over the store intercom system for everyone's amusement. It sucked, but it didn't discourage me. Working in that department store was just an unfortunate necessity on my journey. I knew that in time I would leave it and all those insulting assholes behind and be back on my way to stardom. Oh, and by the way . . . that department store chain eventually went bankrupt. Fuck ya! Though an interesting thing did happen one day on the loading dock. . . .

My coworkers and I had just unloaded a semitruck full of mattresses and were sitting or lying comfortably on top of a stack of them, waiting for the freight elevator to arrive. Suddenly, a junker of a car tears into the empty parking lot across the street and starts spinning out doing squealing 360s. "Hey, Rock star," one of the losers on the dock exclaimed, "that guy looks like you!" Focusing on the driver of the car, I saw he did have a massive Afro as I did. We made eye contact and waved to each other, brothers in hair.

At that time, my frizzy brown hair was growing to monsterish dimensions. It had always been just parted in the middle, up until my joining Peacock, when drummer Seth Posner had taken me to his hairstylist to do something with my "mop." In the late sixties, a Long Island, also-ran band called The Illusion had been known for their neatly groomed Caucasian Afros. Seth thought this was a great way to tame my mane, and it was for a while. Not being big on haircuts, my 'fro had got huge! When I was finally promoted from the loading dock to the selling floor of the housewares department, I became the top salesman of *hair dryers*. Even though I didn't use one (other than, from time to time, my landscaper friend's leaf blower with its 100 mph winds), customers just assumed the guy with all the hair must know, so they flocked to me for advice. Eventually, I was told I had to cut my hair or lose my job. Guess which I chose?

Years later, when Mark "the Animal" Mendoza and I finally, officially met (after months of silent acknowledgment as our wall-scraping "hair hats" barely missed each other in the clubs), he told me that he was the lunatic doing the spinouts that day in the parking lot. Animal said he saw my incredible Afro and decided to put on a little show for a fellow "hair farmer," with the auto-parts-store delivery car he was driving. True story.

DURING MY TIME OF recovery, I tried putting a new band together (Heathen), but it never got off the ground and eventually disbanded. Then I heard about something that lit me up: the local band Twisted Sister was performing without a lead singer.

From my last year of high school through my year of college and all during my time in Peacock, I was aware of the band. Born of the New York Dolls and the glitter rock of the early seventies, Twisted Sister—who advertised themselves as Mott the Hoople's favorite band, until Mott got wind of it and sent them a cease-and-desist order—were popular in the tristate area (New York, New Jersey, and Connecticut). Though I'd never seen them perform, I had seen their picture in the local music papers and heard about their act: full-on makeup and bouffant hairdos, platform shoes and glam clothes, playing the best of Bowie, Mott, Lou Reed, and more glitter rock bands of that era.

Formed in 1973, the original band only lasted about eighteen months before imploding. Lead singer Michael Valentine's partying finally got to be too much (though he did come up with the band's amazing name one wild night), and the band fell apart. In early 1975 the band reformed with a new singer and lead guitarist, the new singer was quickly given the boot, and by the summer of 1975 guitarist Jay Jay French had taken over "singing" for the band.

When I got wind that Twisted was without a lead vocalist, I saw a real opportunity. I loved all the bands they covered and was into glitter rock (which was technically over by 1975), but had yet to get into the whole makeup thing. Hell, I had a mustache until I left Peacock! As part of my "fresh start" after I left Peacock, I decided to remove the offending "crumb catcher." Thank God. I never grew it back.

The thing I loved most about Twisted Sister was the name. *Twisted Sister.* Man, did that conjure up some exotic imagery. I had to get in that band.

In August of 1975, they were playing a club in Wantagh, Long Island, called Bobby Mac's. Using my landscaper friend's backpack leaf blower, I blew my hair out to majestic proportions, put on my glitter platform shoes, and headed out to see them for the first time.

I walked into the small, filled, but not crowded club and parked myself on the dance floor. The band's set was composed entirely of songs by Lou Reed, Mott, Bowie, Kinks, the Stones and the like, talk/sung in classic Lou Reed style by guitarist Jay Jay French (he can't sing for shit). The band looked great and Jay Jay French exuded some real rock-star attitude, but they *definitely needed a singer.* I couldn't wait to approach the band.

After the set, I kept an eye on the dressing-room door, waiting for them to come out. Keith Angelino, aka Keith Angel, the band's new guitarist, exited first. A real Keith Richards/Johnny Thunders clone, he seemed approachable, so I made my move. I introduced myself, told him that I sang my ass off and rocked righteously (but not in those words), and said I would love to sing for his band. Keith reacted pretty positively, but told me I would have to speak with Jay Jay.

Keith went back into the dressing room to get him, and a few minutes later out strode Jay Jay French wearing makeup, sunglasses, platform shoes, and appropriate glitter-rock garb. I have to admit I was in awe. This was one of the guys I had seen in all those ads in the papers, which was a big deal to someone trying to get in those papers! This was *the* Jay Jay French!

Jay Jay seemed already well informed about me and why I was there and told me how the band was building all of its material around his "vocal styling" and weren't interested in getting a new singer. Disheartened, I thanked Jay for his time. As I turned to leave, Jay Jay, in what, I would eventually learn, was his true businessman, pragmatist style, called after me, "But give me your phone number just in case." Not seeing a reason, I gave it to him anyway.

I later found out when I finally joined the band that Keith Angel (who was no longer in the band at the time) had told Jay Jay, "This asshole Danny Snider [my name at that time] is out there and wants to sing for the band." Jay Jay assumed that Keith knew me (he didn't, but in hindsight he had *keen* intuition) and wrote me off before he even heard what I had to say. *Where are you now, Keith Angelino?*

It would be almost half a year before I heard from Jay Jay French again.

THERE CAME A DAY when I realized that I had not been in a band, or sung, for close to six months! This was not a good thing on so many levels, the biggest one being getting out of shape vocally.

The voice box is a muscle, and like any muscle, if you work it regularly, it grows strong, but too hard it can get sore, and you can strain or permanently damage it. But if you don't work it out at all, it atrophies and grows weak. Not having sung for such a long time (for a singer), I knew I was ill prepared if the opportunity came along to play with a band. I needed to work my voice out.

I'm not exactly sure how I found the band—probably in the classifieds of the local rock paper or hanging on the board at some music store or rehearsal studio—but they not only needed a singer, they needed a bass player as well. Rather than wander into this band of aliens alone, I put in a quick call to my Heathen bass player, Lee Tobia. I told him I was just looking for a band to rehearse with to keep my chops together and asked if he wanted to audition with me. He was in between bands himself and needed to "work out," too, so we went to the audition together. I don't remember how good or bad the band was (I know I wasn't impressed enough to say "Wait a minute, I've found my next band!"), but it didn't matter, I just needed a band to rehearse with so I'd be ready when opportunity came. Years later, I would become a student of Tony Robbins's (that's right, the man is amazing), and he would verbalize what I instinctively knew: Luck is preparation meeting opportunity. I needed to be prepared because I knew opportunity was coming. Don't ask me how.

Lee and I aced the audition (of course) and were accepted into the band. When we asked the band's name, we were told that they would share that information with us once they were sure we were definitely the right guys. Why? Because the name was so good, theywere fearful we might steal it and use it with another band. Neither Lee or I had ever experienced something like this. *It must be one hell of a name.*

After several weeks of rehearsing (there were never any gigs or even talk of booking gigs), Lee and I were asked to stay after rehearsal for a band meeting. The guys sat us down and told us they were finally sure we were the right singer and bass player for their band (shows how little they knew) and were ready to share their top-secret name with us. (Drumroll, please.)

"This."

"This what?" Lee responded.

"This," they replied.

"This?" I chimed in, confused.

"Yeah. Just *This,"* retorted one of the rocket scientists posing as a band member. "Like 'this rocks' or 'this rules' or 'this is the best'!"

"What about *'this sucks'*?!" I shouted in disbelief.

Needless to say, Lee Tobia and I weren't welcome in This anymore. I wonder what laboratory the former members of This are working in?

BY MID-JANUARY OF 1976, I had been let go from Korvette's department store and started work at Double B Records & Tapes in Freeport, Long Island. Double B was a local distribution company, acting as a middleman between the record labels and stores. I was hired to man the 8-track section (remember those? Anyone? *Anyone?*) of the warehouse—not a very big department—filling store orders, then bringing them to shipping to be packed up and sent out.

I was being trained to replace the guy currently filling the orders. Once I was ready, he was going to leave, and my boss, Zeke, was set to go on a long-overdue vacation. As I filled the orders, I imagined how cool it would be when one day some kid was pulling orders for my albums.

Zeke was a complete asshole (as opposed to the partial assholes I had worked for before) with a squeaky high voice to match. He was a yeller and dogged my ass relentlessly.

One day I was on the pay phone just outside Zeke's office, and he overheard me talking to my This band members about rehearsal that night.

When I hung up, Zeke called me in. "What's this about a rehearsal?"

"Yeah, after work. It's with my band."

Zeke moved in for the kill. "Work comes first; your band is second. I need you to work late tonight. You can't rehearse with your band."

Can't rehearse? I never worked overtime. The prick had given me overtime just to fuck with me. I said nothing and left his office. Nothing was more important to me than my music. I knew my days at Double B Records & Tapes were numbered.

WITHIN A WEEK, AT the end of January 1976, I received invitations to audition for two bands. Man, I'd love to see my horoscope for that week. One was my old high school buddies' fifties band the Dukes. They had become quite a club staple, working regularly with a big following. I had sung in choir with the vocalists in the Dukes, so they knew I had the chops for the doo-wop that was the cornerstone of their show. I love fifties music, so I was pretty excited to get the call.

The second call was from . . . *Jay Jay French of Twisted Sister!* After several months of going it on his own (and the breakup and reformation of the band for a third time), Jay Jay had been convinced by numerous people that the band really needed a singer/ front man.

Remember why I said I left my killer band Harlequin to join the lesser band Peacock? To develop my performing and singing chops and be seen by people. Well, it worked.

Peacock's club booking agent, Kevin Brenner of Creative Talent Associates (CTA), whom I virtually never saw, had noticed me. As the longtime agent for Twisted Sister, he not only told Jay Jay the band needed a front man, he suggested Jay check out "Danny Snider."

"Danny Snider?" Jay Jay replied. "That guy approached me to join the band months ago."

You know how when you have never heard a certain word or seen a certain thing before, and after you do, it seems as if you're hearing or seeing it everywhere? That's kind of what it was like with Jay Jay and me. After I introduced myself at the club that night, it seemed Jay was constantly hearing my name.

Long before Kevin Brenner brought me up to Jay, a barkeep named Phil Zozzaro, whom everyone called Wha,* from one of the clubs both Twisted Sister and Peacock played, was constantly telling Jay Jay about this kid who sang for Peacock. "You gotta check him out, Jay Jay! The kid's amazing!" Thanks for that, Wha.

DO YOU KNOW WHAT LSD is? No, not the hallucinogen. *Lead Singer Disease.* Oh, it's real, and all front men have it. I won't deny it. Of course we do. Front men have chosen a profession where we are expected to stand in front of a crowd with only our voice and personality to entertain with. We have no guitar or drums between us and the audience, no buttons, knobs, pedals, or screws to futz with when the music stops or the crowd gets antsy. We're out there with our dick in our hands. All we've got to protect ourselves is the massive ego it takes to get up there in the first place. It's that we're so full of ourselves that makes us believe people will actually want to listen and watch us do the things we do. Front men are fucked in the head by definition.

It's been said that most people are more afraid of public speaking than they are of dying. We are the nuts who choose the former as our livelihood. Of course we're fucked-up. You need us to be! Our band members want us to be cocky, egotistical, and defiant onstage, but then "lose the 'tude" the minute we get offstage. Ha! It doesn't work like that. It's not a switch we can just flick on and off; it's who we are. It's what makes us tick. It's what makes us rock. I appreciate your (the band's) frustration, but the "ego-less front man" is a mythical creature, like a unicorn or Bigfoot. They don't exist.

The point is, all bands hope against hope that somehow they can manage without a front man. Maybe one of the guys in the band, one of the *musicians*, can handle the job and they'll be able to get by without one. While it can happen, and there are some great guitar or bass-player/vocalists, keyboard or even drummer/vocalists, the terrible truth is LSD is contagious. Eventually, whoever that "lead

---

* Phil was called Wha because every time someone talked to him, he responded, "Wha?" (Get it?)

guy" is, will catch it and become just as bad as any other front man. It comes with the territory.

After dealing with two nightmare lead singers, Jay Jay was hoping that maybe he could make a go of it without one. He even brought his childhood friend Eddie Ojeda into the band on guitar and vocals. Eddie's got a great voice . . . but he's not a front man. Jay Jay tried to do it without one, but he couldn't, so he made the call. Maybe this Danny Snider won't be like the others. *Fat chance.*

It didn't take me long to choose between the Dukes and Twisted Sister. I knew the whole fifties thing was just a craze; there was no future in recording old songs (Sha Na Na had already milked the hell out of that cow), and I would have to cut my hair! Deal breaker. I saw a real future in Twisted Sister, so I jumped at the chance to audition.

There was one problem. I had just finished training at my job, the guy I was replacing had left, and my boss was scheduled to go on vacation the week Twisted Sister wanted me to go away with them to audition. Wait a minute! I was looking for a way to get even with Zeke the Asshole. Problem solved! I quit my job without notice and left that prick hanging (no pun intended). It not only destroyed his vacation, but had him pulling 8-track tapes himself while he looked for a replacement for me. *Payback's a muthafucker!*

6

this is twisted sister?

My audition for Twisted Sister was not going to be typical. The band had a long weekend of shows booked in a club at an upstate New York ski area called Hunter Mountain. Jay Jay had made a deal with the Turtleneck Inn to spend the week there. The plan was for me to drive with the band to the club, audition, and, if all went well, rehearse with them during the week for the weekend shows. I don't know if they were confident I would pass muster or just hopeful, but I readily agreed to the plan. I had never lost an audition in my life, but I still brought money for a bus ticket home. The last thing I wanted was to be stuck for a week with a band that didn't want me and then have the long drive home with them as well. Besides, Queen (when they were still metal) were playing while I was away, and having not missed any of their previous tours (this was before they broke big—I'm an original fan! *Queen II* is the best), I wasn't going to blow the audition *and* a chance to see my then-favorite band in concert.

I felt everything I'd done in my life up until that point had led to this audition. I was ready.

On February 1 (my dad's birthday), the night before we were supposed to leave, a major ice storm hit the region. I was sure my big audition would be postponed, but despite all travel in the area being disrupted, the plan remained the same. Kenny Neill, the original Twisted Sister bass player, was going to drive the band station wagon (they had a band car!) from his home in Upper Montclair, New Jersey, out to Long Island (normally a three-hour drive; with the weather it must have taken him at least four) to pick me up at my parents' house in Baldwin, then we'd drive and pick up the new Twisted drummer, Kevin John Grace (drummer number two, for those keeping count), a couple of towns over from me in Levittown. Next we'd get Jay Jay in Manhattan, then head to the Bronx to pick up guitarist Eddie Ojeda. Only then would we all head upstate to Palenville, New York, to the Turtleneck Inn. *Sounds easy enough.*

I had seen photos of Kenny Neill and he looked like a pretty wild guy, but the person who arrived to pick me up was anything but. Looking and sounding incredibly normal (and a bit nerdy; sorry, Kenny), he seemed extremely *mature.* All of the members of the band (besides Kevin) were three to five years older than me. It doesn't seem like much now, but when you're twenty, that's a significant difference, and I think it played a role in some of the problems that developed between the guys and me later.

Still, I was superexcited and loaded my bag into the car to begin my adventure. On our ride, I quickly found out that Kenny was a recovering alcoholic (a bit more rock 'n' roll) and attending several AA meetings every week. I was amazed that he was able to work in a bar/club environment and control his disease. He did, and never fell off the wagon during the couple of years we worked together. To the best of my knowledge, Kenny is now around thirty-five years sober. Good on you, Kenny.

When we got to drummer Kevin John Grace's house, he seemed young (maybe even younger than me) and came out to the car wearing glasses and *galoshes*! I had seen a photo of Kevin; he looked great and didn't wear glasses (or galoshes). I guess he took them off for the band stuff. Not that there's anything wrong with needing them (all of Jay Jay's sunglasses are prescription), but the effect of the glasses, the galoshes, gloves, and winter coat was . . . very dorky. This was *thee* Twisted Sister and I was driving in an olive-green station wagon with two nerds! Next stop, New York City to pick up the local legend Jay Jay French.

To most Long Island kids, Manhattan is pretty intimidating. This was the midseventies and New York was anything but "the safest big city in America." It was the exact opposite. This was the Manhattan portrayed in *Serpico, The French Connection*, and *Death Wish*, when Harlem was *Harlem* and Forty-Second Street was filled with hookers, sex shops, and XXX theaters. Pre-Disney. Manhattan in those days was riddled with "bad areas" and you needed to know your way around to avoid potential problems. I had rarely been there except for parades with my parents, occasional school trips, and a couple of concerts. On one of my more recent visits, the guys in Harlequin and I had nearly gotten jacked by a gang one night in Central Park, after a Uriah Heep concert (back when they literally used to stop anyone from entering the park at night because it was too dangerous). I was not a NYC fan.

Jay Jay lived on the Upper West Side, where he was born, raised, still lives today, and, I'm sure, they will carry his body out of one day. Hey, nobody gives up a rent-controlled apartment in New York City. In 1976, this was the lower edge of Harlem and *not* a safe place.

The three of us arrived at Jay's place and parked the car. To the best of my recollection, Kevin stayed with the car to watch our stuff (what he would have done if someone tried to rip us off, I don't know. Hit him with a galosh?), and Kenny and I headed upstairs to get Jay.

Jay answered the door wearing glasses, overalls, a sweater, and white Capezio dance shoes. What the hell was going on!? This was not the tall, cool glitter rocker I had met six months before! He was doing some last-minute packing for the trip and invited me into his room to talk.

While I waited for him to get ready, I was introduced to a level of pornography I had never before experienced. This was the seventies, and my exposure was limited to *Playboy* and *Penthouse* magazines; porn was not my thing. It was Jay Jay's. He had imported porn magazines with photo exposés that were staggering to a twenty-year-old bumpkin from Baldwin, Long Island. I'll never forget the one with a beautiful, blond (Swedish?) woman who, after a long day at work, comes home . . . to do five guys at once. The shot of her with one guy in each hand and the other three in each of her orifices mystified me for a long time. I had so many questions. Talk about your first impressions.

Our next stop was the Bronx to pick up Eddie Ojeda. Now, if New York City was intimidating, the Bronx was a whole other level.

I'd only seen it portrayed in movies like *Fort Apache, the Bronx* and heard about it in terrible stories on the news; never in a flattering light. I was more than a little nervous to go there.

Eddie Ojeda is Spanish/Puerto Rican. Growing up in lily-white Baldwin (we had three "Negros" in the whole school), I didn't really know any Hispanic people (I did have one Mexican friend named Carlos), but again, I had seen their portrayals on television and in films. Not so flattering.

When we arrived at Eddie's family's apartment building on Jerome Avenue, the place was buzzing with activity. Just like in the movies. We pulled up in front and Jay Jay jumped out to go inside to get Eddie. I was amazed at how casually this bizarre rocker/farmer/dancer (Jay was now wearing a fur-trimmed coat) walked through all the commotion in front of the building and went inside. Fearless. As we sat and waited (forever), it seemed emergency sirens were constantly going off. So far this experience was doing nothing to dissipate my fears or preconceptions.

Suddenly I heard someone screaming. I turned and saw a woman burst out of the front door of Eddie's building, with her hands covering her face and blood pouring out. *What the fuck!?* Police and emergency vehicles arrived, all hell was breaking loose . . . then Jay Jay and Eddie casually walked out of the building, chatting and laughing as I sat in shock.

Sporting a "disco haircut" and wearing a long, herringbone tweed coat, Eddie did not look rock 'n' roll, but he seemed pretty cool. I quickly impressed him by asking if his last name was actually pronounced *O-hey-da* (three years of mediocre grades in Spanish, finally paying off), and he proceeded to reinforce every stereotype I had about Puerto Ricans.

Before we had driven a block, Eddie asked if we could pull over at a check-cashing place so he could get some money. He used the money to purchase a bottle of booze at a liquor store conveniently located next door, then drank it with a brown bag around it! *Are you kidding me!?* Could he have been any more ethnic? This was atypical behavior for Eddie, and to this day he cracks up when he thinks of how it must have looked to a twenty-year-old, culture-shocked kid from the suburbs. Thanks, Eddie.

Now that we had the whole band, we began our *supposed* two-hour drive upstate to the Turtleneck Inn. The operative word being *supposed*.

As night fell, due to the ice travel became even more dangerous, and as we got closer and closer to our destination in the Catskill Mountains, the roads became downright treacherous. Our pace slowed to a crawl, but credit to our intrepid driver Kenny (who had now been on the road close to twelve hours) for ultimately getting us to our destination safely.

The travel time certainly didn't go to waste. We talked the hours away and got to know each other. I was really hitting it off with Kevin John Grace, probably because he was closest to my age from Long Island and less worldly than the other three. We were both rubes from the suburbs.

While I barely remember any of the conversations we had during that drive, I do remember one clearly. The band was currently going under the name Twisted Sister '76, to acknowledge the new lineup and capitalize on the coming US bicentennial celebration. (Anybody remember the hubbub about that?) The band was even draping the stage in American flags and had a new Twisted Sister '76 logo of a topless girl with a flag on her chest. Jay Jay (always the pragmatist) informed me that with three-fifths of the band (assuming I was brought in) being new, after the bicentennial the band was changing its name. *What?!*

New guy or not, I couldn't sit by and watch this even being discussed as a possibility. I told him that he was way too close to be objective. As an outsider, I could attest to the value of the name within the club scene, and long-term, the name Twisted Sister was priceless. Not only for the band-defining imagery it conjured up, but for the cleverness of the play on words and the sibilance of the two words together. *Twisted Sister!* I'm sure I didn't explain it quite as eloquently as that, but I got my point across, and I think it made sense to Jay Jay. Changing the name was never discussed again.

WHILE THE AFOREMENTIONED QUEEN were my favorite *new* band, a number of other groups were helping to define me as a vocalist and a performer. I loved a lot of the bands of the glitter rock scene. Bowie, Mott the Hoople, T. Rex, Sparks (anyone? Anyone?), Sweet, the New York Dolls, and others were regulars on my turntable, but here are the Big Three: Led Zeppelin, Black Sabbath, and Alice Cooper. The original Alice Cooper band for their attitude and showmanship, Black Sabbath for their riffs and menace, and Led Zeppelin . . . because every member of the band is a god!

If any one band is responsible for my turning to the heavier side, it's Led Zeppelin. If any one vocalist is responsible for sending me screeching into the stratosphere, it is the amazing Robert Plant. I had a poster of Robert hanging over my bed throughout high school, so I would literally bow down before him every time I got in bed. And if I, as a singer was known for one thing, it was for doing a hell of a Robert Plant impersonation.

The tristate bar/club scene was all about playing covers. There was virtually no place to play original material, and the club-going audience didn't want to hear any. Sad, really. Bands were expected to be human jukeboxes, playing the songs people knew and wanted to hear. The hits. When it came to rock bands and rock music, no band was bigger than Led Zeppelin. Bands went to incredible lengths to play the most accurate renditions of Zeppelin songs, and the audiences demanded it. Playing Led Zeppelin poorly was sacrilege. The funny thing is, I remember seeing Led Zep on their 1977 tour and being stunned by how "inaccurate" they were live. Sorry, boys, but if a bar band played your music the way you did that night, they would have been tarred, feathered, and run out of town on a rail. Seriously.

That said, if a bar band could play Led Zeppelin fairly well, they could work, and that I could sing the shit out of Zep songs had always been my meal ticket.

On February 2, 1976, the day of my audition, we ran through a bunch of songs that we all knew, but I know it was my versions of "Communication Breakdown" and "Good Times Bad Times" that sealed the deal. I could sing Led Zeppelin well, and that (to business-minded Jay Jay French) was money in the bank.

A short time after my audition, Jay Jay asked me to step outside with him into the cold winter night. He was complimentary about my audition, but then laid down the rules:

(1) He owned the name Twisted Sister. (This after planning on abandoning it not twenty-four hours earlier.)

(2) He owned the PA system.

(3) Charlie Barreca, the band soundman, was a member of the band.

Apparently, the grand plan was that Jay Jay would play guitar, manage the band, and be the songwriter, and Charlie would be the soundman, tour manager, and producer of the band's records. Sounds impressive, doesn't it? Jay and Charlie came up with this brain fart while smoking a joint on a beach in Bermuda. Must have been really good shit.

Jay Jay was planning on reforming Twisted for a third time, and he knew his old friend Charlie (literally. Charlie was ten years older than Jay) had done sound on a Grateful Dead documentary that had never seen the light of day. (Sounds qualified to do live sound and studio recording to me.) There you have it. Proof positive that marijuana makes you stupider.

After laying down the law with me—to which I agreed readily— Jay Jay says, "All right . . . we'll see how it goes." What? What does that even mean? Was I in the band or not? That was how it was left. With that uncertainty, I sort of joined the band that would take me to the top. This lack of security for my position with the band is another piece in the dysfunctional relationship that ultimately developed between them and me.

Having been *kind of* welcomed into the band, I went back inside to join my *sort of* bandmates. I sidled up to Kevin John Grace at the bar to share my *goodish* news and bond a bit more with my new drummer. As I begin chatting with Kevin about our new relationship and how we were going to rock, Jay Jay French comes up on the opposite side of me and whispers in my ear, midsentence, "Don't get too friendly with him; he's being kicked out." Yikes! Trying not to give anything away to Kevin as we continued to speak, I wondered about "job security" in this band. Clearly, we were all replaceable.

VIEWING THIS OPPORTUNITY AS a new beginning for me in a new life, I approached Jay Jay French for some sage advice. I already looked up to this guy. "I want this to be a fresh start for me," I told Jay. "I want a new first name. What do you think I should call myself?" He looked at me seriously and said, "Let me think about it."

The next day as we passed each other on the stairs leading up to our rooms, Jay Jay says to me, "What about *Dee*, like Dee Dee Ramone, but just Dee?" I thought about it for literally a second and said, "I like it. Tell everyone not to call me Danny anymore." And that was it. Dee Snider was born. God help everybody.

7

wild enema nozzles

I was eased into the show over the next few weeks as I learned more of the band's cover material. They had a few original songs that I hated ("TV Wife," "Follow Me," "Company Man," "Can't Stand Still for a Minute"), but in the seventies tristate club scene, you couldn't even announce you were playing an original. You'd introduce it as an obscure track from a popular band. "Here's one from Deep Purple's first album!" If your original song was good, in between sets people would come up to you and say, "I love that Deep Purple song!"

Besides my taking over the vocals on existing material, the band added songs (starting with more Led Zeppelin) that better showcased my voice. Material that didn't work for me (such as the Kinks, Stones, and Dave Mason) was cut from the sets. The song list wasn't the only evident change. Visually, I was ready to explore the more glam side of rock that I felt defined the name Twisted Sister. While I had worn costumes onstage before, they were nowhere as feminine as the direction I was headed, and I had never worn any makeup.

Now, in 1976, at the age of twenty, I was not nearly as secure in my heterosexuality as I am now. No, it's not that I thought I might be gay, it was just the suburban, adolescent fear of people *thinking* I might be gay that I wrestled with. That said, I was anxious to embrace the whole thing, but from a more theatrical Alice Cooper direction than a gender-bending David Bowie one. Building off a pair of thigh-high, black-leather, five-inch platform boots (very Alice), I pulled together whatever "borderline" feminine outfits I could, without going over the line (read: flaming homosexual.) These consisted of mostly black and white leotards, jumpsuits, and some leftover glitter clothing from my Peacock days. My most outrageous outfit was the aforementioned boots, black stockings, cutoff black shorts (think Daisy Dukes), long sleevelets, and a T-shirt that said I'M DEE, BLOW ME.* Okay, that outfit was pretty tranny-ish. Not that there's anything wrong with it.

Makeup-wise, I was as safe and cautious as possible. Jay Jay (my mentor at that time) showed me how to apply base (foundation), and I would put some gray on my eyelids (going for a bit of a speed-freak thing) and reddish circles on my cheekbones like a doll. *It was a start.*

Joining Twisted Sister, I thought I was entering the real world of rock 'n' roll excess. Jay Jay would tell tales of Twisted's early days (all of two years before), filled with sex, drinking, and drugs, and I would listen enraptured, but I wasn't seeing much evidence of it now. The guys all had steady girlfriends, Kenny Neill was sober, Jay Jay French had pretty much stopped drinking and getting high, Kevin John Grace was a hayseed like me, and while Eddie Ojeda did like to party, with his high-waisted baggies, disco hair, and Gibson 335 hollow-body guitar, he seemed more Latino than rock. Bummer. Still, I felt rock 'n' roll excess was imminent.

WE WERE BOOKED TO play a club in Levittown, Long Island, called Hammerheads. For some reason most of the bars we played had a nautical theme. No matter if they were on a beach or hundreds of miles away in the mountains, a ridiculous percentage of them were filled with portholes, bulkheads, fishing nets, and Lucite-covered bar tops with shells and loose change suspended in them. Hammerheads was no different.

---

* Credit to Alice Cooper for the T-shirt idea. It was a play on an old airline commercial where stewardesses—that's what they called them back then—looked into camera and said, "I'm Cindy . . . fly me."

At one of our early shows, as at most places we played at that level, we were sharing the dressing room with another band. Both groups were at the club in the late afternoon to sound-check. None of the guys in Twisted had heard of our opener before—they weren't from our area—but they seemed cool enough. While the guys in my band were onstage setting up their gear, I went down to the dressing room to hang up my stage clothes. The guys from the other band were already in there, and as I hung up some of my more "feminine" stuff, one of their band members asked suggestively, "Hey, man, are you into wild enema nozzles?"

What?

While I didn't know what a *wild enema nozzle* was, I knew each word in the phrase, and it gave me a fair idea that something wasn't kosher. Shaken, I uttered something pithy like "Thanks, I'm good," and, trying not to appear too panicked, ran upstairs.

Jay Jay and Eddie were on their way down to the dressing room, so I grabbed Jay, pulled him to the side, and frantically told him about my experience. Jay Jay just laughed. In what would be an ongoing issue for me with the senior members of my band, I was treated like a stupid kid from Long Island and not taken seriously. That would eventually change (that's an understatement!), but if ever they felt justified in treating me that way, it was right then.

"Hey, Eddie," Jay called to his worldly friend, "wait'll you hear what Dee just told me." As we walked downstairs together, Jay told Eddie about the other band's question, and now both of them mocked me, singing, "Wild enema nozzles! Wild enema nozzles!" I implored them to believe me.

As we entered the dressing room, filled with the other band's members—wait a minute. Let me rephrase that—filled with the *other band members* (better), Jay Jay and Eddie were well into their second chorus of "Wild Enema Nozzles" (a great name for a song now that I think about it).

Hearing them, the other musicians lit up. "You guys are into wild enema nozzles?"

Jay and Eddie stopped singing. "What?" Eddie gulped.

"Wild enema nozzles," the morally corrupt band leader replied. "Check 'em out." With that, he pulled out a black attaché case, opened it, and, behold, neatly presented were all shapes, colors (mostly pastels), and sizes of definitely wild enema nozzles, and tubing and different-size (pint, quart, gallon) enema bags! Even Mr. Porn, Jay Jay French, was stunned silent.

The other band were "adventurous" sexually, and beside their personal deviant behavior at home (you know, the usual S&M, bondage, fetishism, and early pornographic filmmaking), they quite enjoyed giving each other enemas in the bathroom before they went onstage. Sometimes they even shared one thanks to a Y-shaped, two-headed wild enema nozzle.

Well, Eddie and Jay Jay—no longer laughing—demurred and shuffled out, leaving me with this gang, who were actually cool and matter-of-fact about the whole thing. They answered my many questions and even gave me a really nice wild enema nozzle to take home (kind of a consolation prize) in case someday I cared to experiment. I never used it (sorry to disappoint), but I still have it deep in the bottom of a box of memorabilia somewhere. Man, is that gonna raise some eyebrows when my grandchildren find it after I'm gone!

TWISTED SISTER WORKED FIVE nights a week, Tuesday through Saturday, doing four fifty-minute sets a night. I have always been extremely hard on my voice, so I would do the first three sets with the band each night, and they would do the fourth set without me, Jay Jay and Eddie handling the vocal chores.

Within weeks of my joining the band, two things happened. As promised, Kevin John Grace (Twisted Sister drummer #2) was kicked out of the band (he didn't have what it took to go the distance) and was replaced by drummer #3. Unlike my dear friend Jay Jay, who I feel trivializes the importance of the five core members of Twisted by constantly talking about the band members who were in the band before we even had a record deal (thus underlining that he is the only original member of the band), I want to give the credit and respect to the guys who, as a unit, got us to the top. A. J. Pero is the only drummer that matters, and he played on all of the biggest and best Twisted Sister records, so I'm not going to spend time talking about the five drummers that came before him. Plus, I hated drummer #3.

The second thing that happened was, after years of high singing, I began to lose my upper range and falsetto voice.

For those who don't know, a man's falsetto is that high, "feminine" voice we all have, which, if properly developed, can be used as your actual singing voice. In classical music you can become a countertenor, which is essentially a male soprano. Some of the world's favorite rock voices have used this "developed falsetto voice" and made it their signature. Case in point: Axl Rose of Guns N' Roses.

I had a natural tenor (high) voice, but my highly developed falsetto allowed me to sing songs sung by women and the highest of rock vocalists. Not anymore. Unbeknownst to me, I'd been singing with a throat infection and had damaged by voice. My falsetto disappeared—as did my Robert Plant impersonation—and my range disintegrated. Losing the voice that had defined me my whole life (and got me in Twisted Sister) could have/should have been a death blow to my drive and musical career. I didn't miss a beat.

I began to channel my inner Alice Cooper.

WE HAD YET TO hit our stride or find our own audience, but we were getting there, opening up for some of the biggest bands in the club scene, such as the Good Rats, and Baby. We even opened for some legendary performers, such as Tommy James of the Shondells ("Mony Mony," "Hanky Panky") and Leslie West* of Mountain ("Mississippi Queen"). I remember our first big show opening for the Good Rats. They were a great local band that actually had albums out, on major labels, but still played the tristate club scene pretty exclusively. Why didn't they make the jump to the national scene? I can only speculate.

Back in the seventies, if you were a popular band playing the tristate club scene, it was lucrative. How lucrative? The bigger bands could make $1,000 or more a week, *per man* . . . cash! (A level Twisted Sister would soon get to.) By today's standards, that's a weekly salary for each band member of about $3,500, tax-free. You had twenty-two- to twenty-five-year-old musicians making the

---

* Leslie West, a childhood hero of mine, has since become a dear friend.

pre-tax equivalent of a quarter-million dollars a year! And that's for bands with five members. Some top bands out there had three! You do the math. The top club bands' members were driving Corvettes and Mercedes, buying expensive houses, and literally living like rock stars. In every local scene, there are musicians who think it is the be-all and end-all, and that they are the shit. Well, Dee is here to break it to you . . . it isn't, you're not, you never were, and you never will be. Sorry, dude.

My guess is that the Good Rats just couldn't come to terms with the reality of "going on the road." You'd make little or no money,* be away from home and your family for months on end (some of the Good Rats were married and had kids), travel around the world in rent-a-cars or vans (initially), and share shitty motel rooms with two, three, or four other sweaty guys. (Where do I sign?!) So let's see, sleep in your own bed every night, have money, drive a Mercedes sports car, and live in an expensive house . . . or five guys in an Ugly Duckling rent-a-car, drooling on each other in their sleep?† Decisions, decisions. So the Good Rats stayed home.

OUR FIRST TIME OPENING for the Good Rats was at the 1890's Club, in my hometown of Baldwin. My parents were going to come to the show, but since they would have a couple of my younger brothers with them, instead of coming inside they planned on standing outside the club and listening through the walls.

Now, at this early stage of our career, we had only one roadie, Ritchie the Face, and Charlie Barreca, our soundman, but they couldn't do it alone. Twisted Sister was still unloading the truck, setting up, performing all night, then tearing down and loading our own gear. It sucked. While plentiful, our equipment was nowhere near the mountain of gear it would eventually become with stacks of amps, PA towers, and a full light show. Hell, at this point our light

---

* Back then, your record company would often pay for you to be on a tour, and those costs were billed against your account.

† To Twisted Sister's credit, we chose the latter and chose it early.

show consisted of Ritchie the Face flicking the wall switch for the club stage lights. Impressive.

That opening night, with my parents perched outside the club listening by an air vent, Ritchie the Face flicked the switch and Twisted Sister hit the stage to a packed club. We launched into our then show opener, "Drivin' Sister" (modified to "Twisted Sister") by Mott the Hoople, and tore it up! When the song was over, a thousand people just stood there, completely silent, in shock. (It was exactly like the reaction to "Springtime for Hitler" in *The Producers*.)

Suddenly someone in the crowd shouted, "Fag!"

I strode (all two steps) to the front of the postage-stamp-size stage and glared threateningly at the crowd. "Who said that?!" I shouted into the mic. No response. *Coward!* * The heckler properly dealt with, we launched into our next song and rocked on.

I was still living at home, and the next day when I got up and saw my parents, they asked me, "What happened?" Confused and still groggy from a late night, I said, "What do you mean, 'what happened'?" They told me how they waited outside, watching hundreds of kids pack into the club. When my band finally went on, they heard our first song, but when it was over, they didn't hear any response. "Where did everybody go?"

We opened for the Good Rats a number of times after that, each time winning over their audience a bit more. The night came (again at the 1890's Club) when we blew them off the stage, and that was the last time we shared the bill with them. Eventually, they wrote and recorded a song about Twisted Sister called "Don't Hate the Ones Who Bring You Rock 'n' Roll," which is still in their set to this day. Yes, the Good Rats (with only the original lead singer) are still playing the local club scene, and, no, the money is not what it used to be. Not even close.

---

* I used to get upset when people called me a fag, homo, or gay, getting into confrontations and fights. Considering how I used to dress and what I looked like, what did I expect them to call me, "Macho"?

8

oh, suzy q . . .

Are you familiar with the butterfly effect? Not the movie, but the idea that it is based on. Basically, the butterfly effect, according to Google Answers, is "the observation that an event as seemingly insignificant as the flapping of a butterfly's wings might create a minuscule disturbance that, in the chaotic motion of the atmosphere, may eventually become sufficiently amplified to change the large-scale atmospheric motion, possibly even leading to a huge storm in a distant place."

On April 16, 1976, my life, my band, and ultimately millions of people all over the world were changed forever. I met my future wife, Suzette. Does that sound overly dramatic? Self-important? Pathetic? Pussy whipped?* It's not. Meeting Suzette changed my life dramatically. As a result, my band (on multiple visual levels) and the music I eventually wrote were greatly affected. Twisted Sister's music and live performances have entertained, moved, and even inspired people, all over the world, for over three decades. That's the butterfly effect defined.

Twisted was booked to open for a local popular group called the Bonnie Parker Band at Hammerheads in Wantagh, Long Island. Bonnie Parker was an amazing, cool female (hey, you never know, as ambiguity was part of the scene) singer/bass-player who kicked

---

* Hey, if you have to be whipped, let it be by pussy.

ass and outrocked then-amazing, cool female singer/bass player Suzi Quatro. Suzi Quatro was a huge rock star in Europe, and soon became known in the States as Leather Tuscadero on the seventies hit television show *Happy Days*. But therein lay the problem. There already was a Suzy Quatro. The world didn't need a "better one." (It barely needed one.)

LESS THAN TWO MONTHS into the new and improved Twisted Sister (now with drummer #3), we still had virtually no following and were anxious to perform for Bonnie's audience. Wearing my infamous short-shorts and I'M DEE, BLOW ME T-shirt (well, it was infamous to me), I took the stage that night for our first set . . . unaware that my life would never be the same. As usual, virtually nobody was there to see us. Ours being the opening set of the night, Bonnie Parker's crowd had yet to roll in. I was looking out at fourteen or fifteen people tops, scattered around the room. As we rocked the first song, I looked down at the front of the stage and was bowled over. Staring back at me, her eyes sparkling, her hair golden, her skin tan (remarkable for April), and her smile lighting up the room, was the most beautiful girl I had ever seen. She was bopping and clapping along with the music and smiling at *me*! And every guy knows what (we think) that means . . . she wants me. Some guy was looming protectively behind her, but that wasn't stopping her from giving me the timeless international sign of interest.

I tried to be cool and not stare back too much, but I had to assess the situation. Working my way from top to bottom, I ran through my "guy checklist." The face and hair had already passed muster. Boobs . . . *holy crap, they were huge!* Waist . . . narrow; ass . . . small and tight; legs—she was wearing jeans—long and thin. What a body! Beautiful, petite, and with big tits. This was my dream girl!

She was still smiling at me. Something had to be wrong. Not because she was smiling, but because she was smiling so openly. A girl this beautiful should be acting a little more coy. She . . . must be underage! That had to be it. She wasn't experienced enough at "club etiquette" to put on a front. Since the drinking age at that time was eighteen, I figured that this incredibly hot and beautiful girl had to be seventeen. I had to meet her.

From day one with Twisted Sister I was determined to act and be treated like a star. I always knew I was going to make it, but now I was in the band that I would make it with, so all the silliness, stupidity, procrastination, and dillydallying of "Danny Snider" had to end. *I revamped my entire personality when I joined Twisted Sister.* I was determined to be the person I always wanted to be. Dee Snider was a rock star, and I would damn well act like one.

To that end, the band would show up to the club early to load in and for sound check. This would make sure the band always sounded its best (Peacock never sound-checked), and I would be in the club well before doors opened and the audience came in. Real rock stars aren't seen coming in the front door and walking through the crowd, like a normal person. You see them onstage and that's it. To that end, in between sets I would never leave the dressing room and walk around the club. *Ever.* Even though not a person in the place gave a shit about me, I was determined to carry myself as if I mattered. If *I* didn't think I mattered, how could I ever expect anyone else to think so? Hell, the band placed (stolen) police barricades in front of the stage that said KEEP BACK because what's the first thing people do when they see a sign like that? Get as close as they can. Self-Fulfilling Prophecy 101.

The dressing rooms in these shitholes left more than a little to be desired. I would spend hours every night sitting alone (the rest of the band was having a great time hanging out in the club) in a glorified closet or bathroom before the first show, in between sets, all during the last set that I didn't perform, and after the show until the club closed. Only then would I slip out of the club and into the early morning to head home. I was a star . . . people just hadn't realized it yet.

I mention this to let you in on my mind-set, and so you'll understand just how significant it was that I left the dressing room after the set and came out to find this amazing girl.

I slipped out of the dressing room, still hanging in the shadows at the side of the stage, not wanting to totally blow my rock-star cool. I spotted her by the front of the stage, standing with her girlfriend and the guy I saw behind her, waiting for my band to come back on. Oh, she was totally into me.

I caught her eye and casually waved her over; she immediately came, abandoning the guy she was with. *I was so in!* She looked even hotter close up. I had to have her.

"Hey, how ya doin'?" I said, my Lawng Guyland accent raging.

Her response was completely abstract: "I'm a good girl."

Confused, I pressed on. "*Sure.* Are you with that guy?" Guy code. I didn't want to be one of those assholes who hit on girls with a date.

The insanely hot girl looked back at the guy I was pointing to and, horrified, said, "*Ewww.* No way!" She was abandoning her date for me! This was a lock.

"Cool," I responded coolly. "What's your name?"

The next two syllables she uttered sealed the deal. "Suzette."

Wow. The most beautiful name for the most beautiful girl. It was like a song. *Suzette.*

It was time to stun her with my worldliness and perception. "You're not eighteen, are you?" I asked knowingly.

"No." Suzette was a little embarrassed to have been called on her charade.

"How old are you?" I pressed. It was almost a rhetorical question.

"How old do you think I am?" she said coyly.

Were we really going to play this silly little game? *Fine.* "Seventeen." It wasn't a guess.

"Fifteen," Suzette corrected.

I nearly swallowed my tongue. "*Fifteen?*" I repeated, hoping I had somehow misheard.

"Yes. Fifteen."

Holy crap! Now what? I was head over heels for this girl, and she clearly felt the same way about me. But before I could go any further with this line of thought, Suzette interrupted me.

"How old are you?"

"How old do you think I am?" Two can play at this game.

"Late twenties, early thirties," she responded matter-of-factly.

Late twenties, early thirties?! "I just turned twenty-one!" I protested.

"No way. Let me see your driver's license."

With that, I ran downstairs to the dressing room, got my license, and headed back upstairs. I'd show her.

To be fair, I did look as if I were in my late twenties, early thirties. I've always looked that age. Even when I snuck into a bar at fourteen years old with a bunch of my "older" sixteen-year-old friends, they were all ejected for being underage, while the crotchety old bartender asked me what I wanted to drink! ("What'll ya have, sir?") I had never been proofed in my life!

When I got back, she was still patiently waiting for me. While I was sure she still wanted me, the age thing and her asking to see my ID had shaken me a little. (That and the "I'm a good girl." What did she mean by that?)

I handed the very underage beauty my license.

Suzette scrutinized it, too thoroughly.

"See," I said proudly, "I just turned twenty-one."

Suzette wasn't buying it. "You probably just have this so you can meet young girls."

Was she freakin' kidding me!? Undeterred, I asked her for her phone number. Suzette gave it to me. Further proof she was into me! Just how *little*, I would eventually find out.

THE NEXT COUPLE OF weeks were a blur of Twisted Sister gigs, punctuated with thinking about and phone calls to Suzette. I was obsessed with this too-young girl, and the playful calls and her next visit only made things worse.

To this day, Suzette plays innocent on all accounts of the signals she was sending me. As I would eventually discover, she really had no interest in me at all, which made me want her even more. And that "I'm a good girl" comment? The object of my desire was a total virgin, having only even been kissed by a couple of guys. I was in completely uncharted waters! But she did give me her phone number, and we talked endlessly on the phone. I invited her to come to another local show to see me, and she said yes.

If I had been smitten by Suzette's effervescent glow the first time, the way she looked when she rolled into the club that night delivered the knockout punch. I was devastated by her womanly beauty.

I will readily admit that (like most guys) I am painfully shallow. I won't even try to pretend I saw in Suzette some "inner blah-blah-blah-blah." My attraction was purely physical; my Perfect Woman Qualifications Checklist was pathetically devoid of substance. That said, the way things turned out, I believe a lot more was "at work" in our ultimate pairing. I'm not a spiritual guy, but the way we came together and how well we fit has got to be more than a coincidence. A professional astrologer did our charts the first year we were going out and told us she had never seen two more compatible people. I'm not a big believer in that stuff, but thirty-five years later . . . I'm just sayin'. But back to my shallowness and Suzette's missent signals . . .

Suzette arrives at the club—a slimy biker bar, if you must know—wearing a black, low-cut, knee-length, clinging evening dress with a pair of high heels. Oh my God! On my dream-girl checklist only one box was left unmarked earlier: *legs*. She'd been wearing skintight, bell-bottom jeans the night I'd met her, so I couldn't get an accurate read on what was going on below the knee. But in that dress? *Check!*

One secret box was on the back of the list. It wasn't mandatory, but it would be a big plus if my dream girl had this qualification: Italian.

I had been close with an Italian family named DiBenadetto in Baldwin. Anthony "Nino" DiBenadetto was the drum roadie for Harlequin and the drummer in my band Heathen. I had known his brother Sal, a local rock photographer, from high school. I loved the passion of the DiBenadetto family, the closeness, the support . . . and the food. There was no place like the DiBenadettos' for a starving musician. There was always something delicious to eat and a great vibe. Best of all, I always felt like a part of the family. But that's the Italian way.

I promised myself I would find a beautiful Italian girl and bring the Italian-family energy and traditions into my life through "application," if you get my double entendre. Suzette's last name turned out to be Gargiulo. It doesn't get much more Italian than that. Bada bing, bada boom!

I drove Suzette home from the club after our show that night in the band equipment van and kissed her for the first time, sealing the deal . . . *or at least I thought.*

After seeing Suzette at the club that night, the whole age issue completely went away, for me at least. The reason fifteen-year-old girls were raising families in ancient Rome was because they looked like Suzette! Nothing was going to stop me from making her mine. A week later, we planned to go on our first official date.

WHILE AT THE TIME I could see nothing wrong with twenty-one-year-old me dating fifteen-year-old Suzette, as I sit here writing, with a fifteen-year-old daughter . . . I see everything wrong with it! Sure, Suzette and I have had a pretty legendary love affair, done great things together, raised an amazing family, and stayed together through the best and worst of times, but if some twenty-one-year-old dude who looks like me thinks he's going to roll up to my front door to pick up my hot, fifteen-year-old daughter, he's going to meet the guy on the cover of Twisted Sister's *Stay Hungry* album cover, full-on. It ain't happening! Fortunately for me, Suzette's family gave me a chance . . . sort of.

Our date night finally came and I headed over to Suzette's house to pick her up, dressed to the nines before going there, I had done something I'd done for no other girl: I got my hair trimmed. I must have been in love!

Finding Suzette's house again wasn't a problem. Since dropping her off after the club, I had driven to her house, unbeknownst to her, a few times to commit its location to memory and in hopes of just getting a glimpse of her outside. I know that sounds insane and stalkerish. It is. But when I say meeting Suzette was life-changing, I mean it. I was absolutely obsessed.

I arrived that Sunday evening and strode up to the front door in my rock 'n' roll finest: six-inch, "chocolate-layered" with pink stripe, stack-heeled platform shoes; a short, tight blue-denim-and-black-velvet jacket; and baby-blue, bell-bottom jeans so tight you could tell I was circumcised. What was I thinking!?

Suzette answered the door, blushing profusely (I had no clue she was embarrassed by me), and brought me in to meet her family.

In many Italian families, Sunday is "Sauce Sunday," meaning a pot of meat sauce is made (an all-day process) and the entire family gets together for dinner. Suzette brought me into the formal dining room to meet the adults. Suzette's mom, her mom's goombah boyfriend, Tony (Suzette's parents were divorced), her aunt Ruthie, her aunt Annie, and neighbor Betty were all there having coffee and Italian pastries. I could hear *The Godfather* theme playing (in my mind). Introductions were made, then Suzette brought me into the kitchen to meet her two younger wild animals—I mean, brothers—Vinny and Billy, and younger sister, Roseanne. Several older and younger cousins were there as well, along with a couple of Suzette's friends, all part of the weekly Sauce Sunday gathering. I was introduced, small talk and joking ensued . . . then I was asked to return to the dining room. No problem. I had always done great with parents.

For some reason Suzette opted to stay with her cousins, so I went in on my own. I sat down at the table and shared pleasantries with Suzette's beautiful mom, Jeanette,* the aunts, neighbor, and Suzette's mom's boyfriend. The weather, movies, food, and more were discussed at length, until I realized that one by one all the women were stepping out of the room, leaving me alone with Big Tony the Goombah! Midsentence, he cuts me off.

"What do you want with a fifteen-year-old girl?" he growled.

I couldn't tell him what I really wanted (what *any guy* would want). "Well, you see, Suzette is mature for her age and I'm immature for mine, and, like, we kind of meet in the mid—"

"Cut the shit!" he barked. I did, and he continued, "If you lay one hand on her, this *family* will hunt you down to the four corners of the earth and put you in the bottom of a lake. Do you understand what I am saying to you?"

I remember thinking, *Snider, you have really gotten yourself into it now.* But I was too head over heels for Suzette to let even that put me off. Just about then it did dawn on me that baby-blue jeans might not have been the best choice. The fast-spreading, dark blue spot where I had wet myself was starting to show. I was scared, but I still answered, "Yes, sir." My lot was cast. There was no turning back.

---

* It's been said if you want to know what the girl you're with is going to look like when she's older, take a look at her mom. Suzette's mom was a thirty-eight-year-old knockout. *Check!*

With that, the ladies of Suzette's family all came back into the room as if they'd been hovering outside.

"Did you have a nice talk?" one of them inquired.

"Yes," replied the goombah. "We understand each other now."

And we did.

Suzette had no idea about what was said to me that night. She was mortified when she found out, but it did explain the arm's-length distance I kept from her on our entire, uncomfortable first date . . . and for many dates after. I did not want a pair of cement platform shoes, but even the threat of them couldn't keep me away.

9

the demolition squad

Over the next few months, the new and improved Twisted Sister started to come together. I say *started* because I feel that we were constantly mutating and developing. We always had the master plan in place, but we were forever modifying, refining, and adjusting.

The tristate club scene was just a necessary means to an end. Given the choice of having day jobs and working on our music careers at night in some rehearsal studio, we opted to make our living as a cover band, develop our performing and playing chops as we did, and focus on our original music on our two days off each week. At least the first two parts of that plan worked smoothly.

Our CTA booking agent, Kevin Brenner, started calling us the Demolition Squad because no matter whom he booked us to open up for, we ultimately would dominate, steal their crowd, and blow them away. Soon no bands wanted us to open for them. We didn't fight fair. From day one, Twisted Sister believed in winning at any cost, and we were not ashamed to use every cheap trick in the book. While other bands focused on musical virtuosity, we gave the drunk, stoned, desperate-for-a-good-time, young rock audience exactly what they wanted every night . . . a riotous party.

I remember the night the truth of live performing fully hit me. We had been working our asses off for weeks, and screaming my lungs out every night in smoke-filled clubs had finally caught up with me. We were playing a club in East Quogue, Long Island, called the

Mad, Mad Hatter on a Saturday night. Saturdays were always the best night of the week to play, and the place was crowded. We hit the stage and I started to sing our opening song, only to find that I had a five-note range (instead of my usual twenty-four-to-thirty-two-note range). I couldn't sing!

I turned to Jay Jay with a "What the hell am I gonna do?" look on my face. It was the first song of the night! I had at least thirty more to go! Jay Jay shrugged; he didn't have the answer. I couldn't just stop and say, "Hey, folks, I can't sing tonight, sorry." So I did the only thing I could think of . . . I went fucking nuts! Up until that night I had always been a mover, but now I took it to a whole new level, *and the audience loved it!* They didn't care that I couldn't sing for shit, as long as I could rock, and that I did!

⚜ DEE LIFE LESSON ⚜

The show always comes first; accuracy and quality a distant second.
You can always play and sound good on your records.

I guess this is a lesson Led Zep had already learned.

Meanwhile, things had gone from bad to worse for Suzette and me. By worse I mean I was more obsessed than ever. She was pretty much all I could think about. Every spare moment I had was spent on the phone with her or going to see her. I listened to songs like "She's the One" by Bruce Springsteen and "I Wish I Was Your Mother" by Mott the Hoople over and over because they reminded me of her. When she came to shows to see me, I couldn't stop looking at her. I would make her sit near the stage just so I could keep an eye on her; I was sure somebody else was going to come along and take her away. I was a jealous maniac.

And speaking of coming to shows, Suzette was now coming with me to virtually every gig, five nights a week. She was fifteen and still in high school!

If you are wondering how her parents let this happen, so am I. I've given a lot of thought to it. Putting the cosmic "we were meant to be together" (which we were) shit aside, I showed up at a transitional time in the Gargiulo household. Suzette's parents were divorced; her dad lived a couple of hours away. He came by faithfully every weekend to take his kids out and give them the weekly child-support check, but he never came in the house (at that time the divorced couple weren't getting along) and didn't want to know what was going on there. Each week he and the kids would go to dinner and a movie, and then he'd take them home.

Meanwhile, Suzette's mom and her longtime post-divorce boyfriend, Tony the Goombah, broke up shortly after I entered the picture. His threatening my life on that first date was pretty much his exit speech. The lack of a father figure in the house (Suzette's mom's neighboring sisters were both divorced, too) who would be far more critical of what was going on with his daughter (moms are way too trusting) further assisted me in my mission to make Suzette mine.

To make matters worse, Suzette's mom, Jeanette (may she rest in peace), was still relatively young (thirty-eight), attractive, and vital. She had gotten married young, had four kids in pretty rapid succession, been through a divorce, and just broken up with a longtime boyfriend. The last thing she wanted was to stay at home and be a mom. Jeanette wanted to party, and she did. So when her oldest, mature and together, honor-student daughter told her she was going out each night, Jeanette gave her $20 (in case she got stuck somewhere and needed a cab home) and let Suzette do her thing.*

Suzette would hang with me in the dressing room before shows, in between sets, and after shows (and do her homework) and watch me from the side of the stage during my sets. At one point, the guys in Twisted actually sat me down and told me I had to stop singing every song *to her*. Unaware I was doing it, I would just stare at Suzette throughout the entire set. I was insane for this girl.

At the end of each night, I would drive her home, she'd sleep for a couple of hours, then get up and go to school, starting the whole cycle over again. This went on for about a year! As I look back on it now, it seems incredibly perverse and fucked-up! I swear, I took care

---

* Discussing with Suzette the insanity of what I got away with, she is quick to point out that her mother trusted me and knew I was a good guy. Jeanette was right on both accounts, but still . . .

of her, made sure she ate and helped her with her homework. *Oh my God, that sounds even worse!*

This insanity aside, something more was at work here than just berserker testosterone obsession. Initially, unbeknownst to me (to the fullest extent), Suzette was not only an aspiring fashion designer, but she had a passion for makeup and hair as well. She was gradually working on my stage look. Aware that I was a know-it-all asshole, she slowly but surely got me to experiment. I've already said that I was concerned about taking things too far and having people think I was gay, but Suzette would ease me into going further with my makeup.

One night she suggested I wear lipstick.

"No way!" I said.

"Oh, come on. Just put on a little gloss. Look, *it's clear.*" With that she pulled out of her bag a foot-long tray of cheap lip-glosses, with about a dozen different colors in it. Starting with a completely transparent gloss, the lip-gloss colors in the tray gradually got darker and darker until they reached a bloodred.

"Okay," I acquiesced, putting on the Vaseline-like, clear gloss. It essentially looked as if I had licked my lips; not bad. Besides, I couldn't be gay. I had this hot piece of ass hanging on my arm to prove it.

Eventually the clear gloss ran out, so, what the hell, I went with the slightly tinted "natural" lip gloss. It was practically the same thing. And I knew I wasn't gay.

I'm sure you can see where this is heading. Week after week, another lip gloss shade ran dry, and I'd move to the next darker shade, repeating my new mantra, "I can't be gay. Suzette's my girlfriend," until I was finally wearing the bloodred lipstick at the end of the tray . . . and there I have been ever since.

Suzette did the same thing with nail polish. "Why don't you wear nail polish?"

"I'm not a homo," I responded like a typical '70s-era suburban moron.

"Of course you're not. Just try some black. It's cool. *Please,*" she pleaded.

"Oh, all right." Black was pretty cool.

Well, black led to blue, which led to purple, which led to red, which led to the color I wore onstage for thirty years, pink. That's pretty much how my makeup developed, and my hair gradually went from brown to screaming blond. That girl could get me to do anything. But to tell the truth . . . I liked it.

With my trophy girlfriend by my side, I became fearless. I rapidly developed a face full of makeup, and I was taking more chances with what I was wearing. Trips to shops like Ian's in the West Village would reap postglam clothes and cool boots, but Frankie's (Frankie was the maven of Ian's, known for his one-size-fits-all shoehorning of plus-size people into pint-size clothes) stuff was pricey. Shopping at "Big & Scary" women's stores scored jaw-dropping (for all the wrong reasons) blouses at the right price. A much better bang for the buck.

One night, early in our courtship, Suzette came to a club to see me. As usual, she looked devastating. *The girl knows how to dress!* With the tightest jeans (did she put them on or "apply" them?) and platform shoes, she was wearing the sexiest, fringed, turquoise knit top. I loved it. With it offset by a glowing tan, a killer rack, and a slammin' body, she looked amazing, and I let her know it.

A couple of weeks later, she was coming to a club to see me, and knowing how much I loved her in that turquoise knit the last time, she decided to wow me again. When Suzette arrived at the club, she walked in and looked up on the stage . . . to find me wearing the same exact shirt! To make matters worse, I spotted her in the crowd and started wildly pointing to the tops we were both wearing, as if she didn't notice her towering boyfriend onstage in the spotlight. *I was so excited.* She covered her face in embarrassment and hid in a corner!

At the end of the set I bounded offstage and over to her, compounding the fashion faux pas and humiliating my date on a whole new level.

"You bought my shirt! Why did you buy my shirt?" she cried.

Confused, I responded, "I told you I loved your top. Remember? I said, 'Where did you get that top?'"

It has to be more than a coincidence that a short time after that night Suzette started designing and making clothes for me. She would never have to worry about her boyfriend wearing the same clothes as her again.

◆   ◆   ◆

BY THE END OF the summer of 1976, only six months into the band, we all knew this was the group that was going to take us to the top, and we understood what we needed to do to get there: original material, followed by a demo tape and showcases for record companies. We decided we would achieve this more quickly if we shared a house.

The idea was simple: we didn't have a lot of spare time, so living together would help us maximize our work time and get closer as a band. We all had this vision of a "rock 'n' roll think tank" where our creativity and camaraderie would flow freely.

Sure it would.

Only our bass player, Kenny, opted out of this idea. I don't know if he saw the inherent problems or just needed his privacy (he was a quiet, quirky guy). Either way, he assured us that when he was needed, he would be there. So, Jay Jay, Eddie, drummer #3, my old pal Don "Fury" Mannello (we needed a fifth roommate to make a house financially doable) moved into a ridiculously nice house in the upscale neighborhood of Old Harbor Green in Massapequa, Long Island. I have no idea how we ever got this house. It was a beautiful split-level home with four bedrooms, three baths, living room, dining room, den, *library*, finished basement, *maid's quarters*, and an in-ground pool with cabana. It was amazing! With its being right across the street from the Harbor Green Yacht Club and down the block from Carlo Gambino, the head of the Gambino crime family, they should have had no reason in the world to let a bunch of rocker dirtbags like us rent the place. They must have been desperate.

We moved in . . . and the yearlong wasting of time began. Sure, we worked up a handful of new cover songs for our club gigs (something you had to do to keep your shows fresh, so people would keep coming to see you), but as far as original music goes—our reason for getting this house together—we created one song. But I'm getting ahead of myself.

The house became what you would imagine a rock band's house to become, but that wasn't the problem. After working the ridiculous hours we worked (on average, leaving the house at 5:00 p.m. for a gig and getting home around twelve hours later), Tuesday through

Saturday, the last thing we wanted to do on Sunday was rehearse. I could barely speak by the end of each week, and we all needed a freakin' day off. That left Monday.

Though we felt like and acted like rock stars, we weren't, and we each had plenty of personal responsibilities that needed to be taken care of. By the time we woke up in the afternoon, we only had a few hours to run around doing stuff. One thing would lead to another, and we'd virtually never get any original-music work done.

I REALLY LOOKED UP to Jay Jay French when I first joined the band. He was almost three years older than me, more experienced, cooler, and generally seemed to have it together. I needed and wanted his approval.

One day, Jay Jay showed the band a chord progression and melody he was working on for an original song. It was great, and this was exactly the reason we had moved in together. To encourage a close, creative environment where we could exchange musical ideas and develop them into the songs that would define our band. *Awesome!* Now, I had virtually no songwriting experience (except for the little songs we all make up in our heads and think are incredible), but I wrote lyrics to Jay Jay's song. I was *very* nervous as to how they would be received.

When the band finally found time to get together and rehearse again, I anxiously approached Jay. "I've got some words for your song." Jay Jay peered *down* at me (we're the same height) through his thick prescription glasses, the way only an astigmatic man can, and said, "Whadaya got?" While the band looked on, Jay Jay played his song and I sang, reading the lyrics off a sheet of paper. My face was burning, I was sweating, and I know my lyric sheet must have been shaking.*

When I finished the song, at first Jay Jay said nothing. He took the lyrics from me, glanced at them, and said condescendingly,

---

* To this day, after all the songs I've written and the millions of albums I've sold, I still feel great discomfort showing a new song idea to anybody. Not as bad as that day with Jay Jay, but I still feel very vulnerable having to do it.

"They're about you and Suzette. That's cute." Then he turned away without another word. *Cute?!*

I was devastated. I had humbled myself before Jay Jay, baring my soul and he had the audacity to be dismissive with me?! Embarrassment turned to humiliation, and humiliation to anger. In that instant, our relationship was forever changed. My *former* mentor, Jay Jay French, was added to the growing list of people I had to prove myself to. Along with my parents, teachers, ex-bosses, ex-girlfriends, friends, coworkers, and every other asshole who had mocked, dismissed, or shot down my dreams, now my bandmate—a guy on my own team—was officially an enemy of the state. Years later when I told Jay Jay about this pivotal moment in our relationship, he didn't even remember it. Which is the way it usually is. The "crushee" gets crushed and the "crusher" doesn't even know the significance of what he or she has done. It's like some tank running over a hybrid car. That was the end of my ever trying to write with Jay Jay French.

AROUND THE SAME TIME, I came face-to-face with the reality of the commitment I was going to have to make to achieve my goals. My voice problems were getting worse, and having exhausted medical solutions, I decided to see a voice coach. Maybe a coach could explain what was happening.

I'm not sure who recommended Katie Agresta (probably Kevin Brenner), but she was considered to be a miracle worker with rock singers. Many vocal coaches won't even consider working with rockers—they don't think what we do is real singing—but Katie was building a real name for herself. Cyndi Lauper, the then Janis Joplin–esque former singer of a Long Island–based cover band called Mister Magoo, had gone on to form her band Blue Angel and was starting to get some recognition for her amazing vocal chops. Katie Agresta was her voice coach. That was good enough for me.

I took a train to Manhattan to meet with Katie for the first time. She listened to my voice, but it was the answers I gave to her questions that told what my problem was. How many hours a night did I sleep? *A few.* What did I eat? *You know, fast food and stuff.* What did I drink? *Coffee, chocolate milk, and iced tea.* Katie had heard enough. On the upside, I didn't have issues or the negative effects of drugs, smoking (other than inhaling it all night in the clubs), or alcohol to deal with. But I didn't sleep enough or eat properly, and I drank too much dairy. She explained that I couldn't expect to have a voice every night if I didn't rest it enough, refused it the right fuel to perform, and smothered it with dairy products. I couldn't believe it. I knew guys who smoked, drank, got high, barely slept, and virtually didn't eat, and they sang like birds every night. "Some people can get away with that," Katie replied, "You can't." *Shit!*

As strong a guy as I've always been, as physically fit as I pride myself on being, my vocal cords have *always* been my weak link. Now, even without partying, I was faced with the reality that, if I was serious about going the distance, I was going to have to further restrict my fun and dedicate my life to being a rock singer. Added to Katie's list of musts were vocal warm-ups and warm-downs throughout the night, no excessive talking before, during, and after shows, and drinking hot tea with honey and lemon onstage instead of a nice, cold, refreshing drink (which locks up your vocal cords). Basically no fun at all.

I looked at the lifestyle before me and knew what I had to do. I was committed to making it, and there was virtually no sacrifice I wasn't willing to make.

⚜ 10 ⚜

so *this* is christmas

A t this point in Suzette's and my relationship, I finally figured out something discouraging. She wasn't into me. It took me weeks to fully realize it, but by then I was so committed to winning this girl's heart, there was no turning back.

Apparently, my She Digs Me meter was way off.

Why was she smiling so broadly at me at that first show? Suzette explained that she and her best friend, Wendy, had met these two guys, borrowed other people's proof of age (thank you for that, Cousin Felicia), and come to the club to see the "girl groups" Bonnie Parker and Twisted Sister. When she walked into the club, Twisted Sister was onstage, and from a distance she thought we were just that, *girls*. Once she got up close and saw what we *really* were, she couldn't stop smiling. I was a freak! Though she did think we were great.

Then why did she give me her phone number that night? Because she was *afraid* not to. When I asked her why she didn't just give me a wrong number instead, she said she thought about it, but choked. What about coming to see me the following week at another club? Well, after speaking to me on the phone every day, she thought I was a nice guy (the only thing I actually had going for me) and felt bad saying no when I invited her.

What I gradually discovered in the weeks to come was, not only wasn't Suzette interested or attracted to me, *she was repulsed by me!* She was embarrassed to be seen with me. How freakin' self-absorbed was I? In case you haven't already noticed, I am a text-book narcissist.

To top things off, Suzette had no prior interest in music or bands. She didn't own so much as one record or tape, and she had nothing to play them on if she did.

Suzette repeatedly tried pretty much everything to break up with me during those first few months, but I just wouldn't let go. No matter what her complaint was about me, I adjusted for it. Whatever she didn't like, I changed. When I raised my voice to her for the first time and she opened the door of my car and started to jump out while it was still moving, I swore I would never yell at her again. I still don't.* The more I realized that she didn't want me, and the more I knew about her, the more I wanted her.

This was my theory: I was convinced I was going to make it, and I knew that any girl who was interested in me once I did would be into me for all the wrong reasons. Namely, I was a rich, famous rock star.

My thinking was, if I could win Suzette's heart, get her to love me *for me*, I would always know she was with me for the right reasons. Not because I was in a band or had fame or money or she liked my music.† By starting our relationship as a total zero, whatever happened, I could never go lower than that . . . zero. I would never have to worry about why she was with me. I don't know where I got this odd wisdom from, but I was right.

I need to give credit to Suzette's childhood best friend Wendy Cohen-Yair, who coached me through the rocky shores of dating Suzette. I would often call Wendy for counsel when I was confused

---

* My father was a yeller. I hated the way he would talk to my mom, and I used to pray as kid that I wouldn't grow up to be like him. In spite of that, as I got older, I fell into the same pattern with my girlfriends, screaming at them just as my old man did to my mom. It took a fifteen-year-old Suzette all of one almost-leap from my car and the words "If you ever talk to me like that again, I'm out of here!" to cure me of that. Oddly, my prayers were answered.

† I only recently found out that my wife never liked my voice. When I expressed shock at this, Suzette responded, "You know my favorite singer is Steve Perry from Journey. What about that would make you think I would like your singing?" *Ouch.*

by my girlfriend's actions and/or didn't know what to do. Wendy would always talk me through it, even the time Suzette finally convinced me she didn't want to go out with me anymore. I was going to pack it in and walk away from the relationship, but Wendy assured me that Suzette was totally into me and just didn't know how to express herself.

So I hung in there. As it turned out, *Wendy lied*. Suzette really didn't want anything to do with me anymore. When she asked Wendy why in God's name she told me that she did, Wendy replied, "I felt bad for him. He's so in love with you." Thank you for that, Wendy. Suzette thanks you now, too. I told you we were meant to be together.

I wanted my first Christmas with Suzette to be great. We had been dating now for eight months and were starting to feel like a couple. For Suzette's sixteenth birthday I had wowed her with a white German shepherd puppy. Suzette had had a beloved white German shepherd as a child, so I got her another. She loved it. I had to top the birthday gift on our first Christmas.

Unlike in the "economical" Christmases I had grown up with, I got Suzette four or five different gifts, the capper being a new portable television for her room. Hers had broken, and since she liked to sleep with the TV on, she was frustrated not to have one anymore. I knew I was going to blow her away.

Christmas Eve came and Twisted Sister wasn't working.* I couldn't wait to finish the celebration at my parents' house and head over to Suzette's with my gifts. Both families were Christmas Eve celebrators, but my family celebrated much earlier in the evening. Suzette's family were Christmas Eve traditionalists: no gift was opened before midnight. I arrived in time for the festivities. The Gargiulo Christmas tree was *packed* with more gifts than I'd ever seen before.

Suzette, now in her junior year of high school, was taking an

---

* Twisted always made a point of taking off most holidays so we could enjoy the day and spend time with our families. We still do. We were to have the part of the "house band" in Rodney Dangerfield's movie *Back to School*, but passed because it meant being away from home at Christmas. Apparently Danny Elfman and Oingo Boingo didn't care about things like that. *Heathens.*

accelerated schedule so she could graduate a year early and go to the Fashion Institute of Technology (FIT). She had been interested in clothing design since she was a kid (a much younger kid) and was chomping at the bit to embrace her chosen career. To that end, she enrolled in the fashion-design program at the Board of Cooperative Educational Services (BOCES). BOCES allows students to attend their regular school and classes in the morning, then focus on more career-oriented learning in the afternoon. Anxious to jump-start her career, Suzette attended BOCES classes daily.

Meanwhile, back at the festivities, the gift-giving was in full swing. Now, at my house, we would hand out one gift at a time, watch the recipient open it, and react accordingly. As we did, my mom would pick up the torn wrapping paper from the floor and throw it out, then we would move on to the next gift. *Very civilized.* In the Gargiulo household . . . not so much. They had so many presents, if they went at that pace, it would be the New Year by the time they finished.

I don't recall the exact nuances of the gift exchange, but I opened my first gift from Suzette to discover an amazing, handmade "Suzette original" design top for the stage! White, off one shoulder, with a sleevelet for the exposed arm, it had long, white fringe all over it. It was stunning . . . *ly gay!* I loved it!

I opened gift after gift (Suzette had way more for me than I had for her), to find more and more wild, original designs, which she had hand made for me at her BOCES school. While the other girls were working on designs for themselves—or normal people—Suzette had dedicated her entire fall to creating outfits for me to wear with the band. They were amazing!

Can you imagine what the teachers and other girls in her class thought when they saw Suzette working on these large, superfeminine outfits for her then-unknown, six-foot-one-inch, 180-pound boyfriend? (I was skinnier then.) Suzette didn't care what other people thought. She never has.

The pièce de résistance was a skintight, pink spandex jumpsuit, open in the front to almost my pubes, with floor-length white fringe all across the back and the arms. I had told Suzette that I had always wanted an outfit like this, and she designed and made it for me. Unbelievable! To make the effort even more amazing, Suzette couldn't find long enough fringe, so she and her brothers and sister hand-tied two strands together for each individual fringe, to create the length for the entire outfit! I was blown away.

As I stood in the middle of the Gargiulo living room, knee-deep in wrapping paper (the Gargiulos just let it pile up), I was humbled by the generosity of my girlfriend and her family. Most of the gifts under the tree had been for me. I shuffled through the wrapping-paper pile like a kid through fallen leaves and vowed that Christmas would be like this from now on, if I had to work all year just to afford it. It always has.

More important, and not fully realized at that moment, Suzette's massive effort had just launched me, and ultimately Twisted Sister, to a whole new level. Sure, she may just have been preventing me from ever wearing matching outfits with her again, but she had pushed me to embrace my inner transvestite and be the best Twisted Sister I could be. *Which is all she has ever done*—selflessly help others attain greatness.

There was no looking back!

11

the gauntlet is thrown

In the tristate club scene, Twisted Sister was *the* party band. No one could light up a crowd the way we could, and we quickly became in high demand, especially for holidays and special events. When they were closing the original Hammerheads (the club where Suzette and I met), the owners decided to go out big and hire Twisted for the final blowout. Perhaps that was a poor choice of words. By the end of the night, interior walls had been ripped down and plumbing fixtures torn out, along with most of the drop ceiling, by marauding fans, revved up by the band. Our security that night were some biker/black-belt friends of ours from a karate school known as ACK (American Combat Karate). Founded by martial arts legend Richard Barathy, American Combat Karate was mixed martial arts years before it became fashionable. Credit where credit is due.

At some point during the crazed night, someone maced another in the overcrowded club, it got in the eyes of one of the ACK members, and then all hell broke loose. The scene was reminiscent of the Stones at Altamont with our black-belt/biker security kicking the shit out of pretty much anybody at arm's (or leg's) length . . . and the band played on! People were being taken away in ambulances (some guy actually had his ear bitten off!). My lasting memory of that night is the sight of the club's massive central-air-conditioning unit dropping out of the ceiling and onto the crowd below. Hey, they said they wanted a blowout.

· · ·

DURING OUR YEAR OF living together, many band meetings were held. One infamous meeting was when Eddie—after months of being late, missing things, and generally being less than a part of the band— was to be dismissed and replaced by my best friend and Twisted housemate, Don Mannello. Don was a good-looking, great guitar player who would have made an amazing addition to the band.

Jay Jay, the band manager and spokesperson, was all set to fire Eddie, and then he "called an audible." Without consulting the rest of us, Jay gave Eddie one more chance to get his shit together. We were stunned. Remarkably, Eddie—who always had a "legit" excuse for everything—got his act together quickly, and a band member he remained.

Another meeting was called to discuss the future of the band. Not in an ominous way, but in a positive "What do we do to achieve our goals?" discussion. The special guest at that meeting: Kevin Brenner, our booking agent. Kevin had worked with dozens and dozens of bands over the years, but we were the first that he could see making the jump from cover bar band to playing our own music in concert venues all over the world.

A timeline and game plan were discussed, but when the subject turned to original music, I went off. I couldn't stand the originals we were then playing. Not only did I think they were weak, but they weren't right for my voice, the band, and its ambition. This wasn't the first time I'd griped about these songs, but it was probably the most intense.

Kevin Brenner looked at me. "Can you write songs?"

"Yes," I responded confidently.

"Have you *written* any songs?"

Oops. Brenner had me there. "Uh . . . *no*," I mumbled.

"Then shut the hell up until you've got something better," our intrepid agent barked.

Check and mate! I was red-faced. It was humiliating to be put in my place like that, but it was frustrating, too . . . because he was right. I can't stand people who constantly tear things down with absolutely no suggestion of how to do it differently or better. I sat quietly for the rest of the meeting, and when it was over, I stormed up to my room and slammed the door. I knew I was right about the band's originals, and I was sure I could write songs. It was time to put up or shut up. Inspired by Bad Company's *Burnin' Sky* album, I wrote my first original song for the band a few days later. I presented them with "Pay the Price" * and they liked it. We worked it up (at a club) and added it to our set.

From then on, I was constantly working on new, original songs, and I wrote them all—music, melodies, and lyrics—by myself. Feeling alienated from the band for a variety of reasons, I made it my goal to solely create all the music that would define Twisted Sister.

BY 1977, TWISTED SISTER had solidified its position as a dominating force in the club scene on Long Island and in upstate New York and was beginning to expand its sphere of influence further into New Jersey and Connecticut. The Demolition Squad was on the move. New York City clubs (such as CBGB) were never an option because they were too small and didn't pay well, and because our continued dedication to the no-longer "in vogue" glitter-rock movement of the early seventies made us a pariah to the "too cool for the room" city rockers.

It always blows my mind how New York music industry moguls will wander into some shithole half-empty club (downtown or uptown, take your pick), see a band playing for a handful of apathetic hipsters, and go back to work the next day proclaiming they've discovered the next big thing. Meanwhile, across the bridge (or through the tunnel) some band is rocking the hell out of a dangerously over-filled room of people, literally bouncing off the walls, and it goes completely unnoticed. At the height of Twisted Sister's club days, we were performing in the suburbs to a thousand to three thousand

---

* Though never released on an official Twisted Sister major label LP, "Pay the Price" can be found on Twisted's *Club Daze Volume 1: The Studio Sessions* CD in its demo form. Though not the sound we ultimately became known for, it's still a good song. Especially for my first.

people *a night* (sometimes over four thousand), *five nights a week*, but we had to go to England to get noticed by the music industry! I guess if it's not in the city, it can't possibly have value, right? *Friggin' record company morons.* But I'm getting way ahead of myself. When people would question Twisted Sister's commitment to what was then considered a defunct music trend, I would respond, "If it's that over, why are people still freaking out when I walk onstage every night?" By the time a trend reaches suburban and rural audiences, the urban "cultural centers" have moved on to something else.

I knew plenty of life was still left in the whole glam rock thing and embraced it with a passion. The wild costumes Suzette made were blowing people's minds, though some of the guys in my own band were embarrassed by the more genitalia-revealing ones. Suzette made the pants so tight, they left nothing to the imagination. They didn't call us cock rockers for nothin'! These outfits, combined with my penchant for insane onstage behavior and violent reactions toward hecklers, were building my and the band's reputation as a "don't miss" attraction.

Pretty much nightly, I'd leap off the stage into the crowd and get into a confrontation with some drunk jackass who thought I was going to let his derisions slide. Fuck that! Now they could go home and tell their friends how they got shut down by some huge "fag" in high heels, a shorty satin top, and a purple feather boa. I *loved* that outfit.

I've never been a fighter, but I cannot and will not allow some asshole in the audience (or on the street, for that matter) to dictate what I can or cannot wear or do. Audiences have a mob mentality. If you allow one or two to get away with saying or throwing shit at you, others will get brave, and soon you have a major problem on your hands.

ONE NIGHT, AT A club in New Jersey, I was talking to the club owner, and he made a reference to "my boss."

"My boss?" I said. "Who's my boss?"

"Jay Jay," the club owner responded matter-of-factly, as if he was surprised I even had to ask.

Jay Jay!? My boss?! I was incensed! Did people think that was the case? Jay Jay was still the "bandleader," essentially running the show. He was the consummate carnival huckster, regaling the crowd each night (with my help) between songs with lame, Borscht-Belt humor. To be fair, the audience loved it. The idea that his substance-less bullshit was overshadowing my talent (I was pretty damn full of myself) was flipping me out.

As I drove home that night, I fumed. Talent does *not* necessarily win out in the end. Bullshit beats talent. Then what beats bullshit? I turned this question over and over in my mind, looking at it from every angle, until it hit me.

⇥ DEE LIFE LESSON ⇤
Bullshit beats talent . . . talent + bullshit beats bullshit!

I knew just what I had to do. To dominate, I had to take Jay Jay's shtick, improve upon it, and add it to the singing and performing I was already delivering each night. And I did just that.

As the months rolled by, I continued to write more and more songs and refine my look and my act. The other band members didn't work as hard on their look, so by late '77, people were starting to take the singularity of the name *Twisted Sister* to mean me. I was the "twisted sister." I think the others in the band may have had their own epiphany at that point.

BY AUGUST OF THAT year, the failed experiment that was the band house ended, and we all went our separate ways. Jay Jay and drummer #3 got a place together, and Eddie, who had secretly married his fiancée, Clara, found a place with her. Having graduated high school after her junior year, Suzette was accepted to her school of choice, the Fashion Institute of Technology in New York City, a hell of an achievement for a sixteen-year-old girl. Suzette was going to live in the dormitory at the school. This was a problem.

As I said earlier, New York City could be a scary place for suburbanites. Though I certainly had become more worldly over the eighteen months I had been with Twisted Sister, NYC was still a largely alien place to me. Now I was faced with an even bigger issue: the love of my life was moving there.

Suzette was now officially "in love" with me, though I can't be certain that the Stockholm syndrome didn't play some kind of part in it. We'd been together almost a year and a half, and our commitment to each other was pretty much a lock (not to say that our romance was easy). Suzette's choices had been either to go to school in Paris or New York. Due to the seriousness of our relationship, she chose the latter, but, understandably, was not going to commute. When my high school girlfriend had gone off to college, I'd experienced the growing apart that happens when a couple are away from each other for extended periods.

I wasn't about to let that happen with Suzette. She was to start college the first week in September, so I hopped on a train in the middle of August and headed for the Big Apple to find myself an apartment.

Like a complete idiot, dressed in the nicest clothes I had (a long-sleeved, colorful, man-tailored shirt, high-waisted, bell-bottom slacks, and platform shoes), I made my way to Penn Station, then took the subway, *five blocks*, to FIT. Clearly I had no concept of distance in NYC. I exited the subway station on a steamy mid-August afternoon, dripping with sweat, and stood on Seventh Avenue in front of the school. I looked around, and directly across the street was a lone apartment building: Kheel Tower. I waited for the walk signal (rube!), then crossed the street to check it out.

The building superintendent told me an apartment was available and showed me a killer one-bedroom, one-and-a-half-bath duplex, with a balcony, on the twenty-third floor, overlooking the school (and, as it turned out, right next door to the dean of FIT). The rent was a bit pricey, but I figured with a couple of roommates I could make it work.

At a pay phone outside I called my old pal Don Mannello and my former drummer, turned aspiring actor, Rich Squillacioti. They said they were in, so I told the super I would take the place, got back on the train, and headed home. The whole of this apartment hunting took less than an hour.

When I told everybody I had found an apartment exactly where I wanted it, without a real estate agent, on my first try, nobody could believe it. Apartment finding in Manhattan is long and arduous. Things like that just didn't happen. They did if you were meant to be with the woman of your dreams.

Two weeks later I moved in. Suzette lasted two days in her dorm, then, unbeknownst to her father or my parents, she moved in with me. We've lived together ever since.

⚜ 12 ⚜

leaps and bounds

Having made it to the top of the cover-band bar scene, Twisted Sister had become big money earners. Top local bands lived like rock stars, and now Twisted Sister was making the money to live like them, too. Cars, houses, and more beckoned as we raked it in during the summer of 1977. To our credit, we realized something the other bands clearly didn't. Being and living like a rock star in the tristate area was *not* the goal. It was *not* what we all dreamed about. It felt a lot like it, but it wasn't. Not even close.

The guys in Twisted got together and discussed the temptation of just taking the money and living it up. *Or* we could take minimal salaries and invest in ourselves. Being a top bar band wasn't forever. Having platinum and gold albums hanging on your walls was. So with a vote of four to one, we resolved that after the summer we would cut our salaries by more than half and use the extra money for the things that would help make us *real* rock stars. Truth be told, I never saw myself as playing in clubs and bars. In my mind, every bar was a concert hall, every club an arena. I didn't know it then, but they call that positive visualization: to mentally see things as you want them to be, not as they are.

I said four out of five band members voted in favor of cutting our salaries for the greater good. The holdout was Eddie Ojeda. Eddie claimed he couldn't survive on the minimal money the rest of us were taking. He was married, he needed more. Well, if memory serves, his wife had a really good job, I was living with my girlfriend, and we all were struggling. Eddie wouldn't do it, so he took more money than the rest of us. He paid the band back once we made it, but who needed the money then? So, without Eddie's full support, we invested in ourselves and in our future. Crew members were hired, new lights and sound were purchased. Whatever we needed for the betterment of the band, the money we *didn't* take for ourselves was used for. Then the final piece was put into place.

After seeing the effect Suzette's costuming was having for me, the band hired her, put her on salary and had Suzette continuously designing and making new stage clothes for all of us. From that point on, throughout the history of the band, Suzette has been responsible (or to blame) for the look of Twisted Sister. She eventually guided us to the more "tattered" look the band came to be known for. Suzette knew (well before I did) that I was no pretty boy and I needed to play to my strengths, namely my "badassness." Suzette used to say "You don't wear makeup, you wear war paint." She was right. There was nothin' pretty about me. But I'm getting way ahead of myself. First I *tried* to be pretty.

ODDLY, THE MORE FEMININE I got visually, the more aggressive and hostile I got as a person. I don't think there was a direct correlation between the two, but I'll let a psychiatrist figure that one out. This was around the time that the catchphrase "Look like women, talk like men, and play like muthafuckers" started to be used to describe the band. They should have added "And they'll kick your fucking ass if you don't like it!"

I remember, early on, a gay magazine from New York City sent a writer out to see and interview the new "tranny band" out in the burbs. He showed up at some biker bar we were playing, watched our first set, then came backstage and said, "You guys aren't gay!" Standing there in my high heels and tied-up woman's shorty top, I responded, "Of course not. What made you think we were?" I guess I was sending a mixed message.

An air of violence always seemed to surround our gigs. Part of it was due to the environment inherent to a club show. The shows were in bars, late at night, alcohol (and drugs) were prevalent, and the places were overcrowded with a predominantly teenage, angst-filled audience, ready to mix it up. Add to that a high-energy band such as Twisted Sister, with an incendiary front man (me) stirring the pot, and you definitely had a recipe for potential disaster. I don't think I looked for trouble as much as launched preemptive strikes, but either way, violence often ensued. With so many moments of violence, or near violence, in those days, it's hard to know which to share. The time I had a straight razor held to my throat in a club parking lot? The time I inadvertently "called out" three Hells Angels? How about the time a motorcycle gang descended on one of the clubs Twisted Sister was playing to get our bodyguards and I had to hold a "war council" in our dressing room?

In November of 1977, an incident occurred that I'd like to say was the violence surrounding me coming to a head . . . but I can't. It was really the start of a whole new level.

We were in the middle of our second or third set of the night, at a club called Speaks,* in Island Park, Long Island. Speaks was one of the premier places to play, and Twisted Sister was one of its biggest bands. Almost fifteen hundred people were packed into the place, but we weren't having the best of nights. We were plagued with feedback problems from the sound system (the ultimate mellow harsher), but sometimes the crowd—for whatever reason—just isn't that into it. I tried every party trick I could think of, but we just couldn't get the audience to their usual level of insanity.

Suddenly, midsong, a bottle goes sailing past my head.

There is nothing lower than throwing something at performers on a stage. Deep into whatever they are doing for the audience, with bright lights in their eyes, they are completely vulnerable and incapable of seeing anything coming. Many entertainers have been seriously injured by things thrown at them while onstage. The people who throw things are the biggest cowards and pussies out there. It's like being a sniper. Your targets have no possible means of defend-

---

*   Formerly going under the names The Rock Pile and The Action House. Some of the most legendary bands in rock history had played there, including Jimi Hendrix and Cream.

ing themselves or even a fighting chance of avoiding being hit. Their health and well-being is solely dependent on your inaccuracy. You pieces of shit.

The bottle narrowly missed my head. With the lights in my eyes, I couldn't see who threw it, but I knew the direction it came from. I stopped singing and walked to the front edge of the stage.

"Who fuckin' threw that!" I yelled in the microphone as the band continued to play. My band were experienced in how to handle my confrontations. They would just vamp on the chord progression until I finished my tirade or made my way back to the stage. True professionals.

While no one was owning up to hurling the projectile, fans were pointing to a specific area from where it came. I focused my verbal attack and laid into my attacker, whoever he or she was.

"If you have *half* of one ball—not *the balls*, not *one ball*; *half of one ball, a semicircle*—you'll show yourself and come up on this stage and face me!" I was hoping it was a guy—I wasn't sure what I'd do if it was a woman. The audience always enjoyed my tirades, and even though I was as mad as I had ever been, I still tried to be entertaining. *A semicircle?!*

Still there was no reaction, but my peeps were continuing to point in a specific area. I pressed on, "You're a pussy. Your father's a pussy." I went for the throat: "Your *mother's a pussy*." Technically accurate, but nobody likes when you talk shit about their mother.

With that, a guy directly where everybody was pointing, maybe fifteen or twenty feet back in the packed house, raises his middle fingers in the air and starts yelling, "Fuck you!"

I was incensed. In all the years I'd had things thrown at me, I had never actually found my attacker, *and there he was!*

"You! It was you?!" I screamed over our massive loudspeaker system. "Come up here, you piece of shit! Come up here and face me like a fuckin' man!"

The asshole just stood his ground, cursing and pumping his middle fingers.

I'm not a fighter per se, and I'm definitely not the toughest guy in the world. Besides, no matter who you are, there's always someone tougher out there . . . and then there are guns. With that in mind, every time I've jumped off a stage after someone in the crowd, I've always assessed my options. If I get in trouble, who will have my back?

On this night, I noticed a couple of particularly large biker fans in this guy's immediate area. With my backup firmly in place, I took action. If only I had planned *that* a little better.

Fueled by the frustration of an unresponsive crowd, finding my attacker for the first time and his lack of cooperation, I decided to do something that seemed completely plausible *in my mind*. Rather than climb off the stage or run off the side and take a chance of losing this asshole in the crowd, I would simply dive into the sea of fans below me, they would catch me, and I'd get the son of a bitch. This bad idea was hatched faster than it took you to just read it, and I launched myself from the stage.

To quote Eddie Ojeda, "All of a sudden, I see a pair of red, high-heeled boots sailing past the side of my head."

I definitely got some air.

I didn't account for a few things on that fateful night. The first being human nature.

⧉ DEE LIFE LESSON ⧉

When people see 180 pounds of six-foot-six-inch (in heels) silver lamé and

leather (another killer outfit), made up like the Zuni Fetish Doll from

Karen Black's *Trilogy of Terror*, coming down on them from

ten feet above . . . they get the hell out of the way!

The club was so packed that night you couldn't fit another body in the place, but as I descended, somehow the audience parted like the Red Sea. For the life of me, I don't know where those people went. I hit the ground hard, and as I picked myself up from the floor, I came face-to-face with my attacker, standing in a full-blown *Karate Kid* crane pose, ready to strike. I quickly looked for my backup—the big biker fans—and they were right there . . . clearing an area for the fight to take place.

"Give 'em room! Give 'em room!" *Thanks, guys*. Did I mention the band was still playing? In all the years of my scrapping with people in the audience, it should be noted that not once have any of my band members come to my aid. Roadies, yes. Band, no. I don't know if they were afraid, confused, or just thought it was my problem, but night after night I would be in the shit alone. Except for my faithful backup, our soundman, Charlie "the Sixth Sister" Barreca! I love you for that, Charlie.

One of the things I had learned in my years of barroom confrontations was "When in doubt . . . football!" To remove myself from striking range of this Bruce Lee wannabe, I charged the bastard, grabbed him around the waist, and began to drive him backward through the crowd. (Impressive, in spike heels!) As I pushed him back, my man Charlie came up from behind and grabbed him. Within seconds, every bouncer in the place was on top of the guy and he was being dragged out of the club.

As I limped through the crowd, back to the stage, and climbed up—already I could feel something was seriously wrong with my leg—the formerly placid club erupted. *That's what it took to get a reaction out of them?!* The crowd continued to roar as a girl in the front row signaled me to bend down so she could tell me something. I leaned in to hear what she had to say.

"Was that staged?"

D'oh!

The next day I could barely walk. I had bruised my thighbone in the fall, and my leg had swelled up like a watermelon. I staggered through a handful of songs that night, then had to leave the stage; I was in too much pain. We wound up canceling the next three nights because of my injury.

Upon my return, Jay Jay informed me that the band had decided to hire bodyguards. "You can't be doing security for us."

Ya think?

⚜ 13 ⚜

that "just jailed" look

During the spring of 1978 I made my move. I asked seventeen-year-old Suzette to marry me.

I was tired of being at clubs and introducing the girl of my dreams, the girl I intended to spend the rest of my life with, as "my girlfriend." Every guy in every band introduces every girl he's been with—for even five minutes in a bathroom stall—as his "girlfriend." Complete with quotation marks. It pissed me off that there was no distinction between Suzette and some groupie.

I plotted to pop the question for some time. Jay Jay's dad, Lou, was a jewelry salesman and his girlfriend, Josephine, worked in Manhattan's Diamond District on Forty-Seventh Street. She hooked me up with a good deal on an engagement ring. I put it on layaway and paid the ring off over the next several weeks. When I picked up the ring, I just couldn't wait. The minute I got back to the apartment, I asked Suzette to be my wife. She cried (I think with joy) and said yes. We both knew that we weren't ready to set a date or anything and wouldn't be for some time. Our engagement represented to the world our commitment to each other and our intentions to be together forever.

Unbeknownst to me at the time, Suzette's dad, Vinny, had discovered that Suzette was not living at the dorms. Suzette's a-hole roommate was more than happy to share this information when he called looking for Suzette. *Bitch.* ("Suzette's not here. She's been living with her boyfriend.") Her dad was livid (understandably). Not only was his seventeen-year-old daughter living with a now twenty-three-year-old musician, but Vinny was paying for a dorm room that wasn't being used. They're not cheap.

It should be noted that Suzette's dad had once been a working musician himself. The leader and drummer of the Vinny Garron Orchestra in his youth, my wife's dad tore it up. He gave up his ambitions when he got married and "had to do the right thing," which is a big deal in the Italian-American community. Besides "knowing" what musicians were like, I can't help but think that there was a certain amount of jealousy. I was pursuing my dream and he had given his up.

Vinny Garron also hated rock 'n' roll because it "killed the business," and rockers weren't real musicians "because they can't sight-read music." Even worse . . . I was a "singah"! I couldn't have been lower on his right-guy-for-my-daughter totem pole. Suzette's dad told her he was sending her to Paris to finish school so he could get her away from me. When I asked Suzette to marry me, she says she said yes to kill her dad's plan and be able to finish school in New York. Suzette claims at that time she had no intention of marrying me. Isn't that just like a teenage girl?

While Suzette and my growing love may seem romantic, it wasn't an easy relationship. She was a strong-willed young woman, and I was becoming a more arrogant asshole with each passing day. The more popular my band became, and the more acknowledgment I got for my talents, the more self-centered and self-absorbed I was. And I was just getting warmed up. This was 1978. I didn't hit my stride until 1985! Can you imagine? I can see now that it was only my relationship with Suzette and her seemingly irrational tantrums that kept me grounded in any way. I was heading down a dark path and it was getting darker fast.

EACH YEAR THE BAND took a week or two of vacation after Labor Day weekend, the big finish to a long summer of rock. The riotous closing of Hammerheads happened in August, taking the violent intensity of Twisted Sister shows to a whole new level. The band was ready for a break, and I needed a vacation. Our first in 1977 was relaxing, healing, and good for the soul. The one in 1978, not so much.

ON SEPTEMBER 12, SUZETTE and I were in my car, driving out to Long Island from the city for a dentist appointment in the late afternoon. As I got off the Clearview Expressway and onto the Grand Central Parkway eastbound, some maniac in a pickup truck cut in front of me and slammed on his brakes! I slammed on mine, screeching to a halt and narrowly missing the back of his vehicle. With that, the asshole took off. *Oh, no, you don't!*

Furious, I stomped on the gas and took off after the piece of shit. Swerving in and out of the building rush-hour traffic (with Suzette admonishing me the whole time), I caught up to the dick and pulled alongside. I gave him the middle finger and the nastiest "Fuck you, asshole!" I could muster. Satisfied, I took off . . . only to have this bastard pursue me!

When he pulled alongside me, he didn't curse or give me the finger back . . . he tried to run me off the road! I swerved away, narrowly avoiding being hit and/or hitting another car on the road. It didn't end there. In and out of heavy traffic, he came after me, trying to ram into my vehicle. Traffic on the parkway stopped as this road-rage insanity unfolded.

Finally, the pickup truck sped ahead of me and turned sharply sideways in front of my car, nearly running me off an overpass. When my car came to a stop, this madman (remember: there's always someone tougher than you are) jumped out of his truck and charged my vehicle. Before I could even get out of the car, he blocks my car door (good move, by the way), reaches in through my partially open window, and starts to yank me through the four-inch opening by my hair.

Now I don't want to imply that I was brave or badass in any way. I was scared shitless. This is a cautionary tale I'm telling here. The person who was brave was my five-foot-three-inch, 110-pound fiancée. She leapt from of the passenger side of the car, ran around the back of the vehicle, and jumped on the guy's back! With one arm wrapped around his neck choking him, she started pounding away at his head with her other hand.

What a woman!

At this point the lunatic let go of my hair with one of his hands and started trying to hit Suzette. Seeing she was in danger, I reached under my car seat and pulled out a tire iron I kept there for protection. Reaching through the window opening with my right hand (I was still being yanked out the small opening), I started swinging the tire iron at the guy the best I could. The whole scene was out of control!

Finally, some people got out of their cars and came over to break it up. Probably because it was the only way they were ever going to get home. They managed to pull my attacker off me, but he broke free. He charged the car, blood dripping down his face, and wiped a big smear of blood across my windshield.

When the police arrived, we were both arrested. As we sat there, waiting to be taken in, I asked him why he came after me in the first place. He replied, "You cut me off." *Cut him off?* I didn't even know I cut him off! Then he added, "You're lucky I didn't get one of my guns." The dude had a full gun rack in his pickup.

Our vehicles were impounded, we were taken in and booked. Him for harassment—a misdemeanor—and me for assault with a deadly weapon! The scumbag had tried to kill me and Suzette with his truck, and because I had defended myself and caused him minor bodily harm, I was charged with a felony! To make matters worse, he was released on his own recognizance, and because it was too late in the day for me to be arraigned, I had to spend the night in jail. You know, it's bad enough when your actions bring you down and cause you pain and suffering, but when they hurt innocent people, especially people you care about, it's just fucked-up. My stupidity, my road rage, had endangered the girl I loved, and now she was on her own, dealing with the consequences of my actions.

Its being a typical late-summer day, we left the apartment without jackets. While we were at the police station, a cold front came in and it started raining. Wearing only a bloodstained white T-shirt (which became transparent when it got wet), seventeen-year-old Suzette was let out of the police station, into the cold, in a bad part of the city. She didn't have a clue where she was in relation to our apartment and had to find her way home with only a couple of dollars in her pocket to get her there. This was the seventies; there were no cell phones or ATM cards. To this day I feel like a complete piece of shit for endangering her and putting her through that. I'm so sorry, Suzette.

MEANWHILE, BACK IN JAIL, by the time I was moved from the station holding tank to the jail for the night, I had missed the evening meal. Since I couldn't be arraigned until the next day, they didn't even bother to give me my phone call. Besides Suzette, nobody knew where I was, and she even didn't know they had moved me.

They hold you in group cells filled with all kinds of criminals. There's no separation by the severity of your crime of arrest. Luckily my "felony assault" trumped the hands a lot of my other cellmates were holding and sounded more badass than it actually was, so no one messed with me.

The jail cells were anything but luxurious. They had a common toilet in the middle of the room, and metal "benches" with no bedding of any kind to sit or lie on. I was cold, hungry, scared, and confused. *How did I wind up here?* I had let my anger get the best of me, got carried away with road rage, and met my match. Now I was up on felony charges, punishable by years in jail! Trust me, no matter how you convince yourself that you've got no criminal past (except for some arrests for driving with a suspended license) and there's no way they would *ever* actually imprison you, your mind still messes with you. As you sit in your cell through the night, waiting to face the judge, you are shitting in your pants. I wondered how the hell I had got to this point, examining my whole existence.

In the middle of the night, the jail guards came and took us out of our cell, legs chained us together, and loaded us into a paddy wagon with no windows. I had no idea where they were taking me. How would Suzette or anybody else know where I was? The reality of how, if the authorities want to "misplace" you, they can do it that easily set in, and it was terrifying.

As morning finally came, we were moved for a fourth time and brought for arraignment. My cellmates and I hadn't been offered so much as a drink of water the entire night. When I got before the judge, my attacker was there as well (bet he had a nice night's sleep at his house). I heard the court lawyers saying something about my having no priors, and since prosecution was unlikely, my attacker agreed to drop charges against me if I would drop the charges against him. *What?* Even though I was completely justified in what I had done to him, and that piece of shit started the whole damn thing, I jumped at the chance to get the hell out of there and get my life back. Hallelujah!

When I was released and finally found out where the hell I was, I got to a pay phone and called Eddie Ojeda, who lived the closest. When he arrived, Eddie told me I had the unique look people who had just been in jail have. Ignoring that Eddie had picked up enough people from jail that he would know that we share "a look," I asked him what the look was.

"A mix of shock, disbelief, and humiliation," Eddie replied.

That about covered it.

Over the years, I always remember that night as a turning point for me. I came face-to-face with the terrifying path my life was heading down. I even wrote a song, "Burn in Hell," years later that related my experience of self-discovery.

> *You can't believe all the things I've done wrong in my life.*
> *Without even trying I've lived on the edge of a knife.*
> *Well, I've played with fire,*
> *I don't want to get myself burned*
> *To thine own self be true*
> *So, I think that it's time for a turn*
> *Before I burn in hell!*
> *Oh, burn in hell!*

The odd thing is, it was almost two years before I made a real change. In writing this book, I needed to assemble a timeline for reference. I found that, though my road-rage experience did put the fear of God in me, it wasn't enough to make me get my act together. What an idiot I was.

⚜ 14 ⚜

i'm just a sweet transvestite

I had been aware of *The Rocky Horror Show* since its brief run on Broadway in 1975. From what I heard, the show was a direct link between the glitter rock scene and the fifties nostalgia that was going on at that time, but the run ended, and that was about it . . . for a while.

An ill-fated movie release followed, and again, I didn't see it or even hear much about it.

Cut to the fall of 1977 and, living in Manhattan, we started to hear rumblings about midnight showings of *The Rocky Horror Picture Show* movie at the Waverly Theater on Sixth Avenue in Greenwich Village. When the band finally had a night off that coincided with one of these screenings, Jay Jay, Suzette, and I made our way to the theater. We joined about seven other people in attendance, for an incredible—no audience participation—musical and visual experience. Our collective lives were forever changed.

Inspiration from *Rocky Horror* quickly infiltrated our makeup, costumes, and music. "Sweet Transvestite," first as our intro tape, then as an actual song, was added to our set, as was "Time Warp." For the first time, Twisted Sister had become a trendsetter, as we shared our love for *RHPS* with all of our fans. *The Rocky Horror Picture Show* was undoubtedly an early trigger for the hair-metal craze that was to come.

Twisted Sister were so connected to *RHPS*'s phenomenal growth in popularity that we were asked to perform at the first ever *Rocky Horror Picture Show* convention, held at the Calderone Concert Hall, in Hempstead, Long Island, on February 20, 1978.*

I can still see the stunned look on the faces of Richard O'Brien (writer/Riff Raff), Patricia Quinn (Magenta), and Nell Campbell (Lil' Nell) as they walked, unaware, into the mania that surrounded the *RHPS*.

Priceless.

Twisted Sister's performance at the *Rocky Horror* convention led to our next major career move. We knew we were responsible for putting a lot of the asses in the seats of the theater that night. Looking to take things to the next level, we started to think, *Why not host our own concert event?*

ARMED WITH A BUNCH of original songs and a huge (and growing) fan base, we set out to do what no unsigned club band in our area had done before: stage a full-blown concert event. So, with our own money we rented the Calderone Concert Hall and on October 28, 1978, we went for it . . . but not without some growing pains.

The stress of managing Twisted Sister's day-to-day affairs, playing at the clubs each night, and staging our first concert event ever took its toll on Jay Jay. So many additional issues needed to be dealt with for a show like that. Keep in mind, everything that had to be worked out and set up for that one show were the same things any national concert act would have to do *for an entire tour*. It was an impressive feat for the band, but while most of the creative elements were predominantly mine, *all* of the business and financial elements were on Jay's shoulders.

The night of the show, we overcompensated on every level. We had a comedian and an opening band on the bill with us, and—not having any real idea of what should or shouldn't be in a concert set—we brought the kitchen sink. Every original song we had, plus a bunch of signature covers, were included. I remember being halfway

---

* You can see Twisted Sister's name on the marquee of the Calderone for the convention on the DVD extra "History of the *Rocky Horror Show*."

through the show and getting a stitch in my side, the kind of thing you sometimes get while you're running. I didn't understand. Why was I winded? Sure the stage was larger, but I jumped around for hours each night. Aerobically, I was in incredible shape.

When we finally left the stage, we were told we had been up there for almost three hours! No wonder I got a stitch.

Our first solo theater show was an unprecedented success. It sold out well in advance and took Twisted Sister's live show to the next level. The Calderone Concert Hall event elevated our status in the club community even more. We were now Twisted Sister the "concert attraction." Unfortunately, the ordeal proved too much for Jay Jay, and he announced, understandably, he was stepping down as band manager. If we were going to make it to the next level, we were going to need a manager whose sole purpose was to get us to the top.

As luck would have it, Mark Puma, the promoter of our Calderone show, was looking to get into band management. He was more than a little impressed by this local band who—completely under their own steam—booked, promoted, and sold out the theater, then blew the roof off the place. Start-up manager Mark Puma had found his start-up band.

Hindsight being twenty-twenty, I can now see the folly of this union. Having a manager who was learning how to manage while he managed us was not the best career move we could have made. But we were impressed by his being a major Northeast concert promoter (we had gone to tons of his shows) and his office and staff. Mark Puma seemed the perfect fit, so we signed with him.

15

you're gonna burn in hell

The end of 1978 brought about another major change for our band. Bass player Kenny Neill, a founding member of the band, decided to leave. Kenny's dedication to his sobriety and his being a close "friend of Bill W's" (Alcoholics Anonymous) were making him more and more religious. Sometime during the year, Kenny had officially become born-again and he was starting to have doubts about being a devout Christian *and* in Twisted Sister.

In the fall of that year, several members of Kenny's congregation came down to a Twisted Sister show at Zaffy's in New Jersey to give him the answer to his question. They filed into the room, looking very much like a jury, and sat stone-faced as we did what we did, the way only we did it. After the show, they gave Kenny their verdict. They felt that the devil was working through some of my original songs and through Jay Jay's onstage banter. I'm sure my unwillingness to turn the other cheek didn't help either. Oddly, there was no mention of our cross-dressing or makeup. How Christian of them. Kenny told us then and there that he would be leaving the band as soon as we could find a suitable replacement.

Kenny Neill is a great guy, and we totally appreciated and respected what he was going through, so other than expressing our regrets at his leaving, we accepted his decision as something he just had to do.

Interestingly enough, I was quietly going through my own Christian self-doubt around that time. I was born and raised a Christian and attended an Episcopal church every Sunday—and sang in the choir—until I was about nineteen. Did I lose my faith at nineteen? No. I joined a working rock band (Peacock) and didn't get home from the clubs and bars until about six o'clock on Sunday morning. I wasn't *that* committed to going to church.

I met two of my best friends, twin brothers Willy and David Hauser, in church. They were my partners in crime through a lot of my formative years. Having lost their father at a very young age, they became successful—albeit cutthroat—businessmen. By seventeen they had built up the largest landscaping business in New York State; by nineteen they had bought a large nursery (their second). Helpful and supportive (often giving me much-needed work) throughout my young life, Willy and David were great friends. Somewhere around the latter part of the seventies, the brothers Hauser were born-again. Being the go-getters that they were, they attacked their newly rediscovered Christianity as if their lives depended on it. They aggressively tried to save pretty much everyone who they felt needed saving, to the point of destroying the successful business they had worked so hard to build. I mean, if you're coming in to buy some lawn seed, and a huge sign over the door says ARMAGEDDON IS COMING! (which it did), you might just say "Oh, the hell with it" (pun intended), and skip your purchase. Not good for business.

The Hauser brothers worked on me relentlessly, trying to save my rock 'n' roll soul. They were really good salesmen, and though I wasn't fully buying their whole "end is near" rhetoric (the Rapture was originally supposed to happen in 1984), they did plant a seed of doubt in me. What if they were right and I wasn't one of the chosen and saved? The possibility of being stuck in a postapocalyptic world began to haunt me. What if I was hours away from Suzette at some club when the end came? Since I always wore five-inch, stack-heeled boots in those days—not the best shoes for hiking and negotiating the ruined world that the prophecies foretold—I started to carry a pair of running shoes in my stage-clothes bag just in case the twins were right. I was prepared to run back to wherever Suzette might be when the end came.

The band's star was on a meteoric rise. We knew Kenny's decision to leave could not have been easy for him, but the question of whom to replace Kenny with was not nearly as hard for us to make. Mark "the Animal" Mendoza, formerly of the seminal punk band the Dictators, was our bass roadie at that time and first and only choice for filling Kenny's "platform" shoes.

As I said, Mark and my paths had crossed before, but we became friends when he came down to the clubs to see Twisted during his breaks from touring with the Dictators.

The Dictators were signed to a major label, and they toured with the likes of Kiss, Blue Öyster Cult, and lots of other coliseum attractions of the day. The Dictators were where Twisted Sister very much wanted to be. That we were Mark's band of choice when he was home meant a lot to us.

When Mark quit the Dictators, we were coincidentally looking for a bass tech/roadie. Upon hearing of the job opening, Mark approached us and said, "If I can't play in a band, I'd rather roadie for a band than work a day job." Now that's the rock 'n' roll attitude! He was more than qualified for the job, was a friend of the band's, and had the utmost respect for Kenny. Mark was quickly hired and was a great—albeit overqualified—addition to our crew.

After months of his working on the side of the stage watching the band and Kenny every night, Mark's transition to being in the band was pretty seamless. While we rehearsed the music with Mark, Suzette worked miracles turning a bearded, biker Dictator into a clean-shaven Twisted Sister.

Kenny departed in December of 1978, and Mark stepped in without missing a beat. In Mark I found a peer, agewise (he is a year younger than me) and in background (he, too, had grown up in the suburbs of Long Island), and a brother in my love for heavy metal. To paraphrase *How the Grinch Stole Christmas* . . . "And what happened then? Well, in Twisted Sister they say, when Mark 'the Animal' Mendoza joined, the band's heavy-metal heart grew ten sizes that day."

And I loved it!

With Mark Mendoza in the band and our wagon hitched to

(what we thought was) Mark Puma's formidable "horse," a game plan started to come together. Now we just had to focus our assault on the record companies.

DID I MENTION THAT I was becoming a monster? Oh, yeah, I was. My hostility toward the world was growing at an astronomical pace. My new friend, band bodyguard and Suzette and my roommate (NYC year three) Roger and I were pushing each other to much darker places. I had met Roger after an extremely violent gang-like battle at a club Twisted Sister was playing, and we fed off of each other's worst qualities (and senses of humor). What I had been holding back from a lifetime of indignities (I admit, some perceived) was surfacing with each passing day. I used the band's growing popularity to fire off venom-filled tirades from the stage each night, toward the illusive "they." They could be parents, teachers, adults, politicians, cops, disco assholes, stuck-up chicks, or anybody in the club who wasn't participating, or whom I perceived to have an "attitude." Unknowingly, I was creating a classic "us against them" scenario, with the rockers positioned as the underdogs railing against their oppressors. It worked amazingly well. I just wish I could claim to have known what I was doing. Then again, it was probably the genuineness of my hostilities that sold it to the crowd. I was a vicious, profanity-spewing nightmare with a growing hatred that was coloring my worldview. And the audience loved it! I was becoming the people's champion (before the Rock!).

My anger was not limited to the stage. At the management office, I had the secretary keep an ever-growing list of people and organizations I was going to get even with ("Karen, put so-and-so on the list!"), and I had a saying to go with my mania: PAMF— "payback's a muthafucker!" (a far cry from PMA, I admit). I even had T-shirts made with PAMF on them. I was nuts. Using my rage and hatred to drive me on, I sank my fangs into the task as hand: world domination.

Twisted Sister's grand plan was to "clean up" and properly package our current demo tapes, then showcase for the entire record industry at once. How? By booking ourselves into and selling out the prestigious, three-thousand-seat New York Palladium, an unprecedented achievement by an unsigned band. We knew our rabid fans would pack the place.

The tickets for our March 16, 1979, show sold out in less than a day. To make sure the record industry didn't miss our incredible achievement, we took out a full-page ad in the premier music industry chart magazine *Billboard*. Every record company committed their top people well in advance to be at the show. How could they not? Twisted Sister was doing the undoable, and clearly we were the next big thing.

Never ones to take anything for granted, we decided to pull out all the stops. New costumes for everyone (including multiple costume changes for me), a full-on theatrical light show with staging to match. Spending thousands of dollars that we had not taken as salary (except for Eddie), we self-financed everything, including two massive flashing signs that read DISCO and SUCKS, made to bring home our current battle cry.

In the late seventies, disco was king, and Twisted Sister had always been on a mission to destroy it. From smashing disco albums onstage with sledgehammers (often putting holes in the stages) to burning Bee Gees and *Saturday Night Fever* posters, to electrocuting and hanging various disco stars in effigy onstage, we, the "Rock 'n' Roll Saviors" (one of our biggest songs back then), were spreading the good word: Disco was dead! Long live rock! Though that hanging thing did get us in a bit of trouble one night.

While most of our shows were in suburban areas, we played some rural areas as well. There was one club in upstate New York where the local rockers really loved us. We would pack that place. One night, after a blistering, disco-crushing set, the audience reaction was particularly off the charts. We had finished by hanging disco maven Barry White in effigy, then tossing "his body" into the crowd. The audience tore the dummy to shreds and absolutely lost their minds.

At the end of the night, we were talking with the club owner about the crowd's enthusiastic reaction, and he casually says, "You can never go wrong with hangin' a nigger." *What?!* Idiots that we were, it never dawned on us that it could be interpreted as anything else. We quickly explained that hanging Barry White in effigy was purely symbolic, reflecting our attitude toward disco music as an art form. We certainly weren't racist. We had a Puerto Rican guitarist in the band and one of our former drummers was African-American.*

"You hung a nigger," the club owner reiterated. "People around here love that."

Needless to say, it was the last night for that.

STAGING A ONE-OFF CONCERT event such as at the Palladium required the same effort a major attraction would put into staging an entire tour—and all the expenses as well. We endlessly rehearsed the band and crew, doing full production runs in a huge rehearsal studio. This was our shot and we could leave nothing to chance.

The night before the big show, we rented the Palladium theater—at tremendous expense—so we could have a dress rehearsal on the actual stage where we were going to make our stand. Twisted Sister was making its own luck. But that night, at rehearsal, the completely unexpected happened. Eddie Ojeda had a grand mal seizure onstage.

All of a sudden, in between songs, Eddie dropped to the floor and started violently convulsing. Unconscious, he was rushed to the hospital, and just like that—although we didn't know it yet—our runaway train of a career had been completely derailed.

Eddie recovered surprisingly quickly and we rescheduled our show for April 6; it seemed simple enough. If only. What we didn't realize was, top record executives' schedules are planned well in advance. Because of this, every key person who was to attend on March 16 *could not* attend three weeks later, so they sent their underlings, some as insignificant (to our careers) as their secretaries.

The second thing that happened, which virtually no one (except maybe Nostradamus) could have predicted, was *the music scene changed*. In the three short weeks between Eddie's collapse and

---

* Years later, Twisted Sister would forbid Atlanta Braves relief pitcher John Rocker from using "I Wanna Rock" as his intro music after a particularly scathing racist tirade of his was published in *Sports Illustrated*.

our rescheduled concert, minimalist "new wave" had arrived, and no one wanted to know about some grandiose, over-the-top, big-production, heavy-metal band.

ON APRIL 6 THE rescheduled show went off without a hitch. The place was packed, the response from the fans was staggering ... *and the record industry couldn't have cared less.* Only one label was interested, but they needed a repeat performance—a formality, they assured us—to seal the deal.

Though we were a bit shaken by the limited response from the record companies, we knew it only took one label to say yes, and Epic Records was major. The label president wanted to see us perform, but there was a catch: we had to stage the full concert production at eleven o'clock in the morning just for him. *Are you fucking kidding me?*

It wasn't just the time of day (I didn't get up until the middle of the afternoon), but the expense of restaging this "showcase" was astronomical. The band was still reeling from the expense of Eddie's cancellation. Epic Records assured us we would be reimbursed, and again, this was just a formality; we were going to be signed.

I hated the idea of doing this—it was insulting to ask us to perform like that—but when the day arrived, with only a few hours' sleep I got up at 6:00 a.m., so I could be ready to rock by showtime. It takes me two hours to prepare for any performance, so at 9:00 a.m. I was at SIR studios, putting on my makeup and warming up my voice. By 11:00 a.m. we were dressed and waiting for Epic Records to grace us with their presence.

At 11:30 a.m., the asshole rolled in with two others and, without a word, sat down *on a couch* set up in the middle of the room in front of the stage. We launched into our show and performed the entire ninety-minute concert set, including audience-participation numbers—which they didn't participate in—as a "formality" for getting signed to Epic Records; *it was a done deal.*

When we finished our show, the Epic Records label president and his cohorts walked out without saying a *word* to the band. I wanted to verbally and physically tear that piece of crap apart.

⸱   ⸱   ⸱

YOU'LL NEVER GUESS WHAT happened next. Yep. Epic Records passed on the band, saying we were "dinosaurs" and no one was interested in "arena rock" anymore. And they didn't reimburse us for the expenses of the private showcase. Needless to say, the president of Epic was added to my PAMF list. *The prick.*

Of course, as the band continued on after our "Epic" failure, we convinced ourselves that being rejected by every label in the country was merely a bump on our road to stardom. The marketplace had completely changed, and industry insiders said there was absolutely no interest in a band like ours. *Oh, yeah?* Try telling that to the *thousands and thousands* of rock fans who were coming to see Twisted Sister in the clubs *every week*. Twisted Sister wasn't just a *big* band in the tristate scene, we were *the* band in the tristate scene. Our achievement at the Palladium that night sent our status on the local scene into the stratosphere. Playing to thousands of people every week we were affecting the musical tastes of a generation of rock fans in the region and the music future generations *internationally* would listen to. How can I say something as insane as that? Read on.

Twisted Sister was defining the local music scene and setting the standard by which other bands were being judged. Clubs were built to accommodate our crowds and staging needs, and the young musicians who would be the future of rock were flocking to study everything we did. In our audience, or in bands opening for us on any given night, were members of Bon Jovi, Cinderella, Billy Idol's band (Steve Stevens), Kix, Poison, Anthrax, Overkill, and more. Even the original Metallica—then totally unknown—opened for Twisted Sister at one of Metallica's first East Coast gigs in front of almost four thousand people.*

Twisted Sister was defining what would become hair metal, thrash metal, and the coming new wave of heavy metal in the United

---

* I didn't remember them opening or even seeing them that night, as I was always backstage getting ready for our show. When we toured together years later, they told me about their opening. Someone eventually sent me the ad from the local paper a few years ago. *Amazing.*

States. Even punk bands found inspiration in what we were doing. For years Green Day played "We're Not Gonna Take It" in their set.

This explains the disconnect you'll find between people's perceptions of my band. If you lived and grew up in the Northeast (or in Western Europe), you were aware of the effect and importance of Twisted Sister. If you were from the rest of the country (and world), your awareness began and ended pretty much with our couple of hit records, and we tend to be dismissed as a one-hit wonder or a flash in the pan.

With rejections coming in almost daily from out-of-touch record execs sitting in high towers in big cities, the visceral response of thousands of rabid rock fans each night told us to stay the course. I mean, who better knew what record buyers wanted to hear—suits in the city or the kids who actually bought the damn things?! We were reminded daily that the record-buying public was dying for recorded music from Twisted Sister.

In July of that summer, Twisted Sister was asked to play in a Long Island amusement park's weekly concert series. Every Tuesday night, a local band was hired to give a free show in the huge parking lot behind Adventureland in Farmingdale. The average weekly attendance was about three or four hundred people, but we were told that one of the bands (I think the Good Rats) drew around eight hundred. Twisted knew we could draw a lot more than that, and we pulled out all the stops (as usual) to make this *the* concert event of the summer. We even hired a plane to pull a sign over the beach, the weekend before, to help get the word out.

The night before the Adventureland show, Twisted Sister was invited to a going-away party for a mutual band friend, Barry Ambrosio. Barry was a well-liked local musician who had been busted for cocaine possession and had to do time. A local club was booked to house all of Barry's friends, and a couple of notable rock stars were there as well: Billy Joel and Ritchie Blackmore of Deep Purple and Rainbow.

Meeting these two hugely successful musicians was eye-opening for me. Where Blackmore was weird, standoffish, and unlikable, Joel was the exact opposite. Welcoming and self-deprecating, with virtually no ego, despite his multiplatinum status, Billy did everything to show how gracious and down-to-earth a star can be. When people spoke of Ritchie, it was with disgust and loathing. With Billy, it was only with praise and admiration.

After the party that night I reran the experiences I had had with both rock luminaries. I started to wonder how *I* came off to people and what they said about me after I left. In my heart I knew the answer: I was way more of a Ritchie Blackmore than a Billy Joel. I vowed to make a change, promising myself I would be more like Billy. I kept that promise . . . but it did take me a few years to put it into full effect.

HAVING ARRIVED AT A new level of success and stardom, the band decided we needed to hire an official "road manager." He would handle a lot of the stuff that was starting to overwhelm Jay Jay. As good as he was at handling the band's club business, he was our guitarist first and needed to focus his attentions on that, not dealing with club owners and the minutiae of Twisted gigs.

A longtime friend of the band, Joe "Atlantis" Gerber,* was brought on to handle the job. He had no prior experience, but Joe was smart, trustworthy, a good friend, and looking to get out of the audio business and into the world of rock 'n' roll. Did he ever.

The Adventureland show was Joe's first day on the job. It was a bit different from the typical club show, but pretty straight-ahead as shows went. Crew sets up, band arrives for sound check, band

---

* From this point forward, Joe Gerber's name will be popping up frequently. So frequently in fact that my editors decided there would be no need to continually reintroduce him every time he is mentioned. That's just as well, given how many titles he held. Joe began as our Road Manager (Joe essentially functioning as our day-to-day manager). He eventually earned Co-Manager status. At various points along the way, Joe also served as Tour Manager, Stage Manager, Production Manager, Monitor Engineer, Lighting Designer/Board Operator, Advance Man, Security Director, Video Liaison/Supervisor, Executive Tour Manager, Travel Agent, Truck Driver, Bus Driver, Indie Record Company President/Field Rep/Distributor, Merchandise Salesman, Enforcer, Bookkeeper, Bouncer, Bail Bondsman, Consigliere, Confidant, Father Confessor, and Designated Scapegoat. You get the idea. Whatever needed to be done, he did it . . . *he's my dear friend and will be a great supporting role for some actor in the film adaptation of this book.*

gets ready for show, band performs. After that, the crew tears down, band goes home, and the road manager settles up (collects the money) with the people who hired us. It's not rocket science.

After sound check that evening, I headed into the trailer provided as a dressing room behind the stage to start getting ready. About an hour before showtime, Joe Gerber came into the trailer, white as a ghost. Continuing to apply my stage makeup, and without acknowledging his condition—it was his first day—I asked, "How's it lookin' out there, Joe?" Since I never left the dressing room, I always wanted to know how the crowd was.

"You don't know?"

"I've been in here since sound check. Why?" My curiosity was piqued.

"Take a look for yourself."

I got up from my seat in front of the mirror and peered out the trailer-door window.

Now I knew why Joe was so pale! A sea of people were waiting for Twisted Sister to hit the stage. The parking lot was so jammed with fans that they had climbed onto the roofs of adjoining warehouses to better see the band.

The Long Island newspaper *Newsday* would report the next day that attendance at our Adventureland show was more than twenty-three thousand! *This was for an unsigned local band!* It should be noted that Kiss was playing to two-thirds of a house at Madison Square Garden that night. I can only imagine how many people would have been at our show if Kiss weren't playing.

The massive crowd caused all sorts of problems. There wasn't nearly the parking needed (especially since the massive back parking lot was being used for the concert), and people were abandoning their cars miles away so they could see the show. The security for the event was woefully understaffed, and as a result, a lot of damage was caused by the riled-up, overcrowded, unsupervised fans, and Twisted Sister got all the blame. We were banned from all outdoor shows in the Northeast for years after on account of the problems with the crowd that night.

The show was an incredible success and only added to the band's growing legendary status. No one could compete with Twisted Sister—apparently not even Kiss! Twisted Sister would not be deterred by corporate rejection, and though we were being dismissed as a "regional phenomenon," we pushed on. This said, we weren't complete idiots (we were "incomplete" idiots).

We knew it couldn't last forever. There was no way to make a real career out of our local microcosm of rock stardom. The band needed to do something to make the leap from local legend to rock icon, but I couldn't see what. That's when Twisted Sister's devoted fans brought us our next windfall on our path to the top.

⇥ 16 ⇤

o come, all ye faithful

As a songwriter, I was beginning to focus my writing method. I quickly figured out I couldn't be limited by depending on my modest guitar-playing skills.* Even without a true understanding of any musical instrument, my mind was capable of at least imagining more inventive musical parts. My strength is melody. Some great songwriters write the lyrics first, but I quickly discovered that for me it only produced monotonous melodies. Case in point, "Lady's Boy," the flip side to Twisted Sister's self-released "Bad Boys of Rock 'n' Roll" single.

My best work always came from the songs that I wrote the title to first. I'd take a song title that made a statement or captured an attitude I was looking to convey, decide on the feel I wanted for the song (fast, slow, swaggering, headbanging, etc.), then I'd just let it flow out of me. I am blessed with a mind that can constantly create, so I trained myself to only turn it on (like a faucet) when I had some way of capturing the idea. Too many times I had come up with a great song or concept in my head and been unable to later remember it. *Very frustrating.*

---

* The only song I ever wrote on the guitar is "Destroyer" on Twisted Sister's first album. Though a longtime fan favorite, it does underline my limitations as a player.

I would continually build a list of good song titles, and when I was ready to write, with recorder in hand, I would look at a title and see if I got any inspiration from it. If I didn't within a couple of minutes, I would move on to the next title. If I got an idea, I would sing the parts into the recorder. Usually an idea would start with the drumbeat or groove for the song, then I would sing the guitar part, followed by the song's verse, bridge, then chorus. Sometimes I would even come up with the release (that part of some songs that only happens once) on the first try. More often than not, some of the key words or lines of the song would just pop out of my mouth. When they did, I would use them as the starting point and inspiration for the rest of the lyrics. I would repeat the above method for my entire list of song titles, which usually stood at about fifteen or twenty at any given time.

To gain objectivity, I wouldn't listen to the tape again for some time. The other reason for that is, with a cassette filled with ten, fifteen, or twenty song ideas, I needed to have time to take notes as I listened, so I would remember where the best ideas were contained.

The average person always seems to imagine that songs are written and created in a complicated process. Unlike romanticized television and movie portrayals of bands and artists, the reality of it is mostly mundane and undramatic. People expect the birth of a great song to be much like childbirth itself, some intense, painful, loud experience with a lot of people yelling and cheering the idea on, until it finally comes into the world and is given a name. I don't think the idea of me, alone, singing in a quiet falsetto into the built-in microphone of a cassette player, would be satisfying to the average music fan, but that's the reality.

The process would get even more primitive when I needed to transfer my good ideas from the original tape. I would cue the song idea up on my handheld cassette player, hold it up to the built-in mic on my boom box, hit RECORD on the boom box, PLAY on the handheld, and record from one machine to the other. I'd repeat the process with all of the ideas I wanted to work on, until I had a new cassette tape with just them. Hysterical, really.

I guarantee, if you heard any of these tapes I made with my singing softly on them, you would be hard-pressed to make *anything* out of what was on them. *But that's how I did it.* I am blessed with the ability to create virtually effortlessly and endlessly. I'm never at a loss for ideas.

Don't let my having only a couple of hits fool you. Hit records are no reflection of songwriting ability or quality. Making a song a hit is a whole other process, in most ways beyond the control of the creator. Some of the best things I've ever written have never even been available to the listening and buying public.*

IN 1979 I WAS songwriting in the spare bedroom of our tour manager Joe Gerber's apartment. I don't remember the exact reason I was writing there, but I'm sure I couldn't get any privacy at my apartment. Suzette and I always had roommates. During that writing session, working off my song-title list, I wrote just the chorus of a song that would change me and my band (and the world if you count the butterfly effect) forever.

We're not gonna take it
No, we ain't gonna take it
We're not gonna take it anymore

That's it. I couldn't figure out the rest of the song. It makes me laugh when people cite that song as the "selling out" point of Twisted Sister, when we became "fat cats" and went commercial. In 1979 I couldn't have been more broke and the band was desperately struggling. The inspiration for that song came from genuine emotion—anger and frustration. It couldn't have been more real, which I suspect is one of the reasons it resonated so soundly with the rock audience.

---

* I feel the best stuff I've ever done was with a band called Desperado. The project was shelved in 1989 by our label (more on that later) at the eleventh hour and didn't see the light of day until recently, on a small indie label. Seek out "The Heart Is a Lonely Hunter" and you'll know what I'm talking about.

I'm pretty sure I immediately knew I'd created something amazing (which was confirmed when I listened back much later), but I couldn't figure out what to do with it. I didn't have any ideas for the rest of the song. Which was probably for the best. I think now, if I had completed "We're Not Gonna Take It" back in '79, when I first wrote the chorus, it would most likely just have been fodder for some ill-fated demo tape, or sacrificed on the altar that was our first indie record, *Under the Blade*. It's doubtful the song would ever have become the juggernaut that it is. The way things worked out, the world will be singing it long after I am gone and forgotten. Hopefully my heirs will still be collecting the royalties! I have often thought of using those royalties to set up a "rhinoplasty trust fund" so future generations of Sniders who inherit my considerable proboscis can afford relief.

I wouldn't finish "We're Not Gonna Take It" until 1983. In the meantime, Twisted Sister needed a new, more professional demo tape to play for the record companies, and into our lives walked engineering/producing legend Eddie Kramer. Literally.

EDDIE KRAMER HAD WORKED with the Stones and Led Zeppelin, was Hendrix's exclusive engineer, and produced *Woodstock*, *Frampton Comes Alive*, and *Kiss Alive*, just to name a few. Yeah, the guy's a recording god. Now, Twisted's die-hard fans have always been our strength (as you will discover more and more), and our meeting Eddie Kramer is a prime example.

We were playing at a club called Detroit,* in Port Chester, New York, one night, and unbeknownst to us, some of our fans had run into Eddie K. Ever the professional (and looking for new talent), he asked what local bands the girls were into. They told him he had to come and see Twisted Sister. Eddie walked into the huge, mobbed

---

* The club Detroit has often been confused with the city. It's not. It was named after a great Good Rats song called "Takin' It to Detroit" (which is about the great rock city of Detroit), used as the club's theme song on commercials. Confusing, I know. New York club-goers referred to it as "Detroits," as in "Hey, youse goin' tuh Detroit's tonight tuh see Twisted?" Adorable.

club* and was knocked out by Twisted "fuckin'" Sister, as we had come to be known (and still are). He came backstage after our set and told us he wanted to work with us. We were blown away! After all, he was Eddie "fuckin'" Kramer!

Eddie was known as the man who helped build Electric Lady Studios with Jimi Hendrix. He had designed all the studios. When Eddie told us he could get a deal at Electric Lady for us to record, we were sold. Some of our favorite records of all time were made there. Twisted Sister were going to work in the hallowed halls of rock royalty.

The Electric Lady sessions in November of 1979 gave us our first real demo tapes. Working closely with Eddie Kramer in rehearsals, we tore apart our original songs and rebuilt the best ones from the ground up. "I'll Never Grow Up, Now," "Under the Blade," "Lady's Boy," and our cover of the Shangri-Las' classic "Leader of the Pack" were chosen to be recorded.

The process was grueling and Eddie Kramer was a taskmaster. He was particularly tough on drummer #3's timing and brought the man to tears at one point. As much as I didn't like drummer #3, I actually felt bad for him. Eddie Kramer would pound a bar stool with a drumstick as if he were some kind of human metronome and scream at drummer #3 that he was off time. It was brutal.

The Good Rats' drummer, drum-book writer, and friend of both drummer #3's and the band's (and future Twisted Sister drummer #7), Joey Franco, was brought in to see if he could do anything to help. While Joey could hear what Eddie Kramer was talking about, he had to say that the inconsistencies were barely perceptible, and at the end of the day *it's only rock 'n' roll.* Some of the biggest hit records of all time have had drum timing issues, and nobody even notices or cares. All in all, I have to say I learned a hell of a lot from Eddie.

The Electric Lady recording sessions themselves were *incredibly* eventful. While we were in our studio recording, Mick Jagger and the Rolling Stones were doing some overdubs and mixing their hugely

---

* Detroit was one of the growing "megaclubs" built to handle the massive, young audiences turning out to see the bigger area bands such as Twisted Sister. It was cavernous and held close to fifteen hundred people.

successful *Some Girls* album down the hall. Eddie had worked with the Stones on *Their Satanic Majesties Request* and knew the guys well. One of the more surreal moments in my life occurred while we were mixing "Leader of the Pack" (not the one on *Come Out and Play*). We were listening to a playback and Eddie's got the mix cranked. Suddenly, the door to the studio flies open and in dances *Mick Jagger*! As I sat there, Mick does his classic "chicken dance" around the room to the song and exits as quickly as he came. Kramer never stops mixing (as if this is a normal occurrence), and I'm sitting there stunned, wondering if it had actually happened. Weird.

Another night, people are hanging out in the common area of the studio. Now, Ric Ocasek from the Cars is there with Ronnie Spector, whom he was producing in one of the other studios. Eddie Kramer is talking to Jagger and takes the opportunity to introduce his budding star (me!) to the rock legend.

"Mick Jagger, I want you to meet Dee Snider. Dee Snider, this is Mick Jagger."

As I reach to shake Mick's hand, I hear my own voice saying, with ridiculously forced casualness, "Yeah, I've seen you around." *What?!* What did that even mean? *What kind of an idiot says that?!*

Eddie Kramer just shakes his head in disbelief as Mick smiles knowingly (I'm sure he's seen that deer-in-the-headlights reaction a million times) and shakes my hand.

Did I mention . . . I'M A FRIGGIN' IDIOT!?

The one other Rolling Stones moment of note was the day Mick was waiting for Keith Richards to show up and record some guitar overdubs. Mick arrives, as he did every day, promptly at 11:00 a.m. Keith was scheduled to be there at about noon. Mick waited *over twelve hours* for Keith, who never showed up, so Mick finally leaves for the day.

At about 1:30 a.m. in rolls "Keef," posse, kids (I remember young Marlon was with him), guitars, and all, ready for his session. Someone explains to him that Mick had been waiting all day and finally gave up and left.

"Awl-right," Keith says in his classic gravelly voice, and up the stairs, out the door, and into the night he and his entire crew go. I never saw him at the studio again.

•　　•　　•

THE ELECTRIC LADY RECORDING sessions were eye-opening. I stayed with Eddie Kramer and his engineer Rob Freeman every second of the process and learned a boatload about song construction, studio performances, the recording process, mixing, and more. I loved working with Eddie, and my only complaint about him is that he just didn't know when to quit. We would be there for hours on end, and he would literally fall asleep at the console, midtake. I'd do a pass at a vocal, he would nod off during it, and when I'd get to the end, he'd wake up and say "One more for the machine, mate!" What did that even mean? I'd start another take, and he'd fall asleep all over again! It's nice to know my performances had him so riveted.

With the Electric Lady tapes finished, we had a big piece ready for another major assault on the American record labels. Twisted Sister was once again on the march!

17

i'm snider than you are

Twisted Sister ended the decade with a real bang, and I'm not talking about one of our legendary New Year's Eve parties. Tired of waiting for the record companies to acknowledge us and looking to take things up yet another notch, we decided to use the Eddie Kramer demos and release our own single. In December, on Twisted Sister Records (TSR), "I'll Never Grow Up, Now!" with "Under the Blade" was released on an actual 45 rpm seven-inch! "I'll Never Grow Up, Now!" was the archetype for what would eventually become our calling card: the rebellious, teen-angst anthem. The formula I discovered writing this song would be replicated by me, culminating (but not ending) with "We're Not Gonna Take It." My addiction to the music of the early-seventies English glitter-rock band Slade taught me everything I needed to know about writing these types of songs.

With a (terrible) professionally designed TS logo* on the cover and a new photo shot to go with it for the back, Twisted Sister gave

---

* We hired a top Manhattan ad agency, at great expense, to produce the definitive Twisted Sister logo. When they asked me to tell them about the band and to give them a feel for what we needed, I said something like "We're metal, but we're glamorous. Think black and pink, leather and satin." Weeks later we received their best effort: the block letters *T* and *S* in black leather with studs, on a pink satin background. *Thanks.*

their fans what they wanted, and all five thousand copies we printed quickly sold out.

The single got some "homegrown" radio airplay, was added to a lot of local jukeboxes, and gave Twisted our much needed, next degree of legitimacy with the fans. The flip side, "Under the Blade," was even added into rotation by upstate radio station WPDH in Poughkeepsie and became a minor hit in their broadcast area. WPDH was the first station in the world to recognize Twisted Sister as a legitimate rock act. Thank you, WPDH! You rock!

JAY JAY AND I were still sharing the onstage banter, but his raps leaned more toward selling merchandise, promoting the band's mailing list, and his usual Borscht-Belt comedy. I was handling the rabble-rousing and fanatical tirades.

Having become one hell of an orator (if I do say so myself), I was more than capable of communicating the Twisted Sister doctrine to our rabid fans, nightly, with both hostility and humor. No, they're not mutually exclusive! Each night the audience had two choices: join the Twisted Sister nation or get the hell out of the club. Or suffer a personalized, blistering verbal assault, from the stage, by yours truly. Okay, three choices.

As the months and years passed, my ego and my anger grew, as did my ability to express it with laserlike accuracy. My friend and now band bodyguard Roger was not only a physical lethal weapon, but he had an incredibly bright mind and acerbic tongue. He and I would spend hours each day riling each other up and pushing the limits of acceptable sarcasm. Referring to each other as Godachi and Messiarah, we walked around verbally tearing people apart, with the full weight of Roger's Hulk-like strength to keep people from resorting to violence as a defense. These daily verbal sparring sessions resulted in even more focused and debilitating oral assaults on the audience each night . . . and they loved it! The band . . . not so much.

Guys make fun of each other. It's what they do. When any group of men—or even boys—get together, it's not long before the insults start to fly. It's how men are wired. The guys in Twisted Sister were the same way. We spent hour upon hour together, and a good part of that time was passed joking around and goofing on each other.

When it came to insults, I had become really, *really* good. I have often said my last name is not a proper noun, it's an adjective. It wasn't just because I had a quick wit and was good with a comeback, but because nothing hurt me. Over the years I had gone from being a painfully sensitive kid (I would cry at sad songs) to becoming stonelike, virtually incapable of being offended or embarrassed in these exchanges.* In my life, people had said a lot of cruel, offensive things to me, and I had been teased a lot, so my skin got real thick. Night after night, day after day, I would go from destroying people on the street and in the audience, to destroying the guys in my band backstage. I could not be beat.

One day, a band meeting was called. I didn't think much about it; we had pretty regular band meetings. Immediately, the focus of the gathering became *me*. The guys were tired of my abuse (I thought it was dressing-room banter!) and voted—unbeknownst to me—that I could no longer participate in the exchange of insults between band members. Supposedly my lack of giving a shit, and my Swiss-Ukrainian-Transylvanian heritage, left little for the guys to work with when they retaliated. I think they just aren't good at it.

Bottom line? I was too vicious for them, and so I would sit in dressing rooms, hotel rooms, car rides, tour buses, plane flights, etc., not joining in the "reindeer games." *Forever.*† Which made me feel even more alienated from the band. (To be fair, I guess I was doing my fair share of alienating.)

To his credit, Joe Gerber pulled me aside and said, "Don't you

---

* Years later, when I started acting, one of the most difficult emotions for me to portray was embarrassed. After all the years of looking the way I have, that feeling has become completely disconnected!

† When the band starting performing together again in the early 2000s, I had forgotten about the ban (it had been over twenty years since it had been instituted) and got into an exchange with Eddie. It ended with Eddie on the verge of quitting the band and calling me a "white supremacist" (which I most certainly am not). I have since gone back into self-imposed "insult exile." I can't take me anywhere!

dare stop exchanging insults with me. *I love it!*" And I love you, too, Joe. At least I had him and Roger* to joke around with.

THROUGH THIS ALL, SUZETTE was there. Not coming to the clubs every night anymore, but still with me.

Having graduated from the Fashion Institute of Technology at the top of her class, she turned down a job offer from Betsey Johnson and was now working on Twisted Sister costumes full-time. She continually tried to break up with me (I can't imagine why, I seem like such a treat), but I wasn't letting go. Something told me not to screw this one up, and I barely didn't. Somehow I hung on.

No matter how maniacal I got, my tough, little, Italian hottie refused to allow me to get away with any of my arrogant, asshole shit in our private life. It couldn't have been easy, but she remained (and remains) the singular grounding force in my life.

THE NEW DECADE ARRIVED and the cloud over Twisted Sister continued to darken, as did my disposition. The energy from the release of our first single quickly dissipated, and the fans' attention began to wander. They had joined our mad parade to rock stardom, and when the payoff for our endless chest pounding and fist pumping didn't come, I'm sure we started to look like we were full of shit.

While we continued to scramble and clamor for record company attention, now we had to work even harder to sustain our tristate popularity as well. The early part of 1980 called for a masterstroke of some kind, and in the spring of that year I came up with just the thing.

AMONG THE MANY NAMES and phrases used to describe Twisted Sister (besides *fags* and *assholes*), "the Bad Boys of Rock 'n' Roll" was

---

* Roger Offner remains my best friend to this day. He is godfather to my son Shane and I to his son Roger Jr.

one that stuck. Following the template of "I'll Never Grow Up, Now!" I wrote our new battle cry using that exact turn of phrase. With the song as a spearhead, I worked with Suzette to create a new look, then revamped our staging, lighting, merchandise . . . everything.

The one thing the band still lacked was a definitive Twisted Sister logo. Since the top design agency had delivered total garbage, this time, we decided to work with someone local and younger; someone who would let me have input on the work. I don't remember exactly how we found Ellie Hradsky, but we did and I laid it out for her. We were not only looking for the ultimate Twisted Sister logo, but it needed one specific quality—carvability. Like the Van Halen *VH*, the Twisted logo needed to be cool enough that fans would want to carve it into their desks, and simple enough that they could.

Working closely and combining our ideas, Ellie and I finally came up with a great design. A bent and stylized *T* connected to a bent and stylized *S*, forming one diamond-shaped symbol. It was simple, strong, *and eminently carvable*. It was the definitive Twisted Sister logo.

In May we released our second single on Twisted Sister Records, "Bad Boys (of Rock 'n' Roll)" backed with "Lady's Boy," emblazoned with the new "floating" TS logo, and launched our "Bad Boys of Rock 'n' Roll" tour of the tristate. It was just what the doctor ordered and reinvigorated our local career. The record companies . . . not so much.

Our management made another go-round with all of the major—and minor—labels of note, with a new press kit, demo tape, and offer: if any A&R person or record company executive was willing to come to the suburbs and see our band, we would provide them with a limo and dinner. Seems fair enough, right? We made this offer to every single credible industry person . . . and we had *one* taker: Reen Nalli, president of ATCO Records. She was limoed from Manhattan to the Mad Hatter nightclub in Stony Brook, Long Island, and in that packed club, she saw Twisted *fuckin'* Sister do what we did every night . . . light up the record-buying public! At the end of the evening, Reen got back into her limo, pledging to sign our band to ATCO. She knew we were going to be the next big thing . . . until she got to work on Monday morning.

The problem with people—successful people especially—is they tend to second-guess themselves. Reen was convinced by what she saw that Friday night on Long Island, and when she got to work on Monday in New York City, and started telling people about an amazing new band, I'm sure her subordinates and coworkers were pumped.

"Really?! Who is it?!" they must have clamored to know.

"Twisted Sister!" I bet Reen said with great excitement. After all, she'd discovered the next big thing, and nobody else knew about it.

"That bar band? They're a regional phenomenon. Everybody passed on them already. They're a joke" are just some of the wonderful accolades I'm sure Reen heard *from people who had never even seen the band!*

At this point self-doubt began to set in. *What if I'm wrong? What if I've made a terrible mistake?* Reen even received a call from her superior at Atlantic Records, ATCO's parent company and a label that had soundly rejected us a couple of times already, telling her to forget about this Twisted Sister silliness. Did she really want to take a chance of looking foolish by signing a band that looked like us? She didn't . . . and the phone calls to our management about signing us soon ceased.

You have to keep in mind this is 1980. Glitter rock was over. "Hair metal" didn't exist yet—Twisted Sister were the sole purveyors of that glitter/metal amalgam. There was no Mötley Crüe or Ratt or Poison. Even Kiss had made a disco record (which I can't believe their fans ever forgave them for) in a desperate attempt to regain favor. We were in uncharted waters. Signing a band such as Twisted would take a lot of 'nads . . . or simply the belief in your own eyes and ears. Unfortunately, those kinds of record men and women are few and far between.

Twisted Sister were heading toward the end of 1980, still unsigned, with only a pile of rejection notices to show for our whole Bad Boys initiative. There was, however, one glimmer of light. An adventurous young English rock photographer named Ross Halfin was in New York, on assignment, I believe, to cover a bunch of English and Australian metal bands currently touring in the United States. He ran into a couple of female heavy metal fans somewhere who insisted he come see this amazing band playing in New Jersey.

God, I love our fans! They carried the torch for our band when no record company would touch us.

Ross walked into our show and was knocked out by what he saw. A new wave of British heavy metal was brewing, and whadaya know . . . a young American band was waving the new wave of heavy metal flag, too. He whipped out his ever-present camera and snapped away. The photos made their way back to the home office, and on Ross's word about how great we were, editor Geoff Barton published a shot of me in the *Sounds* music paper. *And English metal fans took notice.*

⟡ 18 ⟡

bang the drum slowly

By September of 1980 a couple of major things in my personal life came to a head. My terrible money-managing skills caused me to get—once again—into a ridiculous amount of debt. I don't know what it was about me (besides that I'm foolishly optimistic), but I *always* owed somebody money. When I was a kid, it was friends, and as a young man, it was friends and landlords and phone companies and insurance companies and . . . you get the picture.

The funny thing is, I didn't drink, do drugs, gamble, or spend a lot of money on my fiancée (Suzette was incredibly low-maintenance and not big on jewelry)—all the typical things people blow money on. I was just insanely irresponsible with the limited money I made.

Cases in point: Some credit company gave me my first credit card, with a $500 limit on it, and I bought a dog with the entire $500 the first week! What?! Another time the bank mistakenly credited my account with several hundred dollars, and what did I do? I immediately withdrew the money and spent it on . . . stuff. Of course the bank discovered the mistake and I had to pay it back over time. I was an idiot.

By the end of my third year in New York City, I was deep in debt (for a twenty-five-year-old) and had to give up the apartment. It had always been too expensive for what I was making, which was the key to my economic crisis. But it had been across from Suzette's school!

• • •

SUZETTE, OUR TWO DOGS (Tosha, Suzette's birthday-gift white German shepherd, and Woofie, my credit-card-bought chow chow), our three cats, and I moved back to Long Island and into a three-bedroom storefront apartment with my brother Matt (and his then fiancée, Joyce, and their black Lab), and various people in the third room. One couple had a Saint Bernard! It was like living in a kennel. Keeping the animals apart, feeding and walking them (sometimes on the roof of the neighboring business), required military-like planning and execution. But split three ways, the rent in the "Wantagh Roach Motel" was low enough that we could afford to live and I could pay off my debts.

Another upside: after being engaged for a few years, Suzette and I decided we would get married when I finally straightened out my financial problems.* Good incentive.

The other thing I was finally coming to terms with was the dark path my life had been on. The violence, the arrests, my eye-opening experience with Billy Joel, and the repeated questioning of my Christian beliefs by my born-again friends, the Hausers, were all finally having an effect. I was, and still am, a Christian, but clearly my behavior didn't always support those beliefs. I could be a nasty, cynical, angry asshole, and it was spilling over into my personal life. Moving out of New York and digging myself out of debt was the beginning of a new page for me. I could now separate truly negative and evil thoughts from my natural intensity and drive. I was *starting* to become more of the person I wanted to be. Even though I had a long road ahead of me—and I would falter along the way—at least I felt I was finally on it.

BACK IN AUGUST OF 1980, drummer #3 tried to take our dislike for each other to the next level and introduce violence to our relation-

---

* For the record, Suzette wants it known that she didn't want to get engaged or married. Are any of you buying that this strong-willed young woman had absolutely no say in the course her life was taking? Our kids don't.

ship. It wasn't major; actually it's almost comical in retrospect. I had always attested that drummer #3 was not a good guy, yet nobody else saw it. He was so good at appearing innocent, the others started to think *I* was the bad one for trying to get drummer #3 in trouble. Realizing the reverse effect my finger-pointing was having, I stopped my active campaign.

DEE LIFE LESSON

If someone is a bad person, they are not only going to be bad to you. Given enough time, they will always show their true colors.

Drummer #3 had yet to reveal his evil side to the band when, one night, he disappeared at a gig. When it came time for the band to go on, he was nowhere to be found. He was repeatedly paged over our PA system, and the crew searched everywhere for him. After delaying the show as long as we could, Jay Jay, Eddie, and Mark took the stage and started making noise, hoping that drummer #3 would hear it and come before we had to forfeit the night.

I was still waiting in the dressing room to go on when drummer #3 slipped in, smug as can be. He thought it was funny. He had been in the club the whole time, ignoring the calls. I started giving him shit about his selfish behavior, and he picked up one of his platform boots and threw it, with force, right at my head. I ducked and he missed, but that was it. As I said earlier, the one thing I will not stand for is physical violence between band members, and his action toward me crossed the line. When I got onstage for the set, I walked directly over to Jay Jay and said, "Drummer #3 just threw a boot at my head. Either he goes, or I go."

The band didn't have much of a choice, and they informed drummer #3 that he was going to be replaced. At first, he was classy about it—acting all innocent and protesting his dismissal, expressing his willingness to stay on until the band found a suitable replacement. *Classic drummer #3.* Once again, the band were looking at me as if I were the fucked-up and unreasonable one.

But then an interesting thing happened. As the weeks rolled by, and we started auditioning new drummers, the reality that he was going to be replaced started to hit drummer #3. And he didn't like it. Slowly but surely, he began to show his true, dark colors to the rest of the band. After over three months of looking, we still hadn't found the right guy, but now the entire band knew exactly the type of guy drummer #3 was. He had to go.

Twisted Sister was so popular and successful in our region that every area drummer wanted to be in the band. They all knew we were poised to go on to greatness, and potential candidates were auditioned by invitation only. The last thing we wanted was an open call.

The difficulty we had finding a replacement for drummer #3 wasn't always that the drummers weren't good enough. After all, this was Twisted Sister, not Rush. Sometimes it was the regimen of being in Twisted Sister that scared potential candidates off. Twisted Sister were a machine. Being true professionals, everything was about the show . . . and I was a miserable taskmaster.

The fun in playing in a band ended for me in 1977 when my vocal coach explained the sacrifices I had to make if I wanted to go the distance. In many ways for me, that was the day the music died. My ongoing throat problems never got better. I had a sore throat pretty much every day, for close to a decade. Can you imagine? It was always uncomfortable for me to even talk or laugh. By the end of each week of shows, I couldn't even speak. With two days off, I'd barely get my voice back by Tuesday for the week to start all over again, week after week after week.

And my physical performing style? I performed so aggressively that I felt like Linda Blair in *The Exorcist* when the demon inside her was whipping her back and forth on the bed! ("Make it stop! Make it stop!") But if I wasn't pushing myself to the point of pain every moment I was onstage, I would feel that I was phoning it in, that I was cheating the audience.

Do you know what my favorite part of each night was? *When it was over.* I could stop the self-flagellation and rest, knowing I had blown the audience away. Though, being my own worst critic, I was rarely happy or satisfied with my performance. (Anyone who's any good at what they do rarely is.) Talk about self-loathing! I know what you're thinking. Why didn't you just quit? I couldn't. It was like a drug, I had to have that feeling of being completely spent and knowing I had given my all, and I couldn't get that satisfied feeling without actually doing shows. Now that's a catch-22.

Each night I left everything I had on that stage. No voice or energy was left over for partying. I laugh when I hear about bands "going out and jamming" after their shows. As far as I'm concerned, if you have *anything* left after your performance, you've ripped off your fans. There was no socializing for me backstage. Other than band and crew, nobody was even allowed in the dressing room except for Suzette, but as I grew more manic and intense about my performances, she didn't want to be around me. Like the band, Suzette would leave to have fun. Who would want to sit in silence and watch me? But I was on a mission.

I remember we auditioned one drummer who was perfect for the band: Walter "Woody" Woodward III, aka WW III. Woody looked the part and had a great playing style. The job was his; he was going to be in Twisted Sister. Then I told him "the rules." I told him about our "no friends or groupies" backstage, the restrictions on drinking, drugs, and general partying, and our taking less of the money we made (except Eddie) to reinvest in ourselves. I told him of the Twisted Sister commitment to excellence and becoming international rock stars . . . *and he passed!* What?! Yup. Walter said thanks, but no thanks. Being in our band (and he was a *huge* Twisted fan) sounded like being in prison! He asked if he could just play his favorite Twisted Sister song with us one time before he left. We did (he played it great) and he said good-bye. Hey, if you can't stand the heat . . .

In the next couple of years, we would go through two more drummers before finally finding the perfect match.

Drummer #4 was Ritchie Teeter, formally of the Dictators. He had played with Mark, was a solid drummer and a good guy. It was understood from the beginning that he would only be an interim drummer, until we found the right fit. Ritchie wasn't heavy enough for the band and just wasn't into the whole costume and makeup thing. He would actually take his stuff off between each set, then put it on all over again, so he wouldn't be seen wearing it in the club. Drummers would have killed to have his job, and he didn't care. It just wasn't the right fit for him. I can respect that. He was stupid . . . but I respect it.

Drummer #5 was Joey Markowski, aka "Fast" Joey Brighton. At first we thought we had found our perfect match. Joey was a prodigy with an impressive résumé. He was a drum teacher at the prestigious Carmine Appice* School of Drumming, actually filling in for Carmine when he was on tour. Joey had also been the original drummer in the Good Rats (one of his students, Joe Franco, replaced him) and had been immortalized in the popular Good Rats song "Tasty."

> We had a drummer name of Joe
> He played so fast we let him go
> He ran away with all our songs
> Now he's in school where he belongs.

You'd think we could take a hint. The only thing we got from that song was to call him Fast Joey. *Idiots.* Turned out Fast Joey ran away (tempo-wise) with all our songs, too. Apparently, he had a drug addiction, which culminated in his having a full-blown seizure on our dressing-room floor, the (rare) night an important record industry type came down to see us. *Next!*

---

* Carmine Appice is a legendary drummer who has played with the likes of the Vanilla Fudge, Cactus, Rod Stewart, and Beck, Bogart & Appice, to name just a few. His incredible style helped to define heavy metal drumming.

⚜ 19 ⚜

the doldrums

Historically, Great Britain has always been a trendsetter on the international music scene. Geographically not even the size of some of the larger states in America, pound for pound no other country or place is more influential. The bands that have launched their careers out of the UK are legion, and not just English, Irish, Welsh, and Scottish acts. More than a few recording artists who couldn't get signed or attention in the States had to head to Blighty to find a warmer welcome. Jimi Hendrix, Joan Jett, and the Stray Cats had all been "discovered" by way of Great Britain . . . so why not Twisted Sister?

While we hadn't completely given up on the States, with a glimmer of a positive reaction from the UK press, we decided to send our "A team" overseas on an exploratory mission—was there life for Twisted Sister in England? In November of 1980, our manager, Mark Puma, and our psuedomanager, Jay Jay French, got on a plane, armed with Twisted Sister demos and press kits, determined to plant some seeds with the UK record industry.

They returned several days later with tales of a land where a renewed interest in heavy metal was growing. They had met with Doug Smith, the band manager of the biggest metal group in Britain at the time, Motörhead. The bass player/vocalist for the band was there, too. Jay Jay told me that the guy from Motörhead— Lemmy something?—was really dirty and scruffy and looked more like a biker than a rocker. Then he handed me an advance tape of an album from a new band coming up. The band, virtually unknown at that time in the States, was Iron Maiden; the album, *Killers*.

I listened to the amazing Maiden album and saw a glimmer of hope. *We weren't alone out there.* All over the world, a new movement of heavy metal was starting up. Disco was dead, new wave was fading, and punk was dying. The punk fans, in particular, were looking for some kind of intense music to invest their righteous anger in, and the new heavy metal—much of it with punk influence—fit the bill.

Jay Jay and Puma had planted some seeds for us in the UK and developed some new relationships, but we still hadn't given up on getting signed in the States. This was our home. We didn't want to leave our massive Northeast fan base and everything we knew to get a deal. Why should we? We were the hugely popular Twisted fucking Sister and it was just a matter of time before a major American record company realized what was rocking, right under their nose, and snapped us up. All we needed was another grand gesture to get their attention. So, we booked the New York Palladium for a second time, on January 3, 1981. *Happy New Year!*

AS I SIT HERE writing, I don't remember anything about our second New York City Palladium show. Maybe because it represents when I truly began to realize that things were coming apart for the band (or maybe I'm just getting old). Unfortunately, this would not be the last time I would know that terrible feeling.

The only actual memory I have of the event is the image of one concert photo—that's it. I'm bent over to the left and singing, and Mark the Animal is wearing fur boots. The only reason I remember it at all is because I see it in my photo album from time to time. That concert did nothing to change Twisted Sister's trajectory, which at that time was horizontal, *and it even hurt us.* The show didn't sell out and the record companies cared less about it than the first time we performed at the Palladium.

We had been together for almost five years, built what had to be the largest local following for an unsigned band in history, become true rock stars in our own backyard, and achieved things considered unachievable, yet we were still wallowing in virtual international obscurity, and making $240 a week each. (Except Eddie.)

THE PALLADIUM SHOW RESULTED in all of one offer, from a start-up boutique record company called Handshake Records. It was run by a *former* industry heavyweight named Ron Alexenburg, and the deal he offered amounted to little more than an employment contract. Handshake would own the rights to everything we did and pay us a salary! Handshake Records indeed. Hand job is more like it. We declined.

DO YOU KNOW WHAT the Doldrums are? They're a region of calm winds, centered slightly north of the equator. With virtually not a breeze to speak of, sailboats can get mired in them for mind-numbingly long periods. Now, imagine being stuck there . . . with a hole in your boat. That was 1981 for Twisted Sister.

After the failure of our second Palladium show, not only were we dealing with, once again, essentially no label interest, but our local fan base was beginning to erode. You can only scream "We're gonna make it!" for so long before people start to think of you as "the band that cried wolf."

Throughout the Doldrums we continued to work on ways to freshen things up on every level. I realize now that this time saw our most creative advancements as a band, which may be what ultimately led to our breaking out.

Staging-wise, we made some significant changes. I got the idea for what came to be our signature stage look: the pink, barbed-wire chain-link fences. The idea was to create a prison yard or inner-city schoolyard vibe for the band onstage. The fans loved it.

Suzette started hitting her stride with the band's stage clothes as well. Her method of designing and creating for artists (she's worked with other people besides Twisted Sister) has always been to help them look their best at how they want to look. Suzette will guide you and give you input, but she understands that if you don't feel confident in how you look, it will affect the way you perform. If sometimes that means sending an entertainer out looking terrible, so be it . . . as long as the performer *thinks* he or she looks great. Savvy?

This said, Suzette had known for a long time that the whole "sweet transvestite" thing would not ultimately work for Twisted. I was starting to finally figure that out for myself, too. I couldn't help but notice that when I picked photos of myself to use for promotion, they were always the "pretty" shots, which had no connection to the reality of how I looked. When fans would present me with a gift (as they often did) of some blown-up and beautifully framed photo of me, it was always some hideous shot of me snarling or screaming or just looking generally insane. Clearly, they saw me differently than I saw myself. Suzette's costume designs for the band (always with my and the band's approval) were starting to look less femmy and a lot more tough. Belts and straps, buckles and tatters, were becoming prevalent, and the band's stage outfits were becoming unified. Sure they were still spandex, but they were harder-looking. We now had costumes that complemented each other's, and we even started to establish colors that represented each of us. I was pink, Jay Jay was yellow, Eddie was red, Mark was green and animal fur (get it?), and our drummer "du jour" was blue.

Our sound started to become more defined as we got turned on to new five-piece, two-guitarist metal bands. Judas Priest and AC/DC became templates for the twin-guitar sound we wanted, and my songwriting began to better reflect it.

SONGWRITING IS LIKE ANY craft: the more you do it, the better you get at it. Since we were constantly in need of new originals, I was always working on songs . . . and I was starting to home in on our band's sound.

In recent years, Twisted Sister has released more "postmortem" *

---

* As of this writing, Twisted Sister is still reunited, but our original recording days are far behind us. Hence the "postmortem."

CDs/DVDs than Tupac Shakur. My least favorite of the bunch, orchestrated by Jay Jay French and Mark Mendoza, are *Club Daze Volumes 1 & 2*. The first time I listened to this early original material of mine (forget the songs of Jay Jay's that I always hated), I was stunned. *They suck!* No wonder we didn't get signed. I apologize to our fans who grew up with that stuff and love it (some of our early fans like it better than the stuff we became famous for), but as the songwriter, I have to be honest and recognize that it is weak.

The good news was, I was getting better—a lot better. All of the writing—and rejection—was making me work harder at my craft. Interestingly, nobody else in the band was contributing any ideas. Though I was still very much a loner when it came to creating my own songs, I had become confident enough in my ability that I would have been willing to work with the guys on their ideas. But with me pumping out an endless—and growing—stream of original material, the band seemed to be content to let me do the work.

Jay Jay always felt he deserved more than the rest of the band because he was the sole founding member left, he owned the name, and most important, he had managed the band for the first few years. He still worked closely with our manager, Mark Puma. The other band members didn't want to give Jay Jay anything, but I recognized the value of his additional contributions.

Publishing is the money a songwriter gets when his or her songs are sold in any capacity. My songs had not sold a thing, and my publishing was worth zero dollars, but I knew it would be profitable one day, so I gave Jay Jay 15 percent of what I would make. It was the right thing to do . . . and I knew it would keep him from ever thinking of submitting any more terrible songs.

Eddie "Fingers" * Ojeda submitted all of one song from 1976 to 1983, "Working on You Baby." I'm not sure why. Eddie is a riff master, and I begged him to record a bunch of riffs for me that I could write from, but he never did. Once I started to make money from my publishing, Eddie gave me a couple of things to work on, which

---

* Contrary to popular belief, the nickname Fingers was not given to Eddie because of his guitar-playing prowess. It comes from a joke I made about Eddie after he had cut his fingers repeatedly and, temporarily, screwed up his ability to play guitar.

I did, but they didn't make the *Stay Hungry* record. As I said, song-writing is a craft. By the time Eddie decided to get his ass in gear, my craft was way more developed than his. He never even submitted a song after those last two.

Mark "the Animal" Mendoza will tell you that I would never listen to or consider his ideas. I swear to you on my children's lives that is not true. I remember one night in particular, sitting with Mark in the dressing room of the Detroit nightclub, in Port Chester, New York, putting on our stage makeup together and his telling me he had some song ideas. I told him to just give me the ideas on tape and I would see if I could do something with them. *I swear.* Mark was my best friend. There was no reason I wouldn't want to work with him.

Not being a musician beyond playing a little guitar and drums, my songwriting tends to suffer when it comes to its musicality. Sure, I have had my moments ("Under the Blade," "You Can't Stop Rock 'n' Roll," "Burn in Hell"), but for the most part my songs are strong on melody, but simplistic musically. I would have killed for some more musical ideas from the guys in the band. Maybe I was just overwhelming the guys with my output? Or maybe they just didn't have any real ideas.

DURING THE DOLDRUMS, WE did have some brushes with record deals, but they were nothing, little companies, with oddly ambiguous names. An ill-fated deal with Combat Records never came to fruition. I only remember that the guy who let Twisted Sister slip through his hands from that company was fired when the band finally broke in the UK. Then there was Camouflage Records. How's that for an ambiguous name? The president of Camouflage, Peter Hauke, flew to the States to see our band, loved us, and right then and there worked out a deal with our manager. He then got on a plane with the intention of finalizing our deal once he got back to Germany. On the flight back, the president, a robust twenty-six-year-old man, had a total circulatory system collapse, and Camouflage Records was shut down. Set and match.

With our slimmest of leads overseas drying up, we turned once again to the labels in the States for another try. But how do you go back to companies who have already said no several times? Faced with the choice of packing it in or continuing to do the only thing we knew how to do, we came up with what he called the Burger King approach to shopping a deal: "Have it your way." In desperation, as a last-ditch effort to get US record-industry attention, we put together a new demo and press kit with two different photos of the band. One with makeup, and one without. We didn't care about why they signed us as long as we got a freakin' deal.

The "no makeup and costumes" photo session was pretty funny because I put on "just a touch" of makeup for the session. You know, base, blush, light eye shadow, mascara, eyeliner, lip gloss; just the necessities. I looked more like a drag queen—and creepier—in those photos than in the regular Twisted shots. Ha!

Thankfully the "Have it your way" never saw the light of day . . . we were saved.

SOMEWHERE DURING THE DOLDRUMS the band performed its two-thousandth show together. *Two thousand shows!* People were always asking me (when we made it to "the Bigs") how I got so good at handling audiences. They had no idea of my band's history and assume that Twisted Sister had been together a few years, mainly rehearsing and doing the occasional show. Say what you want about playing in a cover band, but all those years and all those sets prepare the hell out of you for live performances. Dealing with forty thousand angry headbangers at Castle Donington is nothing compared to five hundred post-happy-hour drunks at a club on the Jersey Shore during the Memorial Day weekend. Now that's a tough audience!

REMEMBER THE BUTTERFLY EFFECT? Remember what I said about Twisted Sister's fans being our greatest asset? Remember that English rock photographer, Ross Halfin, our fans brought to a show in Piscataway, New Jersey, and how he took photos that were put in the biggest UK rock paper, *Sounds*? *Flutter, flutter, flutter* (the sound of a butterfly's wings).

Not only did the English metal fans start to take notice, but so did the *Sounds* editorial staff. Editor Geoff Barton sent a punk/metalhead staff writer, Garry Bushell, to find out what all the Twisted Sister hubbub was about in the States. In the spring of '81, Garry showed up at a club in New York, was completely blown away by the band and the fan reaction, and headed back to Great Britain filled with Twisted tales. He wrote about his Twisted experience in America, creating further interest in the band in England. Thankfully, the butterfly flutter was stirring into a breeze that would change the course of the band's life forever. And it was about fucking time!

❧ 20 ❧

i got you babe

In the midst of the Doldrums and all this career insecurity and worry, one of the greatest things in my life happened. After being engaged for three and a half years, living together for four, and dating for five and half years, Suzette and I got married!

I never was one for thinking things through or looking at the big picture. I tend to "use the force" and go with what my gut—or whatever body part is doing the talking—tells me. I screw up from time to time, but in the scheme of things, my overall hitting percentage is definitely Hall of Fame worthy. While I always figured I would hold off on marriage and a family until my musical career was better situated, the way things were going, I couldn't wait any longer to get my *real* life started.

Getting married and having a family was always a major part of my life's plan (okay, sometimes I did look at the big picture), and though the world, and my peers, viewed having a family and being a rock star as mutually exclusive, I never did. To me, that was the promise of being a rock 'n' roll star—living the way you wanted to, without the limitations or rules of a traditional life.

Though I'd only just finished ridding myself of debt and had no money saved and no real financial support from our extended families to pay for it, I charged headlong into getting hitched. Did I mention I wanted to have a big wedding? Suzette will be the first to tell you that while she wanted a traditional wedding, I wanted a *big* wedding. I was consummating the greatest conquest of my life—getting Suzette Gargiulo to marry me—and I wanted everyone we knew (and then some) to bear witness!

To this day, if someone asks me what the greatest achievement of my life is, I respond, "Getting Suzette to love me and be my wife." That's the truth. It's the most difficult thing I've ever done. You don't think so? I got a girl who had absolutely no interest in me—was repulsed by me—to love me, marry me, have my children, and stay with me for more than three decades. That's a miracle. Becoming a rock star was tough, but at least rock 'n' roll showed signs of accepting me from day one. I always believed, and knew, I could go the distance with music. With Suzette, not so much.

I can see now that the lengthy planning of our wedding (and finding a new place to live and furnishing it) helped to keep me sane during this dark career time. It gave me something else important to focus on and made me feel that my life was going someplace even if my career wasn't.

During all the ups and downs of my career, my home life has been a singular stabilizing and grounding force. In my darkest times, I always had Suzette (and my kids) there for me, and during my career highs, they have always kept me from getting carried away with my own self-importance. Thank you for that, Suzette.

OUR WEDDING DATE WAS set for the fall, and while we dealt with all the details of having a three-hundred-person wedding, my rock 'n' roll life continued. Part of the "Have it your way" plan was a new demo tape, and that meant new, original songs. During this time the seminal Twisted Sister songs "Shoot 'Em Down" and the aptly titled "You Can't Stop Rock 'n' Roll" (amongst others) were created. As Twisted Sister's songwriter, I was hitting my stride. During those demo recording sessions, the band also recorded a song I wrote as a wedding present for Suzette, "You're Not Alone (Suzette's Song)." *

I presented it to her at our reception.

---

* This can be found on Twisted Sister's *You Can't Stop Rock 'n' Roll* album.

•   •   •

ON OCTOBER 25, 1981, Suzette and I had a traditional wedding in a beautiful little church, in Huntington, Long Island. With Mark "the Animal" Mendoza as my best man and Wendy Cohen (now Yair)— Suzette's best friend, who helped keep us together—as her co–maid of honor along with Suzette's sister Roseanne, we pledged our undying love to each other. Actually, I'm not so sure about Suzette. She was so nervous on the day that when repeating the vows, she said, "I take Mr. Snider to be my husband. . . ." I think she may be married to my dad!

Suzette and I started down the path of holy matrimony in the best style we could afford at the time . . . at least from the neck down. My bride looked absolutely stunning, but with me in my white tuxedo and Mendoza in his "morning" tuxedo, you would swear our big-haired heads were photoshopped onto other bodies. If Photoshop existed in 1981.

With some financial help from Suzette's father on the reception (with an assist and temporary loans from Jay Jay French and Mark Puma), we had a legendary party! The reception was packed with family, friends, business associates, and other people who for the life of me, when I look back at our wedding pictures, I don't know who they are! What a motley crew. The classic Brooklyn/Staten Island Italians of Suzette's family with the suburban Eastern European Snider family, our rock 'n' roll friends, and the borderline thugs who were the invited club owners were quite a sight. But to a man, woman, and child, it is still talked about as one of the greatest weddings anybody has ever been to.

Suzette wanted our wedding song to be "I Got You Babe" by Sonny & Cher, but I felt it made a joke out of our relationship—the lyrics hit too close to home. We wound up using some Stevie Wonder song I don't even remember. Suzette was right; "I Got You Babe" would have been perfect.

Thanks to my parents, the next day we headed off to Jamaica for a much-needed honeymoon/vacation, and I started "planting the seeds" for our next big adventure. Get it? Planting? Seeds? Do I have to draw you a picture!?

❖   ❖   ❖

IN DECEMBER 1981, MARTIN Hooker, the president of the British indie label Secret Records, contacted our manager about Twisted Sister. The writer from *Sounds* magazine, Garry Bushell, had been so impressed with the band that he reached out to Martin and gave him our demo tape. (Thank you, Garry!) Martin Hooker loved the tape and wanted to see the band immediately.

Coincidentally, Twisted was giving a concert a few days later at the Mid-Hudson Civic Center in Poughkeepsie, New York, about seventy-five miles north of New York City. Twisted had a huge following in the Hudson Valley region of New York State and had sold out the over-three-thousand-capacity arena multiple times. Martin Hooker seized the opportunity to see the band in a concert environment (as opposed to a club), and a few days later he was landing at JFK International Airport and being driven upstate.

We did what we always did, and the Secret Record's president was appropriately impressed. He came backstage with our manager, Mark Puma, and told us that he was going to sign the band. Our reactions were . . . *controlled.*

"Cool."

"Great."

"That's nice."

Confused, Martin Hooker left the dressing room with our manager. He knew our history. He knew how long we'd been trying to get a deal. Yet, when he told us he was ready to record an album with us, we were anything but enthusiastic.

"They're happy, Martin," explained Puma. "It's just that they've had so many near misses and collapsed deals, they find it hard to get their hopes up."

It was true. Besides . . . Secret Records? Talk about ambiguous. We'd never even heard of the label. *Must be because it's so secret!* Handshake, Camouflage, Secret—what we wouldn't have given for a label with a name that didn't sound like Abbott and Costello's "Who's on first?" sketch when you told somebody about it.

"What label did you sign with?"

"It's Secret."

"C'mon, you can tell me."

"It's Secret."

"I promise I won't tell anybody."

"I told you, it's Secret!"

You get the picture. Martin Hooker headed back to the UK promising to make good on his word, and we prayed that something tragic wouldn't happen to the fine young man before he did.

Though Secret Records *did* eventually sign us, these things tend to take a long time and leave you guessing if they will ever get done. With our track record, we didn't bother to get our hopes up.

As Twisted Sister continued to slog its way through the winter, the ugliest time of year to play, a notable bright light was shining in the darkness . . . and it wasn't an oncoming train. In March of 1982, Suzette and I found out she was pregnant with our first child. With a floundering career, a small weekly salary, and a studio apartment, we couldn't have been happier!

Some people say babies are good luck. I'm a believer. From the moment I found out Suzette was pregnant, things, unbeknownst to me, began to get better.

❧ 21 ❧

drums, drums, drums, drums!

With drummer #5 turning out to be everything we hoped *he wouldn't be*, the search began for his replacement. Joey Brighton was destined to be the Pete Best of Twisted Sister. Once again by invitation only, myriad drummers made their way to the rehearsal studio to see if they might be the chosen one, and we held our breath and prayed.

One of the toughest failed drum auditions for me was Neil Smith of the original Alice Cooper band. We had known Neil for a quite a while. As I was a *huge* Alice Cooper fan, just being friendly with the guy was an honor. His band's music changed my life. As we were looking for a new drummer, we thought, how cool would it be if Twisted Sister was joined by a rock legend like Neil Smith?! Neil was currently in a band, Flying Tigers, playing a lot of the same venues as us. I put in a call to Neil, and he said he would love to join Twisted. Now, there was just the formality of the audition—or so we thought.

Neil came down to the studio with his own roadie and massive road cases. Inside were his legendary mirrored drums! These were the first-ever mirrored drums, which saw the world on the Alice Cooper *Billion Dollar Babies* tour, and we had all seen them gracing the pages and covers of so many rock and music magazines. They were amazing, and as a fan I was in awe of having *the* Neil Smith playing my songs, on those drums, with my band. It was absolutely surreal ... *until he started to play.*

Neil Smith is an innovator as a drummer whose style helped change the face of modern drumming. He bridged the gap between the styles of the sixties and the early seventies and what came to be contemporary heavy-rock drumming (in the eighties). But that was the problem. Heavy drumming had evolved, and Neil's transitional style just wasn't right for the band. No matter how bad we wanted this to work, it just didn't. The call I had to make to Neil Smith, one of my childhood heroes and now a friend, to tell him he didn't pass the audition, was one of the toughest phone calls I ever had to make. Man, did that suck.

Somewhere along the way in our search for drummer #6, a friend of the band's gave me a tape of a drummer friend of his. "This guy's amazing," he said with his thick Staten Island accent. "You should check him out."

I took the cassette tape—it didn't have a case and wasn't even labeled—and threw it into my gig bag with my stage clothes. It quickly sank to the bottom.

Months later, on my way out of my apartment to a dentist appointment, I was looking around for something to take with me to listen to.*

I spotted the cassette tape of the drummer that had been getting banged around in my gig bag (I can't believe I didn't lose it). I grabbed it—not expecting much—and took it with me. As I sat in the dentist's chair with dread, my mouth filled with dental apparatuses, fighting to keep my mouth open, *I heard a powerhouse of a drummer!* I couldn't believe it. This guy's tape had been in my bag for months.† If I thought he sounded good now, imagine how much I would like him when I wasn't getting my teeth drilled.

---

* My dentist had a state-of-the-art ... *Walkman cassette player!* What better to listen to while you're getting your teeth drilled than blasting heavy metal? The opening, whining guitar lick in "Under the Blade" was inspired by a dentist's drill. I told Jay Jay, "Play something that sounds like you're getting your teeth drilled," and that's what he came up with.

† A.J. was stunned to find out that the professional press kit—complete with bio, photo, and résumé—he had given his friend had been reduced to an unmarked cassette by the time I received it. I guess it was just meant to be.

Tony Pero, from Staten Island, New York, officially auditioned for Twisted Sister and impressed the hell out of us. With arms like ham hocks, this guy hit the drums harder than anyone else I had ever seen. And he could play technically, too. *He could play anything!*

Tony had been a child prodigy, taking lessons from greats, like Gene Krupa. By the age of ten he'd already toured Europe playing with a big band. This son of a bitch could play! He was the perfect complement to Mendoza's pummeling bass playing, and musically the two of them connected immediately. This was the missing piece to the Twisted Sister sound.

But there was one problem.

Tony Pero's name, and physical appearance, were close to drummer #3's. I didn't want people to mistakenly think he was drummer #3, and I couldn't bear to call him by the same first name. I explained my dilemma to Tony and asked if he had a middle name. He did, Jude. Thinking quickly, I asked how he felt about being called A.J. instead of Tony. Sure, we already had a Dee and a Jay Jay, but can a band ever have enough names that are initials?

I don't know if Tony actually had a problem with it or not, but he *really* wanted to join our band and agreed to the change. Twisted Sister had finally found its perfect musical match.

NINETEEN EIGHTY-TWO TURNED OUT to be one of the most tumultuous years of my life. It started as a continuation of the career downward spiral that was 1981 and finished on the highest of highs with some crazy-ass peaks and valleys in between.

A. J. Pero officially performed his first live show with Twisted Sister on April Fool's Day. The difference in our sound was tangible. You could feel it as well as hear it. We had always been a sledgehammer of a band live—now we were a twenty-pound sledgehammer! The work of preparing A.J. to step in, and the subsequent break-in period as with any new player (although A.J. was amazingly prepared for rehearsals and shows), did take time and effort. I definitely feel this helped divert our attention from the reality that after *six years* we still did not have a deal. Keep in mind, for Jay Jay it was *nine years* since he joined the band. *Yowza!*

That all changed when Martin Hooker of Secret Records made good on his word and negotiated a deal to sign Twisted Sister.

Secret Records' roster consisted then of one band, to my knowledge, neo-punks the Exploited (there may have been more, but I didn't know of them). The Exploited made quite a bit of noise in the UK. Much like Twisted Sister, they refused to allow their favorite music form to die. Hence the name of their first album, *Punks Not Dead*. In truth, punk—if not completely dead—had suffered a genre-ending injury (for the time being), and most punks and skinheads were looking for a new musical home. Thanks to crossover bands such as Motörhead, heavy metal was fast becoming a haven for the working-class youth of the world.

Martin Hooker saw what was going on and, in an attempt to create a "one-stop shop" for said youth, signed a heavy metal band, so Secret Records could serve all facets of the aggressive rock market. Smooth. Back then, Twisted Sister had genuine punk appeal.* Our first shows in England were attended by a mishmash of metalheads, punks, and skinheads. (Having Mark "the Animal" Mendoza of the seminal punk band the Dictators in our band didn't hurt).

The only problem was, in signing Twisted, Secret Records had bitten off way more than it could chew. We weren't some local minimalist punk band. Twisted Sister was a larger-than-life heavy metal monster from America, which brought with it a whole range of issues, as Martin Hooker would soon find out.

To capitalize on the growing buzz on the band in the UK and set the stage for our album release later that year, Martin wanted to release the demo tape that had turned him on to our band in the first place, as an interim EP—a four-song album—and call it *Ruff Cutts*. Happy to get any product out into the marketplace, we readily agreed.

On April 15, 1982, on the sidewalk in front of Eddie Ojeda's apartment building in Queens, Eddie, Jay Jay, Mark, and I met and signed our contract with Secret Records. Why we weren't invited in to Eddie's apartment I have no idea. Next up, we needed to find a

---

* To this day, "We're Not Gonna Take It" is considered a punk anthem, owing some of its own inspiration to the Sex Pistols, for sure.

producer for our record, and Martin Hooker had an idea: Pete Way of the band UFO.

UFO was a favorite band of Mark and mine, and Pete Way—the bass player and one of UFO's songwriters—was legendary. Pete had recently done a nice job of producing the album *The Wild Ones* for the UK Oi!* band the Cockney Rejects. We were recording a low-budget indie record album. Pete Way's price was right and he brought quite a bit of credibility with him, as well. He and UFO were full-fledged legends in the UK and Europe. Having Pete produce us was like getting a pope's blessing. Now we just had to meet with him to seal the deal.

As luck would have it, UFO was currently on tour in the States. Pete Way was interested in working with the band and agreed to fly in to catch one of our New York–area shows.

To say Pete traveled light would be an understatement. He stepped off the plane, a drink in one hand, wearing only a T-shirt and a pair of jeans, with sneakers, and that's it. No carry-on, no luggage—I'm not sure he even had a wallet. (This was the early eighties, when all you needed to fly was a valid ticket.) Pete was brought straight to the club to see the band. He was (and still is) an extremely likable guy, whom I can only describe as a rock 'n' roll version of Dudley Moore's "Arthur," but without the money. Not that Pete was poor; he just never seemed to have any actual money on him and was always looking to cash a dog-eared check he carried around that his wife had given him.

Pete and the band immediately clicked and a partnership was formed. Pete Way would be our producer, and we were ready to rock.

---

* According to world-class authority Wikipedia: "Oi! is a working-class subgenre of punk rock that originated in the United Kingdom in the late 1970s. The music and its associated subculture had the goal of bringing together punks, skinheads, and other working-class youths."

⇜ 22 ⇝

lemmy kilmister: fairy godmother

In June of 1982, Twisted Sister played its farewell tristate-area show at the North Stage Theater in Glen Cove, Long Island. Fueled by the fire of knowing we were finally making good on our promise of heavy metal glory, and with our loyal fans giving us a hell of a send-off, we gave one of the greatest live performances of our careers.* Three days later, we were on a jet to England.

I reluctantly left a very pregnant Suzette. Six months into her term, my petite wife had been overstuffed by her mother and grandmother ("You're eating for two now") and looked about to burst. There was never a question of *if* I should go; Suzette never uttered a word of negativity or protest. It was just understood. This was what we both had been working for for so long, and it was finally coming together. Besides, I would be back in August, in plenty of time for the birth of our first child, who was due in September.

Leaving A. J. Pero—temporarily—behind to marry his first wife, Joanne (he joined us a few days later), after six and a half years of waiting (eight-plus for Jay Jay), we finally headed off to England to take a giant step in our musical careers. *Twisted Sister was recording its first album!*

---

* The North Stage Theater Concert DVD, found on the *Double Live: North Stage '82–New York Steel '01*, is a must-have for any true fan of the band. I don't say that about too many things we've done, but filmed on the eve of our initial breakthrough, the band was at its best!

We were booked to record at Kitchenham Farm studios, in Ash-burnham, England, where Def Leppard had just taken a year to record *Pyromania* and Paul McCartney had finished his latest record. This place was the real deal! Our agreement with Secret Records was that they would provide the studio, housing, and meals. The studio and hotel were in the English countryside, which was absolutely beautiful in July. Our hotel was this amazing old place, originally built by William the Conqueror in the Middle Ages. *We're talkin' the eleventh century!* In the States, we call things that are seventy-five or a hundred years old "antiques." In Europe, that's considered "relatively new." We couldn't have been more blown away. The studio, on the other hand, was a different kind of surprise.

Kitchenham Farm itself was pretty cool, but we weren't record-ing there. I can't remember if it was purely a budgetary thing or if it was thought to be "more metal" (that was probably our justification for the budget issues), but it was decided we would record our basic tracks and guitar overdubs in a local barn, using a mobile recording unit. Amps and drums were set up, bales of hay were used as sound baffles, and the recording truck was parked right outside the emp-tied barn, in the middle of a working farm. Things were going well until the first time we asked our engineer to play something back in the mobile unit. The condescending, arrogant asshole (that was how he acted to us) refused to turn up the volume. Apparently he had tinnitus or something like that and couldn't listen to playback loudly, and by loudly I mean anything greater than normal speak-ing volume. Was he freakin' kidding!? We were a damn heavy metal band for God's sake! We were loud by definition!

Needless to say, my reaction to this guy's "condition" didn't endear the band to him, or the rest of the people working at the stu-dio. Screaming at a guy with tinnitus tends to be counterproductive. Talk about your ugly Americans.

AS A RECORDING ENVIRONMENT, the barn did the trick. We were able to get some kind of sound out of "the room," but the local residents seemed none too pleased with us. And by *local residents* I mean farm animals. I remember being outside looking at a cow while Mark "the Animal" Mendoza was getting ready to test his equipment. The minute he started playing his bass (blisteringly loud, of course), the cow started uncontrollably shitting. That poor bovine didn't know what hit her. Maybe it was commentary on Mark's playing?

The songs we were recording for our first album were ones we had been playing in the clubs for years, so there was no wasted time writing, creating parts, or even discussing what we needed to do. It was pretty much just laying down what we did live. Regardless, any recording process is long and pretty boring. Like movie- and video-making, the industry mantra is "hurry up and wait." Now, I'm sure that "partying" bands have a lot more fun, adding friends and girls and booze and drugs when recording. That wasn't for me. I was on a mission, and I'd finally been given the keys to the kingdom.

I already had a cassette full of song ideas for the next album, which I had worked on in the months before we left. On the seven-hour flight to England, I went through the ideas and selected the best twenty or so. Now, while the guys were in the barn getting sounds, recording tracks, or just fooling around, I sat alone in the band van—or in a spare room or in my hotel room; whatever was available to me—developing those song ideas. When I wasn't actually working on the recording and mixing of our first record, I was writing lyrics and/or further preparing the songs for our second, so they'd be ready for the band when the time came. This is how I worked for the first three albums. We didn't even have album one out and I was ready for number two. I was that sure and committed. Remember Tony Robbins's "luck is preparation meeting opportunity"? I knew this instinctively. Nothing was going to stop me.

With Mark Mendoza working by Pete Way's side (Mark was interested in the art of recording) and the engineers assigned to our record (Craig Thomson, Will Gosling, and Dave Boscombe), we made our way through track after track, pretty much live to tape, with the exception of vocals. Those were recorded at various available studios.

Pete Way, though his rock 'n' roll heart was definitely in the right place, wasn't much of a producer. His greatest value was the credibility he brought to a bunch of relatively unknown, crazy Yanks. Fans and musicians loved Pete, and to have his seal of approval opened a lot of doors for us.

Motörhead had recently gone through an ugly "divorce" with Fast Eddie Clarke, their lead guitarist, leaving the former band members on terrible terms. As bad as the breakup had been, the media were making it ten times worse, pitting the band members against each other in the press. It was sad to see. Pete was good friends with all of the Motörhead guys and put in a call to Fast Eddie asking him if he would play some lead guitar on one of our songs, "Tear It Loose." Fast Eddie didn't have a clue who we were and didn't have to. His pal Pete asked and that was good enough.*

The legendary Fast Eddie Clarke arrived at the barn with a guitar in one hand and a bottle of Jack Daniel's Old No. 7 in the other. It was only midafternoon, but Fast Eddie was ready to get his game on. The plan was for Jay Jay and Fast Eddie to exchange lead guitar licks with each other on the track. Even though Jay Jay's hard-partying days were behind him, he stood toe to toe with Fast Eddie Clarke in that barn, trading guitar licks and hits on the bottle of Jack, one for one.

I don't know when I felt prouder of Jay Jay.

In the short time I got to hang with Fast Eddie, I shared with him my thoughts on how the press were manipulating the feud between him and Motörhead's singer/bass player Lemmy Kilmister. I told him how his relationship with Motörhead was like a marriage. They had some amazing years together, and even though they didn't get along now, it couldn't change the time they shared and what they had achieved.

What a pushy ass I was! Who was I to lecture him on anything? I would find out for myself, in just a few short years, how difficult it was to keep a positive attitude about your band members after you broke up. Did I mention I was an ass?

The track turned out great, and Fast Eddie became a friend of the band's for life. We would see him again soon enough, but not before we met the remaining members of Motörhead in a way-more-intense environment.

---

* Pete Way and Fast Eddie Clarke (along with Jerry Shirley of Humble Pie) would later form a band called Fastway, who would have some success, despite Pete's leaving before the band recorded their first record.

• • •

WHILE WE WORKED TO finish our first album, the *Ruff Cutts* EP was being readied for release in early August. It would contain two Eddie Kramer–produced tracks, "Under the Blade" and "Leader of the Pack," and two self-produced songs from our last demo: our long-time show opener, "What You Don't Know (Sure Can Hurt You)," * and "Shoot 'Em Down." But before either of these records would hit the stores, Twisted Sister was offered an opportunity that would become one of the pivotal moments—*if not thee pivotal moment*—of our career.

Motörhead was returning to the UK after their worldwide *Iron Fist* tour and headlining a heavy metal festival at the football stadium in Wrexham, North Wales. Their manager, Doug Smith, had been helping our manager with Twisted Sister's logistics in the UK and offered us a slot on the bill. Not just any slot, but the "special guest" slot . . . *third on an eight-band bill*. Twisted Sister readily accepted our first chance to perform for a British audience, after months of hype in the local rock press.

Our guardian angel, Pete Way, couldn't come with us to the show, so he called one of his mates who was going to be there. Pete told him that we were a great bunch of guys and he should watch out for us. That mate? The original pirate of rock 'n' roll—headliner Lemmy Kilmister of Motörhead.

When we arrived at the stadium, the true reality of what we were undertaking began to set in. On a bill filled with bands with records in the stores, Twisted Sister had none. Nobody in this country had even heard one of our songs or even seen us perform, for that matter. Add to that, makeup-wearing bands were not only nonexistent but completely unacceptable to English metal fans. Any band that showed even a hint of glam had been brutalized by the notoriously hostile British metal fans. The Canadian metal band Anvil had been given the nickname Canvil after they were bottled off the stage because lead singer/guitarist Lips wore fishnet "sleevelets." The band

---

* Considered by many metal fans to be one of the greatest opening songs of all time.

Girl (first recording band of Phil Collen from Def Leppard and Phil Lewis from L.A. Guns) were pounded mercilessly at a festival for wearing a hint of makeup. Wait until they got a load of us!

As we looked out at the gathering crowd of metalheads in the stadium, things went from bad to worse. Motörhead's fans were some of the nastiest and ugliest-looking muthafuckers we'd ever seen, and the few female fans they had . . . well, let's just say you'd rather have sex with one of the guys!

To top it all off, the second band on the bill, Budgie, canceled at the last minute, pushing us up to the number two slot, right before Motörhead. Then we found out we'd be going on before sundown.

Because of people's often negative reaction to Twisted Sister's appearance, I had written "What You Don't Know (Sure Can Hurt You)" to open our shows. The only song I've ever written to fit a stage-lighting plot, the idea was for the band to be lit only in silhouette for the first third of it. This would give the audience a chance to hear us, *before they saw what we looked like.* The song had always been effective, and we'd get a strong reaction when the front lights finally came on, revealing our "unique" appearance. The key to the success of the song was that the stage and the band would start out almost totally in the dark. Twisted Sister had never performed in the daylight, and we were terrified of what might happen with Motörhead's audience.

The band gathered in our dressing room to discuss a plan of action. We'd been warned about the potential reaction to how we looked and we were freaking out. Our first UK performance might well be our last. I don't remember whose idea it was, but somebody suggested that we not wear our makeup and costumes for the first time in our career.* This was met with a pretty enthusiastic response from most of the jittery band members. Not me. I told the band that I was as afraid of going onstage that day as they were, but I hadn't come this far, looking the way I did, to back down now. It had not been an easy road for us; I had been in a lot of scrapes and alterca-

---

* That's not completely true. Every Halloween, Twisted Sister would perform in street clothes. We figured while the world was dressing up, we would take that one day off each year.

tions because of our image. If I was going to take the costumes and makeup off for fear of a negative audience reaction, I would have done it a long time ago.

While the band did wear their makeup and costumes that day, some of them wore their Twisted Sister denim vests over their stage clothes and sunglasses covering their eye makeup.* *Not me.*

As we stood in our dressing room nervously debating what we were going to do, Lemmy Kilmister passed our open door. I've always joked that Lemmy stopped and came in because he knew the smell of human excrement (from us shitting in our pants), and it was wafting out into the hall. Whatever the reason, he did come in and made an unsolicited proposition that blew us all away. *Lemmy offered to introduce the band.*

I'm sure the magnitude of this gesture is not being fully appreciated by most of you. Motörhead were the headliner. Traditionally, the top dogs don't even make their presence known to the bands backstage, let alone let the audience see them before their own set. It kills the suspense. Fans wait ravenously all day for their heroes to finally come forth, in that mind-blowing first moment of the concert. For the front man to walk out onstage, without an introduction, before his or her show is unheard of. *Let alone to help out an unknown band that the artist has no affiliation with!* To this day, I am still not sure why Lemmy showed us this kindness. It's probably just the way he is wired and one of the reasons he is so beloved. He may be a pirate, but he's a benevolent pirate.

When it was finally time for our set, we solemnly walked the *long* stadium hallway leading to the stage, heading to our doom. The end of our intro tape (AC/DC's "It's a Long Way to the Top [If You Wanna Rock 'n' Roll]") played, and the band walked out onto the stage. The instant the British fans saw us, they began to react hostilely. Before we had played our first note, arms throughout the crowd were cocked to throw bottles, cans, and more at us... *then Lemmy Kilmister walked onstage.* The crowd was shocked to see him and froze midthrow. Lemmy's voice is notoriously unintel-

---

* It should be noted that Jay Jay always wore sunglasses onstage. At that time, nobody else ever did.

ligible to untrained—especially, not British—ears, but his fans heard exactly what he said.

"These are some friends of mine from America. *Give 'em a listen.*"

That was all it took. A dozen hoarse words from a U.K. rock god and Twisted Sister was given some blessed breathing room to prove our worth. We launched into a blistering set of what we did best, but with one caveat. Over the years, I'd slowly been losing the more campy elements of my live performances. The more I discovered my inner badass—and realized that *pretty boy* were two words that would never be used to describe me—the Frank-N-Furter trappings of the early Twisted Sister years had gradually disappeared. On that day, during that performance, in front of that crowd, the last vestiges of camp went completely out the window, and I fully released my true inner monster . . . *and I never looked back.* The ovation from the Motörhead stadium crowd was staggering, and when we finally left the stage, we knew the Demolition Squad had done it again.

Ten minutes after our set was over, we were sitting in our dressing room, cooling down, feeling good about what we had done, laughing and making a lot of noise. At first, I thought I heard thunder. Oh, shit! Was it going to rain? But the thunder was rhythmic . . . and there were voices. Joe Gerber told everyone to quiet down, and it all became clear.

"Twisted! [STOMP-STOMP!] Sister! [STOMP-STOMP!] Twisted! [STOMP-STOMP!] Sister! [STOMP-STOMP!] Twisted! [STOMP-STOMP!] Sister! [STOMP-STOMP!]"

We could hear the crowd still chanting for more! *This was the greatest ovation of our careers!* What I'm about to tell you next is a violation of trust, but I won't mention the person's name, and I think thirty years is the statute of limitations on something like this. Someone from the Motörhead camp came to me and said they overheard Lemmy saying "This is the first time I've ever been afraid to go on after a band." I couldn't believe it. *No way.* This was Motörhead. *Impossible.* The door to our dressing room opened and in walked Lemmy. He came straight up to me and said, "I introduced your band . . . *now you introduce mine.*" Holy shit! Me introduce Motörhead at *their* headline stadium show?!

And that's just what I did. I walked out onto the stage, and the crowd went absolutely mad. Twisted Sister had won over their little, black heavy-metal hearts. I introduced Motörhead, then went to the side of the stage and headbanged to every song along with all the other fans. Halfway through their set, Lemmy turns, points to me, and says, "This one's for him. It's called 'America.'" For me?! The crowd cheered and Motörhead roared into the song.

A day that had started out as a nightmare had turned into an incredible dream. After six and a half years, five guys from the New York area—led by a rube from Long Island—had arrived. I will always be grateful and have nothing but love for Lemmy Kilmister and the kindness he showed my band and me that day. If he had not done what he did, there could have been a very different outcome, and our career might have ended before it began.

⚡ 23 ⚡

scarred for life

Flying high after our slam-dunk performance at Wrexham, we headed back to London to mix our album at Whitehouse Studios and take photos for the album cover.

Originally, the record was going to be called *You Can't Stop Rock 'n' Roll* (after our song of the same name), but Secret Records' president, Martin Hooker, had a change of heart. For some reason, at that time, songs and album titles with the words *rock 'n' roll* in them were out of vogue in the UK. Hooker was fearful that Twisted Sister's first record would be rejected before it even got out of the gate. With that kind of overly cautious approach, I'm surprised he didn't ask us to change our name. As that time, it was oft noted by rock critics that bands whose name began with the letter "T" (Tank, Terraplane, Tygers of Pan Tang) were doomed to fail. Be that as it may, "You Can't Stop Rock 'n' Roll" was removed from the track list, and *Under the Blade* chosen as our new album title. Why? Because it was one of our most sound-defining songs, a fan favorite . . . and fucking metal!

The idea for the cover art came from the photographer (I think). When we arrived at the studio, a backdrop, with a swinging axe painted on it, was already hanging for us to throw shapes in front of. The guys posed intensely and I did my (new) thing for the camera. Fresh off my performing revelation at the Motörhead festival, I now knew exactly what my audience wanted and I gave it to them. I was a full-on rock 'n' roll monster.

The back-cover photo was taken without our makeup and costumes to establish a core belief of the band: we were not hiding. Twisted Sister wore costumes to enhance our live performances, more as a special effect. By putting a photograph of us without our makeup and costumes on the back cover, we felt it instantly communicated the message. The band didn't want this point to be lost.

One other precedent I insisted be set from album one—my lyrics had to be printed on the inside record sleeve. I pride myself on my atypical heavy metal messages and wanted people to know exactly what I was singing about (or at least have a shot at understanding). I made an effort to use traditional heavy imagery to communicate more positive, empowering, and inspirational messages in many of my songs. "Bad Boys (of Rock 'n' Roll)" was about being misjudged and standing tall as an individual. "Sin After Sin" was a warning about the path of evil (the first of many). I knew that most listeners would never get past the dark imagery, but some would. I wanted them to know what I was saying.

I TOLD YOU PETE Way was the Man and pretty much friends with everybody. You want more proof? We were mixing *Under the Blade* one night, the door to the studio opens and, completely unexpected, in walks Ozzy Osbourne. No bodyguard, no posse, nobody at all . . . just the Ozzman. Clearly feeling no pain, he and Pete exchanged the greetings of longtime friends, and Ozzy explained that he had just shot his dog (or had to go shoot his dog—I can't remember which) for biting his wife (Thelma, not Sharon). Pete made the unnecessary introduction of Ozzy to our stunned band, then cranked up our mix of "Destroyer" for Ozzy to check out. Ozzy seemed to like it (he should have, it's one of my most Black Sabbath–influenced songs), and then he proceeded to hold court.

Ozzy was in the middle a major rebirth on the *Blizzard of Ozz* tour, and his career was firing on all cylinders. His band had just played a major UK homecoming, in front of thirty thousand headbangers with Motörhead, at the "Heavy Metal Holocaust" festival at Vale Park, and the man was flying high again (pun intended). Ozzy had every right to feel vindicated. Since nearly fading into obscurity after leaving Black Sabbath, Ozzy had fought his way back to the top, and he told us—at length—all about it. ("I saw my empire crumbling all around me!")

Not that we minded. He was Ozzy fucking Osbourne, for God's sake—he was Mr. Heavy Metal!

Meeting and hanging with Ozzy was the capper on an amazing first trip to Great Britain, and the recording of our first album. The *Ruff Cutts* EP was ready for release, and the *Under the Blade* album was headed for final postproduction.. Before we left for home—*my wife had a bun in the oven*—we had one more bit of business. We needed to perform at the legendary Marquee Club in London for all the rock press to see. They had heard about our taking of the Wrexham festival, but we wanted them to witness the power of Twisted Sister for themselves. If only the weather had cooperated.

In the early eighties (and still today to some degree), air-conditioning and refrigeration in Europe weren't up to US standards. For sure we are a wasteful bunch, but the UK was at the opposite extreme. Things we Americans see as necessities were/are considered luxuries over there. You need to request ice for your drink at a bar, and then they'll drop *one cube* in your glass. Ask for another and they'd look at you as if you were insane. It wasn't unusual to walk into a butcher shop and see raw meat sitting uncovered or unrefrigerated on a counter, with flies crawling on it. Open the door of a soda cooler for a cold drink and it would be warm inside. And air-conditioning? Don't make me laugh! To this day, only the best hotels in Europe have air-conditioning, and you still have to check with the hotel to make sure it's available. To be fair, Europe doesn't get quite as hot as it does in the States, but when it does, people literally die from the heat. Case in point . . .

Twisted Sister's first true performances in Great Britain were two nights in August at the legendary Marquee Club. The Wrexham festival was a month earlier, but that was a supporting slot, with a short set, and in the daytime. We would be headlining the Marquee shows at night. We'd finally get to use dramatic stage lighting and play our full set.

The Marquee Club is essentially London's CBGBs, but with

a much longer history and a more amazing roster of bands who have played there such as Hendrix, Bowie, Led Zeppelin, and the Who. The Rolling Stones were fired from there. You get the picture. Twisted Sister's selling out two nights at the Marquee—without any recorded product—was a major statement about an emerging rock band.

The average high temperature in London in August is seventy-two degrees Fahrenheit. Quite a bit different from New York. That summer, a heat wave hit London during the days of Twisted Sister's Marquee shows, topping out in the low eighties. This was certainly manageable for a bunch of New Yorkers used to anywhere from the nineties to over a hundred degrees. That was until we met our match in the Marquee Club.

Like any nightclub, the Marquee Club had no windows, but unlike the clubs we were used to playing in the States, the Marquee had no air-conditioning either. Not that the air-conditioning in a packed, smoke-filled club (remember when it was legal to smoke in public places?) on a hot summer night did much to cool things off, but at least the clubs started out cool. Not the Marquee.

While I was in the dressing room getting ready for the show, it already felt hot and humid, but seeing our crew rushing in and out dripping with sweat, and saying things like "It's gonna be a hot one," started to get me concerned. I was used to being drenched by the end of a show,* but not before I had even hit the stage.

The club was packed, wall to wall. Between the hype in *Sounds* and *Kerrang!*—the UK's enormously popular weekly and monthly rock magazines, respectively—and the buzz about our performance at Wrexham, every headbanger worth his or her salt wanted to see the Bad Boys of Rock 'n' Roll.

Suddenly, the door to our dressing room opened and in walked Lemmy Kilmister from Motörhead.

After the show we did together, Lemmy became an ardent supporter of Twisted Sister, coming to many of our gigs, introducing us

---

* I once weighed myself before and after a show, and I had sweat off eight pounds! Sometimes I would take off my shirt and wring it out—sweat pouring off it—in front of the crowd to show them how hard I was working and motivate them to rock harder. My roadies would have to mop up the sweat on the floor beneath me so I wouldn't slip on it and fall.

and sometimes jamming with us as well. Lemmy had been around for a long time and seen it all. From rocking to the Beatles at the Cavern Club in Liverpool, to being a roadie for Jimi Hendrix in his early days, to touring the world with just about everybody with Motörhead, Lemmy Kilmister is a true rock 'n' roll dog. He was blown away by Twisted Sister, and to have Lemmy recently tell me I am one of the three greatest front men he's ever seen—and the best at speaking to an audience—is one of the greatest compliments I have ever received. But I digress.

The time came for us to deliver our goods to the rabid crowd, and we did in true Twisted Sister style . . . for a few minutes.

The first thing that hit me—like a wave of nausea—was the fetid smell of the crowd. Packed shoulder to shoulder, in one sweaty mass of denim and leather, their odor was palpable, and almost unbearable. We would come to learn that this was the 80's default smell of a British metal crowd, but I can't say it ever became something we got used to. That said, the heat was something else entirely. The air was so thick, we could barely breathe: the temperature and humidity, unbearable; unlike anything we had ever experienced before. When the stage lights came on (the ceilings in the Marquee are low so the lights are close to the band), they felt like the heat lamps. As the set went on, it became more and more difficult to sing or even move. Eventually I begged Joe Gerber (doing double duty during that era as our light man), over the mic, to keep most of the lights off.

It wasn't just the band who were suffering. The audience, packed tightly together, were dropping like flies. People were being carried out of the club and taken to hospitals. It was a total nightmare. When we finally got to the end of our seventy-five-minute set, I could barely move. I stumbled off the stage, a sweat-soaked mess, with the rest of my band, collapsed in a chair, and did something I had never before done and haven't done since . . . I cried.

I cried out of frustration and anger at being unable to give people the kind of performance I was capable of. I cried because, in our first true performance for an audience that had heard and expected so much, I had failed to deliver. I cried because, in my mind, everything had built up to this moment, and in front of the rock press and the heavy metal elite I had failed. I cried over being defeated by an unseen enemy that, try as hard as I might, I could not beat.

Lemmy—and others—came in to congratulate us, but wound up consoling us instead. There are no worse critics of Twisted Sister than the members of Twisted Sister. I believe it is what makes us so great live. The dressing room vibe seemed like somebody died rather than a celebration after a sold-out rock show.

The next day—the second of our Marquee shows was to be that night—the reviews came out in the dailies. They were great. They acknowledged the brutal conditions in the club and couldn't believe the band were able to perform *at all*. The audience was incapacitated, yet somehow Twisted Sister was able to rock on. We were so caught up in the misery of trying to perform, we were unable to be objective about the situation. The fans and press loved us!

That night, we got huge fans (the rotating kind, not the fat kind) for the stage, blowing over trays of ice (primitive, yes, but technically air-conditioning), and reduced the wattage and re-aimed all the lights onstage to cool things down a bit. It worked. It was still hot, but it was bearable.

After that first show—for decades—I could not perform without feeling some kind of air blowing onstage. If I didn't, and it started heating up, I would begin to have flashbacks of that terrible night and start to panic, feeling as if I were suffocating. That show scarred me for life.

Oh, yeah, one other thing. We found out later that the managers of the Marquee Club had turned on the fucking heat—during a heat wave in August!—so people would drink more! Sometimes I just want to kill somebody. . . .

⚜ 24 ⚜

i can't believe they threw a shite

Word of the knockout punch Twisted Sister delivered at the Wrexham show in late July quickly spread throughout the UK rock scene. While we were back in the US enjoying life with our families, awaiting the release of *Under the Blade,* a call came into our management office—the Reading Festival wanted to add us to the bill!

England's Reading Festival used to be the premier rock-music festival in the UK. It's still a major player, but now there are a bunch of other equally competitive festivals. Unlike Castle Donington's "Monsters of Rock" (all heavy metal and now known as the Download Festival), Reading always mixed things up, having more than thirty bands, playing different types of rock music at the three-day event. (Now Reading offers as many as fifty bands.)

We were stoked to be asked to perform at such a prestigious event. The lineup that year was the festival's heaviest yet, including Y&T, the Michael Schenker Group, and Iron Maiden.

Our *Ruff Cutts* EP had just been released, so this seemed like the perfect opportunity for us to make further inroads within the UK metal community, promote the EP, and build anticipation for our September album release. Leaving Suzette behind, *again,* heavy with child, we jetted back to England for a weekend romp at Reading.

We would be taking the stage in the early afternoon for a short set, but we made sure to stack the deck in our favor. (Twisted Sister were never ones to fight fair.) A call was put in to our friend and producer Pete Way, inviting him to join us on our last song of the set, a cover of the Rolling Stones classic "It's Only Rock 'n' Roll (but I Like It)." Twisted Sister had been closing shows with an anarchic rendition of the song for years, and it had always been a crowd-pleaser, but why not bring out a bona fide English heavy metal legend to further legitimize us? Pete was currently in the studio rehearsing with Fastway, so he suggested bringing Fast Eddie Clarke along to jam as well. Even better!

We arrived at Reading at just past noon, a few hours before our set, and the place was already up and rocking. On this third day of the event, more than thirty-five thousand people were in attendance. Finally, a bigger crowd than we had ever played to on our own. The band and I made our way to the stage to get a better look.

With a large camping area off to the right, the two stages were side by side, and the huge crowd was split between them. The people who wanted the best view of the band currently on would pack themselves in front of that stage. The people who were more interested in the band coming up next would wait impatiently in front of the second stage while it was being set up. This way they could still see the band currently on while securing a good spot for the next band. This alternating system allowed for no major break between bands.

The band Terraplane was currently performing, opening the day, and they were getting quite a bit of stuff thrown at them. Apparently, the just-waking Reading crowd didn't like having their beauty sleep interrupted.

On my way backstage to check out the dressing room, I ran into our new friend Lemmy Kilmister, who was there for the weekend's festivities. I gave him the heads-up that Fast Eddie Clarke was going to be jamming with us, then shared with him the same little lecture I gave Fast Eddie when we were recording. You know, the one about how the press were manipulating the feud between them and their relationship was like a marriage? Did I mention I was an ass? I don't think I can say it enough.

My first official realization something wasn't quite right was when Terraplane finished their set. The throwing of things didn't stop. Now the audiences in front of each stage were pelting each other. When I inquired about the reason for this, I was told it was a band thing. The fans of the band about to go on and the fans of the band going on after them were going at each other. It seemed idiotic to me, but whatever.

As we were getting ready for our set, the whole truth of the Reading Festival audience's bizarre actions became clear. They throw things at every band and each other. This violent behavior had become so epidemic, and so many bands and fans had been hurt that the promoters had banned all glass bottles and metal cans from the festival grounds. This shit was moronic and serious!

It was finally time for our set.* As we stood off to the side, waiting for the point in our intro tape when we walk out, *stuff was being thrown at the empty stage.* I guess they were warming up their arms because when we made our entrance, all hell broke loose. That we were performing in broad daylight turned out to be a blessing in disguise. At least we could see the deluge of projectiles being hurled at us. What's that line from the movie *300?* "Our arrows will block out the sun." "Then we shall fight in the shade." Well, we rocked in the shade.

We were bombarded with anything and everything those assholes could throw. Glass bottles and metal cans being banned didn't slow them down one bit. They would throw plastic liter bottles filled with soda, water, *or even urine* at the stage. Some members of the Reading audience even took the time to slowly, methodically fill the bottles with dirt or small rocks and then hurl them at the stage. It was insane! The truly terrible thing was that a lot of the stuff would never even make it to the stage and slam down into the backs and heads of the concertgoers closest to the band. Some of them even wore helmets for protection, in anticipation of this happening. I was livid!

Under the heading of "the coolest thing I've ever seen a record company executive do," our label president, Martin Hooker, caught a peach that was thrown on the fly, gave it a quick once-over . . . then ate it! Waste not, want not, I guess.

---

* When I put on my costume that day, I realized I'd left my armbands, gloves, and neck chain back in the States. I got ahold of roll of black duct tape and used it to make armbands and wrap my hands with. If you look closely at photos from that day, you can see it. The crucifix around my neck is a blessed one I wore every day.

As the band tore through "Bad Boys (of Rock 'n' Roll)," followed by "Shoot 'Em Down," I was getting angrier and angrier. It was so incredibly frustrating to be unable to do anything about what was happening, standing high above the crowd on a stage, with a moat of a space between us and the barricade.

Our recording of "Shoot 'Em Down" on the *Under the Blade* record ended with the sound of a machine gun firing. While in the new millennium a song about shooting people who mistreat you (albeit in metaphor), finishing with a gun firing, would be considered insensitive and un-PC, this was 1982. No asshole had yet taken song lyrics that literally. At my request, Secret Records had rented a military-grade Uzi filled with blanks for me to fire off dramatically at the end of "Shoot 'Em Down." Like I said, Twisted Sister doesn't fight fair.

When we got to the end of the song, I pulled out the Uzi. It was a damn good thing I didn't have live rounds in it because, I'm telling you, I would have used them on those fucking pieces of shit. I was out of my mind with rage. When the song finally ended, I had my first opportunity to tear into the audience. And I did.

I had been warned about using profanity and told our band would be banned from all outdoor venues if I cursed. Though I was (and still am) a renowned user of expletives in concert, this was not a problem. Not being drunk or high, I have total control of the language I use (which has come in handy) and can fairly easily modify my speech, while still getting my point across . . . though there is nothing quite like the F-bomb to communicate one's innermost feelings.

I told the crowd that the people throwing things were a bunch of pussies who didn't have the balls to say or do something to my face. I told them those same pieces of crap were hurting innocent people in front of the stage. Then I delivered my ultimatum. I called out the entire audience—all thirty-five thousand of them. I said if they were men and women enough, I would meet them all on the side of the stage after the show and fight every one of them, one at a time; I didn't care how long it took. And I meant it!

Suddenly, the audience stopped throwing things and began to laugh. Not at me, but at the audacity of this makeup-and-costume-wearing Yank who was clearly out of his mind and not kidding.

They'd never heard or seen anything like it. The band then ripped into "Destroyer" and the tide turned. The Reading audience started to rock! By the time we got to "It's Only Rock 'n' Roll," the crowd had been completely won over, but the best moment was yet to come.

Toward the end of "It's Only Rock 'n' Roll" we have a breakdown where I get the audience to yell "I like it!" after I sing "I know, it's only rock 'n' roll but . . ." Using various audience-participation tricks I'd perfected over the years in the tristate club scene, I would never fail to get the audience screaming their lungs out. And tonight I had an ace up my sleeve.

After a couple of okay tries, I introduced Pete Way and Fast Eddie Clarke. The audience lit up! These guys were rock gods and totally unexpected by the crowd. The two deities plugged in their "axes" and joined the band for another go at getting the audience screaming . . . and scream they did. While I was talking to the crowd, getting them ready for the big finish, they suddenly, inexplicably started to roar. I was confused. Being a professional "crowd revver-upper," I was an expert in cause and effect. I say something reaction inciting—the crowd reacts. That's how it works. But this audience was reacting and I hadn't initiated it. And now they were pointing at something. I turned to look where the audience was gesturing and saw an unmistakable figure, dramatically backlit at the rear of the stage. With his Rickenbacker bass guitar (did he bring it with him just in case?) slung down by his side, Lemmy Kilmister walked out to join the fray.

For the first time since their breakup, Lemmy and Fast Eddie Clarke were brought together. The crowd absolutely lost their minds! Lined up across the front of the stage, guitars pointed at the crowd like the Magnificent Seven, were myself, Eddie, Animal, Jay Jay . . . *Pete Way, Fast Eddie, and Lemmy!* Holy shit! We tore into the finale of "It's Only Rock 'n' Roll" and completely turned the Reading Festival on its ear.* What a complete audience turnaround in forty short minutes!

We exited to the backstage area where cameras were flashing and everyone wanted to know about this crazy makeup-wearing

---

* You can find this killer Reading show in Twisted's DVD box set *From the Bars to the Stars.*

band from New York who had not only won over the vicious Reading crowd, but had just orchestrated the reunion of Fast Eddie and Lemmy.

Maybe I'm not such an asshole after all.

After the press barrage, Mark Mendoza, A.J., and I headed over to the side stage to see if there were any takers on my offer to fight. The place was packed . . . with new Twisted Sister fans ready to do battle against any would-be takers with us! *There were none.*

Later, after we'd changed out of our stage clothes and taken off our makeup, the band and crew were standing around, marveling at what had transpired. What a day! The drummer (Danny "Piss Flaps" Heatley) and guitar player (Big John) from the Exploited had done us the enormous favor of being roadies for us that day. Eddie Ojeda joked that we should have put our amps *in front* of us as a protective wall.

The usually quiet Big John piped up, in his thick Scottish brogue, "I canna believe-a someone-a threw-a shite."

"What?" I said, completely confused by what Big John clearly thought was English.

"Someone-a threw-a shite."

"A what?"

"A shite man, a shite!" Big John exclaimed again, frustrated by my inability to understand him.

"A what?"

Danny Heatley chimed in with his "Scottish to East London" translation: "A shit man, somebody threw a shit!"

Wow. Somebody had thrown human shit at the stage. My mind was blown. So many questions about this needed to be answered. How much do you need to hate a band to throw human shit? Whose shit was it? The thrower's, or somebody else's? Where did they get the shit? From a Porta Potti, or did they just have it on standby in case they hated a band enough to throw it? Or were they so angered by us, they dropped trou, laid a fresh one, then hurled it? Which brings me right back to my first question: how much do you need to hate a band to throw human shit? It's a conundrum.

I pondered that brainteaser on and off during my flight home to the States, but I had other, more important things on my mind. It was time for my wife to have our baby.

* ◆ *

ON SEPTEMBER 19, 1982, my life was changed forever. My son Jesse Blaze Snider was born.

Suzette, my twenty-two-year-old wife, had a brutally long labor and natural birth, and I sat by her side through it all feeling completely useless. Sure, we took Lamaze classes, but let me tell you, saying "Breathe, breathe" and "It's going to be all right" to a woman dealing with the pain of mind-numbing contractions rings hollow and makes a man feel impotent. Men are instinctively programmed to protect the women we love and want to help them, but as women go through this incredible ordeal, we are helpless to do anything but stand and watch.

After a long night of suffering (my exhausted wife slept through painful contractions that would bring a grown man to his knees), Suzette was finally brought to the delivery room. My feeling of helplessness was never greater than when I watched her pushing so hard to deliver our baby, blood vessels were bursting in her face. What had I done to the woman I loved?

Then suddenly, a baby's cry and the words "It's a boy," and my emotions completely reversed; from the lowest of lows to the highest of highs in a split second. Was this what it felt like to do drugs? Maybe I was missing out on something after all. Moments later, without warning, the nurse put my newborn son into my arms. I had heard about and thought I understood the incredible feeling of being a father. It seemed a simple enough concept. The reality is, you cannot understand the feeling until you experience it yourself.

Back in the day, the guys thought they appreciated what I was going through, being so far away from my family for such long periods. Years later, Jay Jay, who had a daughter *after* our heyday, asked me, "How did you do it? I can't imagine being away from Samantha the way you were away from Jesse." Well, we do what we have to do.

From that day forward, the road was total misery for me. I couldn't *not* pursue my life's work, but the only place I ever wanted to be was home.

⪡ 25 ⪢

man-o-wimp and the new flower children

With Jesse born and Twisted Sister's first album released (albeit available only as an import in the United States), I was sitting on top of the world. Then the news came that we would be touring England, in support of our album, with the band Diamond Head. Today, they are best known for being a major influence on Metallica (who have famously covered a few of their songs); in 1982, they were a popular English metal band, and we were stoked to tour with them.

With our dream of being an international recording and touring rock band finally beginning to be realized, we hit the tristate club circuit one last time, for a big, farewell run of shows. The time had come to officially say good-bye to our longtime, stalwart supporters in the bars before we left in October for good. With an album in the record stores (remember those?) and international stardom on the horizon, every one of those shows was packed to the rafters. Every loyal Twisted fan wanted to see their rock 'n' roll heroes off. It couldn't have been more glorious.

Upon finishing our run of club shows, we were readying ourselves to leave on the Diamond Head/Twisted Sister tour, when the bottom fell out of our world.

There had been ongoing delays with Secret Records getting us our plane tickets to the UK, but they always seemed to have a good reason. We had no reason to doubt them, so we continued with our preparations. Just days before we were scheduled to leave, we received word—Secret Records was unable to put up the tour support for the band. Without their economic backing, we could not afford to do the Diamond Head tour.

It had been incredibly ambitious for this microlabel to sign and import an American rock band. Unlike the Exploited, who all lived "down the road," Twisted Sister required plane flights, accommodations, ground transportation, per diems, equipment rentals, and more. Bringing us over for the recording of *Under the Blade*, then back again for the Reading Festival, must have pushed the label to its limits. The tour was off. Twisted Sister was facing a long, cold winter ahead.

Without a tour, we had no income. Having just played our big "farewell tour" of the tristate area, we couldn't very well go back to the clubs for a "Psych! We Were Just Kidding" tour (though that does seem to have worked for Kiss). We did have some money in our war chest, but who knew how long that would last, or even how long it would have to last for?

In October of 1982, only weeks after the birth of my son, I sat with Suzette and Jesse, in our studio apartment, essentially hiding, because everyone thought Twisted Sister was on tour in England. After all my preening about how we were leaving the bar scene behind, I was too embarrassed to have people know the truth. I had no record deal, no shows or tours—and I had no idea what the hell I was going to do next. Twisted Sister had pretty much run out of options. Now what?

AS THE NEW YORK weather got colder, the band's spirits took a nosedive. Just when we thought we were finally getting a leg up, we had slipped and fallen to our lowest point ever. Weeks turned to months, and though—remarkably—our ability to draw minimal salaries held out, without an end to our problems in sight, we had no idea for how much longer it would.

But how *were* our salaries holding on? Had we really saved so much cash we could continue to float the whole band and key crew personnel indefinitely? Not quite. Unbeknownst to the band, our intrepid tour manager, Joe Gerber, feeling our plight, and being one of the most loyal and dedicated people I have ever had the pleasure of knowing, began to put his own money into the band's coffers so, as the holidays approached, we wouldn't be quite destitute. It wasn't that Joe was independently wealthy or anything like that. He had received a small inheritance and was loaning it to the band—no interest; no guarantee of repayment.*

Our temporary ability to pay our bills aside, the frustration and anger, already raging inside me, were compounding exponentially.

ONE COLD AND RAINY, nasty fall day, while Twisted Sister was sitting out those dark months, Suzette and I were out running some errands in our older but mechanically sound and dependable '76 Mustang. We had just picked up dinner for the night and a cheap video rental (ninety-nine cents!), and as we drove along, safe and warm from the bone-chilling weather outside—a delicious, hot cup of coffee in my hand—I had this wonderful, all-consuming feeling of contentment. Our healthy newborn son was in his car seat, I had a precious few dollars in my pocket, and somehow the bills for our studio apartment were miraculously paid (thanks, Joe Gerber) for another month . . . and I realized that this was *it*. That intangible thing we all struggle to find and achieve . . . was right here. I realized that it's not money or success, fame or extravagant worldly possessions. *It* is all around us, all the time . . . we're just so busy looking for some big, significant moment, thing, or "sign," we don't even see *it*. This would be the feeling I would fight to re-create the rest of my life. If I could die with this feeling, I would go a happy man. I knew from that point on that all the things I was so desperately struggling for were merely the icing on the cake. No doubt it would

* We didn't find out about Joe's grand gesture until a couple of years later, when a bonus structure was being discussed for him because of his years of service. When his generosity was revealed—as an example of his commitment to the band—some of the band members were unaffected by his kindness, and one—in an effort to further discredit his action—actually said, "You didn't ask us if you could do that." *Unbelievable.*

make, did make, and has made my life that much better, but it all would be nothing without *it*. Before I had even come close to making my mark in the entertainment business, or realizing my rock-star dreams, I had already achieved my life's goal. I'd found *it*. So know that throughout the rest of this tale, I was never without the joy, warmth, and love of my amazing wife and children. I am blessed. They are my everything; I am *nothing* without them.

IN NOVEMBER OF 1982, a couple of disturbing articles came out in *Sounds* and *Kerrang!* One was an interview with the Finnish band Hanoi Rocks, the other with fellow American metallurgists Manowar. Hanoi Rocks—another makeup-wearing band—had made a joke at Twisted Sister's expense, calling us "Cinderella's ugly stepsisters." Manowar called us a joke and said, "Back in the States, Twisted Sister plays wet-T-shirt contests and dollar beer nights." Both lies.

While Hanoi Rocks' comments were an affront (in retrospect, it was a great line), Manowar's comments were particularly infuriating. Their guitar player "Ross the Boss" was a former band member and touring roommate of Mark Mendoza's in the Dictators, had been to Twisted Sister shows, and had even jammed with the band. We considered him a friend.

As trivial as both bands' comments sound (and are to me now), in the darkness of my mood at that time, they were fighting words. The only problem was, I was in America, they were in Europe, and I could do nothing about it. Or was there?

They say the pen is mightier than the sword, so with a razor-sharp pen (actually a typewriter), I wrote a letter to the editors of both *Sounds* and *Kerrang!* In it, I broke down the lies, indignities, and aspersions cast on both myself and my band by Hanoi Rocks and Manowar and demanded a public apology. Either that, or Twisted Sister and I were calling them out.

A couple of weeks later—much to my relief—my letter was published for all of the English heavy metal community to see, and both Hanoi Rocks and Manowar were contacted about my challenge.

Hanoi Rocks completely laughed off my letter—further infuriating me—and Manowar accepted my challenge for what they thought was a battle of the bands.

My response—this time by phone, in an interview—was swift. My calling them out was not meant to be musical, it was meant to be physical. "My fist, your face" I believe were my exact words. If Twisted Sister didn't get an apology from both bands, there would be a nonmusical, physical showdown the next time we were in England . . . whenever that might be. We still had no clue as to what the hell we were going to do next.

I now see the complete stupidity of the whole thing. A psychiatrist once explained to me that when we lose control over the bigger, more significant issues in our lives, we tend to lash out at little things we feel we should have control over. The husband who has to put up with his demanding bosses and clients all day, catering to their every whim, flips out when he comes home and dinner isn't on the table. Why? Because in his mind it seems reasonable that at least *this* he should be able to control. With my whole world crumbling around me, this bullshit from these bands was something I *could* do something about. And I was pissed!

When the opportunity for us to return to the UK finally presented itself in December (much more on that shortly), I made good on my promise. I notified the rock press that we were officially challenging Hanoi Rocks and Manowar to a fight in London's Covent Garden on Sunday, December 19, at high noon. Very dramatic.

When the day finally arrived, we charged into Covent Garden— with press in tow—to face our accusers and have our revenge. Not surprisingly, a lot of fans were awaiting this confrontation. We prowled Covent Garden looking for Hanoi Rocks and Manowar (both had made it clear, in advance, they had no intention of showing up and fighting us) in every possible location, from garbage cans to even the ladies' room. Shouting into a megaphone (or *loud-hailer* as they call it in England), I did my best impression of David Patrick Kelly from *The Warriors* (which would come in handy on a future album).

"Hanoi Rocks . . . come out to plaaaay! Manowar . . . come out to plaaaay!" Everyone enjoyed a laugh at Hanoi's and Manowar's expense.

Young and so innocent. Who could imagine what was to come?

Gettin' an attitude by 1972. Maroon and tan clothes? Apparently, I was an "autumn."

Performing with my high school band Dusk in 1973. Sparkle velvet pants with a pink-and-white top. My flamboyant side was starting to show!

With my sister Sue and my youngest brother Doug at my high school graduation in '73. Check out the 'stache!

Kickin' ass with Harlequin in the parking lot of a McDonald's. Hell yeah!

Very early shot from 1976 B.S. (Before Suzette) with only a touch of makeup.

The night I met Suzette wearing the now legendary T-shirt. Wasn't I the catch?

The beautiful Suzette, age seventeen. Yowza!

Rockin' my favorite Suzette Christmas gift with Jay Jay French, circa 1976.

The game-changing fashion faux pax, as me and Suzette bought the same shirt. For the record, it looked much better on her.

Yet another "Suzette original" Christmas gift in action, this time with a very disco-looking Eddie "Fingers" Ojeda.

Twisted Sister promo photo, 1978.

"Sweet Transvestite" —era Twisted Sister, circa 1979. Look at those legs!

The view from the stage at the sold-out Palladium show in NYC, circa 1979.

Clowning around on our wedding day. That's Suzette's co-maid of honor/sister Roseanne on the left.

Me and my best man, "The Animal." If it weren't taken in 1981, you'd think the heads were Photoshopped onto the bodies!

Broke, record deal-less, out of work, and happy, fall 1982. I had discovered "it."

Picture from home, winter '83. I see my son sit up for the first time, inspiring "The Price."

Twisted Sister '81/'82. The look
is finally coming together. I have
released my inner beast!

Post show, Marquee Club dressing room, 1982. I'm sure I was telling somebody how hot it was the first time we played there!

In the thick of things at Castle Donnington, UK, 1983.

A literally "cocky" bastard, backstage at Donnington.

In all my glory B in the D (Back in the Day)!

When men were women . . .
who were men!

The record that I am presently working on with "Twisted Sister" is guaranteed to go at least platinum or I resign. .....

Signed

Geoff Werkman

Witness: Gary McGorman

The handwritten guarantee by engineer Geoff Werkman (RIP) that *Stay Hungry* would go platinum.

Mark Metcalf, Marty Callner, and me during the "We're Not Gonna Take It" video shoot.

The original Twisted bone logo sketch that Suzette did in five minutes.

Yes; that was my real hair! But clearly the "car-pits" don't match the drapes!

Busted in Amarillo, Texas!

Meeting up with my family in Florida mid-tour, October 1984. I was happy to see them, too.

Hangin' out at MTV, 19

Me with A.J. Pero and Brian Johnson in 1985. Really! That's Brian Johnson!

Just an average dad washing the family car!

Playing with my baby boy Jesse backstage after show at The Pier in NYC.

Me and Shane, 1989.

The Snider family happy in Florida, 1990. You wouldn't know the bottom had fallen out of my career, would you? That's because I had "it."

Me and Bernie Tormé backstage at the only Desperado gig we ever did. Check out the beard! I had to grow it after a boating accident. Did I forget to tell you about that?

Me and the great Howard Stern (both sans sunglasses) backstage at a Widowmaker show on Long Island in 1990.

Lean and mean fronting Widowmaker in 1990.

Me, struggling but happy and celebrating my fortieth birthday with Cody Blue in 1995.

Me and the love of my life, Easter '92.

The Snider Family, aka "It" (l. to r.): Cody, Shane, Suzette, Dee, Jesse, Cheyenne.

After a thorough search, it was officially declared (by the press) that Hanoi Rocks and Manowar had "chickened out."

While Hanoi Rocks weren't tough, image-wise, to begin with, this declaration was more than a bit damaging to Manowar, whose entire shtick was built on "mannishness." Performing and being photographed in loincloths, with oiled bodies, they prided themselves on being heavy metal warriors (more like medieval Chippendale's dancers), ready to do battle for the cause. I guess they just weren't ready to do battle for their *own* cause.

The press proclaimed them "Man-o-Wimp" and a photo was taken with the victors (Twisted Sister) and all of their supporters. In the post-"nonconfrontation" interview, I let it be known that it didn't end there. If they weren't men enough to face us, unless they formally apologized, we were going to come for them. My plan was to show up at one of their concerts, climb onto the stage, and throw them a beating right in front of their audience. I'm nothing if not committed.

Shortly after the article about the showdown came out, Hanoi Rocks sent a letter to the rock press apologizing for what they'd said about us and declaring themselves the "new flower children." Fair enough.

Man-o-Wimp—er, I mean *War*—took another tack. Ross the Boss directly contacted his old friend Mark "the Animal" Mendoza. While I can't reveal what was said, there were no further issues between Manowar and Twisted Sister. But if they do mouth off again, Ross's plea—er, I mean *request*—will be fully disclosed.

By now you should be wondering, "What the hell were Twisted Sister doing in England in December of 1982?" Ahhh, the plot thickens.

⇥ 26 ⇥

it's only rock 'n' roll . . . but they like it

Remember what I said about our fans being our greatest asset? Well, Twisted Sister had one hard-core fan in particular who was going to bat for us in a big way. Jason Flom, the former head of Lava Records, Atlantic Records, Virgin Records, and Capitol Music Group, and now back at Lava—responsible for the sale of more than 200 million records during his career—was then just an annoying stoner (sorry, Jason). He used to come down to our shows—with his fried buddy Zemsky—and use his low-level involvement with Atlantic Records to get backstage, so he could party like a rock star. Bands (including ours) were so desperate for any kind of label attention, they would fall all over themselves catering to every whim of this hot mess.

That said, Jason loved Twisted Sister and did everything he possibly could to get us signed to Atlantic Records. Jason was so unrelenting, the then president of the label—who was absolutely not a fan of ours and had personally rejected us multiple times—threatened to *fire* him if he ever mentioned our name again. Despite that threat, knowing the head of Atlantic Records Europe, Phil Carson, was coming to the New York offices, Jason assembled a dossier on Twisted Sister as thick as a phone book and shoved it into Phil's hands, begging him to take a look at it on his flight back to the UK.

Phil Carson is responsible for the sale of more than 275 million albums worldwide. Among others, he has signed ABBA, Genesis,

Yes, Mike Oldfield, AC/DC, and Emerson, Lake & Palmer. He also worked with Led Zeppelin from album one as their record-label liaison. The dude is the real deal.

When Phil finally settled into his first-class seat for his flight home, he pulled out the manuscript Jason had handed him and gave it a quick look. Between the crazy photos of us and the density of the text, Phil closed the massive presentation, rolled it up, and crammed it into a vomit bag. So much for that . . . for now.

AT THE BEGINNING OF December, our manager, Mark Puma, received a call from a popular English television show called *The Tube*. One of the producers had seen Twisted Sister at the Reading Festival, and the show was interested in having us on. Knowing how far in advance television shows like to schedule, we were clearly a last-minute replacement, which makes what happened that much more incredible.

Every week, *The Tube* would invite three bands. Each band would play live to a "clublike" studio audience, and the show would be broadcast live. The show offered to Twisted was on December 16, joining the Tygers of Pan Tang (with a pre–Thin Lizzy/Whitesnake John Sykes) and the legendary Iggy Pop. This was the lifeline we desperately needed, but there was one catch . . . they would pay us nothing and cover none of our expenses to get over there.

Our management team (Mark Puma, Jay Jay, and Joe Gerber) immediately went to work, figuring out how we could make this happen. By booking a couple of shows while we were in the UK, we could offset our expenses, but not nearly enough. We needed to fly five band members plus an equal number of crew there, and transport, feed, and house everyone for the duration of the trip. The band was broke, but we saw this as our last chance for salvation. We *had* to borrow the money. Turning to family, friends, and business associates, we pulled together the twenty-two thousand dollars needed to make it happen.

My younger brother Matt and his wife, Joyce, lent us five grand. I don't think I ever properly thanked them. Thanks to both of you for taking a chance and helping to make my dream a reality. Along with Matt and Joyce, the band was loaned money by Joe Gerber's mom, Sophie, and Charlie Barreca's brother-in-law Johnny Rutigliano. Our club agent, Kevin Brenner, came through for us, as did a number of our faithful club owners, who gave us advances on future club dates, including Tony Merlino of the Gemini nightclubs, L'amour's owners, Mike and George Parente (who later managed such bands as White Lion and Overkill), and the Salerno family of the Fountain Casino in New Jersey. Thank you all so much for what you did. None of it could have happened without you.

With less than two weeks until Christmas, we arrived in Great Britain for our last gasp. That's how it felt. If we didn't create some kind of energy out of this appearance, we were done. In our never-ending quest to stack the deck in our favor, we asked Lemmy and Motörhead's new guitarist, former Thin Lizzy axe master Brian "Robbo" Robertson, to join us on our show closer and they accepted.

The day of the broadcast, as we sound-checked and prepared for the show at the studio, my mind raced. This was an incredible opportunity for us, but I needed some grand gesture to seal the deal and win over not only the studio audience, but the viewers at home as well. I had an idea, but I wasn't absolutely sure I would go through with it. Unbeknownst to the band, I gave Joe Gerber a couple of things to have one of the roadies ready with if I asked for them.

The show opener was Tygers of Pan Tang, whom I don't remember anything about because I was deep into my preshow preparations while they were on. Iggy Pop was next, and he lived up to his reputation. At sound check, Iggy had fallen into the drums, knocking them completely over. During the break before the show, he disappeared, and after a frantic search and concern that they would have to do the show without him, he was finally found. The one thing all the bands had been warned about was playing beyond our allotted time. This was live television, with no wiggle room in the schedule. If you did not finish on time, they assured us, they would cut the power. Iggy found that out the hard way. Now it was our turn to rock.

Remember Phil Carson, the head of Atlantic Records Europe? Well, as luck would have it, he was attending that *Tube* broadcast.

Mick Jones, the lead guitarist and primary songwriter for Foreigner, was being presented an award on the show, and Phil, Mick's longtime friend and head of Foreigner's record label, had accompanied him to the presentation. Upon their arrival, Phil inquired of the show's producers, who else was on the show that night?

"Iggy Pop, Tygers of Pan Tang . . . and Twisted Sister."

Mmmm? Phil thought. *Wasn't that the band that annoying kid was all over me about?*

Before he could even give himself an answer, Mick Jones chimed in, "Twisted Sister? You can't turn your radio on in New York without hearing them."*

Phil was nonplussed. How was it that seemingly everyone knew about this band Twisted Sister while he, one of the most powerful men in the recording industry, did not? He sought out Mark Puma and inquired about us. Mark told Phil the band was currently without a deal and looking for a new home. Phil Carson took note.

We opened *The Tube* with our usual "What You Don't Know." The studio, which was set up like a nightclub, was filled with rock fans who had waited for hours to be part of the audience. While a couple dozen metalheads/Twisted Sister fans were at the front of the stage, the majority of the audience were spread out around the room, too cool or indifferent to care about a bunch of makeup-wearing "poofters" from America. As the band performed, my brain churned. I had to win this crowd over.

"It's Only Rock 'n' Roll" was our final song, and when we got to the audience-participation breakdown in the middle, I revealed our secret weapons. Hanging out by the bar, as if they just happened to be there, Lemmy Kilmister and Brian Robertson charged the stage to a huge ovation. Robbo, in a drunken attempt to make a dramatic entrance, decided to climb down to the stage from a balcony above, but fell. The crowd loved it. We blasted into a jamming solo section of the song, with even more of the studio audience getting into it,

---

* We did have a song being played on a couple of New York stations. Our demo of "Shoot 'Em Down" was part of a radio-station compilation album (along with a then unsigned Jon Bon Jovi's "Runaway") being played on WAPP, and WPLJ had added the song off our *Ruff Cutts,* then *Under the Blade* records.

but it still wasn't enough. A full third of the in-house crowd were sitting us out. Without any warning to the band, show, or crew, I decided to make my surprise move.

Addressing the audience in the studio, I noted that not everyone in the room was getting into it, and if *they* weren't into it, how could I expect people sitting in their living rooms watching on TV to get into it? Playing off my knowledge of the disdain for makeup-and-costume-wearing bands at that time (remember, this predates hair metal), I asked the crowd if they weren't getting into it because of my makeup? Already shirtless (meaning the costume element had essentially been removed), I moved in for the kill.

I told them I'd give them an early Christmas present if they'd give Twisted Sister one in return, their participation. I signaled my roadie to bring me what Joe had given him earlier: *makeup remover and a towel.* I told the crowd, if the makeup was the thing stopping them, it was time to take the makeup off. Grabbing a big handful of Albolene (the greasiest and most effective of removers)—much to the surprise of the audience *and the band*—I rubbed it all over my face. Then I took a towel and completely wiped off my makeup (as much as I could). Looking at the audience, my face a sweaty, grease-smeared, makeup-less mess I asked, "Now what's stopping you?"

With that, the band, Lemmy, and Robbo launched into the final audience-participation part of the song . . . *and the entire place was up and rocking!* We finished to a thunderous ovation, with Lemmy grabbing the mic from me and shouting in his classic voice, "Twisted Sister, all right?!" It was.*

Not only did the in-house audience love us, the at-home audience did, too.† We had three record deals offered to us immediately following that show, and Phil Carson told Mark Puma he was interested in the band, too. Phil just wanted to see us performing a full

---

* This performance can be found on Twisted Sister's *Video Years* DVD.

† That year, our performance of "It's Only Rock 'n' Roll" was voted one of the top five videos of the year, in the *Sounds* readers' poll, even though it was never released as a video. Several years later, I would return to the *Tube* studios to find one entire wall of the greenroom with a blown-up picture of the last anarchic moments of Twisted, Lemmy, and Robbo performing. I'd say it was a memorable performance.

set at a Marquee Club show we had booked for a couple of days later to be sure.

True to his word, Phil came to the sold-out show, watched us do our thing, and afterwards told Mark Puma he was going to sign the band.

"To Atlantic Records?" Mark replied in disbelief.

"Of course to Atlantic Records. I work for Atlantic Records. Who else would I be signing you to?"

"That's great! Do you want to come back and meet the band?"

Having just watched our maniacal performance, Phil responded, "That won't be necessary. I want to sign them; *I don't have to meet them.*"

Mark Puma wouldn't take no for an answer.

Phil quickly discovered that we left our crazy on the stage and were an incredibly focused, intelligent, sober, and professional bunch of guys (for the most part).*

The next day, we headed back to the States for the holidays with the greatest Christmas present of all: a deal with a major international record label, and the knowledge we would be heading back to England, after the holidays, to record our next album. Phil Carson knew our band had a building energy in the UK, and he wanted us back there to record as soon as possible to capitalize on it.

It was a very merry Christmas, indeed.

THE RECORDING OF THE *You Can't Stop Rock 'n' Roll* album would be the best recording experience of my career. The band spirit, camaraderie, and recording environment would never be matched.

As I wrote earlier, while we had been recording the *Under the Blade* album, I'd been hard at work writing songs for the next record. During the dark months after the Diamond Head tour was canceled—though we had no idea what we were going to do with them—we continued rehearsing, and recording the basic ideas for

---

* I remember Phil's being particularly surprised when one of the band's main concerns was if there was a gym close to the recording studio. He said most bands wanted to know how close the nearest bar was.

the new songs. I would always write way more songs than the band needed, so we wouldn't work on the final song arrangements until we knew which ones were going on an album. Mark Puma had given our new demo to Phil Carson when he met him at *The Tube*. I'm sure Jason Flom had included some of our music with his presentation to Phil as well.

Weeks after our victorious *Tube* appearance—with plans well under way for the recording our next album with Atlantic Records—the phone rang in my tiny studio apartment. Suzette answered (obviously this predates ubiquitous answering machines and caller ID). Covering the mouthpiece as she handed me the phone, Suzette said, "It's some English guy. The phone sounds really weird."

In the eighties, international phone technology was far more primitive than it is today, being more akin to using a ham radio than a telephone. The only thing I can compare it to is some of the wonky connections we still get when we talk cell phone to cell phone. ("No, you go first. No, you.")

I took the phone from Suzette and said hello.

"Dee? This is Phil Carson from Atlantic Records. I was just listening to the new demo." In complete disbelief he added, *"There are hits on here!"*

"Sure, Phil, I'd like to think so." Then it hit me. "You're *just* listening to our music?"

"Yes; it's great!"

I couldn't believe what his statements implied. Now, in my own disbelief I said, "You signed us to a recording contract without listening to our music?"

"Of course. I saw the band and the audience's reaction, and it just worked. There was a connection. I don't have to like it or listen to it to know it will sell."

Unbelievable! What Phil said was absolutely true, but for a record executive to not only state this truth, but to act on it as well, was unheard of. Young, upstart A&R* guys and girls might go with their gut like that, but never high-level record executives. They've got way too much to lose. Once a record man or woman gets that

---

* "Artist & Repertoire." The term coined to describe the function of people at record labels in charge of finding and developing new talent.

corner office with the big salary, objectivity is lost and the willingness to take chances is over.

Phil Carson was the last of a long-gone breed of record man who knows what he knows and doesn't allow others to alter his opinion or make him start second-guessing his decisions. Phil had signed AC/DC off a 16 mm film of the band performing "It's a Long Way to the Top (If You Wanna Rock 'n' Roll)," shown to him on a self-contained projector, with a little screen, at two o'clock in the morning. After seeing the film, Phil said he'd sign the band, and had their representative wake Angus Young up in Australia so he could tell him. Phil Carson trusts his instincts and that's what it took to finally get Twisted Sister signed. Someone self-assured and powerful enough to go back to the office, be unaffected by naysayers, and have the clout to get what he wants done.

When Phil told the international executive board of his intentions to sign Twisted Sister, he ran head-on into the president of Atlantic Records' strenuous objection. You remember him, the one who rejected us multiple times (including overriding ATCO Records' decision to sign us) and threatened to fire Jason Flom if he ever mentioned our name again. *That guy.* Phil had to put his entire reputation on the line to get us signed to Atlantic Records internationally. Phil Carson's signing record within the company was legendary, and he got his way. I owe you my life, Phil Carson.*

Before hanging up, Phil said these fateful words to me: "'I Am (I'm Me)' [one of the songs on the tape] is a hit. We are going to the top of the charts with that one!"

And we did.

IN THE WEEKS BEFORE we left to record, I tried to savor my home life as much as I could. I knew I would be gone for a few months, and during that time, due to my finances, I would have virtually no contact with my wife and son. Bringing them with me wasn't an option,

---

* Full disclosure: Phil is now my manager, business associate, and lifelong friend. In all my years in the record business, he is the only record-company person I have had an ongoing relationship with. He is the real deal.

and phone calls home at that time were prohibitively expensive. I often think how much easier it would have been on Suzette and me with today's technology. Face-to-face Internet calls are ridiculously inexpensive and an incredibly satisfying way of staying connected. But this was the early eighties, not the 2000s, and seeing and hearing from each other while I was away just wasn't possible.

One afternoon before I left, Suzette told me she was going to run out to the supermarket. Three-month-old Jesse was asleep, so with me there to keep an ear out for him, she was going to pick up something for dinner. When Suzette left, I realized that I had a few moments to myself. This would be a good time to write some new songs.

What I'm about to tell you is not ego talking, just the truth about how blessed I am when it comes to writing and creating. My mind is fertile and *always* ready for creativity. For me it's just a matter of being able to focus and capture the ideas so I don't forget them. Because of this, I have trained myself to literally turn off my creativity, and turn it back on when I need it. This is an incredible gift.

I grabbed my list of song titles (remember, I work off those), got my recorder, turned on my "mental faucet," and sang song ideas to tape for the next forty-five minutes. By the time Suzette had come home from shopping, I had basically created all of the songs (except for "The Price") that would become Twisted Sister's *Stay Hungry* album. I had even finished—after writing the hook three years earlier—"We're Not Gonna Take It." "I Wanna Rock," "Burn in Hell," "Stay Hungry," "S.M.F."—all of our best-known Twisted Sister songs—spilled out of me while my son slept and my wife was out getting groceries. I knew I had some good stuff, too.

With our formal record contracts still being negotiated (not that there was much negotiating), the band and I boarded an Air India flight* bound for Great Britain to record our next album. With me, I had the makings of the album—after the one we were about to make—that would change our lives forever.

---

* Atlantic Records had a trade deal with Air India and flew all of their fledgling acts on it. Imagine Twisted Sister sitting in coach amongst a 747 full of Indians, eating curry and watching Bollywood movies. *Hysterical.*

☙ 27 ❧

the price

Recording at Jimmy Page's Sol Studio, in Cookham, Berkshire, England, was like a rock 'n' roll fairy tale. Originally built by Elton John's producer, Gus Dudgeon, in the late seventies, Gus was forced to sell it due to rampant overspending on the project, poor accounting, and a temporary crash in the music industry postdisco. Jimmy Page literally helicoptered in, took a look, and bought it for a fraction of its actual value.

Built on the site of an old river mill, the recording studio is on one side of the river, and it is connected by a covered bridge to the living quarters on the other side. With beamed, vaulted ceilings, French doors, and picture windows looking out at the river and open meadows, the band house is like something from a storybook.

The studio was nothing short of amazing as well. Custom mahogany cabinetry, split-wood, matched-panel doors, and brass abounded. The console room had a working fireplace, and both it and the recording room had large picture windows looking out over the landscape. One of the worst things about recording (for me) is that there are never windows in studios, and thus you lose contact with the real world. Windows are virtually impossible to sound-proof, but Gus spared absolutely no expense (which is part of the reason he lost the studio) to create two-foot-thick walls and ceilings with special sound-deadening qualities that allowed for these unique portals. I remember recording a vocal one day when snow started to fall, as horses ran free across the field. I'm telling you this so you'll understand just how magical the recording environment and experience was while we made the *You Can't Stop Rock 'n' Roll* album.

Removed from our friends, families, and other distractions, we focused completely on the work at hand and bonded as a band as never before.

We worked all day, had an in-house cook and housekeeper, hung out, watched movies, and laughed. Each morning, Jay Jay and I would go for long jogs to stay in shape or hit the gym at the local recreation hall nearby. Through it all, I continued to work on the songs for our *next* album.

Why didn't I use the great (or so I thought) new songs for the album we were currently working on? Simply, they weren't ready to be presented to the band or record company. Since I didn't really play an instrument, I needed to show the band my ideas slowly on guitar (I couldn't possibly sing as I played), then we would rehearse and demo-record them. Finally, I would sing the melodies onto the recordings so the whole idea could be understood. It was a process. Plus, I just felt the new ideas I had weren't meant to be on the current record, for whatever reason. If they were, I would have come up with them before. Timing is everything, and if I had finished "We're Not Gonna Take It" in 1979, it would have never become the song it did. It was meant to be recorded in 1984.

While the recording process and hang time with the band was amazing, the heartache of being away from my wife and son was brutal. I wrote a letter to Suzette religiously, every day and waited for the occasional letter from home with precious photos of my son. Jesse was growing up without me (the growth a baby experiences the first year is exponential), and all I had to savor the first time he sat up, the first time he watched TV, the first time he said "Da-da" (to a stuffed frog!) were these photos.

Suzette was having a hell of a time on her own. At just twenty-two years old, she had to take care of the baby and our apartment. Her family now lived in Florida, too far away to help out, and my family weren't supportive at all. After the first month or so, she gave our two dogs up for adoption, closed up shop and went to Florida to stay with her mother—a much better situation.

As the months rolled on, I became more and more homesick. One day, the studio phone rang and it was Jay Jay's sister-in-law Ricky. We spoke for a minute and she asked me how things were going. I told her that the recording experience was amazing, but I was missing my wife and son. To this, Ricky responded, "Well, Dee, I guess that's the price you have to pay." Her words hit me hard. I gave Jay Jay the phone, grabbed my handheld recorder, went into the bathroom (a place I've always gone for privacy), and wrote "The Price." It would become one of our biggest songs.

REGRETTABLY, WE NEVER SAW Jimmy Page. He was a pretty legendary recluse, living nearby, in a high-security, gated mansion once owned by Michael Caine. Jimmy didn't drive and only went out at night. On a number of days, we'd come into the studio to find things had been moved around and other evidence that Jimmy had been there during the night. It was a little creepy.

Jimmy Page's well-known affinity for the occult had us overanalyzing everything in the building, trying to find evidence of his mystical hand. Though we never found anything out of the ordinary, we did discover one amazing thing. One day, while we're in the studio, Mark Mendoza rushes in—a look of awe on his face—and says to me, "You have got to see this!" Without asking what it was, I followed him to the upstairs offices of the studio. Mark takes me to an unlocked closet, opens the door, and turns on the light. Inside were shelves filled with large master tape boxes. This was nothing unusual for a recording studio; they all have closets like this.

"Take a look at the labels," Mark says.

As I read the labels on each of the reels, I was stunned to discover that every one was a *different, legendary Led Zeppelin song*. In this unlocked closet, in an unlocked building, in the lazy little town of Cookham, were the original recordings of some of the best-known, biggest-selling, greatest songs in the history of rock 'n' roll! You name it, it was there. From "Whole Lotta Love" to "Immigrant

Song" to "Kashmir" to "Stairway to Heaven," *every single Led Zeppelin song ever recorded was there on the shelves.* For us as Led Zeppelin fans (and who isn't?), it was like finding the Holy Grail . . . *in a bathroom.*

For the record, we didn't take any of them. We definitely touched a lot of the boxes, but we left them in the closet.

LIKE TWISTED SISTER, PHIL Carson was a man on a mission. His grand plan for us, while we were in the UK, involved a lot more than recording an album. Phil wanted to set the stage for the release of the *You Can't Stop Rock 'n' Roll* LP by first putting out a single: the "There's hits on this tape!" track "I Am (I'm Me)." To ensure it a high chart position, Atlantic planned on releasing three different versions: a seven-inch two-song single, a twelve-inch four-song single, and a picture disc, with different additional tracks on each one. The idea was for fans to want all of the songs and their various formats, tripling the single sales and pushing it farther up the charts. Great plan, now we just needed something for the flip sides on the variants. We couldn't use the tracks from the actual album.

Phil Carson had that figured out, too. We would perform a couple of shows at the Heat Club, er, I mean, the *Marquee* Club and record them. The live tracks from the show would provide the unique content for the B-sides. *Brilliant!*

"I Am (I'm Me)" was released on my twenty-eighth birthday, and Phil's plan worked like a charm. All of London and the surrounding areas were plastered with giant pink-and-black posters of my screaming head, announcing the single's release, and "I Am (I'm Me)" was soon flying out of the shops. The most popular of the extra tracks was the uncensored recording of "It's Only Rock 'n' Roll (but I Like It)." More than one heavy metal fan was turned on to the band when they heard that track for the first time. (Right, Sebastian Bach?)

Still finishing our album at Sol Studio, we got the word that legendary heavy metal DJ Tommy Vance would be debuting our single on his national BBC weekly radio show. We were stoked! Tommy

Vance was *the* national voice of metal at that time, and we knew the core metal audience would all be listening.

The night of his show, we gathered around the radio, waiting for Tommy to introduce our song to Great Britain for the first time. When it finally came time, Tommy gave the proper buildup for an anticipated release and started the record . . . *at too slow a speed!* Having received the twelve-inch version of the single, he had assumed that it was an LP to be played at 33⅓ rpm. It was in fact intended to be played at the same speed as a seven-inch single, 45 rpm. Like most radio DJs, Tommy wasn't actually *listening* to the music he played. Once a song starts, DJs (as I now know from personal experience) turn down the studio volume and busy themselves getting the next song ready, setting up commercials, talking to people in the studio, etc.

The band and I sat, listening in agony, as our song played on at almost half speed. It was barely distinguishable as a song! This lasted for a seeming eternity until suddenly Tommy Vance stopped the record, opened his mic, and said, "Oops. That can't be right. Sorry about that, lads. [He knew we'd be listening.] Let's try this again." With that, Tommy restarted our song and played it at the right speed, in its entirety.

Years later, I ran into somebody who was listening that night. He said when "I Am (I'm Me)" first came on, he thought, *This is the heaviest fucking song I have ever heard!* He was disappointed when Tommy Vance corrected his mistake.

As we hoped, "I Am (I'm Me)" jumped right into the Top 20, putting us squarely in the sights of the mega weekly music show *Top of the Pops*. At that point, for close to twenty years, it had been *the* televised show on which to get your band noticed, but—primarily because their records didn't make it into the top of the charts—it rarely featured heavy rock bands. It was an amazing opportunity to get our name and music out there, and to jam heavy metal down the throats of the mainstream.

Doing the show was unique. Due to union rules, you (any appearing act) were expected to go into a studio, of your choosing, and rerecord your entire track in one afternoon, under the watchful eye of some union representative. This new recording of your song would be the one you lip-synched to when you were on the show. Understand, it takes days to get just the sounds for your record, let alone to record every part and mix the damn thing. Twisted Sister is just a straight-ahead metal-rock band. Can you imagine how long it takes to record a Pink Floyd single? This said, the whole "rerecording" thing was a ruse. Toward the end of your session, the union watchdog would *conveniently* step out of the room, allowing the recording artist to slip in the original master. The union got its money, and the artist got to lip-synch to the original track. Freakin' ridiculous!

Our first of three visits to *Top of the Pops* stunned Great Britain, and not because of my horrendous first attempt at lip-synching.* Despite the fact that we were on with Boy George and Culture Club, the *TOTP* viewers were mortified by our appearance and demeanor. Us?! Of course the metal fans loved having one of their own on the show for a change. Keep in mind, the UK had all of four television stations back then, so there wasn't a lot to choose from. Whether you liked it or not, on Tuesday nights *Top of the Pops* was the show the entire country tuned in for.

Meeting Boy George for the first time was interesting. He was the poster boy for everything headbangers loathed about insipid pop music. I had used him and his band as a target of my vitriol in my UK on stage rants, vowing to punch him in the face if I ever ran into him. Imagine my surprise when I found out Twisted Sister and Culture Club would be on *Top of the Pops* the same week.

As I walked down the hallways of the *TOTP* studios, who should suddenly step out of a dressing room? The Boy himself, in all his glory. Before I could utter a word, Boy George says, "So where's the slap?"

I was totally thrown. *He knew that I said I was going to hit him.* "What?"

"The slap. *The makeup.* Where's your makeup?"

Turned out, Boy George *was a Twisted Sister fan* and had been following us since our first album. Go figure. And therein lay the problem.

* I later read an interview with Mick Jagger where he said the key to good lip-synching is singing along with the track. I've done that ever since. Problem solved.

⇌ DEE SNIDER RULE #1 ⇌
You like me, I like you.

⇌ DEE SNIDER RULE #2 ⇌
You don't like me . . . we got a problem.

Clearly, Boy George fell well inside the protection of rule number one. So much for hitting him.

TWISTED SISTER WOULD PERFORM two more times on *Top of the Pops*. Once more for "I Am (I'm Me)" and again for our second single, "The Kids Are Back." We would perform on the show with other up-and-coming international stars such as the Eurythmics, Dexys Midnight Runners, Kajagoogoo, and the Thompson Twins. Why I even bother to mention them will become clear later.

THINGS WERE GOING BETTER than expected in the UK. We had two Top 40 hits, our album was high in the charts, and Twisted Sister was on the covers of all the rock magazines and even spilling over into pop and mainstream press. Even better, it was almost time to go home, and I would return victorious. I couldn't wait to be reunited with my wife and baby boy.

Unfortunately, that was going to have to wait a bit longer. Twisted Sister was so hot, Phil Carson wanted us to stay in the UK another month, do a headline tour of Great Britain, and film a video for our next single, the title track from our album. MTV, then only a year and a half old, was going to be a force to be reckoned with, and Phil saw the writing on the wall. Before we headed back to the United States (where I'm sure he knew we would get little help from Atlantic Records US), he wanted us armed with this latest tool in breaking a band.

Having been away from home for close to three months, the last thing I wanted to do was spend another month overseas. I had missed Valentine's Day, my birthday with my family, Suzette's and my anniversary, and I'd had all of about two phone calls home my entire time away. I was homesick! But this was the opportunity and the support from a record label the band had been looking for; there was no way I could pass it up. I broke the news to a *way* too understanding and supportive Suzette, and Twisted Sister hit the road in the UK.

THROUGHOUT THE HISTORY OF rock 'n' roll, many bands have had "band jackets" with the band name and whatever other information they care to impart (person's name, tour, etc.). These jackets—usually baseball-style, satin or something along those lines—conveyed the upbeat, clublike feel of a group and its surrounding organization. Twisted Sister was anything but an upbeat club. More of a hardened "band of brothers," it was us against the world. We viewed ourselves as outlaw rockers, descending upon an unsuspecting community and leaving devastation in our wake. Because of that, we decided to have "colors" like a motorcycle club, instead of jackets.

The band colors were black and pink, so of course those had to be the predominant colors of our back patches. The top rocker read TWISTED and the bottom rocker said SISTER. The TS logo over the pink and black rings made up the center patch.

Twisted Sister always had a sense of humor and an appreciation for the absurdity of how we looked. Putting the "registered trademark" symbol on our logo and having a patch that said RB (rock band) instead of the traditional MC (motorcycle club) was our way of giving a little wink, while also making it clear we were not a motorcycle club. Most people got that.

Only a handful of people (maybe two dozen in total) have ever been given a set of patches by us, and those earned them through their loyalty and dedication to the band.

While out on the *You Can't Stop Rock 'n' Roll* UK tour, we did a show in Nottingham, home of the legendary Sherwood Forest. It was strange to arrive in a town so much a part of history. You just assume these places don't exist, but like Sleepy Hollow, New York, Nottingham is a very real place. Who would have thought we'd run into problems with a motorcycle gang there? Then again, that is where Robin Hood's Merry Men hung out. After our show that night, as we were getting ready to leave, Joe Gerber came into the dressing room to share a concern. A Nottingham motorcycle club had seen our Twisted Sister colors and were demanding we take them off while on their *turf*. Some gangs can be very territorial and view another club's wearing colors as confrontational.* We understood the club's concerns, but there was one problem—we were a fucking rock band! No motorcycles, just guitars.

I wasn't taking off my band colors for some stupid idiots who couldn't see that. The motorcycle gang was waiting outside, and some of the band were concerned that they might take physical action against us if we didn't remove our colors. I didn't care. I was adamant . . . no way was I taking off my Twisted Sister denim vest for these morons! I'm not sure what the rest of the band and crew ultimately did, but I walked out of the hall proudly, past the gang members, got in the tour van, and we drove off. Fuck 'em.

A few weeks later, we were backstage at a Motörhead show in London. Motörhead has always had a relationship with the Hells Angels, and as usual a bunch of them were hanging out. Jay Jay was talking to a couple of them at the bar (isn't it amazing how much nicer everyone seems with an English accent?) and took the opportunity to ask what they thought about our Twisted Sister patches.

Jay Jay turned around and showed one of the HAs his vest, to which the Angel responded, "Nice pink." Clearly, *real* bike gangs aren't threatened. Years after that meeting, Jay Jay's testicles finally dropped.

THE FINAL SHOW OF our UK *You Can't Stop Rock 'n' Roll* tour was a triumphant return to London. The last time we'd played there was at

---

* As exemplified in the movie *The Warriors* by the rivalry between the Orphans and the Warriors.

the Marquee Club, before the release of our hit singles or album. This time we would be headlining the much larger, two-thousand-seat London Lyceum . . . and the show was sold out.

Throughout the tour, we had done "in-stores," personal appearances promoting our album. With a top-selling record, two hit singles, three appearances on *Top of the Pops*, mega media coverage, and a sold-out show that night, was there a better place to have our final in-store than in the heart of London? Unfortunately, we didn't ask ourselves that question in advance.

Heavy metal has never been an urban music form. Thriving in suburban and rural areas, it speaks to the angst of disenfranchised teens who yearn for more out of life than their limited environment allows them. Teens in urban areas have greater access to a much wider variety of entertainment and culture. They still have angst, but it doesn't require the same sort of expression.

For this exact reason Los Angeles became the center for the eighties explosion of heavy metal. LA has always been known as a suburban city. It's spread out and residential, not traditionally city-like at all. Yet, it still is a city, a cultural center, and has the music industry firmly entrenched within. Now, driving a car is the first true expression of every suburban or rural kid's young adulthood. There is no more independent feeling for a young man or woman than cruising and listening to your music. This is one great experience urban teens rarely have . . . unless you're from Los Angeles. You need a car to survive in Los Angeles, and heavy metal thrives in cars.

Heavy metal concerts in urban areas succeed because they are the epicenters of surrounding suburban areas. Metal fans in a fifty-mile radius will travel to an urban concert venue to see a favorite band. If only the same held true for in-stores.

Twisted Sister arrived at the Virgin Records store in London and discreetly slipped in through the back door, to avoid being mobbed by the fans we knew would be waiting outside. We'd done this many times before. As we entered, we heard the strains of our new album playing from inside. That was part of the deal. While you were there, your new music would be played on a loop, to expose people to the record and encourage them to purchase it. Some artists will only sign their new product, but Twisted Sister made it a rule to sign pretty much anything a fan brought.*

Before we could even enter the main floor for the appearance, Artie Fufkin from Polymer Records intercepted us. Actually, it was the label representative from Atlantic, but he was doing his best Artie Fufkin from *Spinal Tap*, apologizing endlessly for the debacle we were about to walk into.

Only *one fan* was waiting to meet us! A few other people meandered around the store looking at records, but they obviously had no idea who we were, or what the hell we were doing there. To make matters even worse, that one fan had an *insane* amount of Twisted Sister material for us to sign. Nigel had brought (of course I remember his name, I wrote it like a hundred times!) every record— self-released, indie-released, and major-label-released—plus count- less magazine and promotional photos for us to sign. This guy was hard-core!

As we signed—for what seemed like an eternity—every item this fan had brought, I picked up a definite negative vibe from the people working in the store. This shop was no friend to heavy metal or Twisted Sister. If anything, they were obvious about their disdain for our music. The store put up no signage regarding our coming appearance, and when we investigated further, we found out it had done virtually no advertising at all. Why the hell did they even book the in-store in the first place?

When we finally finished the humiliating appearance, we exited the building the same way we'd come in. Before the last of us had physically left the room, I heard the sound of our record being liter- ally ripped off the player, midsong, the stylus dragging across the grooves of the record. Those arrogant bastards!

That night, Twisted Sister played to more than two thousand screaming fans in our triumphant return to London, cementing our position as contenders in the UK metal scene. Our victorious per-

---

* The strangest things I ever signed were plastic fetuses. At a festival, an "anti- choice" group was handing them out to show people the horror of abortion. I was doing a signing there, and fans were waiting on line to have me sign them. Weird. Of course I signed them. They weren't *actual* fetuses.

formance wiped away virtually any memory of our embarrassing appearance at the record store that afternoon. Virtually . . .

A few days later, my hair pulled back and wearing a baseball cap, I wandered into the record shop, alone and unnoticed, and set off a stink bomb! PAMF!

28

welcome to the real world

Recording contracts are not the "band-friendly," dream-come-true documents you might think they are. While the label *is* taking an investment risk, the repayment of the money laid out on behalf of the band can most closely be compared to repaying a loan shark. Unless you really, *really* break through, you could be paying the vig on that investment forever. Which is pretty much what happened to Twisted Sister.

I've already told of my love, respect, and appreciation for Phil Carson, the man who made it happen for my band, but that doesn't mean he didn't sign us to a draconian record deal. Our contract ranks up there with some of the worst, but we were not duped or lied to by Phil. We knew full well what we were getting into. With our choices being zero or something, we signed on the dotted line and were damn happy to do it. This is just the reality of the business.

So what was our record deal like? Well, back in the eighties, a *great* record deal could get a new band twelve to fifteen "points." A *point* is a deceptive way of saying "percent." So, a great deal would get the band 12 to 15 percent of the net profit from sales. Of course, out of that percentage would come repayment of *all* recording costs, tour support, and video production. The record company's economic responsibilities (besides laying out the money) are marketing, pressing up the records, and distributing them. To recap: the record company would take 85–88 percent of the net profit and the costs of recording, touring, and video came out of the band's percentage. Some deal, huh?

Did I mention that 10 percent of all sales were deducted by the record company for "free goods"? This suggested that on a platinum-selling record they would *give away* one hundred thousand records. Really? The company also took another 10 percent for "breakage." This deduction was instituted when LPs were made out of an almost slatelike substance and could shatter like plates if not handled properly. By the sixties (maybe even fifties) this problem had been completely alleviated by producing records on flexible, virtually unbreakable vinyl. Yet still the 10 percent deduction for breakage remained. Add to that the 15 percent and 25 percent packaging deductions for cassettes and CDs, respectively. Are you doing the math?

I said that Twisted Sister signed a sucky deal, right? Well, we got only eight points, and all above-listed expenses came out of our share. *That's 8 percent of the retail cost of the album.* With some of our producers taking two of our points (the label gave the producer any additional points) from record one—meaning *before* we paid back our debt—all the other deductions were taken off the top to pay back the money we owed. When all was said and done, we were averaging about *forty-six cents* per unit sold. And don't get me started on how they ripped off my writing royalties.*

I want to reiterate, this is not unusual. Most bands start out with these kinds of crummy deals. So we gladly signed. The only way to rise above this is to be successful long enough to demand a contract renegotiation. That's why you have heard of artists such as Michael Jackson, AC/DC, and Metallica receiving $2 or $3 *per album sold.* Once you get signed, every band assumes their career will have that very arc, yet sadly few do.

As I said earlier, MTV was becoming a force to be reckoned with, and Phil Carson knew it. In continued support for his up-and-

---

* All labels would only agree to pay the band songwriters three quarters of the statutory rate (union-defined royalties). They would give the writer a choice of signing a waiver giving up his or her right to the full royalty or they wouldn't sign the band.

coming baby band, Phil got Atlantic to come up with a few thousand dollars for us to make a video for our next single, "You Can't Stop Rock 'n' Roll." Fully recoupable against our royalties, of course. I've often thought, why didn't we shoot a video for our UK hits "I Am (I'm Me)" or "The Kids Are Back"? Our chart-topping peers in Great Britain were starting to make major inroads into the US market with *their* hit songs. The American arm of each of their labels was using the energy and positive press of the bands' success in England to launch the same records Stateside. Wouldn't Atlantic Records US be doing the same thing for Twisted Sister?

Phil Carson knew how little support we were going to get in our homeland. He had put his reputation on the line to get us signed internationally in the first place. I don't think he had much hope for his detractors' helping him succeed. So Phil armed us with a video for the less commercial, much heavier song, knowing it would better connect with our core audience.

Now generally, a lot of the decision making for this album was taken completely out of our hands. The producer, the album-cover art (loved the "metal TS," hated the cover colors and typeface), and now the video director were chosen by Phil Carson. Oh, we were shown the choices for tacit approval, but there wasn't anything we could do about them. "This is the producer I want you to use. What do you think?" or "This is the album-cover art. How do you like it?" Not much wiggle room in those questions. They were rhetorical at best. This said, we were just happy to have an album to be produced and cover art for; we weren't even thinking about making choices.

Our video director was Arthur Ellis for Limelight Films. He had just done "The Last in Line" video for Ronnie James Dio and it was pretty cool. We sat with Arthur and he laid out his idea. Our music video had a story line about the Taste Squad, an organization whose sole purpose was to monitor and track the activities of Twisted Sister. Ultimately, the band's nemesis would be "converted" to heavy metal and the ways of the band.

With no idea as to what constituted a "rock video," we ran with Arthur's idea. He seemed to get our overall attitude. The video showed us both with and without makeup, which we liked, and it had a sense of humor. While Twisted was serious as cancer about what we were doing, we definitely saw the humor in it. I mean, we were a bunch of badasses wearing women's makeup! *Self-deprecation* is my middle name.

The shoot was an education to a world I knew nothing about, but the possibilities were not lost on me. This new medium allowed music to be communicated with a visual component, something the band and I had always embraced. The big difference was that we as a band could only present ourselves in one city or town, and for one limited audience, at a time. With a rock video, your musical presentation could potentially reach millions at a shot (the operative word being *potentially*). This was exciting. Arthur Ellis taught me that the visual element for a song didn't have to be exclusively traditional performing. You could do a lot with this medium.

THERE WAS A MOMENT during the shoot, where my entire band's lives could have been dramatically changed for the worst had things gone differently. At the beginning of the "You Can't Stop Rock 'n' Roll" video, the band races out of an empty lot in a van, followed by the Taste Squad. Nothing crazy speedwise, but as I drove the van during one of the takes, with the entire band on board, it bottomed out, hit a curb, and ripped the gas tank open! We didn't realize what had happened until the van stalled a couple of blocks away, out of gas, but it would have taken only a small spark to ignite that ruptured tank. We thought we might get some press from out near catastrophe, but not one press outlet was interested since no one was actually hurt. Hey, "if it bleeds, it leads."

With the album done and released, two hit singles, a sold-out tour, and now a video in the can, it was time for the band and me to head home. We had been gone almost five months . . . and I'd missed *more than half* of my son Jesse's life.

THE THING I REMEMBER most about Twisted Sister's triumphant return to the States was the confused look on my eight-month-old son's face when he saw me. He had no idea who I was. I'd left when he was three and a half months old and returned almost five months later, having had no contact with him whatsoever.

I didn't expect much from him as he stood there (he was standing?!) in his adorable khaki outfit, all tanned and his hair (he had hair?!) bleached blond from spending so much time in Florida, with his mom. I didn't allow myself to feel hurt by my son's lack of reaction. This was the life I had chosen; what did I think would happen? I just scooped Jesse up in my arms and hugged and kissed him until he got used to me. The kid loved (and still does love) the Muppets. I must have looked like a real-life Sweetums (one of the biggest, hairiest Muppets).

My choice of employment isn't the only job in the world that requires a parent to be away from home for long periods. The only thing you can do is be the best father you possibly can when you are home. Two things I have no doubt my kids always knew: I'd only be away as long as I absolutely had to . . . and I would always come back. I love being a dad.

WE ALL START OUT thinking we live in a yes-or-no world, everything black and white, good and bad, right and wrong. Vanilla or chocolate? Ah, the innocence.

As we get older, the reality of life begins to hit us. One is rarely confronted with easy choices.

⊰ DEE LIFE LESSON ⊱
Life is shades of gray, and our goal becomes trying to pick
the lightest shade possible, and hope for the best.

Sad, really. We start out with such conviction and strong beliefs, and life slowly beats us down and forces us to accept and compromise for the so-called greater good.

The summer of 1983 I was forced to make one of those adult choices. *I still feel bad about it today.*

＊　　＊　　＊

WHILE THE BAND HAD finally broken into the big league and accomplished an incredible amount in the UK, it quickly became apparent we would get no help from our record label at home. While the New York office had some "friendlies," such as Jason Flom, our label president was less than happy (understatement) to have our band on the Atlantic Records roster. To compare the two, Phil Carson and the UK branch couldn't do enough for us. *Atlantic Records US made us a poster.* Seriously. They made a poster, announcing the album's availability, to be hung in stores. Other than that, the only evidence we had that the label gave any thought to our record or band at all was that the back-cover photo on the album was changed. Atlantic's US president demanded it, saying, "What the hell are we doing, advertising dentistry!?" He wasn't a fan of my "wide-mouthed, showing all my teeth" pose—you know, the one I became famous for? So, the back-cover photo was changed, as well as the color of the US-released album cover (to black) and the typeface as well (both for the better).

What wasn't the record company doing for us? Any kind of promotion at all and no tour support (money advanced to offset the costs of a new band's touring). Our video was submitted to MTV, but at that time most record labels still didn't take the "music television" network seriously.

Without strong label support, a new band is left completely to their own devices to finance any performances to promote themselves and the record. This meant touring conditions would be rough at best. Not to whine and moan—Twisted Sister was always prepared to do what it had to—but with other new bands out there being fully supported by their labels, it sucked to have a sometimes daily reminder of just how little your label cared.

We'd been home for a several weeks when our manager called us all into his office for a "career meeting." We had these from time to time, but only when a "dinner with the band" or "everyone listen up" quickie meeting in a gig's dressing room wouldn't do. We all sat and listened as Mark Puma told us that while we had done some amazing work in Great Britain, we had hit a wall in the United States. Of course, the tristate area fans were gobbling up the album, but without the support of the label, our chances were slim to none of doing something with our record in the States. The band's spirit completely deflated.

Mark Puma continued, informing us there was *one* ray of hope. We had been offered a tour in the United States—the band was instantly reinvigorated—but there was a problem. Uh-oh. The tour was with Blackfoot (a Southern rock band, looking to go more mainstream, hard rock) . . . *and Krapus.** With that utterance, the entire band slowly turned and looked at me.

WHILE WE HAD BEEN on tour in the UK, I'd received a message to call home. I was assured Jesse and Suzette were fine, but I needed to call immediately.

Suzette didn't just make costumes for Twisted Sister. Another band who had hired her were Swiss heavy-metal rockers Krapus. Being half-Swiss, I actually liked Krapus and was proud of a metal band from my mother's native land. That pride was about to disappear.

Upon hiring Suzette, Krapus had paid her the traditional half of the total cost down (for materials), the other half due upon delivery. While I was away, Suzette agreed to meet with Krapus and deliver some of the costumes she had finished. She showed them the pieces she'd made and they loved her work. Naturally, Suzette asked for the balance of the money, $1,500. Krapus's towering, six-foot-five-inch, 275-pound tour manager tells my wife that they're not going to pay her. Suzette immediately tells him she wants the costumes back. With Krapus looking on, he steps up to my five-foot-three-inch, 110-pound wife, holding my five-month-old baby boy, and tells her they aren't giving them back, they aren't paying her any more money, and if she doesn't send them the remaining costume pieces she's working on, they are going to have her "taken care of." *What the fuck!?*

---

* That's not their actual name, but I won't give them the pleasure of having their actual name in my book. Some of you will know exactly whom I'm talking about.

I was on a pay phone, in England, hearing this story and losing my friggin' mind. These guys threatened my wife—with my son in her arms—ripped her off, and I could do absolutely nothing. However, other people *could* do something.

My wife's godfather and uncle, Hugh MacIntosh (RIP), was at that time the enforcer for the Persico crime family. "Hughie Apples" was a real-deal, no-bullshit mob hit man, and he didn't deal in idle threats. Google him. "The Icepick" fucked people up. When Suzette's family got wind of what had happened, *the call* was made to have Krapus and their management taken care of . . . *for real*. But Suzette wouldn't have it.

"You don't kill people for fifteen hundred dollars," she told her family. (They did in Uncle Mac's world!) My wife is a too kind, and benevolent woman. Krapus, you have no idea how close you came to buying the farm . . . or should I say, the bottom of a lake. Be careful whom you rip off.

SO NOW THE CHOICE was mine. Would I stand strong for my wife's honor and say, " 'Fuck that! I'm not touring with the assholes who threatened my wife, with my son in her arms!" It would effectively kill my band's chances of promoting our record and pull the plug on what we had all worked on for over seven years. Or, would I swallow my pride, opt for the big picture—the greater good—and agree to grab on to the one vine left for the band to swing out of that suffocating jungle of defeat. (How's that for a metaphor?)

On the one hand, it was nice of the guys to leave the decision up to me—they would back whatever I chose. On the other hand, *they left the fucking decision up to me!* No one said "Don't do it." "We wouldn't do it if the same thing happened to us." "Don't worry, Dee, something else will come along; the band will survive." No. They just looked at me with puppy-dog eyes (they hate it when I say that), and said, "It's up to you, Dee." And I caved.

As I agreed to do the tour, in my mind I was plotting, *Okay. When I see Krapus and their piece-of-shit tour manager, I can get even with those fucks for the way they treated Suzette. PAMF!* That's when my manager added a caveat.

Krapi's (that's the possessive plural for *Krapus)* management had anticipated my plan and stipulated that if I did *anything* to their band in retaliation, Twisted Sister would immediately be kicked off the tour. To that our booking agency had added that Twisted Sister would be blackballed from any future tours, that they would cease to represent us and that no other agency would take on a band that beats up the bands they tour with. Curses . . . foiled again!

I went home and broke the news to Suzette, who could not have been more disappointed in me. She could not understand or accept why I was doing the tour. I felt like shit and still do. Though years later, when our fame and notoriety surpassed Krapi's, I would have them banned and dropped from concert bills and refuse to play them on my international radio show, *The House of Hair* (effectively killing a prime source of airplay for their music), it still is not enough to make me feel I got even with them for what they did. I let my best friend down. That can't be changed. *I'm sorry, Suzette.*

THE BLACKFOOT TOUR WAS "bargain basement." With no financial support from the record label, Twisted Sister traveled in a motor home (as opposed to the tour buses Blackfoot and Krapus traveled on), which quickly turned to two Ugly Duckling rent-a-cars* when the motor home's engine blew up in the middle of nowhere in the Southwest. We stayed, three to a room, in the cheapest fleabag motels we could book and lived off a *$7-a-day* allowance.

I became an expert at finding buffets for the band. Mendoza, our resident wheelman, would drive and I'd ride shotgun with all of my senses on high alert, barking out seemingly nonsensical directions, which would ultimately lead to the promised land . . . EAT, SIT 'N' GULP! ALL-U-CAN-EAT BUFFET! (or the like). I got so good at nursing my daily pittance, at the end of the week I'd have money left over for toiletries and gifts to bring home.

---

* Ugly Duckling rent-a-cars are the cheapest rental cars you can get because they only rent used cars. There is nothing luxurious about the beaters you rent. They truly live up to their name.

∗   ∗   ∗

FROM THE MOMENT WE played Salt Lake City, our first non–East Coast stop in America, I knew this axiom would always hold true:

⯇ DEE LIFE LESSON ⯈

Great heavy metal fans are fans of great heavy metal,
no matter where they are from.

It's always held true. Along the way, some people have warned me that Twisted Sister wouldn't be as successful in non-English-speaking countries, believing that all of our success in concert stemmed from my ability to verbally interact with and incite a crowd. Not only is that a total pile of jealousy-driven bullshit, but Twisted Sister has been able to win over virtually any crowd—no matter what language they speak. As long as they want to rock, we can rock 'em!

City after city, Twisted Sister—the opening band on a three-band bill—were taking the show. Blackfoot were a great Southern rock band with a couple of big songs, but they were on their way out. Krapus were a typical, AC/DC-esque, also-ran metal band, who understandably never did much in the United States. Twisted Sister were pure aggression, with everything to lose. We were the band to beat.

Having to see Krapus and their tour manager backstage and not say or do anything was tough. Being at the hothead stage of my career, and coming off incendiary live performances each night, I was pretty much terminally angry. With great effort I would walk past PU or the Krapus band members without so much as a hostile glance at them. But those were the rules for being on the tour, and I was keeping my eye on the prize.

That wasn't good enough for Krapi's asshole American-tour manager. He decided to try to push my buttons and make me snap. That was one way of stopping Twisted Sister from making his band of Lilliputians look bad every night! One night, as I walked offstage, their tour manager was waiting for me with a big smile offered me a towel and said, "Great show, Dee!" What the fuck!? Was he kidding?! Without a word I walked past him and went to the dressing room. *The fucking asshole!* The next night, he did the same thing . . . and the night after that . . . and the night after that. Each occasion I did the same thing: bit my tongue, refused to take the bait, and walked past the piece of shit. I knew what he was up to.

After about a week of this, I got a call from my manager. Puma had received a call from our agent saying he was getting reports that I was being rude to Krapus. *What!?* Not being able to get me to break, their tour manager was using our nightly *lack of exchange* to try to get the band and me tossed off the bill! That was it! I didn't give a shit if we lost the tour! It was bad enough that I had to endure being around them each night without confronting them; now they wanted me to smile and be nice! Fuck that!

Quickly calming me down, Joe Gerber (who I know would have had my back in a second if I ever threw down with Krapus) decided he would take one for the team and be friendly to the tour manager and Krapus, intercepting him each night before he got to me. We made it through the rest of the tour without any further problems.

TWISTED SISTER BECAME AN international sensation; Krapus an also-ran. My career continues to thrive; Krapus is a dime-a-dance shadow of their limited past. Life is filled with shades-of-gray decisions that move you forward on your path to ultimate success, and the memory of most of those choices fades with the passing years. But not that one. Accepting that tour with Krapus, and never truly avenging the way they treated my wife, still haunts me and will until the day I die. *I should never have done it.*

❧ 29 ❧

welcome to the promised land

By the summer of 1983, Twisted Sister had been fighting the good fight for glitter-rock-infused heavy metal for almost seven and a half years. Fighting for our right to rock the way we wanted to rock, at times we felt we were up against insurmountable odds. Discovering the burgeoning new wave of British heavy metal certainly gave us hope, a much-needed boost, and reason to keep believing, but it was still a struggle.

In August, the band and I drove through the heat of the night to Los Angeles, for the first time. With the sun coming up behind us, coming out of the Mojave Desert and the San Gabriel Mountains, we were at last in range to tune in the LA radio station KMET and discovered Iron Maiden's "Flight of Icarus" playing. We could not believe it! We had heard that heavy metal was big in Los Angeles and KMET had garnered the nickname K-Metal, but we never imagined it would be like this. Metal on the radio in the morning? We had reached the promised land!

We pulled into West Hollywood to find a major metropolis that had completely embraced heavy metal. It was actually in style! Heavy music and headbangers had *never* experienced this before; our music was being accepted on a cultural level. Everywhere I looked, I saw evidence of this acceptance. Kids walking down the street were imitating the style of dress of their rock heroes, more often than not that of David Lee Roth of Van Halen. And the women? Metal had never been that big with the female rock audience, but they, too, had found the style and attitude in it, particularly from Pat Benatar. Pat wasn't metal, but she definitely rocked and had attitude. The girls were totally hooking into that. But something didn't feel quite right.

As I read the local papers, saw the billboards and marquees, and simply met the metal fans in LA, it became clear they were more into the look and attitude of heavy metal than the music. They were clearly more interested in stylized heavy-metal bands and less so in the traditional "denim and leather." Mainstay Sunset Strip clubs such as Gazzarri's openly advertised bands with "only the best-looking guys" to entice the local rock chicks. Where the girls go, the boys follow. Much of the LA metal scene was hollow—like the facades of Hollywood sets—mostly about style and not substance.

This is not to say there were no real metalheads or metal bands in Los Angeles. Slayer—one of heavy metal's Big Four—were from Huntington Park, just outside LA, but I could see what was fueling the Sunset Strip scene . . . and it wasn't the heaviness of the music.

Los Angeles was set to brand its own specific form of heavy metal, and Twisted Sister was a perfect fit for the LA metal scene at that time. We were a metal band first and foremost, but stylized with our extreme makeup and costumes. Eddie and Jay Jay certainly had female appeal, and I was just . . . Dee. While I most definitely fell short in the "pretty boy" department, I was an over-the-top wild man, and the LA metal scene loved that. But for how long?

Usually when we hit the stage as the opener on a three-band bill, the venue would be maybe half to two-thirds full. Not in LA. When we took the stage at the Hollywood Palladium that night, the place was wall-to-wall. While there was interest in Krapus, the buzz on Twisted Sister was huge. Metal fans out there had been hearing about us long before our *You Can't Stop Rock 'n' Roll* or even *Under the Blade* albums had been released. Word of the East Coast phenomenon, the makeup-wearing heavy metal band, had reached the Left Coast when we were still in the bars.

We did our usual thing (including verbally tearing apart an arrogant LA elitist in the VIP balcony who deliberately dumped her ashtray on the crowd below), and after the show we got our first exposure to the whole *Hollywood thing.* Local notables all wanted to meet the band, and even a fellow up-and-comer from a band we'd heard about called Mötley Crüe, came back, excited to meet us. I remember Vince Neil asking me if his girlfriend "da jour" could come back and take a picture with me ("She's a big fan!").

The big surprise was when Atlantic Records' West Coast senior VP, Paul Cooper, came backstage to meet us. Resplendent in an expensive suit, manicured, tanned, coiffed, and walking with an elegant-looking cane, he told us how much he enjoyed the show. Stunned that any executive from Atlantic Records US had come to see us period (hadn't he got the memo?), I expressed my appreciation, especially considering this was clearly not his cup of tea.

That upset him. "Not my cup of tea? My cup of tea is making money. Your band is going to make this label a lot of money. *You're my cup of tea.*"

I liked this guy! To have an Atlantic Records exec—who wasn't Phil Carson—say that meant the world to us. And seeing firsthand the heavy metal explosion that was happening in Los Angeles gave us incredible hope. After missing the boat in 1979 (when Eddie had his seizure and new wave took hold), it looked as if, four years later, the music scene was finally coming back around. Twisted Sister was going to have a real chance.

IN SEPTEMBER OF '83, my childhood dreams of being a rich, famous rock 'n' roll star started to become a reality. I already had a degree of fame and was *technically* a rock 'n' roll star (at least to some people), but the rich part had definitely been eluding me. With the signing of Twisted Sister to Atlantic Records came two other economic pieces to every band's rock 'n' roll pie: a merchandising deal and a music-publishing deal. While Twisted Sister shared the monetary signing advance and proceeds from merchandise sales, that wouldn't be the case with the songwriting/publishing advance.

Since many hit songs are not written by the band or the artist performing them, the songwriters get an independent royalty (free of all record company recoupment) per song, per record sold. As the band's sole songwriter, *all* of the publishing money and the five-figure advance coming with it from the publishing deal was mine. While some bands take the all-for-one, one-for-all approach to royalties and share them equally (Black Sabbath, Van Halen, etc.), I didn't consider sharing the wealth with my bandmates for a second (other than the 15 percent of my publishing royalties that I had given Jay Jay). I was finally receiving compensation for all my hard work and sacrifice.

It should be noted, an advance is just that: money given against your share of future earnings. While it's a great thing to get, it's only *your own money* being given to you ahead of time. Of course, the company is taking the risk that you may not sell enough to pay it back, but they get a larger percentage of the total receipts for extending you this courtesy. Few young artists can resist the offer of an advance. It's usually the first time you ever see a sizable amount of money in your career.

Upon returning home from the Blackfoot tour, I had my first chance to do something with the publishing advance for the *You Can't Stop Rock 'n' Roll* album. I had already had the immense pleasure of depositing said check into my bank account. With my son's first birthday approaching, the fact that I had now been away for more than seven months of his life was not lost on me. Not to mention, my young wife had been left to raise him on her own. At last I was in the position to start to making good on the promise of being a rock star. That fall we bought our first house and a brand-new car.

After being mostly in the red my entire adult life, it felt great to walk into a place and tell them what I wanted and how I wanted it, but it was the start down a slippery slope.

IN AUGUST OF 1983, Twisted Sister was booked to play the legendary Monsters of Rock Festival, Castle Donington, in the UK. Not only was this the premier heavy metal event for a band like ours to play, but after the amazing response we'd had with our album and singles earlier in the year, Twisted Sister's playing Donington would be a triumphant return to Great Britain.

The bill spoke volumes about how far we'd come. It was the original Whitesnake (with Jon Lord, Ian Paice, and Cozy Powell), Meat Loaf (his career was dead at that time in the United States, but in Europe he was still a viable *heavy metal* act—go figure), ZZ Top, Twisted Sister, Dio, and Diamond Head. Just nine months earlier, we were going to open for Diamond Head, and to be higher on the bill than a legend and hero such as Ronnie James Dio was just amazing.

The Castle Donington audience were of the same ilk as the Reading crowd, expressing their dissatisfaction—or whatever—by throwing things at the bands, crews, metal-DJ/host Tommy Vance (who wore a lacrosse helmet for protection when he was onstage)— pretty much anything that moved. We were sure that our major success in the UK would keep the "shite" throwing to a minimum, but when we hit the stage, it was worse than Reading. It was raining garbage!

We couldn't believe it! The band and I had every reason to believe that the headbangers in the UK liked us. But let's do the math. Say we were beloved; what would you say is a great percentage of a festival audience to like us? Ninety percent? Surely even the Beatles couldn't expect a much greater number than that. Which means, in a crowd of over forty thousand people . . . four thousand didn't like the band. Do you have any idea how much stuff four thousand people can throw? I do. It was off the hook! So much garbage and food and so many liter bottles—filled with everything from dirt to piss—were descending onto the stage while Twisted Sister was on, some of the guys in the band wanted to walk off.

In an ultimate act of futility, the intrepid Joe Gerber jumped off the stage into the front section of the audience and began running through the crowd, punching the people throwing things in the face! I asked him later what he could possibly have hoped to accomplish against so many aggressors, to which Joe responded, "Hey—that section stopped throwing things!" I love that guy.

No way were we walking off the stage. It would have meant admitting defeat, and Twisted would never have lived it down. Instead, I resorted to my effective Reading Festival rap and challenged the entire crowd to a fight. By that time, everyone had heard about my now legendary Reading ploy and weren't backing me as they had at Reading. They threw even more stuff. Thinking quickly, I pulled out an old nugget I'd used in the tristate clubs on occasion, albeit on a much smaller scale.

"How many friends of Twisted Sister do we have here?!" I bellowed.

Ninety percent of the crowd went wild.

"Well, we're stuck on this stage and some assholes out there are throwing stuff at us, and there's nothing we can do about it!"

Our fans heartily booed the "throwers."

"All I know is, if we were out there and somebody was throwing shit at you, we'd kick their ass!"

The crowd roared.

"But we're not out there . . . you are! So if you see somebody throwing stuff at us . . . kick their ass! And if they're too big to beat up on your own, get a bunch of your friends, pull 'em to the ground, and kick the fucking piss out of them!"

The crowd went absolutely insane.

We launched into the next song with a vengeance. As Twisted Sister played, fights erupted throughout the massive crowd. At one point, a large fire started blazing for some reason. It was out of control! But nothing further was thrown.

The rest of our set went incredibly well, with the Donington metalheads rocking Twisted Sister–style. When we got to the big audience-participation part of "It's Only Rock 'n' Roll," after getting the crowd to throw their fists in the air and scream, "I like it!" . . . I decided to up the ante.

"This time when I say 'It's only rock 'n' roll,' I want you to scream 'I like it' . . . and jump!"

The crowd laughed.

"I'm not kidding!" I said as if I'd read their minds. *"I know not everyone will have the balls to do it. Some of you are worried someone might laugh at you! Poor babies!"*

The crowd laughed, cheered, and jeered.

"The true sick muthafucking friends of Twisted Sister will jump! Are you ready to jump, SMFs!?"

The crowd were beside themselves with excitement.

"Then let's do it! 'I know it's only rock 'n' roll, but—' "

Allow me to tell you what happened next by quoting the words of the writer from *NME* (*New Musical Express*) who reviewed our set at the festival. *NME* is no friend of heavy metal—they pretty much hate it all. After brutally tearing Twisted Sister's set apart in her review, the writer said of the last moments of "It's Only Rock 'n' Roll," "I have to admit, seeing 40,000 punters, leaping into the air in unison, *is a sight and memory I will take to my grave.*"

It *was* incredible. Too bad they were all so drunk the entire crowd fell over like dominoes!

WITH THE FALL AND winter approaching, the band had a lot more work to do. On the plus side, Twisted Sister was selling a steady three thousand records a week—not too shabby for a band with no record company support. Every Monday, during the weekly Atlantic Records telephone conference with all of the national reps, the New York office was forced to hear tales of how Twisted Sister had come into some region and totally dominated—our record was flying off the shelves. While it was nice knowing how much that had to annoy the powers that be, it changed nothing for us as far as support from Atlantic went. We were still on the road, completely on our own.

Meanwhile, Twisted Sister was starting to get noticed on MTV. Not that they were playing our video all that much, but they did use a piece of it in a heavily played promotional clip for the network, and people were noticing. Outside of the tristate area I kept hearing, "Hey, you're that guy from the MTV commercial!"

MTV struck gold with heavy metal. The very idea of music television was to add a visual element to the already-existing musical one. Many hugely successful recording artists had nothing to offer on that front. The first song played on MTV, "Video Killed the Radio Star" by the Buggles, was prophetic to say the least. When people got a good look at artists such as Joe Jackson and Supertramp, their careers were over. There was a reason Joe Jackson's biggest record had his shoes on the cover . . . and it wasn't just the album title. MTV needed bands and artists with a visual element, and they readily found it in heavy metal. For metal bands, giving a compelling, live visual performance had always been a priority, and the imagery of much of the music lent itself to rock video. MTV's embracing of heavy metal as a staple of their video playlist was key to the major breakthrough eventually experienced by the coming wave of bands, and what later became known as "hair metal."

OUR FALL RUN OF dates paired us up with Queensrÿche, fresh out of their rehearsal space, as our opening band. We didn't know much about them, other than that they had a pretty cool four-song EP out on a major label and were getting some radio play and MTV rotation. When Twisted arrived in our beat-up van at the venue in Kansas City for our first show together, we pulled alongside a shiny, new tour bus. Whose the hell was that? Once we got inside, we found out.

Queensrÿche was one of those bands whose record company support was the exact opposite of ours. Their label, EMI, was giving them everything they needed to make sure they succeeded. To quote their then manager, "We told the label if you want them to be rock stars, you have to treat them like rock stars." Amen. If only someone had told our label the same. Not only did this band, fresh out of their Seattle basement, doing their *third* live show that night, have a tour bus, they had new equipment, stayed in nice hotels, and each had a credit card just in case he needed anything! Try as we wanted to hate them, we couldn't. They were all cool, unpretentious guys who had drawn the long straw when it came to record companies. It wasn't their fault our label sucked.

That night, we took Queensrÿche to school. Not intentionally; it's just what Twisted Sister does. You have no idea how many bands and front men stand on the side of the stage, or out by the soundboard, studying the band and me (right, Jon Bon Jovi?), trying to figure out the secret of how we did what we did (and still do).

Queensrÿche opened the show in Kansas City that night, looking and sounding great. They were well rehearsed, dressed, equipped, and staged and went through their set with mechanical precision. Then Twisted Sister went on. During our usual chaotic sixty-minute set, pandemonium ensued. Two women climbed onstage and had a spontaneous "strip-off" to one of our songs, and a guy in the audience I'd verbally been tearing to shreds decided he wanted a piece of me. He climbed onto the stage to attack me, and I one-punched him back into the crowd. Through it all, Queensrÿche stood side-stage, watching the whole thing, their mouths agape.

As Twisted left the stage at the end of our show, guitarist Chris DeGarmo grabbed me. "Is it like that every night?!"

"Only the good ones," I said, and ran off.

All in all, the Twisted Sister/Queensrÿche tour went well. Some shows were wetter than others (the sprinkler system went off in the packed club during our set in Chicago), and rumor has it, the Queenrÿche boys were a bit disenchanted with some of the more clublike venues they were playing (poor babies), but Twisted Sister was kicking ass and selling records.

In November, during the final weeks of our tour with Queensrÿche, our manager got *the call*. The president of Atlantic Records in the US wanted to meet with the band.

⚜ 30 ⚜

that's a horse of a different color

I t came as no surprise to us that our record continued to sell at a steady pace. Now approaching 150,000 units in the United States alone—*with no record company support*—Twisted Sister's commercial value could no longer be denied. We were becoming a force to be reckoned with.

As we headed into New York City for our big meeting with the all-powerful Oz—I mean, president of Atlantic Records—we were sure he was going to tell us the label was ready to fully get behind our *You Can't Stop Rock 'n' Roll* album. Every band we had shared both the top of the charts and *Top of the Pops* with in Great Britain were having major hits in the United States with their UK releases. It was our turn to shine.

We arrived at Atlantic Records to find a very different label from the one we had been so unwelcome at before. As we walked into the lobby, a placard said WELCOME ATLANTIC RECORDS RECORD-ING ARTISTS TWISTED SISTER! with the band's picture on it. We were immediately ushered inside, toured the Twisted Sister–poster-adorned office complex and were warmly greeted by every person in the place. Everyone seemed to be a Twisted Sister fan and had a story to tell about how he or she had always championed the band. It was completely confusing. When we were finally brought in to meet the president of the label, we couldn't believe it. Was this the same guy who had personally rejected our band multiple times, threatened to fire Jason Flom if he mentioned our name, and fought to have Phil Carson not sign us? He was so welcoming and nice!

Once all the glad-handing was done, Mr. President got down to business. He told us that Twisted Sister were going to be huge. We'd proven ourselves in the UK and had continued to sell—on our own—in the United States. Now it was time to push the button and make things happen.

At last! Twisted Sister and our *You Can't Stop Rock 'n' Roll* album were finally going to get the support and attention we deserved!

The president's next words were career-changing on so many levels, both good and bad: "But let's not throw good money after bad. It's time to focus on a new record."

What?! A *new* record? We hadn't even scratched the surface of this album's potential. We had two hit singles in Great Britain with *You Can't Stop Rock 'n' Roll*; they could be hits in America! While it was amazing to hear him say that Atlantic Records would "push the button" and make us real stars, why not maximize the financial potential of the record they'd already paid for?

I'll tell you why.

Imagine *you* were the president of Atlantic Records. You fought tooth and nail, for years, to keep Twisted Sister off your label. You personally rejected the band, threatened people's jobs for even mentioning their name, and had been shut down and overridden by a fellow executive, in front of your peers, over this band and this very album. Now, the band and album you did *nothing* to support and *everything* to stop had survived and were threatening to break through, leaving you as their sole naysayer. Not an enviable position to be in, was it?

By playing the "let's not throw good money after bad" card, Mr. President had shown a change of heart and real support for the band, while shutting down the offending record. This allowed him to distance himself from the album and appear to be the giving god, shining his grace on the new Twisted Sister record . . . which he will make sure everyone knows he was very much a part of. Nice move, asshole.

If our label president had done the right thing (instead of the self-protective thing), *You Can't Stop Rock 'n' Roll* could have been a platinum or multiplatinum album (instead of eventually going gold years later), putting Twisted Sister at the forefront of the new metal movement in the United States and setting a strong foundation for a much-longer, hit-filled, and illustrious career. Instead, we were set to be a *part* of the initial wave of heavy metal and hair bands, with a much shorter life expectancy.

We left the Atlantic offices that day pumped by the amazing new support we were getting from the label, but disappointed our current record would not be given the chance to shine and do what we all knew it could. Still, the holidays were coming, and 1984 held incredible promise for the band. Big Brother was gonna be rocking to Twisted Sister.

WHEN SUZETTE WAS PREGNANT with Jesse, she would come down from time to time to see the band perform. She would tell me, when Twisted hit the stage, the baby would go crazy in her belly, kickin' and rockin'. The heavier the song, the wilder it went. Our unborn child wanted to rock just like its dad. Now, at fifteen months of age, I had been away for almost two-thirds of Jesse's life. I wanted him to see what his daddy did when he was away.

Upon returning home from our tours, the band took a victory lap of the Northeast to celebrate our major-label album and trouncing of the UK metal scene. The self-fulfilling prophecy had come true, and the "bad boys of rock 'n' roll," whom the SMFs had believed so strongly in, had made it to the next level.

One of those victory shows was on December 29, 1983, at the 2002 Roller Rink—turned concert hall for the night—in Sayville, Long Island. An all-ages show, the place was wall-to-wall with thousands of teenage kids clamoring to see a band they'd heard about from their older brothers and sisters for so long and who were putting the Long Island rock scene on the map. As Twisted Sister rocked the house of nearly two thousand, it was pandemonium. But what I was most focused on was my son Jesse Blaze, standing on the side of the stage for the first time . . . and rocking out to his dad!

During the show, our eyes locked, and Jesse, with a look of determination, started to head out onto the stage to join his old man. I blanched, realizing that the band were deep into performing and oblivious of Jesse's potentially dangerous action. Luckily, he only got a couple of steps before Suzette grabbed him by the shoulder and reeled him in. I was amazed. My little more than one-year-old son understood what his dad was doing and wanted to do it with me. How cool was that?

NOT SURPRISINGLY, ATLANTIC RECORDS felt time was of the essence. They wanted to capitalize on the energy and goodwill Twisted Sister had already created before it went cold. Nothing releasing a couple of singles and videos off the *You Can't Stop Rock 'n' Roll* album wouldn't have fixed. *Oh, all right, I'll let it go.*

The first thing we needed to do was choose a producer. Our choice and his availability would decide the recording schedule, and everything else would roll out from there.

The band was asked to submit a list of producers we would like to work with, and we did. Martin Birch (Iron Maiden), Max Norman (Ozzy Osbourne), Dieter Dierks (Scorpions), Mack (Billy Squier), and more were all submitted for approval. Nowhere on our list, or even considered or thought of *in any capacity*, was the response from Atlantic Records. "How about Tom Werman?" *Who?*

Tom Werman was a former record company A&R man turned record producer out of sheer necessity. Having signed Ted Nugent, Cheap Trick, and Molly Hatchet, he subsequently "produced" their records and had been credited for taking bands that were rough around the edges and making them commercially viable.

Now, the term *producer* is very general, covering any person responsible for overseeing and delivering a record. Some producers are hands-on engineer types, who actually push the buttons on the board and technically help get the sounds, while others are musicians who contribute to the writing and construction of songs. Still others are truly old-school (remember, the recording process started out with some microphones in a room and the band playing live to tape) and just listen. Tom Werman is the latter. To quote the man himself: "I don't write, I don't create, I don't touch the board. I'll just tell you if I like it or not." He said it, I didn't.

Werman had just finished the *Shout at the Devil* record with Mötley Crüe, and it was looking as if it was going to be huge. Noting Tom Werman's work with the Crüe and the other bands he had "cleaned up" in the past, Atlantic thought Tom was the perfect choice.

We listened to the *Shout at the Devil* record and were unimpressed. The guitars and drums sounded pretty good, but overall it was not the sound we were looking for. Not heavy enough. Still, the label wanted Tom to hear us, and for the band to meet him, so Werman was flown in from LA to one of Twisted Sister's "Northeast victory-lap shows," in Washington, DC.

Arriving late, Werman came in midshow and saw Twisted do what it always did—destroy a packed house. After the show, we met and had a chance to chat. Tom seemed nice enough. Upon explaining his A&R background to me, and how he came to be a producer, I decided to ask Tom a simple question. If he were still an A&R guy, would he have signed Twisted Sister?

Werman answered me simply and directly, "No."

While I appreciated his honesty, this clearly was not the producer for our band. We didn't care for his work, and he didn't care for the band. Done and done.

A few days later, Mark Puma and I took another meeting with our label president to discuss the issue of Tom Werman and the choice for producer in general. During the discussion, I explained the kind of producer the band was looking for and why Tom Werman just wasn't the guy for us. El Presidente pressed hard for Werman, and I countered, explaining how we needed to make a true heavy record for our fans. We went back and forth on the issue for a few minutes, until exasperated, our label head exclaimed, "Exactly how many fans do you suppose you have?"

Thrown by the question and his intensity, I replied, "I don't know, 200 thousand."

"What do you want, those 200 thousand fans, or the 800,000 others that will make your next record platinum?"

Just like that, I was shut down. I didn't have a response. I wanted a platinum album. Of course, I now know the correct answer was "both." There's no reason a band can't have both their core audience and the mainstream rock fans. (Just ask Metallica.) But I was intimidated by our label president's intensity and the pressure of the whole situation. This was our shot.

So it was decided that Tom Werman would be producing Twisted Sister's next album. *That was the beginning of the end.* I know it seems crazy to say that when our biggest album and greatest success hadn't yet even happened, but I firmly believe the decision to hire Tom Werman was the start of a butterfly effect that eventually destroyed the band.

❦ 31 ❧

the ayatollah of rock and rolla

By this point in Twisted Sister's career, Suzette and I were a creative machine, always working way ahead, in anticipation of the band's next move. As I finished writing the material for Twisted Sister's next record, Suzette was already coming up with ideas for the band's next look.

The "tattered look" of the *You Can't Stop Rock 'n' Roll* tour had gone down well (and inspired many other bands) and taken a major step closer to the ultimate look for Twisted. I always had a lot of rules as to what was and wasn't acceptable for Twisted Sister costumes. Suzette would often come up with new ideas that I would reject out of hand, but slowly I would come around to her wisdom (much the same process that got me to wear more makeup).

Suzette's concept for Twisted Sister's next costumes was to take the tattered look to a whole new level. As huge fans of *Mad Max* and *The Road Warrior* (aka *Mad Max 2*) movies, Suzette saw an opportunity to introduce elements of postapocalyptic style into the outfits. Wait'll they get a load of me!

THE DEMO PROCESS FOR the next album was identical to all previous ones. The songs I'd been working on during the recording of *You Can't Stop Rock 'n' Roll*, along with two songs Eddie and I wrote (yes, Eddie had finally written some guitar riffs for me to work on) and a couple of fan favorites from the club days ("Rock 'n' Roll Saviors" and "You Know I Cry"), were rehearsed in their most basic form (intro-verse-chorus-verse-chorus), then recorded as demos. The versions of the songs were truncated because we always had so many more than we needed—only ten to twelve would be chosen for the album. We didn't want to waste time fully arranging all of them.

Once a demo was finished, we would give the tape to all the interested parties (band, crew, management, record label, and our producer), then vote for our favorite tracks. The ones with the most votes would be the songs for the record.

As a songwriter I was hitting my stride. I knew some *really* strong songs were on the new demo. Particularly, "We're Not Gonna Take It" and "I Wanna Rock."

"I Wanna Rock" was inspired by the galloping rhythm of many Iron Maiden songs. I thought if I could combine the metallic drive of a Maiden song with the anthemic feel of many of my songs, I would have a winner.

One note: When I originally wrote the song, I envisioned the "gang (chant) vocals" being sung *on* the word *rock*, as in "I wanna *rock*!" When we were working up the songs for the demo, I was explaining it to Eddie Ojeda.

"Oh, you mean like 'I wanna rock! *Rock!*'?" Eddie asked.

That was a much better idea! "Yeah," I replied, taking full credit, "like that." *Thanks, Eddie.*

I'd been sitting on the chorus for "We're Not Gonna Take It" since 1979. I knew the hook was a killer, but try as I would, I could not come up with a suitable verse and B-verse (the second, different part of a verse). I'm a *huge* fan of the English band Slade (as are many other prominent hard-rock and metal bands) and their incredible rock anthems. Most of you will know them best for the Quiet Riot smash hit "Cum On Feel the Noize" and follow-up, "Mama Weer All Crazee Now." No, Quiet Riot didn't write those songs, *Slade did.*

Slade songs are usually uniquely comprised of a hook (catchy repeated melody and lyric) for the verse, a hook for the B-verse, and a hook for . . . *the hook.* Jim Lea and Noddy Holder are amazing songwriters! "We're Not Gonna Take It" is a full-on Slade-inspired romp. *All of my anthems are.* Thank you, Noddy and Jim, for the inspiration and songwriting lessons. I couldn't have done it without you.

Credit for the crowning touch on the song has to go to my drummer, A. J. Pero. I had the idea of starting the song with a drum cadence, like in a marching band. When I asked A.J. to come up with something, he created a hell of an identifiable beat! The minute people hear those drums, they know what song it is. *More cowbell!*

Many years after I'd written the chorus to "We're Not Gonna Take It," I was riding in a van on tour with my band Widowmaker (more on them later). My guitarist Al Pitrelli was driving, and we were discussing song plagiarism. Over the years, many songs have been ripped off both unintentionally . . . and intentionally. We were running through different songs that had been "appropriated" (i.e. George Harrison's "My Sweet Lord," taken from the Chiffons' "He's So Fine," and Bon Jovi's "Who Says You Can't Go Home," borrowed from Sam Cooke's "Cupid [Draw Back Your Bow]") when Al says, "And, of course, 'We're Not Gonna Take It' is 'O Come, All Ye Faithful.' "

"What?"

"You didn't know 'We're Not Gonna Take It' is 'O Come, All Ye Faithful'?" asked Al.

As I sat there dumbfounded, Al sang, *"O come, all ye faithful— We're not gonna take it."*

Holy shit! I sang in the church choir until I was nineteen years old. I must have sung "O Come, All Ye Faithful" hundreds of times. Somehow the first six notes of it infiltrated my psyche and were transformed into "We're Not Gonna Take It!" *Thank you, God!*

Elton John once said that his biggest hits were based on the chord patterns of church hymns. He says the comfort and familiarity in them connects with the listener. I guess he's right.

ONE MORNING DURING THE demo process, I was having coffee in the dining room of our home and listening to the basic tracks of the new songs, without vocals. Vocals were always the last thing added, and I was studying the tracks in anticipation of recording.

The minute I pressed PLAY on the portable cassette player, baby Jesse Blaze came running in, wearing only a diaper, planted himself in front of the boom box, and started headbanging incessantly for the entire tape! I'd never seen anything like it. The kid was glued to the music and would not stop until it was over. *He loved it.* I took that as a good omen.

FROM THE MINUTE TOM Werman arrived on the scene, things began to degrade with the band. The majority of us had accepted the reality of a world filled with shades of gray, but Mark Mendoza was still very much living in an unrealistic world of black and white. He refused to accept that any compromise needed to be made, under any circumstances, and the fact that he was being outvoted on the issue of production—something he'd always been actively involved in—set him on a path of constant passive-aggressive resistance. Oh, but it was okay for me to tour with Krapus for the greater good, right?

We sent Tom Werman a demo tape of close to twenty songs of new material. These were the songs that would become our multiplatinum *Stay Hungry* album. "We're Not Gonna Take It," "I Wanna Rock," "The Price," "Burn in Hell," and every other track on that album were on the demo tape we sent Tom Werman, in a totally recognizable form.* We were excited to have him hear our new stuff.

The first day of preproduction, Tom Werman handed me a tape, saying, "Here are some songs I think you should consider covering."

Slightly taken aback, I asked if he had listened to our new-songs demo.

"Yeah, it's good," he said dismissively, "but I think you should listen to these songs."

Not wanting to be accused of being closed to Werman's ideas—

* Some of these original demo tracks can be found on Twisted Sister's *Stay Hungry 25th Anniversary Edition*. They are almost identical to what you hear on our album.

especially the very first day of preproduction—I took a look at the tape. Listed on it were three songs by the heavy metal band Saxon. I was totally confused. "These are Saxon songs."

"I know," replied Werman. "They're great songs."

"They *are* great songs. We've toured with Saxon. They're a great band."

"So what's the problem?"

"*We tour with them!* We can't be playing Saxon songs when Saxon are playing them at the same show!"

"That's just in Europe," Tom countered. "Nobody knows them over here."

"We tour in Europe and our fans know them! It would make our band a joke. *We can't record songs by Saxon!*" I was dumbfounded by the man's inability to grasp the situation.

Werman gave me a dismissive shrug (he was dismissive a lot) and said, "All right, I'll give 'em to some other band to have hits with."

Journal entry: *Day 1 of preproduction with Tom Werman. Things are not going quite as well as we had hoped.*

The next hurdle was getting Werman to put the right songs on the record. He was adamant about including "Don't Let Me Down" ("'Don't Let Me Down' is *a hit*," insisted Tom) and the two songs on the tape that I had decided not to use for this record, "Captain Howdy" and "Street Justice" (these were meant to be a part of a "rock opera" I was developing). Those three songs are the only songs from the *Stay Hungry* record *we never played live* (until recently). They are the *least popular* songs from that album.

On the list of songs Tom Werman did *not* want on the record? "We're Not Gonna Take It," "I Wanna Rock," and "The Price"— *our three biggest songs!*

Using our traditional voting process to pick the songs from our demos, these three songs were the top picks by everyone else who voted. Still, Tom didn't want them. Werman insisted "The Price" was a typical ballad; "I Wanna Rock" was just a "Molly Hatchet thing"; "I've done that already. *Dump-dada-dump-dada-dah*"; and "We're Not Gonna Take It" was too singsongy—"*Nah-nah-nana-*

nah-nah," he sang mockingly. This A&R man turned producer, who said he *wouldn't* have signed our band and *didn't* want the songs that would become our biggest hits on the record, was in charge of steering Twisted Sister's ship and was getting five figures and four points on the record to do it?! *What the fuck!?*

At one point I literally got down on one knee next to Werman's chair and pleaded with him to put those three songs on the record. I promised him they would be more impressive when they were finished. Finally he caved.

"Oh, all right," Tom said indifferently. "If you *really* have to have them."

"Thanks, Tom," I replied, fighting the urge to blow this condescending, arrogant piece of shit right out of his seat. As I struggled with that feeling, the first of what would become ongoing stomach pains dug into me. I knew then that recording our album with this man was going to be a constant battle and it was up to me to fight.

Mark Mendoza, the band member who usually handled the studio duties and was the bellwether of Twisted Sister's sound, had washed his hands of the situation. He didn't agree with our using Tom Werman (who did?) and spent little time in the studio with the man. So, instead of my working on material for our next record during recording (as I always did), I was forced to stay in the studio most of the time and make sure Tom Werman didn't completely screw things up.

If Mark had continued to handle the production, I would have written a very different follow-up record to *Stay Hungry*. It would have been written when the band was still struggling, a much better place for great metal to be written than from a plateau of comfort and success. I truly believe the band's entire career arc would have been different, and way more in line with how it should have been. Shoulda-woulda-coulda.

The rehearsals themselves went exactly according to Tom Werman's prime directive: "I don't create anything, I just tell you whether I like it or not." Song after song, we'd play something, ask Tom what he thought, and nine times out of ten he would say "Fine." On occasion he would say "I don't like that." The band would come up with an alternative way of playing it, and Werman would say "Fine." You gotta love that creative process!

THE FIRST DAY OF recording basic tracks, at the Record Plant in New York City, we met Werman's secret weapon. Geoff Workman, Tom's engineer, was the guy who *did* push the buttons and get the sounds. Anything good about the sound of our *Stay Hungry* record is thanks to Geoff Workman.

Geoff had been legendary producer Roy Thomas Baker's engineer on all of the first five Queen albums, the first four Cars records, and two Journey albums. Geoff then went on to coproduce, with Journey, Journey's multiplatinum *Departure* record. The guy had mega-experience and chops.

For me, Geoff Workman was the only bright spot in the entire recording process. He was patient, tireless, and a funny SOB. I remember, the first few days of recording, Geoff labeled everything in the studio that was his. GEOFF'S PEN, GEOFF'S TAPE, GEOFF'S ASHTRAY, GEOFF'S COFFEE MUG. At one point, Geoff hung a sign from the ceiling, suspended over his chair (also labeled), that read GEOFF'S AIR. Funny shit.

Geoff chain-smoked Gitanes cigarettes, drank a magnum of Johnnie Walker Black on ice a day, and pretty constantly— discreetly—snorted cocaine, but I didn't care. The guy was always even tempered and not a "shape-shifter" (someone whose personality changes when he or she gets high). If only the same thing could be said for Tom Werman.

AS SOON AS BASS and drum tracks were laid down in New York, the band headed to the West Coast to finish tracking the record (guitars and vocals), record overdubs, and mix. Tom Werman's choice was Cherokee Studios, so that's where we set up shop.

For the first time, Suzette and Jesse were able to accompany me, and we moved into the Oakwood Apartments in Burbank. The Oakwoods are legendary, furnished rental units (complete with bedding, kitchen appliances, and utensils) that have housed so many "entry-level" musicians and actors. I remember being blown away by how nice they were. At that point in my career, it was living the high life! ("Look, this switch turns on the gas fireplace!")*

It was great having my wife and son with me. I almost felt like a "real dad," working all day, then coming home to my wife and kid. On my days off, we would go to family-type places, such as Knott's Berry Farm, Universal Studios, and Disneyland. On our visit to Disneyland, things began to change forever.

Suzette, fifteen-month-old Jesse, and I were having a great time at the park . . . when someone recognized me. Keep in mind, Twisted Sister was not really famous yet, other than within the hard-core heavy metal scene. But some headbanger spotted me and asked for an autograph and picture. *Sure.*

As I signed and posed, other people started to notice. "Hey, that's that guy from the MTV commercial!" Now *they* wanted autographs. *Okay.* Quickly, more and more people started to gather around for autographs and pictures. After I signed for several minutes without my even looking up, a deep male voice said to me, "Make it out to *Lashonda.*"

I lifted my head to see a large black man standing in front of me. "Your name's Lashonda?"

"No! That's my two-year-old daughter." He laughed. Then he leaned in and asked, "Who are you?"

What!? I was spending my family time signing autographs for people who didn't even know who I was? And speaking of family, where the hell were Suzette and Jesse?

I looked around to find the crowd had literally pushed my wife and son away, who were now a good distance from me. I made my apologies to the disappointed crowd ("Where's he going? Who *was* he?") and ran to Suzette and Jesse. The crowd followed. We quickly headed onto a ride. When we got off at the other end, people were

---

* A couple of years ago, Suzette and I were booked into the Oakwood Apartments for a few weeks when my son Jesse Blaze was starring in MTV's *Rock the Cradle*—we didn't last a night. ("What am I, an animal!? Get me a *real* hotel!") Funny how people adjust their standards.

there waiting for us. Most of them didn't even know who I was! That is the insanity of celebrity. People are obsessed with anybody who is anything, even if they've never heard of or seen the person before. Imagine what it's like when they actually know you? (I would soon find out.)

I grabbed Suzette and Jesse, and we quickly exited the park, vowing not to return, unless it was for a parade in my honor. (That never happened, and I've been back to Disneyland and Disney World many times, in disguise.)

Regrettably, that day set a new standard for our family extracurricular activities . . . which essentially became none. My notoriety continued to increase, causing me to become more and more reclusive. For practically my entire life I'd wanted to be famous, and now I was beginning to discover the downside. The saying "Be careful what you wish for . . . because you might get it" rang in my ears. I finally understood.

﹩ 32 ﹩

the guarantee

Recording with Tom Werman continued to be torturous. I fought a constant battle to keep the integrity of our band intact from someone I knew was not a fan of my band or even heavy metal.

Tom Werman drove an expensive Porsche, with the custom license plate 33 RPM, which represented the rotational speed of a long-playing record. Cute. Every day he would pull up to a reserved spot in front of the studio, park his car, then laboriously set the car alarm, put on a car cover to protect his "baby" from the sun, and run a cable lock under the vehicle to secure the cover. It probably took him ten minutes each day to complete this task.

Now, sometimes Werman would drive me so crazy I would have to leave the studio to get away from him and go outside for some air. One time, while I was out, a devilish idea struck me. I went over to Tom's beloved Porsche and rocked the car, setting off the alarm. I then ducked into the alleyway alongside Cherokee Studios and waited.

In a flash, Werman burst out of the front door of the building, looking around frantically. Seeing no suspicious activity, he must have assumed a passing truck or something set off his alarm. Tom then went through the lengthy process of undoing the lock, taking off the cover, opening the car (the whole time with the alarm screaming), resetting the alarm, relocking the car, putting the cover back on, running the cable lock back under the car, and securing the cover once again.

Once he was sure his baby was all right, he headed back into the studio. I'd wait a minute or so until I was sure he'd be settled in the studio, sitting comfortably in his chair, then I'd dart out and shake his Porsche, setting off the alarm again. Back into the alley I would duck, and moments later Werman would come bursting through the door, cursing and fuming, and start the entire process all over again. It was great!

DURING MY FRUSTRATION OF recording with Werman, Geoff Workman was my only solace. The guy would make me laugh, deflect Werman for me, and figure out ways to get what my band needed for the record. Workman believed bands didn't need producers, they needed an objective additional "band member" to help them get what they instinctively knew was right. Geoff was a smart man.

One day I was particularly down and feeling beaten by Werman. The daily battle with the guy was really getting to me. Tom wasn't in the studio at that moment and Geoff asked me what was wrong.

"Tom's destroying my band's album."

"Don't worry," Workman replied without a hint of a smile, "it will be fine. This record will go at least platinum, or I'll quit the business."

This was some statement. Geoff had worked on a lot of hugely successful records. "Yeah? Will you put that in writing?" I joked.

"Get me a piece of paper," Workman commanded his assistant engineer, Gary McGachan. With that, Geoff wrote, *The record I am presently working on with "Twisted Sister" is guaranteed to go at least platinum or I resign. . . .* He then signed his name, and Gary signed as witness. It really cheered me up.

I still have that piece of paper. It's laminated and sits in the frame of my now triple-platinum *Stay Hungry* album. Thanks for that, Geoff. You have no idea how much I needed that emotional boost at that moment. You saved me.

• • •

DURING RECORDING, WE DECIDED our new record would be called *Stay Hungry*. The band always used one of the song titles from the album. It focused attention on a "nonsingle" track of our choosing (radio always gave airplay to title tracks), which would inevitably be one of our heavier songs.

The song "Stay Hungry," and the rest of the music on the *Stay Hungry* album, was inspired by a book I had read in the early eighties, by Arnold Schwarzenegger. Published in 1977, during his bodybuilding heyday, *Arnold: The Education of a Bodybuilder* was part-autobiographical/part-motivational. One of Arnold's motivational edicts was to "stay hungry," to always keep that feeling of desperation and drive you have when you're just starting out. He believed if you become too content, you will lose your edge and fail. (Boy, did I ever learn that the hard way!)

Predating *any* of his later career successes, in the book Arnold laid out the game plan for his life. Paraphrased, he said, "First I will become the most successful bodybuilder in the history of the sport, then I will invest my winnings and become a real estate tycoon, then I will become the biggest movie star *in the world*, and then I will go into politics." This was 1977! At the time I was inspired by Arnold's "aiming for the stars in hopes of hitting the moon" attitude. As the years went by, and step by step he did *exactly* what he said he was going to do, I was completely blown away. I was one of the few who was not stunned when Arnold decided to run for governor. It was all in his book!

Reading *Arnold: The Education of a Bodybuilder* taught me to never give up and inspired the biggest album of my career. *Stay Hungry* was dedicated to Arnold Schwarzenegger.

Many years later, my music publishers received a call from Arnold's campaign headquarters in the early days of his run for governor of California, requesting the use of "We're Not Gonna Take It" as his campaign song. I was blown away. I had written that song (and the others from the *Stay Hungry* album) fired up on "Arnold-speak." Now he was getting inspiration from a song he inspired me to write?! Talk about "going full circle."

I granted usage to Arnold gratis and wished him well. Arnold Schwarzenegger is a man who does what he commits to do, and even though I was not a resident of California, I fully supported him. You may not like the way he gets the job done, but he *always* achieves his goals. I respect that.

When I was asked to perform my song at Arnold's final rally, I jumped at the opportunity, mainly because it gave me the chance to meet a man who had changed my life for the better.

As I stood on the stage, in front of the California state capitol, at the epicenter of a media maelstrom the likes of which I hadn't seen since the PMRC hearings decades earlier (much more about that later), singing "We're Not Gonna Take It" over and over and over to a roaring crowd, it was surreal. Who woulda thunk it?

Suddenly, Arnold appeared in the distance at the end of a ridiculously long red carpet and began to approach the stage. I was thrilled when my hero* came right up to me, warmly shook my hand, and rocked out to the song he inspired me to write! When Arnold acknowledged and thanked me to the crowd—with his legendary Austrian accent—it was the icing on the cake. Stay hungry indeed!

I'M THE ASSHOLE. *I admit it.* I'm the one the band blames for all of their woes, all of the band's failings and our eventual demise. Why not blame me? I wrote every song and was responsible for virtually every bit of creativity (with the help of Suzette) within the band. Besides . . . it's a hell of a lot easier than taking responsibility for your own failings, or accepting one's own inabilities.

While my bandmates are at it, they should blame me for the success of the band, too. I'll take personal responsibility for every bit of inventiveness, originality, and manic drive that made the band a success. *That's all my fault as well.* Though my band will probably say nothing could be farther from the truth, I'll let my post–Twisted

---

* Arnold Schwarzenegger's and Robert Englund's autographs are the only ones I have ever asked for.

Sister success do the talking. I haven't noticed the rest of them doing all that much. I'm just sayin' . . .

During the recording of *Stay Hungry*, I was doing daily battle with Tom Werman to keep the integrity of our band intact. You would have been hard-pressed to find another band member there with me to fight the good fight, other than when they were needed to record something. Believe me, no one was stopping anybody from hanging out for hours on end, babysitting our producer.

To make matters worse, the growing resentment Mark Mendoza had for me, along with his secret passive-aggressive behavior toward everything I tried to do, was making it increasingly difficult for me to get things done. The biggest problem was, I had no idea that Mark was upset with me. He never said anything to me about it. Maybe I should have been less oblivious.

Still, I was sensing a problem, and when, from time to time, the band would have meetings to discuss various issues—even when asked directly if he would like to discuss anything—Mark would *never* say a word. I would hear about how he would bitch and moan to others about things—never offering an alternative plan of action—but when it came to openly discussing the issues with me, he would clam up or, even worse, deny there was a problem.

I remember one meeting in which Jay Jay tried to clear up some issues he knew—but I didn't—existed between Mark and me. When Jay Jay carefully worded some of Mark's concerns, in an effort to help him communicate his feelings, Mark hung Jay Jay out to dry, saying, "I never said that."

Jay was livid! "You told me you were going to throw a wrench into anything Dee tried to do until you got what you wanted!"

I couldn't believe it! I had sensed something like that was going on, but to hear that Mark had actually verbalized it to Jay Jay (and Jay is no liar) absolutely stunned me! We were on the same fucking team! I was killing myself trying to make the band a success, and Mark was trying to stop me?!

Mark just sat there in silence.

At one point during the production and preparation for the *Stay Hungry* album, Mark proposed the band *stop* wearing makeup and costumes.

What?! After eight years of championing a lost cause (wearing makeup and costumes)—fighting for the right to look the way we did—when the tide was finally turning and wearing makeup and costumes was being accepted, he wanted to take them off? If we were going to do that, we could have done it years earlier and had a far easier time getting accepted.

Because Mark was a band member, his idea had to be put to a vote. Our partnership agreement stated the majority would rule in any band vote, so I had to stand there and make my case for continuing our course, while Mark argued against it. *I still can't believe it!*

Our drummer, A. J. Pero—being the youngest and the "new guy"—was a real follower at that time and very much into imitating everything Mendoza did. When the votes were cast, makeup and costumes won, three votes to two. In other words, if one more person had voted against makeup and costumes, by partnership rules the band would have had to abandon the image our very name was based on! *How fucking ridiculous would that have been!?* I'm not sure what I would have done if the vote had gone the other way. I would probably have quit the band.

For all my band's complaining about my not letting them be a part of the creative process, I am hard-pressed to remember them ever even making suggestions. Actually, one major idea does come to mind. . . .

❧ 33 ❧

twenty pounds of shite in a five-pound sack

When we finished recording and mixing our new album, we all headed back home to deal with some of the other elements in record-releasing.

Stay Hungry was the first album cover we controlled. It was finally up to us to come up with an idea. I don't remember if I had any specific ideas for the cover—I'm sure I did—but Mark Mendoza made a great suggestion.

His concept was to have the band—sans makeup—in a run-down tenement, gathered around an "electrical-cable spool" for a table, with a large bone, stripped clean of meat, on a plate in the middle. Around the "hungry" band would be, superimposed, pictures of us in full stage regalia, holding bottles of champagne and living the high life, representing our dreams of rock stardom. It was a brilliant idea, and I told Mark so.

Since this was Mendoza's vision—and I was always being accused of controlling everything—I suggested he run with it. We had a budget for the cover art and an enthusiastic photographer— a young gun from New Jersey named Mark Weiss—so the cover was Mendoza's baby. Mendoza accepted the task willingly, and I was overjoyed to finally share the creative responsibility with someone who had a good idea. Finally, something I didn't have to do.

When the day of the cover-photo session arrived, Suzette—our intrepid hair, makeup, and wardrobe person—and I headed into New York City for an 11:00 a.m. start, and a long day of picture taking. Along with the cover photos, we were scheduled to take a wide range of shots both with makeup and without so we would have a variety of pictures, for various uses during the coming months. Both the label and our management knew their long-range plans for the band, and it behooved us to have a stockpile of photographs. It wouldn't be easy to book photo sessions once the band hit the road.

When we arrived at the photo studio, we were blown away to see Mark's vision brought to life. They had actually built a rundown apartment room in the studio, just like Mendoza described. It looked great.

That day, for the first time, we all put on Suzette's new costumes together. They, too, were amazing. She had taken our tattered style to the next level, giving everybody in the band his own great look. For me, gone was any remnant of my past "sweet transvestite." I was now—to quote one reviewer—"Raggedy Ann on acid," fully embracing my hulking, inner monster. The use of football shoulder pads added mass to both me and my already voluminous hair (now reaching down to my chest, with the addition of two long, black streaks (a first). I loved it!

Now seems as good a time as any to talk about my legendary mane—it pretty much put the *hair* in *hair band*.

First off, that was *really* my hair. Of all the misconceptions about me and the band, people's thinking I wore a wig (even a fright wig!), had hair extensions, and/or used cans of hair spray to make it as big as it was, are at the top of the list . . . and drive me nuts! *Other people* used extensions and hair spray to make their hair look like *mine*, but my hair was the real fucking deal.

Being of Eastern European descent my hair had a natural curl and buoyancy, which gave it said volume. It was mousy brown by nature. But when Suzette started bleaching it blond for me around 1980, it was the final, missing piece to my unique "theatrical" look (though some say I was a real-life "Quay Lude" from the Tubes' "White Punks on Dope").

◆   ◆   ◆

BACK TO THE PHOTO shoot.

My new boots hadn't yet arrived, so I was forced to wear my old pink boots (as seen on the cover) from the *You Can't Stop Rock 'n' Roll* tour. Bummer. The one thigh-high, one low, asymmetrical boots were the finishing touch to my new outfit when they finally arrived.

When we all got onto the set, dressed and ready to shoot, we had a terrible realization . . . the room was too small! We couldn't see how "the Marks" would fit photos of both the band gathered around the table—as now seen on the *back* cover of the *Stay Hungry* album—with the band "living the high life" superimposed behind us! Bear in mind, this was 1984; amazing computerized tools such as Photoshop didn't exist. Trying our best to make it work, the band flattened—unnaturally, especially for a band "living the high life"—against the walls of "the apartment." It made us all look way too stiff.

The photos of the "starving" band, gathered tightly around the table, were taken next. All we could do was hope for the best.

Before we finally left the photo session—at 9:00 a.m. the next morning!—we had put that room Mendoza and Weiss had built to good use, doing all kinds of pictures—both group and individual—with makeup and costumes and without. We also did shots on a number of different backgrounds, everything done to achieve the goal of stockpiling photos for the weeks and months ahead.

I'm not exactly sure what Mark Mendoza's rationale for his actions were—sabotaging the photo session, or just an overt hatred for taking photos (though now that I think about it, I can't remember his ever causing problems during photo sessions before that)—but he screwed up shot after shot after shot. Whether it was deliberately not following the directions of Mark Weiss—usually saying "Fuck you," "Shut the fuck up," "I'm gonna kick your ass," or the like—or giving the middle finger, pretending to pick his nose, or other such behaviors, Mark made it impossible to use a wide range of the group photos. Mendoza's "parrot," A.J., joined in Mark's "merriment," further contributing to the growing count of unusable shots.

I particularly felt bad for Eddie and Jay Jay, who—like me—fully committed and posed for every picture, trying to look the best they could. What ultimately happened with the group photos was no fault of theirs, yet they suffered the consequences.

After an insanely long day and night of shooting, we were finally ready to wrap. Mark Weiss was a real taskmaster, always calling for "just one more roll" (thirty-six pictures—remember, there was no digital photography back then) on every setup we did after already shooting several rolls of film. As we all dragged our exhausted asses to the dressing rooms to at last take off our makeup and costumes, Weiss says to me, "Dee, I've got one roll of film left. How about taking *one last roll* of solo shots of you in 'the room'?"

I'd come this far . . . why the hell not?

Now, the large bone you see on the *Stay Hungry* album cover is not a prop bone. It's a real cow's femur Mark Weiss had gotten from a butcher, *days* before the shoot . . . and neglected to refrigerate. The thing smelled like death. The stench was so bad, no one could bear to be within a few feet of it!

As I prepared to pose for the final roll of pictures, I looked at the gnarly, fetid thing on the table and said, "What the fuck? I can always burn my glovelette later." I scooped the bone up and began frantically posing with it. I was really feeling the horror of being desperate, hungry, and trapped in a terrible world of hopelessness. Thirty-six quick clicks later, I was finished for the day.

THE FOLLOWING WEEK AFTER all the rolls of film had been developed, the real tragedy of our twenty-two-hour photo session became clear. Mark Mendoza's cover concept wasn't achievable. Not only was the room too small to accommodate both the non-makeup "starving artist" shot and the "living the high life" with makeup and costumes shot, but Mendoza and Weiss had hung a drop lightbulb for effect over the "bone table" and it blocked the face of whichever band member was positioned behind it. *The cover idea was undoable.*

Now, in the eleventh hour, we needed to come up with a suitable picture that would work for the cover. The no-makeup photos were out, as were all the pictures, with makeup, of the band pressed up against the walls of the run-down apartment; they just looked too unnatural.

Next, we looked at all the other group photos and—surprise, surprise—they were unusable for a variety of reasons, and Mark and A.J.'s clowning around in so many of them killed a lot of potentially good shots. Now what?

The only individual-band-member photograph that can represent a band is one of the front man. That's just the way it is. When people see a shot of the singer, they connect it with the band. The same does not hold true for an individual photo of other band member. There *are* exceptions with some bands once they are established (Led Zeppelin, Van Halen, the Rolling Stones, and the like), but certainly not when a band is just starting out. And when you have an outrageous, enigmatic front man who embodies the name and image of the band—such as *moi*—you don't need anyone else. Did I mention *egomaniacal*?

As the record label, our management, and I went over every photo for a possible replacement shot for the failed cover, we all kept coming back to virtually the last shot taken, on that last roll of film, at the end of that long day of shooting. A photo of me, crouched in the corner of the room, like a trapped animal, holding the bloody bone out in front of me and screaming. The shot was the definition of *Stay Hungry* and it became the album cover... exposed dental work and all.

The shot of the band in street clothes (nice Capezios, Eddie) around the table with the bone on it became the back cover, but the lasting image that would come to represent the band all over the world was a picture of yours truly. The band couldn't have been happier. *Yeah, sure.*

This album cover was probably the biggest slight of all to the band, and the thing that truly set things on a downward spiral between us on a personal level. While I had always known that when we finally broke through I would be the one everyone focused on, I believe the band was fooled by the attention each of us had received during our years in the club scene. Playing night after night, two, three, or even four shows, the audience had time to get to know and love *each* member of Twisted Sister. Before we had albums out and toured, it was definitely more of a "John, Paul, George, and

Ringo" vibe with our fans. Once a group got out of the clubs and on tour, with only thirty to ninety minutes to get to know a band, the one time of the year they came around, all the attention would be on the front man or the most outrageous member of the band or the creative force. All of those were me. Twisted Sister was way more of an Alice Cooper than a Kiss.

The posters, T-shirts, magazine ads, and more resulting from the Dee-only album cover, and the additional attention it brought me, just added insult to injury and were a constant reminder to the guys of the horrible turn (for them) the band had taken. Meanwhile, I couldn't have been happier.

BY OUR THIRD RECORD, the idea of the TS logo being interpreted differently for each album and tour was starting to set in. I envisioned the logo out of bones for the *Stay Hungry* record and tour, but needed a mock-up to show the Atlantic Records art department. I turned to my in-house *everything*, Suzette, to do a quick sketch.

She had just woken up and was in her pajamas and robe, having her morning cup of tea. I asked her to knock out a quick representation of my vision.

Half-asleep, Suzette grabbed a pen and a sheet of paper and in literally five minutes banged out a TS bone-logo sketch. With no erasures (it was pen) and one try, it was definitely close enough for the art department to understand what I was going for. Suzette is so damn talented.

A few weeks later, I paid a visit to the record company. I stopped by to say hello to Jason Flom, and on the wall behind his desk was a TS logo sticker . . . with Suzette's bone-logo sketch!

I asked Jason where he got it from, and he told me the art department had given it to him. I quickly headed down to the office of Bob Defrin, the label's art director, to discover Suzette's sketch of the bone logo—not someone's polished interpretation of her sketch, but her actual sketch—had been used on *everything! It was on the cover of our album, for God's sake!* Somewhere along the way, my "here's the idea of the logo I'm looking for" had been translated to "here's the bone logo, run with it."

Nobody at the label or my manager's office understood why I was so upset. They all thought the logo looked great, as did the band.

When I broke the news to Suzette, she was mortified. She is a perfectionist and would never have allowed something that important to go out that rough and unfinished.

"If I knew it was going to be the actual logo," Suzette exclaimed, "I would have spent ten minutes on it!"

Suzette's bone logo—as is—has been in use on records, merchandise, print ads, and more, all over the world, for more than twenty-five years. Suzette says Twisted Sister owes her money!

≈ 34 ≈

the game changer

One more piece was needed before we could pull the trigger and launch our *Stay Hungry* album and tour . . . a video. Though we had stuck our toe in the water with the first one, nothing could have prepared us for what was about to happen.

Ever since we had done the *You Can't Stop Rock 'n' Roll* video, my mind raced with thoughts about the true potential of the medium. MTV was growing at an exponential rate; making a video to go with your album and single was now expected. Believing that "We're Not Gonna Take It" would *unquestionably* be our first single, I conceived an elaborate, story-driven video, with an actual "acted-out" opening, something I didn't realize hadn't been done before in this format.

My idea was for a father—like my own—to be yelling at his son to turn down his music, and the kid would transform into me and blow his father out a window. The song would kick in, and Looney Tunes–esque high jinks would ensue.

Unbeknownst to the band, an established, award-winning concert and comedy-show director, Marty Callner, was looking to make his entrance into the world of rock video. He and his partner, lawyer Mickey Shapiro, approached Atlantic Records with the idea of producing both a video and live-concert special for a "promising, up-and-coming band." Atlantic accepted Creamcheese Productions' proposal and offered them three new bands for consideration: INXS, Zebra . . . or Twisted Sister.

As luck would have it—or by design, on the part of the wily director—Marty Callner brought his teenage son Dax with him to check out the music of the three bands. The story goes that Dax lit up when he heard Twisted Sister, and his dad trusted his son's instincts.

I flew out to LA with Mark Puma and we joined Atlantic Records' senior VP Paul Cooper at the Palm Restaurant in Beverly Hills for a meeting with Creamcheese Productions to discuss the video and concert shoots. I took to Marty Callner immediately, and he to me (I think). Though he lived and embraced the Beverly Hills lifestyle (Johnny Carson once quoted Marty, saying, "Beverly Hills is like being in high school with money"), Marty was anything but West Coast. Growing up a street-tough kid from Cincinnati, Ohio, he embodied the American dream, yet kept the "Cinci" attitude.

Before the meeting even officially started, Marty noticed my eyes grow wide at the sight of massive jumbo shrimp served as an appetizer. Having only ever had the "all you can peel-n-eat shrimp" off of a salad bar, I wasn't prepared for these baby's-arm-sized, already peeled—and cleaned—beauties. What a rube I was! Marty told the waiter to bring out a large bowl filled with them for me. Welcome to high school with money!

Once all the introductions and pleasantries (and behemoth shrimp) were behind us, we got down to business. Marty immediately asked if I had any thoughts for the video, and I shared my concept. *He loved it!* This is one of the things that makes Marty Callner the great (and hugely successful—just check his history on IMDB) director that he is . . . he is not threatened by good ideas from other people. Even though my video experience was practically none—and I was so wet behind the ears that big shrimp left me dumbfounded—Marty recognized, welcomed, and encouraged my creativity.

Marty told me he and I would work side by side on the project, asking only that I not undermine his authority with his crew by correcting him, or telling him to do things, in front of them. That was it. From that moment on, and throughout the project, Marty Callner and I were attached at the hip, becoming better and better friends the longer we worked together. We're still great friends to this day.

UNFORTUNATELY, BEFORE WE EVEN got out of the video-production gate, I was pulling my insanely long hair out of my head over a major issue with the choice of first single. People's preferences were all over the place! Every "country" was being heard from, including various clueless record-company types . . . and they were gravitating away from the obvious lead track.

When I got word that it looked as if the record company would go with "Burn in Hell" as the lead single, I pretty much lost my mind. Great as that song is, it would have been album suicide.

Seeing how upset I was, Marty Callner made me get in his car (the beautiful Jaguar XJ6 that Tawny Kitaen would later be seen doing splits on, in a Whitesnake video Marty directed); he said he wanted to show me something. With the windows rolled down and the air-conditioning blasting (something else I learned in Beverly Hills), on a beautiful spring day, Marty took me to a huge cemetery and stopped the car.

"You see that?" he said emphatically, pointing to the sea of gravestones. "That's a real problem. As long as you're aboveground, you're okay. In the end, none of it really matters anyway. Don't let the bullshit get to you."

His point hit me hard.

"So what's the matter?" Marty asked.

I told him about the record company's stupidity over what the single should be.

"I'll take care of it," Marty said.

Later that same day, I received a call saying the president of Atlantic Records had pronounced that "We're Not Gonna Take It" was to be the first single. I couldn't believe he had finally come around!

He hadn't.

You see, when Marty and I got back to the house, Marty sent El Presidente a telegram that read HARD AT WORK ON VIDEO FOR

TWISTED SISTER'S "WE'RE NOT GONNA TAKE IT" STOP SEE YOU AT THE TOP OF THE CHARTS! STOP MARTY.

The minute Mr. President thought money was already being spent on a "We're Not Gonna Take It" video, he changed his position on the choice of the single and made his new "decision." To this day, that man claims he was the one who picked "We're Not Gonna Take It" as our lead track. Yeah, sure you did, dude. *Thank you, Marty!*

THE VIDEO MAKING THIS time around was much more involved for a couple reasons. For one, the budget was not only *way* bigger than for our first video, but it was way bigger than *most* video budgets at that time. This was Marty Callner's foray into the world of MTV and he wanted to make a statement. The six-figure budget we had for the shoot was a huge amount to spend, and a big budget with an ambitious concept meant a huge production and crew. And we were simultaneously setting up the *Stay Hungry* concert for filming as well, so you can see what a tremendous undertaking this was.

Marty Callner was true to his word and made me his partner every step of the way, the first step being laying out the entire story on index cards so we knew exactly what the hell we wanted to do. Together we developed the story line, pretty true to my vision, but for some reason he wanted me to knock out an elephant. *You heard me.* We both thought the scene in *Blazing Saddles* where Mongo knocks out a horse was hysterical, and it would be a laugh riot if I knocked out an elephant in my full Twisted Sister regalia. It had nothing to do with the story of a son rebelling against his father, but Marty became pretty obsessed with proving he could make it happen.

As the days went by, and the story became more and more refined, the elephant scene hung on. Just days before shooting, one of the producers pulled me to the side and begged me to convince Marty to drop the idea. It was prohibitively expensive and didn't make any sense. I couldn't disagree, so I spoke with Marty, and he begrudgingly removed it. Knowing Marty as I do, I'll bet he still regrets we didn't do it.

◆ ◆ ◆

LOCATION SCOUTING, CASTING, STUNT coordination, wardrobe, even what the family in the story were eating for dinner, were all run past me for my input and approval. I learned so much by Marty's side during this incredible experience. When it came time to cast the role of the father, Marty asked me whom I envisioned.

Now, *Animal House* was always a Snider family favorite. My four younger brothers and I loved nothing more than quoting lines from the film to each other. If we could incorporate the dialogue into daily conversation, even better. That's exactly what I did at the end of "We're Not Gonna Take It." While riffing on the repeat choruses at the end of the song, I spontaneously broke into Doug Neidermeyer's "ROTC rap" from *Animal House*:

You're all worthless and weak!
Now drop and give me twenty!

Everyone thought it was hysterical, so we kept it in the final mix. At that time I had no idea that I would have some future affiliation with the man who made those lines famous.

Neidermeyer is one of my favorite characters in *Animal House*. Though the father, son, and entire family portrayed in the "We're Not Gonna Take It" video are supposed to represent *my* family, I told Marty that someone like the guy who played Neidermeyer would be perfect to capture the screaming tyrant my dad could be.

Marty looked at me, confused. "Someone *like* Mark Metcalf [the actor's name]? Why don't we get him? What's he doing, working on a cure for cancer?"

Oddly, while in my world Mark Metcalf was a "superstar," in reality he had all but retired from acting and gone into producing. A few quick calls were made, and for a thousand bucks and the price of a round-trip coach ticket from New York, we had *the actual* Douglas C. Neidermeyer in our video!

I remember the day Mark Metcalf was to arrive at LAX airport, and Marty was going to send a production assistant (the lowest position on a film set) to pick him up.

"*Oh, hell no!*" I exclaimed. "I'm picking him up!"

Later that same afternoon, I was standing in the baggage-claim area of the airport looking for our video's star when I heard from close behind me, in that Neidermeyer voice, "You lookin' for me, mister?" (a classic line from *Animal House*). I spun around and there he was . . . *Neidermeyer!* I don't think Mark could believe my genuine childlike glee at meeting him. The entire ride back to Marty's I made Mark regale me with *Animal House* tales.

Mark Metcalf's dialog for the video was worked up by Mark, Marty, and myself. My idea was, contrary to the *Animal House* movie, Douglas C. Neidermeyer had *survived* being shot by his own troops in Vietnam and was now the married father of six kids and none too happy about it. Metcalf's improvisation was designed to incorporate things my dad had always said to me growing up (the most famous being, "What do you wanna do with your life?!") while paraphrasing his character's dialogue in the movie. I've always joked that the sole reason I came up with the idea for the video was to give my brothers and me some fresh *Animal House*–type dialogue to play with.

The video shoot itself was an amazing experience. Videos are like little movies (especially the way Marty Callner and Twisted Sister were doing them). For an outcast kid from Long Island to have his crazy ideas brought to life like that was almost overwhelming.

THE *STAY HUNGRY* LIVE concert was an entirely different animal. Marty Callner specialized in filming concerts, having done some legendary specials for HBO in the late seventies and early eighties. The hugely successful Cher, Diana Ross, Pat Benatar, Fleetwood Mac, and other concert specials were all his.* I just stepped back and let him do his thing.

Marty had a reputation to uphold and wanted to make a powerful statement to the rock-video world. His plan was to make Twisted

---

* Marty Callner is *still* the premier director of live-concert filming, including concerts by Justin Timberlake, the Rolling Stones, Britney Spears, Garth Brooks, and many more.

Sister even larger-than-life than we already were. To achieve this, everything was done on a grander scale. The stage Marty picked for the show was wider and deeper than most others, and our signature "pink, barbed-wire fences" were doubled in height and width to give the stage a massive look. To bring out the "bigness" of the whole event, Marty wanted to use a Louma crane. The Louma jib crane allows for simultaneous, sweeping lateral and vertical movement, with 360-degree rotation of the camera. It changed filmmaking, and the invention even received an Academy Award in 2005. Though they're now a standard in the film industry, only two of these cranes existed at that time, and they were run by Jean-Marie Lava*lou* and Alain *Mas*seron, the creators and namesakes. Hang the expense, Marty had to have one.

Filmed in San Bernardino, California, at the Orange Pavilion, the show sold out nearly instantaneously. The West Coast buzz on Twisted Sister was huge, and because the event was being filmed for a home video and to be broadcast on MTV, the fans would do just about anything to get tickets.

The night of the filming couldn't have been more tense. Though it wasn't going out live, we only had one shot at getting it right. Do or die. This was a huge opportunity for the band and we could not afford to blow it.

One major concern was the barricade the film crew had set up to keep the audience back from the stage and allow room for the film crew and Louma crane to move about. For one, it left a wide chasm between the band and the crowd, something that would definitely affect our connection with the fans. Second, it was freestanding, meaning nothing moored the barricade to the ground so it could resist any force from the crowd. It pretty much depended on the audience's voluntarily not pressing up against it. What kind of useless, fucked-up barricade was that?!

The band and our crew tried to impress our concerns upon Marty and the production staff, but having never worked with a raucous, heavy-metal crowd before, they just didn't understand the potential problem. We were pretty much told not to worry our pretty little heads about such things and focus on the show. *If they say so . . .*

When the audience was let in, there was initially no problem, though I could see by the looks on the faces of the fans, on the video monitors, even they were confused by how the barricade was supposed to work. A short time before the band was supposed to go on, the pressure of the packed house became too great, the barricade collapsed and thousands of fans surged forward. It was terrible!

Down the barricade went in splinters, with the fans spilling onto the broken shards, falling onto one another and into the camera crew and their expensive equipment. The entire filming plot was wiped out in a second, and injured fans were being carried out of the place by EMTs. The fire marshal arrived and was ready to shut down the event!

An announcement was made: "Dee Snider says the band isn't coming out unless you all back up!" *Uh oh*. Joe Gerber saved the show by grabbing the mic and emceeing the near riot. He talked the packed house through a step-by-step backing up, so injured people could be helped and the film crew could regroup.

When it was finally time to start the show, another reality became painfully evident. While concerts are traditionally dark events, with the stage dramatically lit, they don't provide enough light to "read" well on film. To accommodate the lighting needs of the camera, additional lights are added onstage, and the houselights are left on the audience. When you watch a filmed concert event, you don't notice the extra light because the film "swallows" it up, making the final product look pretty normal. Unfortunately, having your dramatic lighting effects nullified by lights that stay on during the filming of your show screws up the band's head, and nothing kills the crowd vibe like turning on the houselights.

On top of all this, the worst thing of all happened to me . . . I had a wardrobe malfunction.

This was the first time I was wearing my new stage outfit under "battle conditions." Over the years, Suzette and I had pretty much locked in what worked and didn't work for me onstage . . . *pretty much*. To keep my pants from pulling down in the back, Suzette had designed stylized suspenders that V-ed up from the front and back and went under my shoulder pads. Great idea . . . in theory. The first time I violently threw my body forward onstage that night, the stitching on the back of the suspender gave out and it tore free. Not only did I have a dangling suspender like a vestigial tail, but my pants kept pulling down in the back every time I bent over . . . which was a lot. *Having the crack of your ass hanging out is not metal!*

On top of my woes, the band was having all sorts of technical issues. Eddie had an equipment issue that made the opening solo on "The Price" sound as if he were playing a banjo!

Overall, it was a self-conscious performance for a self-conscious audience. To top it all off, when we finished the show, Marty said he needed us to go back onstage and redo the opening song and a couple of others. Talk about anticlimactic!

When the show was finally *over over*, the band went back to our dressing trailer and stood in stunned silence. *We blew it! We sucked!* It could not have been worse. Knowing that we have always been our toughest critic—which I believe is the reason we are so good live; we're never satisfied—I told everyone not to say a word about how horrible we knew we were. Maybe people didn't think it was that bad.

Minutes later, the dressing-room door flew opened and in poured Marty Callner and his production staff. *They were blown away!* Everybody was blown away! Nobody noticed *any* of the issues we were having, and when the show was all edited and overdubbed (Eddie even got to fix his solo on "The Price"), it looked and sounded amazing.

Twisted Sister's *Stay Hungry Live* was released on VHS tape and laser disc and aired about eighteen times that year on MTV. Audiences loved it! Unlike so many visually compelling bands before us (Alice Cooper, Kiss, etc.), Twisted Sister got to show our stuff on an international grand scale. Which was a blessing and a curse.

⚜ 35 ⚜

what the hell did he just say?

After spending several beautiful spring weeks in Los Angeles producing and filming our video, the live concert special, and, before that, recording our new record, Twisted Sister boarded a plane and flew (and drove) to New Castle, Great Britain, to start the first leg of our *Stay Hungry* tour.

While it took several weeks for a new release to hook in (get into the stores and on the radio) in the United States, the United Kingdom was much more reactive. The metal press had a stronger connection with the fans, and the metalheads responded more readily to the latest news about their favorite bands. But they couldn't respond to what they didn't know about. . . .

When on May 27, 1984, Twisted Sister got off our tour bus (from Heathrow Airport) in Newcastle, England—nearly twenty-four hours later—the weather was the polar opposite of what we had left in LA. Where it was sunny and warm in Los Angeles, it was dreary and cold in the UK. We had a day off to readjust before our tour began, but the band and I were immediately depressed just being there. As I lay in my hotel room, recuperating from the jet lag, the phone rang and I heard the immediately recognizable voice of a person I had never met.

"Dee Snider? ThesesBrianJohnsonfrumAhseeDahysee."

Ahsee Dahysee? *Was he even speaking English?* I could barely understand him.*

"We cannahafya settinenya 'otelrum onaMundeh-nightenNew-caseh," Brian continued.

What the hell is an *'otelrum?*

"Gatha-up-ya-keeds. Ahmacomin' tuh-gitya, me boy." With that, Brian hung up.

He definitely said something about getting somebody's boy. Just in case, I gathered the band and crew, and a half hour later Brian Johnson and two of his friends showed up in three Mercedes-Benz sedans to take us out on the town. *And did we appreciate it.* We went out to dinner, then to a blues club (Brian got up and sang "Route 66" in his distinctive voice), and finally went to a local pub . . . in Brian's house. While we hung out, drinking (for those of us who drank), throwing darts, and playing pool, Brian told us the story of his rescue from oblivion.

After giving rock stardom his best shot with a band called Geordie in the seventies, Brian had lost hope of ever making it and left his rock 'n' roll dreams behind. He started a business in his hometown, putting vinyl tops on cars. Brian is a "Geordie" (nickname for someone from Newcastle) to the core. When Bon Scott of AC/DC died in 1980, the band asked only a few people to audition for the band as his replacement. Brian Johnson was one of them. He was friends with the AC/DC boys from his Geordie band days and wrote off the audition as a "mercy tryout," done more out of obligation to a friend than anything else.

A couple of weeks later, Brian got a call from AC/DC guitarist Malcolm Young asking him to drop by the studio. Still not thinking much of it, Brian went and paid his friends a visit. When he walked into the room, Angus Young walked straight up to him and said, "You're never going to have to put a vinyl top on a car again." Brian was the new singer and member of AC/DC.

---

* Years later, I would do rock-talk radio on WMMR in Philadelphia, and after an interview with Brian, I played "Guess What Brian Johnson Just Said?" with my listeners. Playing back audio clips from the interview, my audience would call in and try to figure it out for a chance at winning an 'MMR ROCKS! T-shirt. They rarely got it right.

The house in which we were hanging out with Brian, listening to his story, was the biggest house in town. When he was a kid, Brian used to do deliveries, driving past it and telling himself that one day, when he was a rock star, he would live in that big house. Now that's a rock 'n' roll dream come true!

One more thing: Phil Carson, who signed AC/DC to Atlantic Records, told me how he was hanging out at a club with the band one night before Bon Scott died. As Phil sat at a table with the rest of the band, a drunk Bon Scott rolled up, with his arm around Brian Johnson, and said, "If anything ever happens to me, this is my replacement." Now that's just plain eerie.

"FOR THE WANT OF A NAIL"

For want of a nail the shoe was lost.
For want of a shoe the horse was lost.
For want of a horse the rider was lost.
For want of a rider the battle was lost.
For want of a battle the kingdom was lost.
And all for the want of a horseshoe nail.

That's the legendary rhyme about an empire collapsing because of losing a simple—yet important—thing. Twisted Sister had a similar experience with our *Stay Hungry* album in Great Britain, except our "want" was for a postage stamp.

For the want of a stamp the postcard was lost.
For the want of a postcard the announcement was lost.
For the want of an announcement the single was lost.
For the want of a single the album was lost.
For the want of an album the country was lost.
All for the want of a postcard stamp.

The key to the successful launch of any record, movie, television show, theatrical production, book, etc., is the setup. You need your first week of release to be well attended, bought, and/or viewed, so that it will be seen as a hot, successful project. You want it at the top of the relevant sales charts, and to do that, you advertise, promote, and hype your project in any and every way you possibly can. In the case of a new album in the UK, back in the '80s, one of the most important ways to promote a new release is by using the artist's mailing list. You want those die-hard fans to know about it ahead of time, so they will get out to the stores the first week and buy the record and hound radio to start playing your single. This is Record Promotion 101.

With the success of Twisted's *You Can't Stop Rock 'n' Roll* album and singles in Great Britain, we had built quite a following and mailing list. Our fans were primed and ready to buy pretty much anything we put out or did. All our distributor, WEA, had to do was let them know our new record was coming. *And there's the catch.*

The new head of WEA, whom I shall refer to as Rubber Dick—a pretty close play on his actual name—was not what you would call a fan of heavy metal, or Twisted Sister for that matter. When he was asked to approve the expense of *domestic* postcard stamps to do the advance mailing to our fan base, *he passed on it for budgetary reasons!* Stamps?!

As our distributor, WEA's sole purpose was to promote and distribute recorded product. Rubber Dick nixed the cheapest, most cost-effective, and *important* promotion they could possibly have done for our record! *That Dick!*

As a result, our record was released in the UK and didn't sell well enough initially to get us high into the charts. So we didn't get on *Top of the Pops* or find our single on the radio. As a result, our follow-up to a successful record in Great Britain was effectively a flop.* Fortunately, our shows in the UK sold and went great. No thanks to that Dick.

ON JUNE 6, WE joined forces with Metallica for five shows in Holland (3), Germany (1), and Belgium (1) with them opening. Like ourselves, Metallica were up-and-comers and out promoting their new album, *Ride the Lightning*. We had never met the guys before

---

* In spite of the failed promotion of "We're Not Gonna Take It," when we perform the song at any show in Great Britain, it brings the house down every time.

(though they quickly informed us that they'd opened for Twisted Sister at a New Jersey nightclub), and they were all down-to-earth and cool (yes, even Lars). Our first show with Metallica in Holland was eye-opening. Unbeknownst to us, the Dutch were heavily into speed metal. They liked their rock hard. While Metallica's style played perfectly to that, Twisted Sister, with its makeup and costumes and "anthemic metal" leanings, wasn't quite as appealing. No problem. We quickly adjusted our set list to be more metallic, less anthemic, and ramped up our already high speeds to a more Netherlandish pace. Problem solved.

The night before our first show, I was offered the opportunity to promote Twisted's new record on a hugely popular live Dutch radio broadcast. I was taken, along with Joe Gerber—via the band Vandenberg's custom, converted ambulance—to the club from where the show was aired.

Expecting a real metal club, I was stunned to walk into a disco, playing dance music, filled with Johnny Bravos and Janie Bravettes.

The radio station broadcasting the show assured me the audience loved heavy metal and told me what they wanted me to do. They had heard about my onstage "rants" and wanted me to "do one" on the air. I explained to them that my banter was more inspired than planned, and that I had never just "done one" cold. They kept pushing, so I said I would give it a shot. I told the host to bring me onstage (dressed in my street clothes), then engage me in a conversation about heavy metal; I would see if I could muster a full-blown rant. "No problem," the host said in his funny Dutch accent, and headed out to make my introduction.

The music stopped and the host introduced me. I entered with microphone in hand, to a tepid response. The minute I got out there . . . the host walked off the stage without another word. The crowd stared blankly at me, and I stared back in silence. The national radio broadcast was transmitting "dead air." There are radio stations that actually have alarms that go off when there is dead air. This was not a good thing.

My mind racing, I started to rant. About what, I'm not sure, but I was going on about something for a few minutes—with zero audience response—when some guy in the audience yelled, "You look like a pregnant goldfish!" and the crowd laughed. I had no idea what that meant, but the people in the club did, and it clearly wasn't a good thing. I jumped off the stage—microphone still in hand—and charged the asshole who said it.

Well, I'm livid, shoving this guy and muthafucking him—into the microphone of course, always the professional—for all I'm worth, until security pulls us apart and drags me off. Joe Gerber, who, of course, had come to my assistance, says to me, "Oh, well, I guess that's the end of radio airplay in Holland."

But when I walked into the back room where the radio station people and record company reps were, to face the music . . . *I got a standing ovation!* They loved it! As far as the Dutch were concerned, that was great radio. Go figure.

OUR THIRD SHOW IN Holland with Metallica, we pulled into town to find every poster and ad promoting the show had a tiny TWISTED SISTER at the top and a huge WITH METALLICA, and their "troll" logo, taking up 90 percent of the page. Clearly, they were the draw.

Twisted Sister were never ones to headline a show for the sake of headlining, so we sent Joe Gerber to tell James Hetfield and the boys that they could close that night.

A few minutes later, Joe came back to the dressing room with a confused look on his face. "They said no. They couldn't understand why you would want to give up the headlining slot. They think you guys are up to something." That shows you the mentality of the average band. *No one* gives up the headline spot, even if the audience isn't there to see them. Egos.

I went into Metallica's dressing room and explained there was no trick—we weren't up to anything. They were the draw; they should close the show. Once assured, Metallica agreed to the billing swap.

The upside to this was I finally got to see Metallica perform. Due to my two-hour prep time for shows, I was always in the back getting ready while many great bands went on before us. After our set that night, I quickly got changed and went stage-side with Mark

Mendoza to watch this young band who were getting so many accolades from the metal press and fans. Toward the end of their powerful set, I turned to Animal and said, "These guys have got a lot of heart, but they're never gonna go anywhere."

So much for what I know!

MEANWHILE, BACK IN THE States, we were getting reports that our first single was being very well received. Before the *We're Not Gonna Take It* (*WNGTI*) video even started to air on MTV, 145 radio stations nationally were playing the song. I stress that because of the accepted belief that our video *made* the song a hit. While the video undoubtedly *enhanced* the single—and by *enhanced* I mean "supercharged the shit out of it"—"We're Not Gonna Take It" was killing at rock radio from the day it was released. Video or no video, Twisted Sister was set to explode in 1984.

The *WNGTI* video is generally regarded as groundbreaking and game-changing; it altered the face of the medium. In virtually any list of all-time greatest rock videos, *WNGTI* *always* makes it. For better or for worse, it is one of the main things Twisted Sister is remembered for. No one was more surprised than us. This said, the reception the *WNGTI* clip received at MTV is a whole other story.

The video, as delivered to MTV in its original form, had a two-minute-and-fifty-one-second prologue—an acted lead-in, without music. This was unheard of in 1984 . . . *and MTV hated it!* I was told that Music Television cofounder/originator and senior executive vice-president Les Garland was horrified by our effort and said, "That's not a rock video! That's *method acting*!" Needless to say, *WNGTI* was not a "Buzz Clip." Despite its massive success, and the audience's obvious mania for it, the *WNGTI* video was never aired more than in *medium* rotation.

A few months later, when a now hugely popular Twisted Sister delivered the *WNGTI* video *sequel*, "I Wanna Rock" (which also had a prologue), Les Garland was quoted as saying, "Now *this* is a rock video!" It was immediately put into heavy rotation. Egos.

But I'm getting ahead of myself.

After finishing our run of dates in Europe and the UK, we finally headed back home. I couldn't wait to reunite with my wife and son, and *Stay Hungry* was blowing up in the States.

I was not prepared for what came next.

⚜ 36 ⚜

why does the rain smell like pee?

Having been hugely popular in the tristate area, I thought I knew what being famous was. We had thousands of fans clamoring to get into our shows and meet us, we needed bodyguards, our phone numbers were unlisted, and I had to pull my hair back and wear a baseball hat to be less detected on the street. That's a rock star, right? Sure . . . but an average rock star. What I was becoming—totally unbeknownst to me, mind you—was something very different.

It felt great to come back to *my house*, with my wife and son waiting for me. Suzette loved our first little place (it only had two bedrooms) and put her heart into making it look great. Jesse was now almost two years old and a real handful. Coming and going the way I did offered me a unique view of my son's development. People do a third of their life's growth in the first three years of their life, so Jesse's mental and physical leaps—while to Suzette seeming incremental—to me were in huge spurts and a bit overwhelming. I was missing out on so much.

My first night home, I got in my car to run for some milk or something, and I put on the Long Island rock station WRCN. "We're Not Gonna Take It" was playing. Fair enough. It was a Long Island radio station and we were a Long Island band; they *should* be playing our song. On a whim, I flipped over to the other Long Island rock station, WBAB. "We're Not Gonna Take It" was playing. I've never been a gambler, but I decided to go for the trifecta. I spun the wheel one more time, hitting the button for the big New York City rock station and . . . *"We're Not Gonna Take It" was on there, too!* All three rock radio stations in my listening area were blasting my band's song! *We had arrived!* As cool as that feeling was, things soon got creepy and weird.

Suzette, Jesse, and I were shopping at a grocery store, for the first time since I'd got back from Europe, when we heard frantic, hushed calls over the store's PA system for people to "check out aisle three."

"That's the aisle we're in, Suzette. There's nothing here."

A little bit later we heard, "Check out aisle five."

"That's the aisle we're in, Dee. There's nothing going on."

Then a few minutes later: "Aisle seven!"

Hey, that's the aisle we're in, I started to say, but then it hit me.

As we checked out at the register, kids were arriving in droves on their bicycles and smooshing their faces against the glass to look in and see me. This is what I always wanted, but the reality was a bit surreal and even disconcerting. It's one thing to have your every move watched when you are performing, but it's uncomfortable when you're just going about your daily business. We got in our car quickly and drove off. It was cool in a weird sort of way.

The next night, Suzette and I decided to take Jesse out to one of those kid-friendly restaurants with rides and stuff. I wasn't home much, so I wanted to have a nice family evening with my wife and son. We walked in the place and Jesse immediately ran (as any toddler will do) toward some colorful plaything. We weren't five steps in when I realized the entire restaurant had stopped what they were doing, turned, and were frozen, staring at me in shock. Suddenly, the freeze broke, and the wild-eyed masses started to move as one toward me. Realizing this was going to turn into a personal appearance—not a night out with the family—I told Suzette to grab Jesse and we ran for our car.

That was the last time we did anything normal as a family for a long time.

I was becoming more of a star than I ever dreamed of. I wanted to be a rock star, but didn't expect Beatlemania kind of stuff. There was definitely a bit of a mania with Twisted Sister . . . *and it was all being directed at me.* When I went back out on the road with Twisted a short time later, I sent Suzette and Jesse down to Florida to stay with her family. Our quiet neighborhood street, with our quaint suburban house, had become a busy thoroughfare as the word got out where I lived. Cars raced down the block, people honked their horns, shouted and blasted my music. Some even parked outside at night and played Twisted Sister's entire song catalog. Yeah, that's what I wanted to hear when I wasn't recording or on tour playing my music.

And those were the people who liked me. I remember getting a call from my sister-in-law, Roseanne, who was house-sitting. She told me she had awoken the night before because she thought she heard something at the back door. As Roseanne approached the door, she heard the sound of rain. *Funny,* she said to herself, *the weather didn't say anything about rain.* When she peered out the window . . . some guy was pissing on my back door! Clearly, he wasn't a fan.

We hadn't been in our awesome little corner house on the street for nine months and we *had* to leave. It wasn't safe for my wife and especially our baby boy; and it wasn't fun. Everyone wanted to party with Twisted Sister's wild front man, but being wild was what I did for a living. It was the last thing I wanted to do when I got home.

ONE OTHER SAD SIDE effect of becoming "a star" is the way some friends and family treat you.

Caught up in a world of runaway success, you need those closest to you to be a stabilizing force. Suzette sure was. No matter how popular, successful, or famous I got, she remained unimpressed. I'd come home from the road pretty much "floating" into the house, I was so high on being a "rock god," and she would bring me right down to earth. After the initial warm (often passionate) welcome home, the minute I would get egotistical about my accomplishments, Suzette would respond with something like "That's great. Now go and empty the diaper pail, it smells like shit." Instant ego deflation; message received. She couldn't have been happier I was successful, but I was home now, her husband and her child's father. There was no place for egomaniacal bullshit. That is the stabilizing consistency that has kept my feet (fairly) on the ground. Suzette is the one constant in my life. Other people . . . not so much.

When you are a struggling musician, you remain on par—if not below par—with all the people you know. You have always been the one with "a dream," but the odds of your making it were slim to none, so everyone assumes this will be your place in their world: struggling artist. When suddenly you break through, and all the money and celebrity you've worked so hard for comes, it creates a major imbalance between you and them, and they can't help but be affected.

In fairness to those around me, while I wanted them to treat me as they always had, with success I'd proven to the world I was right about the best parts of me . . . and I wanted them to forget the worst. Especially those old stories that made me look so uncool (and human). I guess I was complicit in their change of attitude toward me. This said, does *anybody* want to be reminded of the *embarrassments* of their youth? I rest my case. The fact remains, most of those closest to me *were* affected by my success, and it changed our relationships. I was no longer being held to the same standard.

One of the saddest experiences I had involving this was with a close childhood friend, Eddie G. I didn't have a lot of friends growing up, and through high school Eddie was one of my closest. We had lost touch after he graduated medical school in podiatry, got married, and moved south to Nashville to open up a "drive-through podiatry center." This was a joke, of course. Eddie was funny. When Twisted Sister broke big and we were finally going to be playing down South, I reached out to Eddie to reconnect. I could not wait to see my dear friend and share a bit of normalcy.

The day of the show in Nashville, I rushed to answer a knock on my room door. I was expecting Eddie, and though I was half-dressed and looked like hell, who cared? He'd seen me at my worst growing up; I wasn't making a personal appearance. As I opened the door, there was a camera flash. When my eyes cleared, there stood Eddie with his wife—holding a camera—with uncomfortable, frozen grins on their faces. What was up with that?

Undeterred, I warmly invited them into my room, anxious to catch up and laugh with an old friend. No such luck. Eddie and his wife remained frozen and uncomfortable the entire visit, snapping candid photos of me at the most inopportune times. No matter what I did to try to make them feel at home, they could not relax and act normal. At this point in our rising career the band still stayed at motels, not hotels, so I took my guests to the laundry room with me. What could be more normal and less rock star than doing your laundry? *Flash!* They took a shot of me folding my damn underwear.

That's how our day together began and ended. I never saw Eddie again. A sad casualty of fame and fortune.

TWISTED SISTER HIT THE road *hard,* and this time there was no looking back. With our record and our career taking off, we toured relentlessly for the next ten months. This is the part of every rock 'n' roll memoir where eighties rock stars tell you their stories of sex-crazed, drug-and-alcohol-fueled rock 'n' roll debauchery. After all, it was the "decade of decadence." I have none of those stories to tell.

For a lot of reasons my rock 'n' roll life was so different from that of my peers. For one, I was married and had a kid and a traditional home life. That meant something to me, and I didn't want to screw it up. *I didn't.* More than thirty-five years later, I look at my peers' lives and am extremely happy with the choices I made and grateful to have an amazing wife, family, and life. Then there was my attitude to performing. I said it earlier, but it bears repeating:

If you have anything left after a performance, you cheated your audience. Period.

When I left the stage, I collapsed in my dressing room, guzzling bottles of Gatorade to rehydrate. Then, after warming down my voice, I'd get changed and go straight to the back lounge of our tour bus—no socializing for me. My voice was so shot every night from screaming my lungs out that I couldn't afford to strain my throat talking to people in smoke-filled rooms over loud music. I had to rest.

Making sure I had eight hours of sleep each night to recover (no way was I doing drugs to sustain the energy I needed to perform), I'd wake up in pain every morning, my body aching from my aggressive stage performance the night before. I'd down a couple of cups of hot coffee to loosen my strained and closed-up throat, then climb into a steaming-hot bath. I had to soak my muscles and joints to loosen them up, and the steam from the bath further loosened my vocal cords. This ritual went on every night and day . . . and I was only in my twenties! Once I could move and speak again, I'd start my day. A day of interviews, travel, sound checks, and mentally and physically preparing myself for the next show. Some party, huh?

My mind-set was *terrible*. People always ask Suzette if she traveled on the road with me back in the day. "Hell no!" she tells them. "He was the most miserable bastard to be around. I hated going to visit him on tour." I *was* miserable. It was almost as if I were punishing myself for something. I don't know what.

Mentally I viewed myself as a "hit man" and conducted myself as such. I preferred to arrive in town in the middle of the night and slip into an out-of-the-way hotel, unnoticed. I didn't want to be hounded by fans hanging and partying outside the hotel, sneaking into the lobby and hallways, banging on my door and calling my room (and they would). I needed to be undisturbed so I could get ready for the "hit."

I'd sit in my room all day . . . waiting. Waiting for the time to *kill* my next victim—whatever rock crowd Twisted Sister was going to play for that night. As the killing time approached, like the hit man who slowly and methodically assembles his gun, I put on my makeup and costume, warmed up my voice, stretched my muscles . . . and then the band and I would make the "hit." Every night. Then I'd get back on the bus and drive through the night to the next town, monotonously repeating the whole process, counting the days until my next break from the tour, when I could go home, see my family, and rest. That's what I lived for.

People say, when they see me perform, I seem to be having so much fun. I am . . . and I'm not. I'm completely conflicted. I want and have to do it . . . but I hate doing it. As I've said before, I live for the feeling of exhilaration I get when I *stop* or am finished performing, but I can't get that feeling without performing. The song should have been called "I Have to Rock!" It was a sickness.

⚜ 37 ❧

have some cheese, ratt!

On July 13 we joined forces with Ratt for a monthlong tour. Ratt was also on Atlantic Records and had a head start on the "race for platinum," with an earlier release than ours. Doing dates with various openers such as Lita Ford and Mama's Boys, we covered a lot of ground. From shows in New Hampshire (a festival with Cheap Trick headlining) to McAllen, Texas, on the Mexico border (where after seeing many soaking-wet "visiting" Mexican fans at the show, I learned the pejorative term *wetback* is literal), we switched off as headliners with Twisted closing in the Northeast and Ratt finishing up in Texas.

Besides the oppressive Southwest summer heat, a few memories stand out.

The first is our show at The Pier—an outdoor venue on the Hudson River—in New York City. Being our home base, Twisted Sister headlined with Ratt special-guesting and Lita Ford opening. Lita had been on quite a few shows with us by then, and we had bonded (we are still great friends to this day). That night was her last show with the tour.

Since I was always getting ready when she was on, I never got to *see* Lita perform, but I got to listen to her rock every night, and she was blowing me away. I've been a fan of hers since the Runaways, but now Lita was taking her playing to a whole new level. Besides

April Lawton from the seventies band Ramatam, Lita was the first female guitarist I had ever heard who could hold her own with the guys. Since April Lawton was a transsexual, having originally played with Johnny Maestro and the Brooklyn Bridge as a dude, I guess that made Lita the only one.

When Lita came into Twisted's dressing room after her final show on the tour to say good-bye, I pulled her to the side and told her just how great I thought she was. "You have a great opportunity," I said. "Your killer guitar playing can really show people that women can rock."

Lita was flattered by my words.

"People are going to push you to use sex to sell your music; don't let them," I continued. "To paraphrase Joe Perry, let your playing do the talking!"

Lita thanked me profusely for my inspiring words. She seemed truly fired up to take on the male-dominated guitar-playing world.

The next time I saw Lita Ford was a couple of years later, in a rock video on MTV. She was scantily clad, crawling on all fours, and pretty much humping a block of ice. Her guitar lay discarded on the floor, a few feet away. So much for my impassioned speech.

At that same Pier show, I was inspired to incorporate the giant USS *Intrepid* aircraft carrier, permanently docked adjacent to the concert site, in one of my stage rants.

I told the crowd that I believed they had enough energy to restart the out-of-service ship, and I encouraged them to join me in trying to get it going by shouting "Fuck you!" over and over and over. (Fuck you?) Needless to say, it didn't work.

Several weeks later, Twisted's management received a letter from the mayor's office informing us our group had officially been banned from all outdoor venues in New York City. Why? Well, unbeknownst to us, sound carries really, really, *really* well over water. Apparently, on the other side of the river, New Jersey residents were being forced to listen to Twisted Sister's "Fuck you!" chorus while sitting in their backyards on a warm summer night with their families.

Somehow, I don't think our fired-up, rowdy fans making a huge pile out of all the folding chairs and turning over food carts on their way out of the show helped either.

◆   ◆   ◆

THE ONE SHOW WITH Ratt I remember most in Texas—besides the blistering heat in McAllen (I couldn't believe Ratt abandoned their stage clothes and wore shorts!)—is Corpus Christi.

While my onstage rants are pretty much spontaneous, if I hit on something that works universally, I won't hesitate to reuse it or modify it to fit the current situation. This said, I can't understand how bands can use the same stage patter, verbatim, every night. How can it always be appropriate or not get old? Here are some classic stage-rap faux pas I've heard about.

David Lee Roth had a great line he'd lay on some heckling guy in the audience (you may have heard it): "After the show, I'm gonna fuck your girlfriend!" Cool. Not so cool when he did the same line, at the same time in the show, at a venue only twenty-five miles away, to a lot of the same people who had seen him the night before. Lame.

Triumph used to turn their massive light show on the upper balcony of the audience—every night, at the same moment in the show—and say "How ya'll doin' up there!" It would always get a huge response. Except for the night the show hadn't sold well and the balcony was closed off and empty. The janitor up there by himself, sweeping the balcony, was doing fine.

Paul Stanley from Kiss is renowned for exactly replicating his onstage speeches, every show, on every tour . . . even after they've been captured on live albums. On a tour with Mark "the Animal" Mendoza's band the Dictators opening for them, Paul repeated his raps so exactly and often that even the heroin-addled Dictators' lead singer, Handsome Dick Manitoba, could memorize them. The night Handsome Dick went onstage with the Dictators and repeated Paul's showstopping stage rap, word for word, was the last night the Dictators played with Kiss. I wonder what Paul said that night at that point in Kiss's set.

You gotta keep it fresh, kids, and react to your surroundings— not every venue and audience is the same. This said, in each town we played, at some moment in the show I would rename the town (you may remember a variation of this from the MTV concert):

"You know, Louisville is a pretty lame name for this town."
The audience is unsure how to react. Did Dee just call us lame?
"You guys are way too cool to be called Louisville."
The audience is still confused. Dee did say we were cool.
"From now on I'm gonna call this town Louis-fuckin'-ville!"
The crowd goes wild!
"Let me hear you say Louis-fuckin'-ville!"
"LOUIS-FUCKIN'-VILLE!"
"What?!"
"LOUIS-FUCKIN'-VILLE!"
"What!?"
"LOUIS-FUCKIN'-VILLE!"

I would do it with the name of every town on the tour. It worked every time.

Right before I was heading out to the stage in Corpus Christi, Texas, Joe Gerber rushed up to me.

"Whatever you do, don't say 'Corpus-fuckin'-Christi' tonight!"

"Why not?" I responded, annoyed by his presuming to tell me what to say or not say onstage.

"Because *corpus Christi* means 'the body of Christ.' You do not want to be screaming 'the body of fuckin' Christ' in the Deep South!"

Point taken.

AT THE END OF the Twisted Sister/Ratt tour, the 1984 Summer Olympics began. Americans always get caught up in Olympic fever ("USA! USA! USA!"), but this year was particularly special for both the United States and Twisted Sister. Not only were the games being held in Los Angeles but as our Olympians pursued the gold, so were we. Twisted Sister was approaching our first gold record (five hundred thousand copies) in sales as the Olympic athletes competed fiercely for the dream they, too, had worked so hard for.

As we drove from town to town, rocking our asses off and selling records, night after night, day after day, we tuned in to the Olympic Games and cheered our countrymen and women on. It could not have been more ironic or better timed. Of course, the most inspiring of all was America's sweetheart, gymnast Mary Lou Retton. For a band who had struggled for so long, against such great odds, we connected strongly with the young dynamo, who would not let anything stop her from achieving her goal . . . including a sprained ankle. Mary Lou, you are a true twisted sister! Almost to the day Twisted Sister's *Stay Hungry* album went gold, Mary Lou Retton *stuck it* that one final time to win her gold. Amazing!

We joined Dio's *Last in Line* tour on the final day of the '84 Olympics, and one of our first shows was at the Nassau Coliseum, in Uniondale, Long Island, the arena where I used to go to concerts as a teen. Only miles away from where I grew up, in the heart of Twisted Sister's "SMF stronghold," I couldn't imagine a better place to receive our first gold-record awards.

To make the night even more special, we brought in Mark Metcalf, the star of the *WNGTI* video, to present us our "gold" onstage. Dressed in his character's wardrobe from the video, Neidermeyer "surprised" the band when he walked out onstage. The crowd went wild at the sight of him and as he laid into them "Neidermeyer style."

In the spirit of the Olympics, special gold-record "medals" had been made with red ribbons, and Mark "Neidermeyer" Metcalf draped one around each band member's neck. With our fans, families, and friends all looking on, this was a momentous occasion. After eight and a half years of struggle, more than two thousand live shows, fighting against insurmountable odds, and simply refusing to give up when most others would have, Twisted Sister had finally done it. That gold record could never be taken from us, and no matter what happened in our lives from that point on, we had done what we had set out all those years ago to do. *We had made it!*

BY AUGUST, WITH OUR gold album well on the way to platinum, audiences were coming to see us as well as Dio. We were no longer "some band" opening for the headliner. This said, as is usual, the headliners *are* the main draw, and their fans always snap up the best seats in the house. Night after night, we would have to deal with rows of hardcore Dio fans sitting in the front, many of whom couldn't care less about this new band Twisted Sister. Remember Dee Rule #2: If you don't like me, we've got a problem? As you might imagine . . . I didn't respond well to the negativity. If you were being an asshole, I felt it was my duty to let you know . . . loudly. Not surprisingly, some people had a problem with this.

One night, in Worcester, Massachusetts, there was a guy sitting about seven rows back from the front who was very unhappy with me and Twisted Sister. Since Dio's stage set had my band cramped toward the very lip of the stage—in front of the lights—I could see every subtle, and not so subtle, nuance of his hostility toward us. Apparently, he abhorred the endless ridicule I was heaping upon him and his like-minded brethren and sisthren. Toward the end of our set, his anger got the best of him. As I stood staring directly at him in disbelief, he took careful aim with a bottle and let the lethal weapon fly. I easily sidestepped the projectile, but I was stunned! After all these years of being a blind target on stage, I finally not only saw my assailant but watched as he unabashedly tried to cause me bodily harm.

Sometimes I think people view seeing a live concert like they're at the movies—the characters onstage are two-dimensional and not actually real. Well, I ain't no fucking movie! Dressed in full Twisted Sister regalia (the makeup, the spandex, the shoulder pads, the heels, *everything*), I climbed off the stage, over the barrier, then over seven rows of audience members and chairs, and dived on that fucking piece of shit. Within seconds, crew members—including the intrepid Joe Gerber and our dedicated and loyal stage manager Frank Rubino—came to my aid, scrambling off the stage and into the fray. My band played on.

As my assailant was dragged out of the arena, I climbed back over the rows of chairs and people, over the barricade, onto the stage and finished the set to a stunning ovation from the crowd. *Don't fuck with Dee fucking Snider and Twisted fucking Sister, dammit!*

The next morning I was woken by the phone in my room. On the line were my manager, my lawyer, and my accountant.

"*Are you out of your fucking mind?!*" screamed the usually serene Mark Puma.

"What are you talking about?" I replied, confused. I was still half asleep.

"Last night! What the hell do you think you were doing last night?!" Mark was yelling.

I tried to remember what had happened the night before. After a while all the dates become a blur—as you'll find out in a minute.

"The fight?" I offered. I'd been scrapping with people in the audience for years; I couldn't imagine why they would be calling about that.

"Yes, the fight! You can't be attacking people in the audience anymore," continued Mark. *"You're famous now!"*

"You have money," chimed in my accountant.

"You'll get your ass sued for everything you've worked so hard to get," added my attorney.

The significance of what they were saying began to set into my caffeine-less, foggy mind.

"That piece of shit threw a bottle at me! What was I supposed to do," I parried, my head beginning to clear, "just sit there and take it?"

"We will get you a bodyguard," said Mark Puma.

"A bodyguard?" I replied. "For what? *To protect them from me?!*"

But that's just what they did. They got me a bodyguard so I wouldn't have to do the dirty—potentially litigious—job of defending my and the band's honor. Essentially, *protect the scumbags from me!*

Several months later, I would be on a promotional tour in Australia with my bodyguard, Vic. He was a black, six-feet-tall, 225-pound, ex-military bodybuilder who had worked for Mick Jagger, David Bowie, and Freddie Mercury.*

We were in a limo, leaving an appearance at a nightclub, when my car stopped at a light and a carload of rowdy kids pulled up along side us. One asshole was hanging out the window and yelling, "Twisted Sister sucks! *You fucking suck!*" Vic jumped out of

---

* Vic often said that he never experienced the kind of attention and fanatical behavior I attracted with any of his other clients. I explained to him that it was the "Elephant Man" factor. Looking the way I did, and being as large as I am—especially in five-inch heels (all of his other "bosses" were about five-and-a-half feet tall—totally under the radar)—*you* didn't have to be a fan of my band, or even know who I was to be curious and drawn to me. *Everyone* wants to get a closer look at the Elephant Man.

limo, and let's just say he took care of the situation. He got back in the limo, and we drove off. With pride, Vic turned to me and said, "How was that, boss?" to which I responded:

"A lot like watching someone else have sex with your wife. It may look good . . . but *it doesn't feel the same.*"

❧ 38 ❧

how the hell did i get *both* platform shoes in my mouth?

After touring awhile, the cities become a blur. It's not that you're not into the shows and the audience, but the city and the venue are pretty inconsequential. You're just there to rock.

In the Midwest one of the most ubiquitous concert venues is "the shed." These indoor/outdoor venues are designed to hold from five thousand to twenty-five thousand people with a portion of the crowd seated under an open, roofed-in area and the rest of the audience outside standing or sitting on the lawn behind it.

It was mid-August, and Dio/Twisted Sister had played Chicago the night before, and now we were in Detroit, performing in a virtually identical-looking concert shed. I think you can see where this is going. We opened our set in Detroit the way we did every show, three songs in a row, without stopping, except for the mandatory "If you're ready to kick some ass, we are Twisted fuckin' Sister!" after the first song. The boys and I slammed them with "You Can't Stop Rock 'n' Roll," and the Detroit headbangers were salivating.

Then I opened my big mouth. *"How you doin', Chicago!?"*

The crowd went quiet. *That's odd.* I looked over at Jay Jay, who was shaking his head and mouthing, *Detroit!* Oh, shit! Calling a town by a different name is like calling your girlfriend another girl's name. Calling rival towns such as Detroit and Chicago each other's name is like calling your wife another woman's name . . . *in bed!* No matter what I did, I could not come back from that major faux pas.

I even tried leaving the stage and starting the show over. We never recovered.

Ever since that fateful day, I have been paranoid to say the name of any place I'm performing out loud onstage. I'm terrified I'll get it wrong again. When I first say the city name, I'll slur it and pull away from the microphone just in case I've got it wrong.

"How you doin' [something indecipherable]!"

Did he say "Somethingburgville?"

Now I always have the name of the town or city taped on the monitor or on the drum riser just in case.

Sorry about that, Chicago . . . I mean, *Detroit*.

BY THE END OF August, it was time for Twisted Sister to follow up on our hugely successful *We're Not Gonna Take It* video. WNGTI had changed the face of the format, so the bar was set high. You think I'm exaggerating? Consider the videos that came before *WNGTI* and those that came after. Van Halen was bragging about spending only a few dollars on the "Panama" video, then all of a sudden it's their "all story line and big budget" with "Hot for Teacher." Mötley Crüe were fighting nonsensical Amazonian women in the "Looks That Kill" video in '83, then suddenly they're in a high school setting, complete with a cult actor in the cast, in "Smokin' in the Boys Room" in 1985. What happened? *We're Not Gonna Take It* happened, that's what. Game changer.

The obvious second single from the *Stay Hungry* album was "I Wanna Rock." Besides the fans' love of the song and its natural hook, it had been teased in the first video. The son was listening to the song in his room when his dad burst in, and he said to his father before blowing him out the window, *"I wanna rock!"* *

Twisted once again teamed up with innovative director Marty Callner. In the four months since the release of the *WNGTI* video,

---

* Point of interest: While the son was played by director Marty Callner's son Dax, the voice of the "possessed" son is Marty's. I had envisioned something a bit more *Exorcist*-ish, but I guess it worked. Marty can also be heard "chuckling" when the mother throws water on Neidermeyer, just before the song kicks in.

my pal Marty had become the most in-demand rock-video director in the business. And deservedly so. For the new Twisted video's pre-production, production, and postproduction, I moved into Marty's house in Beverly Hills. That way we could hang out and work on the project pretty much nonstop. These specialized living arrangements created a physical distance between the band and me and definitely further drove a wedge between us.

Having my creative ideas and persona be accepted on such a mass scale made me feel more and more comfortable flexing my "control freak" muscles. I no longer had any doubts (if I ever did) about my abilities and importance. I had all but dropped the ruse of pretending to care what anybody else thought. I knew (and always had) what was best for Twisted Sister and was actively and openly steering the ship. I was becoming a megalomaniac.

MY CLOSEST FRIEND WITHIN the band had been Mark Mendoza; he *was* my best friend. But starting with the bringing of Tom Werman on board to produce the band, we had been drifting further and further apart. We no longer hung out or roomed together (as we always had in the past), and Mark's obvious efforts to sabotage what I was trying to do for the band pushed me away even more.

In fairness to Mark, I definitely created my own distance from the band, as well. The small rifts between Jay Jay, Eddie, and me in the early days of the band had festered and grown. The success we were having as a band—and I was having as a creative and "star" personality—were fertilizer to those seeds of discontent. Negative feelings were flourishing.

Further exacerbating the problem was our manager, Mark Puma. Mark was an easygoing, smooth-things-over kind of guy, quick to put a Band-Aid on a problem, rather than find the cure. Instead of talking directly to each other about our differences (the healthy approach), band members would complain to Puma, hoping he would set the other guy straight. Puma would at all costs avoid asking or addressing the tough questions and figure out a way to assuage the problem for the time being. Unfortunately, the real issue would never be addressed and would continue to grow like some untreated cancer.

MY CONCEPT FOR THE *I Wanna Rock* video was simple: do a sequel to the *WNGTI* video and answer the question "What does the father/ Neidermeyer do for a living?" He would be an even bigger asshole at his job. Marty and I again wrote the video together and brought back most of the people who worked on the first one, especially the now legendary father figure, Mark Metcalf.

Mark Metcalf's acting career had been revived by the *WNGTI* video. His amped-up, overbearing, asshole dad resonated with pretty much every kid in the world and showed Mark to be one hell of a character actor. Because of this, Metcalf didn't come quite as cheaply for this video as he had the first time, and he was a bit more of a prima donna.

The video story played out—as you all probably know—in a high school, where Mr. Neidermeyer was a mean teacher, return-ing on the first day of school. Since this video was to be released to coincide with the start of the real school year, the spirit of the thing truly connected with our audience (though teachers of the era still bust my balls over all the times they had to hear "I wanna rock!" from some smart-ass kid).

By filming in the summer, securing a school for the shoot was not a problem, nor was filling it with high school students. School was out, and Twisted Sister was one of the hottest bands in the world.

The day of the shoot was a scorcher, and the AC at our school was off for the summer. Marty and I arrived at the crack of dawn to find the place mobbed by teenagers responding to KMET's announce-ment for video extras. We had to cast the kids for the classroom, but since I had to get ready for the shoot (makeup and costume), I couldn't participate. I did insist on seeing and speaking to the fea-tured "fat headbanger" before he was locked in.

When Marty brought him into the room to meet the band, I was blown away; he couldn't have been more perfect, but I knew what being featured in this video would do to him. Dax Callner, who played the son in the first video, told me that the recognition he got from being in the video was insane. And not all of it was positive. Some people weren't satisfied with just saying hi or asking for a photo or an autograph. Some kids in school were cruel, and others insisted on reenacting the video, word for word. Not quite what young Dax had expected when he accepted the part.

Where Neidermeyer had just yelled at the son in the *WNGTI* video, I knew the script for *I Wanna Rock* called for him to be a bit more insulting. Borrowing a line from *Animal House,* "I've got a good mind to slap your fat face!" I wanted to be sure the kid knew what he was in for. Not surprisingly, he was totally into it. Imagine you were some kid showing up with thousands of others for a chance to be an extra in a rock video for one of the most popular bands in the world, and you're pulled out of the pack to star in it. Then you're rushed back to meet Twisted Sister, in full regalia, and they ask you if you are okay with what they need you to do. What would *you* have said?

Mark Metcalf showed up to the set a little worse for wear, having been out late the night before with his Left Coast, LA friends. Mark was no longer the easygoing, great guy he had been on the first video shoot. After my experience with him on the *I Wanna Rock* video shoot, I would often tell people that the Neidermeyer persona was the *real* Mark Metcalf, and being a nice guy was just a character Mark played.*

By midmorning, Metcalf was more than a little irritated. Maybe it was the heat, his lack of sleep, or some other X factor. Maybe it was a combination of all three. Mark was in a foul mood and his performance was lacking during the scene where he yells at the Fat Kid. After a few failed takes, Marty Callner started getting a bit firmer with Metcalf directorially, pushing him to give more. Mark was less than pleased. I can't tell you their exact exchange of words or nuance of phrase, but with the entire classroom full of extras, band, cast, and crew bearing witness, it went something like this. After considerable chiding from Marty to Mark to work harder . . .

---

* Mark and I have been in touch from time to time since those crazy video days. As with my own, I can assure you, Mark's "asshole days" are far behind him.

Metcalf (to Marty): "Or what? You don't look so tough."

A hushed silence fell over the room.

Marty: "You wanna step outside and find out?"

Marty Callner is on the shorter side, but built like a wrestler. Mark Metcalf is tall, and very lean. Sort of like Tolkien's Gimli the dwarf versus Legolas the elf. All eyes were on the two potential combatants as they glared at each other. Marty calmly waited while Metcalf's face got redder and redder, as he mentally explored his options . . . then he turned away from Marty without a word. He (wisely) backed down. Gimli would have snapped Legolas like a twig.

Without waiting even a second, Marty Callner yelled, "Action!" and Mark Metcalf launched into the now legendary, spit-flying "I've got a good mind to slap your fat face!" tirade you all know and love. *It was incredible!* While the rest of the long, event-filled day rolled on (Metcalf's stunt double was launched into the ceiling and knocked unconscious; the massive crowd of teenagers hanging out in the heat all day were so hot and hungry, the world's biggest McDonald's order was placed; my face melted off several times; etc.), the band and I passed the time with actor Stephen Furst, aka Flounder from *Animal House.*

I had used my growing influence to hire Stephen to be in the video for a surprise ending ("Oh, boy, is this great!"). Ostensibly he was there only for us to connect even more with my favorite comedy, but the band took great joy in having him repeat every one of his classic lines from the film ("Brother D.D.! Brother Bluto!" "The Negroes stole our dates," etc.). Stephen seemed happy to oblige, but in retrospect I'm wondering if he was too afraid to tell the six-and-a-half-foot-tall (seven feet tall with hair) creatures in the crazy makeup and costumes no. Either way, it was a blast.

MTV and their audience's response to the video was huge. Immediately put in heavy rotation (where it stayed for a long time), *I Wanna Rock* was a major worldwide video hit, and its popularity spilled over to radio as well. Like the *WNGTI* video, it had struck a chord and spoke loudly and clearly for an entire generation of rockers.

◆   ◆   ◆

IF YOU WILL ALLOW me to get even more self-indulgent than I already am, I've been dying to mention something since the day *I Wanna Rock* was released.

In the story line of the video, once the fat kid turns into Twisted Sister, Neidermeyer spends the rest of the video, à la Wile E. Coyote, trying to kill the band. In one of his many ill-fated attempts he tries to blow the band up while they are performing in the auditorium. To this end, Neidermeyer wires dynamite to a plunger, then crawls military-style toward the band—with the dynamite in his teeth—to plant the explosives. Straight out of a Road Runner cartoon, a butterfly lands on the dynamite plunger handle, causing it to depress and blow up Neidermeyer.

That effect was achieved (now it would be via CGI) by exposing a live butterfly to liquid nitrogen, freezing it instantly. It was then placed on the handle of the plunger, with the idea that the warmth of the day would quickly defrost it. Then the butterfly would fly away. Running the film in reverse would give the illusion of its landing on the handle and causing it to depress. In theory.

Sadly, the nitrogen exposure instantly *killed* the poor creatures. To achieve what we needed for the shot, we decided to take one of the dead butterflies, attach it to a piece of clear filament (a long, wirelike stick) that would barely read on camera, put a touch of stickum on the plunger handle to hold the ex-butterfly in place, then lift it off the handle when the camera rolled. When the footage was run in reverse, it would achieve the same effect we were looking for. Great idea. *In theory.*

The first take, a little too much stickum was used, and when they tugged gently on the filament to get the butterfly to "take off," it tore the wings and abdomen off, leaving the head and upper body still sticking to the handle. Subsequent takes worked better, but the footage of the poor dead butterfly being torn in two had Marty Callner and me crying from laughing so hard during editing. I know, we're fucked-up. We decided to put in a quick shot of the "butterfly atrocity"—complete with a tearing sound—as the body came apart. Marty and I were sure that this would have rock fans in stitches.

To this day, not one person has ever mentioned that moment in *I Wanna Rock*! Not once. Not even a "That was fucked-up, dude!" For the life of me, I cannot figure out why that is. It's as plain as day!

ONE OF THE OTHER things I did for the band was promotion. I did all the press, everywhere in the world. It wasn't that the band didn't want to do press—*I didn't want them to do it.* I know, that seems messed up. Read on.

As the creative and driving force behind the band—and the front man—I was the band member interviewers wanted to talk to, and I didn't want anyone else misrepresenting me. Since I created and cowrote the videos, and wrote every song, who better to answer questions? To top it off, I didn't feel any of the other guys gave particularly good interviews, and one of them was trying to sabotage me and the band. What would you have done?

While the vast majority of interviews were done on the phone or in the city the band was in, from time to time I would actually travel to other countries on press and promotional tours. The first ever of these was to Europe. I was flown over to hit a number of Western European countries in September of '84, and in each country I found Twisted Sister had an even greater success story. Everywhere I went, the band had finally broken though the wall of indifference we had faced for so long. Our *Stay Hungry* record and its subsequent videos were making major inroads, not only in the metal world but in the pop world as well. No greater than in Sweden.

I arrived in Sweden to discover our record had blown up. Sales were through the roof and interest in the band had skyrocketed. Oddly, "We're Not Gonna Take It" didn't get the initial reaction there that it got in the rest of the world, but when "I Wanna Rock" came out, the entire country lit up. As much as I abhorred hearing this, it was even a hit in the dance clubs!

Picked up at the airport by a limousine, I was brought to the premier five-star hotel in Stockholm and given the presidential suite. My two-day promotional stay was filled with first-class everything, and dazzling accolades and adoration for me, my band, and our amazing record. *It was incredible!* I was signing albums for the children of the king and queen!

After a dreamlike two days, on Friday of that week, I departed to do a couple of days of press in the UK. I left a beautiful, sunny, spotlessly clean Sweden (it really is like an IKEA over there) to arrive in a cool, dreary, wet, second-hand shop London. I started doing press the minute I arrived by cab at my two-star, run-down, depressing hotel.

As positive and excited as all the other countries' interviews had been, the ones in Great Britain were the exact opposite. Interview after interview was about the failing of Twisted Sister's new record to live up to expectations, and "How does it feel now that the band's success is over?" England was the only country in the world where this was the case, and that was only because of that asshole Rubber Dick's being too cheap to pay for stamps!

When my first day of interviews in the UK finally ended, I was informed I had the weekend to myself, until the torture would start again on Monday. Everybody wanted to talk to the musical flop of 1984. I sat in my horrible little room, in my horrible little chair, feeling horribly depressed and horribly looking at the misery of two long days off alone, when an idea came to me. I had my manager contact Twisted's record company in Sweden and ask them if they could use me over there for a couple more days of promotion. They jumped at the chance to have the front man for the biggest new band in their country back!

Before I had even unpacked my suitcase in London, I was on a plane—in first class, of course—jetting back to Stockholm, where I was picked up by limo and reinstated in my presidential suite. I spent the weekend being wined, dined, and celebrated as the greatest thing since the smorgasbord. *Whew!*

⊰ DEE LIFE LESSON ⊱
You don't need to be king of the world, just king of *your* world.

Swedish krona can buy things, too, you know.

✠ 39 ✠

"these times they are a-changin'"

I returned home in September to a new level of celebrity. *Stay Hungry* had gone platinum, "I Wanna Rock" was a hit, I was making a lot of money, and I now had a full-time bodyguard. While I always expected Twisted Sister to make it, I thought we would be one of those bands that traveled from town to town, blowing audiences away, causing them to run out and buy our records. I never thought we would have traditional *Billboard*-chart hit records. That said, it did make sense. My biggest influences were all bands who had sold millions of albums and *had* hit records. Why shouldn't the product of those influences do the same?

Before Twisted Sister headed back out on the road, there was the little matter of my wife's and son's birthdays.

✠ DEE LIFE LESSON ✠
You can be away the entire year, but if you make it home for the special days (birthdays, anniversaries, Valentine's Day, Thanksgiving, Christmas, etc.), your family will be cooler about your being away.

⊰ DEE LIFE LESSON ⊱

You can be home all year round, but if you miss those same five or six
important days . . . *you're screwed.*

I'm not saying I never missed a special occasion, but I always
made a concerted effort to make it home and celebrate with the family if I could. Jesse was turning two that year, so we had a birthday
party for him with friends and family at our little house in Babylon,
Long Island (the one the guy pissed on). Even though we didn't
spend much time there anymore, it was still our home. In the past
two years I had been away for fourteen months. *Still more than half
of Jesse's life!* Every time I would come home from the road, I'd be
stunned by the changes in him. I had missed so many milestones.
The first time I saw him scurry up a flight of stairs, I nearly had a
heart attack. He'd been doing it effortlessly for weeks, but I didn't
know that—I wasn't around.

Jesse's greatest connection to me as a father was seeing me on
television. Suzette would have MTV on all day (back when it really
was *music television*), listening to the music in the background, and
when one of my songs would start to play, she and Jesse would rush
in to "see Daddy." Suzette told me how he'd get so excited to see me
as she screamed, "It's Daddy! It's Daddy!" Hearing that would make
me smile but break my heart just a bit. I guess that's "the price you
gotta pay." There's that damn song again.

During these hectic times, Suzette stayed home and took care of
Jesse, or they headed down to Florida and lived with her family. We
finally had the money for my wife and son to visit me on the road,
but it was the last place Suzette wanted to be. All I did was hide in
my hotel room, on the bus, or in my dressing room. I would never go
out, not even for a meal. I traveled the world and never saw a thing.
Part of this was because I wanted to experience world travel for the
"first time" with Suzette. I just didn't feel right going out and having
a great time without my wife and son.

The other part of my reclusive behavior? I was completely hung
up on being recognized and hounded by fans. Funny, isn't that what
I wanted all along?

Not that I was all that much more fun and adventurous when I was home. I never wanted to leave the house. For three or four years we hardly ever went out (except for local shopping). No movies, no amusement parks, no vacations . . . nothing. I remember the *one time*, during the heyday, Suzette convinced me to go to a movie. . . .

We went to one of the only single (non-multiplex) movie houses left at that time on Long Island, figuring there would be less people to potentially recognize me. While Suzette got the tickets, I hid in the car, waiting for the line to die down and the houselights to go off so I could sneak in unnoticed. On Suzette's cue I rushed into the theater looking like the Unabomber, wearing sunglasses, a hood pulled up over my hair and head and hiding my face (not too suspicious). Suzette and I slipped into the dark theater and sat down . . . just in time for the *We're Not Gonna Take It* video to start playing on the big screen. *Are you fucking kidding me!?* A rock video was being shown before the feature!? That speaks to the popularity of the band and the video, but it was the last time we went to the movies for a long time.

Living with *this* celebrity wasn't easy.

I'm sure this doesn't sound like a big deal to you. It probably even sounds cool. A good friend of mine, Cooch, once said if he was me, he would announce that he was Dee Snider everywhere he went. Yeah, that's what I thought before I became a celebrity, too. Cooch just couldn't understand my reluctance to be recognized. I can't either. I think it was a combination of wanting to be able to devote myself totally to my family when I was with them, along with my need to always be "the rock star" for my fans. I didn't want to disappoint them. *Does that make any sense at all?* I think another part was that I just liked being so famous I *had* to hide. For what it's worth, I handle celebrity a lot better now.

AFTER THE DIO TOUR, we hit the road with Y&T. A couple of memorable things happened to me during our run. Both were on the West Coast, one bad and one good. Bad first.

Y&T opened for Twisted Sister on all of the shows, except in Northern California, where they headlined. Like Twisted, Y&T had been around for quite a while and had a huge home following. It only made sense that we open for them at those shows. At one Bay Area show, some piece-of-shit Y&T fan (no reflection on the band—they are great guys) started throwing large metal *bolts* at us, with force. I'm talking three-inch-long, three-quarter-inch-diameter pieces of steel thrown like a baseball pitch. These things were positively *lethal* and damaged everything they hit. As usual, due to the lights in our eyes, we could not see them coming until the last second.

I tried everything to locate and call out our cowardly assailant. About halfway through the set I took one of the bolts *hard* in the ribs, and that was it. I couldn't take a chance of somebody in the band or the crew being hit in the face or the head. For the first time in the history of the band, we didn't finish our set and left the stage. I was furious.

Later I realized what I should have done: played with the house-lights on. We'd done it before for other, less threatening reasons. I would have been able to see who was throwing the bolts at the band—if he had the balls to throw them with the lights on—and kicked his ass. Well, my bodyguard would have kicked his ass—since I wasn't allowed to do that anymore. To this day, it bugs the hell out of me that I allowed myself and the band to be driven off the stage by some chickenshit asshole!

Now on to a much better memory.

Alice Cooper is a *major* influence on me. Coming to truly appreciate the original Alice Cooper band and Alice's vocal "attitude" was one of the last pieces in defining the rock singer and performer I would become (the final piece was Bon Scott and AC/DC). Looking at the way Alice and I perform, we are nothing alike. That's because I only had photographs of the band to work off of. In the sixties and seventies there were no videos or DVDs of concerts to watch, and I never got to see the band live. I developed my stage performance the way I *thought* Alice Cooper would perform. Imagine my surprise when I finally saw him onstage when we toured together in 2005! Vocally I'm sort of the upper octave of Alice (as exemplified on our duet of "Be Chrool to Your Scuel").

In the early eighties, Alice Cooper's career couldn't have been more dead. He'd struggled with alcohol and drug addiction and had a series of poorly received records. Saying you were an Alice Cooper fan was not cool . . . but I didn't care. This man and his original band had inspired and defined who I was as a recording artist and a performer, and I owed them nothing but respect and admiration. I continually told the world how I felt about Alice Cooper and his original band . . . and they appreciated it.*

At one of the Twisted Sister shows with Y&T on the West Coast, an unusual floral arrangement was delivered to my dressing room. It consisted of dead, black roses, a small, gnarled tree branch, and an Alice Cooper comic. Along with it was a note from the man himself, thanking me for my unflagging support and telling me he was coming to one of the shows to see the band and meet me. I was blown away!

I'd always thought that of all the rock stars I worshipped, Alice and I would get along. Something in his lyrics and general attitude—and his love of show tunes—told me we would one day become friends. And here was my hero reaching out to me!

I don't remember the exact date Alice came to see the band, but it was like meeting a kindred spirit. Alice is an incredibly affable guy who has been friends with some of the most legendary people in the art, film, and music worlds. Everyone feels they connect with Alice. I guess that's part of his charm. Yet I wonder, who really is Alice Cooper's friend? To quote Inspector Clouseau in *A Shot in the Dark*, "I suspect everyone . . . and I suspect no one."

Physically, he was a lot smaller and frailer than I thought he'd be. Not that he's tiny. I guess everyone views his or her heroes as being larger-than-life. Besides, he came across as such a creature in photos. Monsters are supposed to be big and scary, aren't they? This said, the most constant comment I hear when fans meet me is they didn't think I would be so big. Which kind of contradicts my thinking. Still, getting to meet and know the man is a childhood dream come true. Not many things affect me like that.

---

* I would come to understand just what it meant to have someone championing you when you were down. When Skid Row first broke, Sebastian Bach would sing my praises endlessly, despite that Dee Snider's and Twisted Sister's careers were dead in the water. *Thanks for that, Sebastian.*

• • •

THE DECADE OF DECADENCE didn't just happen on a whim. Like all things, it was the effect of a significant cause . . . the Reagan Era. When Ronald Reagan was elected president, the country took a sudden, wildly conservative turn. I now know the ultraconservative element never goes away, only lies in wait for its opportunity to pounce, but back then it felt as if it sprang out of nowhere. Add to that, thanks to Reagan's ill-fated concept of trickle-down economics (George Bush Sr. took it on the chin for that brain fart), the economy got a steroid shot in the arm and money flowed (until the economy stopped doing the 'roids). Those were exciting times.

But for every action there is an equal (or sometimes stronger) reaction, and the more conservative mainstream America got, the more flagrantly the youth wanted to disregard it. It was a perfect storm. Never was there a form of music more steeped in wretched excess, over-the-top behavior, and hedonism than what became known as hair metal. It was just what the rock 'n' roll doctor ordered. To once again paraphrase the movie *Animal House*, Reagan Era conservatism called for a really stupid gesture on somebody's part . . . and eighties rockers were just the guys and girls to do it!

People often ask me what I think of current trends in music, and for the past twenty-five years or so I've said the same thing: "Not enough middle finger." Since my heyday, I've liked a lot of contemporary heavy music. I even liked grunge—the hair-metal slayer—but in the 1990s and 2000s—and even still today—there's just too much whining and complaining about how life sucks, and not enough middle finger. B in the D (back in the day) we didn't complain about stuff, we railed against it, and if we couldn't do anything about it, we shook our "junk" in its face. That was the youth attitude of the time, and eighties metal bands exemplified that fuck-you state of mind. *We weren't gonna take it!* (See how that works?)

Though woefully misunderstood, Twisted Sister was the visual and musical embodiment of what the kids wanted and everything conservative America feared—in-your-face, outrageous, rebellious behavior. We were a threat to every value they stood for . . . or so they thought.

◆　　◆　　◆

BY THE FALL OF 1984, a change had happened to Twisted Sister's following that we weren't yet fully aware of. We had gone from being the scourge of society—a true underground phenomenon—to "pop rock stars" seemingly overnight. Thanks to the wild success of our videos and the catchiness of our singles, our audience had expanded and attracted mainstream rock fans and a lot of younger kids. The range of a typical Twisted Sister audience now went from hard-core high-school- and college-age metal fans to their younger brothers and sisters, some of who didn't even like heavy metal. *Houston . . . we have a problem.*

Speaking of Houston, Twisted Sister was on the road again in the South and Southwest, and the turnouts were huge. We were a bona fide sensation. While our audience may have been broadening, as a band we had not changed one iota. With our heads down and still putting our shoulders into it, we were giving our fans the same anger-fueled, profanity-laced live show we'd been giving since our days in the biker bars of Long Island. We were anything but mainstream.

Twisted Sister's October 6 concert, at the Civic Center Arena in Amarillo, Texas, was like any other. An aggressive, obscenity-filled, headbanging frenzy for a packed house of rabid SMFs . . . and moms and dads escorting their teenage and preteen children. *Uh-oh.* Toward the end of the show, I got into a confrontation with some hater in the crowd and verbally went off on him in typical Dee Snider style. Nothing out of the ordinary for a Twisted Sister show. The phalanx of Amarillo police waiting for me when I got off the stage, however . . . that was different.

Apparently, one of the parents in the audience, escorting her fourteen-year-old daughter to the show (commendable), had filed charges against me for my obscene language, and I was being arrested. When my tour manager inquired what exactly I had said that upset her, he was informed that the phrase "suck my muthafuckin' dick" had pushed her over the top. I had said it to that guy who was harassing me.

To put this in perspective, I open every show with "If you're ready to kick some ass, we are Twisted fuckin' Sister!" This woman sat through over an hour of profanity that would have given Richard Pryor, in his prime, a run for his money, *then* she decided to press charges? Nice parenting, Mom.

The Amarillo police were kind enough—and wise enough—to allow me to change out of my stage costume and makeup before taking me downtown. They didn't want a scene. I got a bit of verbal harassment from them while I changed, but they stopped once I told them my father was a cop. Once I was in my "street clothes," they slipped me out of the building hoping none of our fans would notice. For the most part they didn't. At the precinct, I was booked on charges of "profane and abusive language," fingerprinted, photographed (can I get a few of those in wallet size?), and released on $75 bail. *Seventy-five dollars!* What the hell kind of bail was that!? I'm a *bad* man! *

My arrest made news all over the world. But it wasn't until we got to the next venue that the seriousness of what had happened the night before hit us.

Word had spread like wildfire in Texas, and the Southern conservatives were in an uproar. It didn't help that by the time we reached East Bumfuck—or wherever we were—the story being reported by the local news had mutated. Now they were saying I had invited underage girls in the audience up on stage to perform oral sex on me! Much worse.

Apparently the New York street colloquialism *suck my muthafuckin' dick* didn't translate well in the South. When we arrived at the venue, the police were there in force with complaint forms already filled out to arrest me the minute I spewed one word of profanity.

Joe Gerber was working the phone trying to hire a local attorney to represent the band's interests in this situation. No luck. While every lawyer in a hundred-mile radius passed on the offer to represent us, one attorney, upon hearing who was looking to hire him,

---

* Point of interest: The scourge of Amarillo, Texas, has been a regular on the radio down there for years now. My internationally syndicated show, *The House of Hair*, is broadcast weekly on KARX 95.7. What was once dangerous and threatening is now comparatively easy-listening and the music of a generation.

hung up with a curt "Why don't you suck my muthafuckin' dick," said with a full-blown Texas drawl. So much for Southern hospitality.

Controlling my vulgarity has never been a problem for me, but not cursing that night just to save my ass didn't seem right. That's when I remembered seeing author Gore Vidal on the *Johnny Carson* show years before. In 1974 he was promoting his new book, *Myron*, the sequel to the controversial *Myra Breckinridge*. In *Myron*, protesting a recent US Supreme Court ruling on obscenity, Vidal used the names of the Supreme Court justices who had voted in favor of censorship to replace offensive words in the book. (Justice) *Burger* = *bugger*, (Justice) *Rehnquist* = *dick*, and so on. I thought it was a brilliant idea—and the perfect solution to my problem.

When we hit the stage that night, cops and various other city-government officials were everywhere. After our first song, I took a moment to point out the authorities in the house and explain to the crowd why they were there. One profane word and I would be arrested. Then I informed the audience what I was going to do *instead* of cursing.

"*What's the mayor's name in this city?!*" I shouted.

"*Miller!*"* the crowd screamed.

"*Well, anytime I say* Miller, *I mean the F-word!*" I railed. "*When I say* Miller, *I mean—*" I pointed my microphone at the crowd.

"*Fuck!*" they shouted.

"*When I say* Miller, *I mean—*"

"*FUCK!*"

"*And when I say* mutha Miller, *I mean—*"

"*MUTHAFUCKER!*"

I then picked a couple of other local officials' names for *shit* and *ass*.

The police and town fathers were besides themselves. They could do nothing but wait for this New York heavy metal asshole to slip up. But I didn't. Being clean and sober, I am always in complete control of my faculties, and I pranced, danced, teased, and taunted, but I never uttered a single curse word that night. The audience was cursing a blue streak, but not me.

---

* I can't remember the city we were in, or the name of the mayor at that time, but *Miller* will work in example.

Oh, I laid "I'm a sick muthafu-fu-fu-fu-*Miller*!" out there a couple times, but those were deliberate. Twisted Sister delivered a killer show and lived to rock another day. Until we got to the next city and our show had been canceled because of my arrest. Not much we could do about that.

STAY HUNGRY WAS A huge record all over the world, and other countries (and our international record label) were clamoring for Twisted to tour. We had done some shows in Europe in the very beginning of the *Stay Hungry* tour, but to actually play in the countries where our record was now a hit would have taken it to the next level. Not to mention gotten us out of the United States, where we were—unbeknownst to us—on the verge of becoming overexposed. Instead, we opted to special-guest on Iron Maiden's North American tour and go back, for a second or even third time, to places and regions we had already been. This was Twisted Sister's first major *conscious* misstep. I don't remember whose decision it was, but I'm sure *I* had a major hand in it.

We'd been supporting the album for eight months, and I was tired of the road. When you tour outside the United States, you are stuck in whatever country you are in, which for me was a nightmare. At least while touring in the United States, when we had a few days off, I could fly home or even fly Suzette and Jesse in so I could see them.

Case in point: In October of '84, Twisted Sister headlined a show at the Sunrise Musical Theatre near Fort Lauderdale, Florida. The theater was near where my wife and son were staying with her mother. Not only were Suzette, Jesse, and her entire family going to get a chance to see me in concert, but we had a couple of days off following and I was going to spend time with my wife and baby son.

The show itself was memorable for a few reasons. I remember the shock of hitting the stage and seeing Suzette's mother, aunts, and *grandmother* in the front row! I had told the promoters to "take care of my wife's family," and in an effort to show me respect they gave these middle-age and elderly women seats right down front, in the epicenter of the insanity (the last place you want to see family for a variety of reasons!).

As I performed "Stay Hungry" to the rabid mob, I was running offstage and barking out orders to my crew to get my in-laws the hell out of there. They were quickly moved to safer seats in the balcony.

During the show, the frenzied crowd started tearing the ceiling and wall tiles down, and I stopped the show and called them on it. The Sunrise Musical Theatre is a legendary venue where the greats, including Frank Sinatra, have played. The beautiful place was quite a contrast to the shitholes we usually had to perform in. Now, I'm the first to trash a dump; my attitude has always been:

◄ DEE SNIDER RULE #3 ►
Treat me like an animal and I'll behave like an animal.
Treat me with respect, I will act respectfully.

Sort of a variation on Dee Snider Rules #1 and #2.

I explained to the crowd how I didn't like going to concerts in or playing in shitholes, and if we tore this theater up, not only wouldn't we get to have shows in nice places, but the Sunrise would become a shithole, too. Needless to say, the vandalism stopped.*

The band had the next day off, and I got to spend some precious time with Suzette and Jesse. My first order of business was to go out with them for breakfast (I loves me some breakfast!). Jesse, now two, resisted sitting in the car seat. He tried every trick he knew (stiffening up, going limp, kicking and screaming, etc.) to keep me from getting him locked in.

No match for his old man, Jesse was ultimately secured, and I got in the driver's seat and started the car. From behind me I heard:

"Not gonna take it anymore, Daddy!"

---

* I found out years later that one of those Sunrise theater vandals was none other than a young and inspired Marilyn Manson. The show had quite an effect on him.

Suzette and I looked at each other, stunned by our infant's proclamation of rebellion. I quickly recovered, spun around, and said, "Write your own song, kid!"

See the cool stuff I would have missed out on if I were in Europe on tour when I should have been? *

---

* Years later (in the 2000s) when the band reunited and *finally* toured some of these countries, it was sad to see and meet now middle-aged fans who had been waiting decades to finally see Twisted Sister.

⚜ 40 ⚜

a rock star is born

*S*tay Hungry was now double platinum in the United States (2 million records sold), and at various degrees of gold, platinum, and multiplatinum in Canada, Mexico, Sweden, Australia, and New Zealand, with no sign of stopping. To pass the time on the road, I would calculate the songwriting royalties I was making with each passing week of massive record sales. All my years of focus, commitment, and effort had finally paid off. I was a rich, famous rock 'n' roll star.

With the band's exploding popularity came increased media attention. Twisted Sister certainly was an oddity with our groundbreaking videos, hair, makeup, costumes, and songs of rebellion, but none in the band more so than me. Add that I was married, had a kid, and claimed to be clean and sober, and the interview requests for me poured in.

The Long Island newspaper—which I'd hated delivering as a kid—sent a reporter out on the road with Twisted Sister to do a cover story on me for the Sunday edition (more on this later). *Rolling Stone* had legendary photographer Annie Leibovitz do a photo shoot with us for their interview. *Entertainment Tonight* flew in a reporter to do a feature on me, and I was on *Late Night with David Letterman*. The pièce de résistance was *People* magazine.

For *People*'s feature they sent me back to my alma mater, Baldwin Senior High School, with a reporter and photographer for a visit. You can imagine the pandemonium when one of the biggest rock stars of the day—a former student—pulled up in a limousine, on a school day with a bodyguard and reporters and photographers.

As I entered the building and walked through the commons area—through which I had crossed daily as a student completely unnoticed—it was like the Pied Piper leading the rats: a swarm of kids followed me everywhere I went. The reporter wanted to take photos of me in my place of high school solace, the choir room. As the mob followed me down the hall, whom should I spot sweeping the floor but one of the guys from the loading dock who used to call me Rock Star. Korvette's department store—which my coworkers were hoping to be working for until they retired—had gone out of business, so *this* was his current place of employment. I stopped right in front of my old "friend," who was leaning on a broom like the one I used to push at Korvette's. The entire procession piled up like a traffic jam behind me.

"Hey, man, it's me, *Rock Star*," I said as if it were just the two of us. *"I'm a rock star!"*

"I know," he replied, a stunned look on his face.

"So, how are *you* doin'?" I asked without a bit of sarcasm.

My former coworker muttered something noncommittal, since how he was doing was pretty obvious.

The crowd behind me in the hall was growing and beginning to get impatient.

"I gotta go do this photo-shoot thing for *People* magazine," I said matter-of-factly. "Tell the ol' crew Rock Star says hey."

With that, my entire entourage piled past my former antagonist and followed me down the hall.

They tell you that revenge isn't satisfying. *I'll be damned if it's not! It is so sweet!*

MY FIRST ROCK-STAR PRIORITY was to find a place for my family and me to live that was safe, secure, and appropriate for a man of my newly achieved means. Suzette and I set out to find a new home with various criteria, but the most important for me was—*I did not want to be able to hear traffic of any kind!* That and the schools.

As for my dream car, I'm a motorhead, and for a few years I had been dragging a basket-case muscle car—a 1969 Boss 302 Mustang—from place to place, wherever Suzette and I moved. I had big plans to restore this rare 'Stang one day, so I was always sure my rust bucket had a garage to protect what was left of the car. A fact that was not lost on my then future wife.

"So *my* car," said Suzette, "*the car that we depend on*—sits outside in the cold, rain, and snow, while *your* car—*that doesn't run*—has its own garage?" She wasn't too happy about this arrangement.

Understanding her justifiable frustration, I tried to assuage her concerns. "Your car is great, but this is one of the ten *rarest* Mustangs. I have to protect it." That logic only worked for so long.

As the years went by, Suzette—now the mother of my child—became more and more annoyed by this indignity. "We live in a studio apartment, we can't even afford a room for our baby, and we're paying for your piece-of-shit car to have a garage?"

When Suzette put it that way, it did seem kind of fucked-up, but I was undeterred. "It's a collector's item. Think of it as an investment. One day it will be worth a lot of money."

That didn't impress my young, sharp wife either.

When the band finally "struck oil," as I like to call it, all plans of me personally restoring the Mustang went out the window (I suck with a wrench, anyway) and Plan B went into full effect. Now that I was a rock star and had money, I would spend whatever it took to make my car perfect. And I did. In fact, I spent more having the premier Mustang restoration shop in the world (Randy DeLisio at Superstang in Clyde, New York) and the top Boss Mustang engine builder (Denny Aldridge at Aldridge Motorsports in Portland, Oregon) restore my car than I would have paid to buy a 1969 Boss 302 Mustang already restored. But that wouldn't have been the same. I wanted *my* car—the one I had been dreaming about for years—to be restored, and money was no object. I actually had the motor *flown* from Oregon to New York so I wouldn't have to wait for it to be shipped by truck. Now that's rock 'n' roll!

◆   ◆   ◆

MY MOST ARROGANT, SELF-SERVING rock-star purchase I ever made had to be a gym.

In the early eighties, when Suzette and I shared that slimy apartment with my brother Matt and sister, Sue, I was an emaciated mess—especially compared to my gymnast/bodybuilder younger brother Matt.

Jay Jay had a theory that girls wanted to be with rockers because we all look like we're about to die and they want to be the last to be with us. But as I looked at my brother's amazing physique, I knew I had to do something about mine. Matt suggested I go to the gym he frequented, Iron Masters in Massapequa, Long Island.

Not long after I started going, the gym's manager started letting me work out for free. The owner, Jim Penney, virtually never came by, so no one would be the wiser. This worked for me because I didn't have the money to afford a gym membership, and getting in for free encouraged me to keep training.

One day, I was at Iron Masters training on the cuff, and in walks *the* Jim Penney, in all his massive bodybuilding glory. Jim was a steelworker (hence the name of the gym) and was a real-life, tough muthafucker. He perused the sign-in sheet and paid members list and quickly figured out I didn't belong. Making an example of me in front of everyone, Jim loudly outed me for being a deadbeat and, after thoroughly humiliating me, kicked me out. Completely embarrassed, just before I exited—and with a safe distance and a counter between me and the ironworking monster—I said with a shaky voice, *"One day I'm gonna own this place, muthafucker!"* Then I ran as fast as I could with the sound of Penney's deep laugh ringing in my ears.

I never forgot that day or my promise, and as soon as I struck it rich, as luck would have it, I discovered Iron Masters was up for sale. I called my people and bought the place.

In a passive-aggressive move of disdain toward Jim Penney, I refused to go to the closing to sign the ownership papers. I wasn't going to let that scumbag have the pleasure of saying he sat with *the* Dee Snider. (I know, I know, I was an egomaniacal asshole.) I sent Suzette with my attorney to take care of the final details. My wife told me afterward that throughout the closing Penney kept saying, in disbelief, "He said, 'One day I'm gonna own this place, muthafucker!'—and now he does." *Now, that's rock 'n' roll!*

It wouldn't be long before Jim Penney had the last laugh. He had thrown me out of his gym for essentially stealing from him. I was the scumbag, not him. As an absentee owner, I would have to deal with people working out and not paying en masse. After losing six figures on the gym and adding significantly to problems that nearly ended my marriage, I would be forced to close the place a few years later. This was in the late eighties, and I'm still writing off the loss on my taxes thirty years later! All I have to show for once owning a gym is a good story to put in this book. *Winning!*

THE FIRST QUARTER OF 1985 consisted of more touring with Iron Maiden, shooting another video, and some Twisted Sister headline shows, including a run through Australia, New Zealand, and Japan.

Our third Marty Callner video was for "The Price," the ballad on the *Stay Hungry* record. This was before the heavy-metal power ballad became a cliché and the lead track for every new metal band (eventually going one step further and getting "unplugged").

Ballads had always been a great way to connect the mainstream rock audience with metal. Affairs of the heart, or any kind of emotional torment, produces forceful and dramatic feelings. The power guitar chord, thunderous bass, pounding drums, and wailing vocals of heavy metal speak to those emotions like no other music form outside of a full-blown symphony orchestra. From Led Zeppelin's "Stairway to Heaven" to Alice Cooper's "Only Women Bleed" to Nazareth's "Love Hurts," heavy metal has always had great success at radio with its ballads. "The Price" was right in the pocket with all those other records, and we had every reason to expect it to be another hit.

Marty and I decided we should go not only with a performance video but with a stripped-down Twisted Sister as well. "The Price" was a heartfelt song (remember its inspiration?) and the makeup and costumes sort of trivialized its true meaning. The idea was to shoot the song with Twisted in street clothes during a sound check, then show the band performing, full-on, in concert later in the song.

The video was filmed at the War Memorial Coliseum in Rochester, New York, during a couple of days' break from our tour with Iron Maiden.

Stay Hungry producer Tom Werman was a great believer in the "radio mix" as key to the success of a single. The thought behind this was that most people experience a new song *on the radio* for the first time. Unlike more deliberate music listening, blasted on your car or home stereo, radio listening is usually at a lower volume and in the background. When listeners hear something that catches their ear, they reach for the volume knob and turn it up for a better listen. That is the real way many people discovered new music.

While songs were usually mixed in the studio at higher volumes through monster—or at least home-size—stereo speakers (this of course predates the iPod), this kind of mixing can be misleading for what the song will actually sound like on the radio. Some record producers *only* mix for the radio. Case in point, Todd Rundgren. He produced the entire Meat Loaf *Bat Out Of Hell* record so that it sounded good on a radio. I'm sure he figures *anything* sounds good when you crank the volume.

To his credit (did I actually just say that?), Tom Werman liked to do a separate "radio mix" for released singles, working on small speakers at low volume to create a mix that would "pop" when listened to in the background. Tom wanted the song to catch your ear even if you weren't focused on it. He even had a car-radio speaker he would plug in and test the mix on, then he would take a tape out to a car with a normal stereo system in it and listen to it again there.

In an effort to get "The Price" out quickly, Atlantic Records never notified Werman of its imminent release, and Tom didn't get to do his special mix as he did for "We're Not Gonna Take It" and "I Wanna Rock."

The song tested well at radio (audience opinion when *asked* to listen to a song) and the video was a fairly welcome departure from our usual fare at MTV, but "The Price" didn't break through the way we all hoped it would. I don't know if the missed radio mix had anything to do with its failure as a single, but I'm sure that didn't help. We expected it to push the album to the next sales level (triple platinum) as yet another hit single off the record. Instead, it was the "event horizon" that signaled it was time to wrap things up and move on to our next album.

WHILE WORKING ON THE "The Price" video with Marty Callner, he imparted to me some bad news. Less than four years after the birth of MTV, they had decided to reduce the amount of heavy metal videos they were airing. After using the genre to help launch their network, they were dropping metal the way a shuttle launch releases its booster rocket. You got us where we need to go . . . *see ya!*

I was blown away by the shortsightedness of this corporate decision; I expected more from Music Television. The heavy metal audience was incredibly loyal. Why cut them completely loose when MTV could have their cake and eat it, too? I had Marty propose to the powers that be for headbangers get their own show to tune in to. Metalhead fans will dutifully tune in once a week, at ungodly hours, to hear a weekly radio show dedicated to their music on the radio; why not do the same thing on television?

MTV soon came back with their answer: if Dee will host it, we will do a metal show. One other caveat. A young MTV producer named Liz Nealon had been proposing the same idea to them. They wanted me to work with her on the show. I didn't have to be asked twice. Here was an opportunity to keep metal alive on MTV, promote the music genre I loved (and still do), and graduate to a new medium as show host. Liz Nealon and I met, connected creatively, and *Heavy Metal Mania* was born. The monthly show eventually became weekly, but I left after working for free for eighteen months because MTV wasn't willing to pay me a dime for my effort. They said it was great promotion for me. By then I was completely overexposed and the most recognizable face in heavy metal. Fuck great promotion! *Show me the money!*

The show Liz Nealon and I created, and that I worked for a year and a half without pay to establish, eventually mutated into the now legendary *Headbangers Ball*. You're welcome.

◆   ◆   ◆

THE *STAY HUNGRY* TOUR would end both auspiciously and suspiciously. Let me explain.

While Maiden played a series of headline shows at Radio City Music Hall and went off to do the first Rock in Rio event, Twisted Sister used the time to take a run at some other countries besides the United States and Canada. Though we would never make it to Europe on that record (other than the pre-album-release dates in England, Holland, and Germany), we did go to Australia, New Zealand, and Japan for a handful of shows. Five, to be exact.

En route to Twisted's first show in Japan, I stopped in Los Angeles with my bodyguard, Vic, to be a presenter on the Grammy Awards. I saw it as an opportunity to further bring the music I loved to the masses. I wasn't nominated or even performing on the show, but back then there was no heavy metal category. The genre was completely ignored by NARAS (National Academy of Recording Arts & Sciences). No one from the metal community had ever even been *asked* to attend. I viewed my appearance as a breakthrough and a major inroad for metal.

I am an original headbanger and I have always had a passion for heavy metal. From the earliest days I believed it was worthy of a much wider audience. It deserved more radio time, television time, press coverage, and general respect and appreciation by the masses. I wanted metal to be the world's music. I wanted to hear it on movie sound tracks, on commercials, and as Muzak on elevators and in banks. I felt it should be heard and played everywhere, and that was a part of my life's mission. Sure I wanted to be a rock star, but I wanted to use my influence to bring heavy metal to the mainstream. Why shouldn't the marching band play heavy metal songs at halftime?

To that end, I accepted every offer I got from the mainstream media. In analogy, I viewed these appearances as the unpopular kid in high school making it with the homecoming queen. I was with her and shouting to all my fellow outcasts, "Look who I'm with! Ha-ha!" The outcasts were having the last laugh. Unfortunately, the metal community did not view it the same way I did. The core metal fan saw my efforts as selling out. They didn't want to share their heroes, especially with the mainstream. If only I'd realized this sooner.

While it can't be argued my dream wasn't heartfelt, when heavy metal did finally make it to the masses in the early nineties, the exposure practically killed it. Metal has always been the cockroach of rock 'n' roll, thriving and surviving on the outskirts of the mainstream while other genres came and went. That under-the-radar quality has kept it alive. Heavy metal was never meant for the masses. It is music by headbangers for headbangers, and that's how it should always remain.

PRESENTING AT THE 27TH Annual Grammy Awards in February of 1985 was interesting, to say the least. The big deal that year was Prince and the Revolution and Prince's movie *Purple Rain*. Everyone was abuzz because Prince had "agreed" to perform on the show. I could not have cared less.

The afternoon of the event, I arrived with my bodyguard for the rehearsal/sound check. Everyone there was either presenting, performing, or working on the show. As I stood backstage with Ray Davies of the Kinks, Stevie Wonder, Leonard Bernstein, John Denver, and other music industry luminaries, it came time for Prince and the Revolution to do their sound check.

At the behest of Prince, the Grammy producers had painted a large dressing room/trailer purple, and set it up backstage. This was so "his royal shortness" and his band wouldn't have to get ready or hang out with the rest of us peons. The door to the trailer opened, and surrounded by nearly a dozen of their personal security, Prince and the Revolution were escorted to the stage. During the maybe 150-yard walk, the lead bodyguard (you may remember the dick— gray-and-black beard, like wrestler "Superstar" Billy Graham?) was barking out orders to the celebrities and crew backstage.

"Don't look at him! Avert your eyes! Look away! Stop staring!"

As Prince and the Revolution passed a bunch of us (I assume they passed, none of them could be seen behind their security), the lead asshole tells Stevie Wonder to *look away!* Are you freakin' kidding me?!

That night, I presented the Best Male Pop Vocal Performance Award, with Sheila E., to no-show Phil Collins, saying as I opened the envelope, "This is the first time a dirtbag presented one of these."

To me *that* was what it was all about. Their being forced to acknowledge and recognize us (the metal community), in any capacity, was a victory. Being on national, prime-time network television—wearing jeans and a cutoff T-shirt—was a moral victory for both me and heavy metal.

I left the theater immediately following my presentation. The producers wanted me to sit in the audience, but I felt it was way too tame and legit for a heavy metal rock star such as myself. I headed back to the hotel and got ready to catch my flight to Japan to rejoin the band. I had more important things to do than hang out with music industry elitists and party.

Not until four years later was heavy metal officially recognized by NARAS (albeit with an initial snubbing of Metallica, when the award went to Jethro Tull), but I'd like to think I helped open that door.

TOWARD THE END OF 1984, I was contacted by the Make-A-Wish Foundation. The last wish of Robert, a sixteen-year-old boy dying of leukemia, was to meet me. I couldn't believe it. Of all the things someone might make his last wish, I was stunned I would be it. I readily agreed to meet him under the condition this would not be a publicity stunt and Robert and I would just spend some time together alone. I wasn't going there to meet anybody else.

My visit was to be a surprise, but the day before I was to arrive at the hospital, I received a call. Sadly, the kid wasn't going to make it until I got there, so in hopes of lifting his spirits and getting him to hold on for a few more precious hours, they told him Dee Snider was coming to see him. He stayed alive just so he could meet me.

When Joe, Vic, and I arrived at the hospital, I first met Robert's family and caregivers, and they informed me that what I was going to experience might be difficult. Because of the advanced stage of Robert's disease, a once strapping young boy now weighed less than sixty-five pounds. As a result of chemo and radiation treatments Robert had no hair and could no longer speak. He was, however, relatively alert and could hear me. I steeled myself and went inside to meet my most dedicated fan.

Robert was as sick as they warned me, but I could see his recognition of me in his eyes. I sat with him for a couple of hours talking about everything and anything, *except* his illness or his bleak future. I spoke only about positive, uplifting things, always in future terms and of "*when* you get better." I shared with him personal stories, spoke of bodybuilding regimens and weight-gain supplements that would help him put on the pounds and regain his strength when he got out of the hospital. I even told him of the possibility of his working with the Twisted Sister road crew in the future.

My whole time there, Robert lay silent and still, a pale skeleton of a boy, but his eyes never left me. After a couple of hours, I could see he was exhausted from the effort, so I told him we'd hang together when he got better and left the poor sick kid forever.

Outside the room, his family's outpouring of gratitude was touching. I had given their son and brother his dying wish, and they were forever in my debt. I left the hospital amazed that what I did mattered so much to some people, and I was glad I'd brought some kind of joy to the final hours of a young man whose life was simply too short. I felt a deep sense of appreciation for how lucky I was and said a silent prayer for the future health of my son. I could not imagine the anguish Robert's parents must have been going through.

IN MARCH OF 1985, Twisted Sister and Iron Maiden played an outdoor show in Tempe, Arizona. I was backstage getting ready when Vic came into my dressing room, a look of shock on his face.

"He's here, boss. *He's here,*" my bodyguard said in disbelief. Vic always called me boss.

"Who's here?" Someone was always "here" in those days, but Vic was being a little vaguer than usual.

"The kid. The sick kid."

I stopped putting on my makeup and turned to Vic. "Robert? The kid from Make-A-Wish?"

Vic nodded.

Robert was still alive? "What's he doing here?"

"Partying," Vic answered, surprised by the word coming out of his own mouth.

And he was. After my departure from the hospital, Robert's disease went into remission and he started a full recovery. Less than six months later, he was out of the hospital, back to "fighting weight" *and then some* (thanks to my weight-gain and training tips), and working construction! Robert was backstage at a Twisted Sister/ Iron Maiden show and making up for the time he lost out on partying when he was sick. It was incredible. Oh, yeah . . . and he wanted to know when he could start working and touring with the band.

I called his mother a few days later to ask what had happened— not that I wasn't absolutely overjoyed. She told me that while Robert had gone into remission, the doctors had told her not to get her hopes up. In time the disease would take hold again and the end would come. In the meantime, she was incredibly happy to have her son back even for a while and so thankful for my help. I assured her that I had done nothing and expressed my joy for her family and Robert's happiness. It was simply amazing.

Decades later I would be contacted by Robert again. He is not only still alive (now in his forties), but married and with children of his own. The leukemia never returned.

A while after my hospital visit, I received a letter from the Make-A-Wish Foundation thanking me for my participation and explaining that wishes are *only* granted to *terminally ill* children. It was the first time *any* recipient had survived.

Do I think I'm special? Sure . . . but not in that way. I simply think positive thought and energy is an incredible thing that has been proven to have life-changing effects. It's that same type of PMA that propelled Twisted Sister's success. Unfortunately, in the band's case my will and drive would one day not be enough.

⚡ 41 ⚡

"click click boom!"

Our return to heavy metal mecca (LA) with Iron Maiden could not have been more triumphant. With now almost 2.5 million records sold in the United States alone (close to 5 million worldwide) in less than a year's time, Twisted Sister had gone from up-and-comers to heavyweight contenders. The Iron Maiden/Twisted Sister tour package was the hottest ticket in town, and every metalhead came to bear witness. But deep inside I sensed something wasn't quite right. I couldn't put my finger on it—and I wouldn't dare put my finger on it if I could—but the night of our first of five Los Angeles–area sold-out performances, I got the feeling Twisted Sister had overstayed its welcome.

The audience was responding, but it almost seemed as if they were afraid *not* to. That wasn't the reaction I was going for. I would later find out that was the case at many Twisted shows. Some people in attendance shouted and cheered out of fear they would either be targeted by me from the stage (no one was safe from my all-seeing eyes) or get their asses kicked by rabid Sister fans. Either way . . . not my goal.

The voice of a single metalhead from that night rings in my ears to this day. As Twisted Sister walked off after our set, I heard a male voice in the seats to the side of the backstage shout down to Blackie Lawless from W.A.S.P., who had been watching our show from the wings, "Twisted Sister sucks! W.A.S.P. rules!"

Out of the corner of my eye I saw Blackie turn to fully accept the accolades of this fan and, with that, silently agree with the fan's assessment. Yes, Twisted Sister does suck, he implied.

Click.

That was the sound of a tumbler to the combination lock of Twisted Sister's *demise* falling into place. Something in the tone of the asshole's voice, Blackie Lawless's silent acknowledgment, and the *measured insanity* of the sold-out crowd that night told me this was more than one idiot's opinion. This was a growing feeling in the metal community. I said nothing to anybody about this—I denied this momentary lapse in positivity even to myself—and went back to my dressing room. Swallowing the bitter, glimmer-of-a-dark-future pill, until now I never said anything to anyone about it again. But subconsciously I knew.

THE SECOND DAY OF our run with Iron Maiden at LA's Long Beach Arena was my thirtieth birthday. While the road to the top had been long and arduous, success was finally mine. You would think it would make the celebration of such a significant birthday that much sweeter. That's what I thought. I had fame, fortune, an incredible wife, and a son. I had achieved my life's goal and I was performing at a sold-out arena show. I was ready for the thirtieth birthday of all thirtieth birthdays. But it wasn't to be.

I hate to admit I had an issue with turning thirty, but I can't deny I had an unprecedented breakdown (for me) that night.

Leading up to the date, I had no trepidations whatsoever: I couldn't have been in a better place at that point in my life. Since that infamous day, I've had a fortieth and a fiftieth birthday, and I've taken them both in stride. My fortieth birthday party was held at a kids' indoor playground, I had Suzette carve the number 40 into the shaved hair on the side of my head, and I wore an adult diaper on the outside of my pants the entire night. *No—I didn't need it!* My fiftieth birthday was televised (maybe some of you saw it?), and I celebrated that milestone for almost two weeks, taking my entire family to Universal Studios, then Suzette and I went away for a romantic week in the British Virgin Islands. I've already got big plans for my sixtieth birthday. I don't shy away from the decade markers of my life. I embrace and celebrate them. (Ignoring them isn't going to make them go away.) But not my thirtieth. Something came over me that night that I just can't explain . . . or maybe I can.

Because of my realization the night before, I was angry and upset when I hit the arena stage and gave one of my stronger performances (anger has always brought out the best/worst in me). I remember smashing my microphone stand repeatedly onstage and screaming with rage (not into the mic) as the raw emotion I was feeling but couldn't explain overcame me. The audience response was particularly great that night.

After the show, Suzette had planned a backstage party for me, but I was having none of it. Feeling on the verge of tears (I'm telling you, it virtually never happens!), I wouldn't come out of my dressing room, and I wouldn't let anybody in besides Suzette and Jesse.

In a fairly famous episode of *The Mary Tyler Moore Show*, Mary throws a surprise party for her boss, Lou Grant, and he flips out when he arrives at Mary's apartment and finds out about it. Lou doesn't want a party and won't let any of the guests enter. One by one, Mary tries to sell Lou on the people waiting out in the hall. "You like Murray. Why don't we just let Murray in?" "It's just Ted. You know Ted. What do you say we let Ted in?" And so on and so forth. Well, that's pretty much what happened to Suzette. As I sat hugging my son like a security blanket, she tried to convince me to let into the room various people who wanted to see me.

"It's Marty. You like Marty. Why don't you just say hi to Marty?"

I was far less cooperative than Lou Grant. Eventually, Suzette told everybody the party was off and put away the cake. I was not in the mood to see anyone or celebrate. We had a custom cake the next day (made with a hand-"painted" picture of me, long before it was commonplace to put photos on cakes), but it wasn't the same. I had ruined my thirtieth birthday and everyone around me was walking on eggshells.

Accepting that I may just have had a problem with turning thirty like so many others, I do have another theory for my reaction that night. Remember that *click* moment I told you about? I think the true weight of what I knew in my heart to be true about the future for the band and me had got to me on a deeper level. I would never have suggested this then, and I know I couldn't explain my behavior at the time, but looking back now, I'm convinced the reality of what I subconsciously knew was happening had shaken me to my core. Somehow I knew I had blown it.

The one thing I did allow myself to acknowledge was that I (Twisted Sister) was *becoming* overexposed. It was time to shut down interviews and press of any kind, but there was one problem. Magazines had a three-month lead time. Meaning, it took three months from the time you did an interview for it to hit the stands. For me to stop doing interviews at the end of March meant plenty of articles and photos would still be published all the way to the beginning of summer. By the time you *think* you may be overexposed, you are done!

Click.

Another tumbler fell into place. I knew inside it was true, but I still wouldn't accept it as a fait accompli. I could fix it. I had everything under control.

TWISTED SISTER FINISHED OFF our last few dates with Iron Maiden, and on March 24, 1985, ending eleven months of touring and four months of recording and preparing for the biggest record and moments of our career. Almost a decade after I joined the band, I was officially a rich, famous rock star (I know I say that a lot but I like the way it sounds.), and I was going to enjoy the fruits of my labor.

Returning home couldn't have been more glorious. Suzette, Jesse, and I had moved into an expensive home on the North Shore of Long Island, in an exclusive area (I still remember singing *The Jeffersons'* "Movin' on Up" theme song as we drove there for the first time), and I had so many "rock-starry" things I wanted to do. We completely fenced in and gated our acreage, installed a built-in pool, and bought a boat and more cars, including a 1950 Cadillac hearse. We had so many *daily* driving cars our insurance company dropped us because they couldn't understand why two people needed so many vehicles. I had a mechanic who would come to the house just to service the vehicles for *lack of use*. They were breaking down because they didn't get driven enough!

We had service people do everything for us: landscapers, handymen, housekeepers, and assorted workmen. I remember one day Suzette, who wasn't buying into the whole "living like a rock star" thing, asked me to help her put down a carpet in one of the small rooms in our house (she's a hands-on kind of person), and I said to her with disgust, "I don't lay carpet, I *pay* people to lay carpet!" Man, did I live to regret making that statement.

I stopped handling my day-to-day finances, opened charge accounts in every store in town, and had my accountant deal with the annoying detail of paying the bills. We would just walk into stores, tell the salesclerk/butcher/pharmacist/grocer/etc. what we wanted, and they would pack it up and send my accountant the bill. Cash? We don't need no stinking cash!

Understand, for a blue-collar guy who grew up in a large, middle/lower-middle-class family, having to work my ass off for anything I wanted, never having any real money or truly nice things, and always having financial problems, this was an incredible dream come true. To not have to do it myself—or get a friend or family member to do it for me—worry about the cost, look for a deal, or ask "How much?" before buying something was positively mind-blowing. I *should have* done all those things, but I didn't. I wasn't rich enough to just throw money away—few people are. But this was *my* rock 'n' roll dream and I was living it the way I envisioned it. Plus I was sure there was a lot more money to come.

I would get up at the crack of dawn each morning, hand-wash my totally restored 1969 Boss 302 Mustang (nobody ever touched my Mustang but me!), then drive to *my* gym (still called Iron Masters) before it opened, weight-train with *my* personal bodyguard, Vic, then head back to *my* beautiful home for a day with *my* wife and son. Rock star time, and the livin' was easy.

THAT SPRING AND SUMMER were great, but I had work to do as well. Each month I would film an episode of *Heavy Metal Mania* for MTV at various locations, including my gym, my mechanic's garage, and touring the town I grew up in, in my open-top Jeep. I had also signed a deal to write a follow-up to Pat Boone's bestseller, *'Twixt Twelve and Twenty*, on the teen years, so I had to do regular interviews/meetings with my cowriter Phil Bashe (more on this later).

Oh, and then there was that day I decided to have my front teeth filed into fangs.

I don't remember exactly where or when, but one day I got this wild (to say the least) idea that it would be cool/crazy to have my two top, front incisors sharpened into fangs. To answer some common questions:

Did it hurt?

No—this isn't the Dark Ages, he used novocaine.

Do I or did I regret it?

No. It was crazy and got a great reaction. If I regret anything, it's that I did it so late in Twisted Sister's career. I could have got a lot more mileage out of it if I'd done it sooner.

What happened to them?

I got them capped a couple of years later. It got old pretty quickly.

I BEGAN TO WRITE songs for the next mega-selling (I hoped) Twisted Sister record, but there was one problem. My inspiration wasn't quite the same.

Every song on every album to date had been written when I was hungry and from a place of desperation and frustration. Now, I was anything but. I remember sitting poolside one hot summer day, with five cars and a boat in the driveway, trying to write the lyrics to my next anthem of teen angst . . . and I had nothin'! No anger, no frustration, not a genuine angst-driven emotion to draw on. What the hell did I have to be upset about? *I had everything I fucking ever wanted!* The true significance of this problem was yet to hit me. I was a musical genius (or so I thought) . . . who needs inspiration?

And speaking of musical genius, I had become a full-blown megalomaniac, defined as in: **megalomania** *n.*, psychopathological condition characterized by delusional fantasies of wealth, power, or omnipotence.

Oh yeah, that was me. In my mind, Twisted Sister's next album was going to be my masterstroke and would bring heavy metal fully to the masses, making my band and me not only the biggest metal band in history, but one of the biggest bands in the world. Nobody could convince me otherwise.

My plan was simple (for someone of my *obvious* abilities): have songs on the album that would appeal to every single segment of the heavy metal audience, from the hit-oriented, pop-metal light-weights to the most hard-core headbangers. I'd have hardcore metal, anthemic metal, speed metal, a power ballad, and every other metal variation on there. I even had the perfect cover song for the record.

In the early days of our career, Twisted Sister used to play the Shangri-Las' classic "Leader of the Pack." Our original fans loved it, and we included it on our first, indie release, *Ruff Cutts*, so I knew even our core audience liked it. Mötley Crüe had just had a hit with their cover of Brownsville Station's "Smokin' in the Boys Room," so I was sure we would knock our cover out of the park. "Leader of the Pack" would appeal to everybody, including the *parents* of our fans who knew the original from when they were growing up. With this song, I was positive Twisted Sister was going to take over the world. Was I an overconfident, self-assured ass or what?! As I said, *a megalomaniac defined.*

This time out, I didn't overwrite for the record and put the songs to a vote. I wrote only the songs needed for the record and gave them to the band, saying, "These are the songs we are doing. Period." Although I'm sure I didn't say it directly to them. We were all way too passive-aggressive as a band by then to be that direct with each other. I probably told our manager Mark Puma, and he prettied it up before breaking the news to them. He always did.

MY FIRST INKLING THAT something might be wrong with my mas-ter plan was when legendary producer Bob Ezrin flew down from Canada and came to my house to hear the new songs. Bob has pro-duced some of the great glam-rock records of all time, such as Kiss's *Destroyer* album, Lou Reed's *Berlin*, and pretty much everything the original Alice Cooper band recorded, so I thought he was the perfect fit for Twisted Sister.

We had all met Ezrin when we were on tour in Canada and liked him. Between Bob's massive talent and great personality, I thought he would be a nice change from our last producer, Tom Werman, the polar opposite.

Atlantic Records did not want us to change producers, per the old saying "If it ain't broke, don't fix it." The accepted thinking was, if you had a hit with a certain combination of artist/producer/songwriter, you didn't mess with the formula for the follow-up record. It makes sense. Mötley Crüe recorded their hit album *Shout at the Devil* with Tom Werman, and despite their feelings about him (I've heard things), they used him again for their follow-up, *Theatre of Pain*, to great success. But if Twisted Sister agreed upon one thing as a band, it was not wanting to work with Tom Werman ever again. At least I think they agreed.

Atlantic Records made us use a producer we didn't want on *Stay Hungry*. Now that I had the power, that wasn't going to happen again.

Bob Ezrin was excited at the possibility of working with Twisted. Why wouldn't he be? We had sold more than 5 million records worldwide, were one of the biggest names in rock 'n' roll, were students of the bands he had helped establish and fans of his work, were *huge* in his homeland of Canada—and to be honest, he hadn't worked with a really big band in a while. This would be a big payday and an incredible opportunity for him.

Bob and I had spoken a lot on the phone about the songs I was working on, and he was pumped to hear them. When he got to my house, I played him the demos Twisted had recorded for the album I was going to call *Come Out and Play*. Yet another decision I'd made without consulting the band. I even shared with him my massive vision for the costumes, album-cover art, videos, and worldwide tour. I told him about the huge amounts of time, effort, and money that were being invested in what I knew would be the apex of Twisted Sister's career. I thought Bob went back to Canada pumped.

A couple of days later, Ezrin called me. Bob's a straight talker, and he didn't think the songs were good enough for the follow-up to *Stay Hungry*. He pointed out that most of the songs on *Stay Hungry* were in major keys, yet all of the songs I had written for the new record were in minor keys. When I pointed out to him "I Wanna Rock" is in a minor key, Ezrin responded, "Yeah, but it *feels* major." (It does.)

After telling me all the things he felt were wrong with the new stuff, Bob respectfully *passed* on the offer to produce Twisted Sister's new album. What!? I couldn't believe it. This was the guy who had cobbled questionable albums from many of his artists into hit records by literally cowriting a lot of the songs . . . *and he was passing?* He didn't even *offer* to work on developing the material for the album!

Click.

There it was again; that sickening sound. My subconscious fully registered it, but my indomitable conscious would not. I couldn't. My refusal to accept things as they were was (and still is) what had got me over and through everything. It's what got me through high school and out of a predictable life defined for me by others. It's what got me Suzette, the love of my life. It's what made me a true-blue, fire-breathing rock 'n' roll star. I couldn't accept any kind of negative final destination. To quote the greatest, most inspiring poem of all time, "Invictus":

> I am the master of my fate:
> I am the captain of my soul.

That *click* sound—my suspicions—couldn't be right. What the hell did Bob Ezrin know anyway?

Apparently a lot.

WITH BOB EZRIN NOW removed from the list, the band and I went through a short list of heavy metal producers whose work we had always enjoyed. After a series of phone calls and letters of inquiry, legendary Scorpions producer Dieter Dierks was hired. We were pretty damn thrilled to finally have a producer whose work we liked, understood our musical genre, and was genuinely excited to work with us.

What we didn't know was that Dieter's biggest successes with Scorpions had essentially been coproductions with the band. We were making a mistake by giving him free rein.

THE *COME OUT AND PLAY* album was recorded in New York City and Los Angeles between August and October of 1985. The record, album cover, costumes, subsequent videos, and tour were all a part of my grand plan designed to have true mass appeal. Every element of this effort was carefully thought out, and with the weight of the *Stay Hungry* success behind me, people scrambled to execute my vision. Why shouldn't they? Besides the band's huge international success, the concept for the *COAP* initiative was truly brilliant . . . if I do say so myself.

I had long been aware of the fragmenting of the heavy metal audience; I was sure that Twisted Sister and I alone could unify them.

In addition to focused song selection, we had a number of guest artists on a raucous, fifties-style rock track called "Be Chrool to Your Scuel." Alice Cooper sang a duet with me on it, Billy Joel played Jerry Lee Lewis–esque piano, Clarence Clemons of Bruce Springsteen's E Street Band tore up the sax solo, and the Stray Cats' Brian Setzer played rockabilly guitar. This star-studded tour de force was guaranteed to garner the entire rock community's attention.

Clarence Clemons was a gun for hire. When we approached him to play, all he wanted to know was if we were willing to pay his rate. Done and done. That said, Clarence was a great guy to work with, and what he did with essentially five notes and a split reed on that saxophone of his was flat-out incredible. There was no one better at the kind of stuff he did.*

Brian Setzer was an old Twisted Sister fan and friend of the band's from Long Island, so it didn't take more than a call to get him on board. If you want authentic-fifties lead guitar, Brian is your man.

I mentioned how meeting Billy Joel for the first time changed my

---

* As I wrote this, word arrived that Clarence had a stroke. Weird. I hadn't thought about him in years. A few days later, he died. Rest in peace, my friend.

life—and I'm not even a fan. He was just such an inspiration as a guy with his feet planted firmly on the ground.

THE AREA WHERE SUZETTE and I had moved to was Lloyd Neck. It's on the North Shore (Gold Coast) of Long Island (immortalized in the book and movie *The Great Gatsby*) and is essentially an island connected to the mainland and town of Lloyd Harbor by a causeway. Billy Joel was the other celebrity resident (actually before me). Subsequent to my moving there, fellow Long Island musicians Taylor Dane (also from Baldwin) and then "Debbie" Gibson also made Lloyd Harbor their "move on up" after they first hit the top of the charts.

At that time Billy was married to model Christie Brinkley, and he was a bit more clandestine than when he was single. It's understandable. In the case of celebrity couples, one plus one equals *three*. You've got each of the partners' celebrity, and then the couple has a celebrity unto itself. I remember driving past Billy's house on the water one day and seeing a huge fishing charter anchored about fifty feet off the shore, with a boatload of fishermen just sitting there and staring into his and Christie's picture windows. Terrible. Anyway, while we didn't hang out together, reaching out to Billy was simple enough. I gave him a call and approached him about playing on the track.

"I know heavy metal's not your thing, Billy," I said, "but this is more of a fifties rock 'n' roll track, not metal."

"*Heavy metal's not my thing?*" Billy responded. "Who the fuck do you think you're talking to?" Billy sounded pissed. "I was playing heavy metal when you were in fucking diapers!"

It's true. After his club band the Hassles, Billy Joel had a band in 1970 with Hassles drummer Jon Small (who went on to direct Billy's videos and a Twisted Sister video as well) called Attila. A two-piece organ—through Marshal amplifier stacks—and drums outfit, their legendary album cover (complete with a very metal Attila logo) was of a long-haired (and mustached) Billy Joel and Jon Small, dressed head to toe in authentic medieval battle garb—including helmets, chain mail, and animal pelts—*in a meat locker!* How freakin' metal is that!?

I humbly apologized and begged Billy—a forefather of heavy metal—for forgiveness. Billy graciously accepted my apology and agreed to rock Twisted's track. True to the man he is, Billy showed up for the session alone, with no fanfare, kicked ass, and left. What a cool guy.

THE ALBUM WAS RECORDED in New York City at the Hit Factory and at the Record Plant in Los Angeles. The Hit Factory was the only studio I have ever been to where a band that sells 2.5 million copies domestically are treated like second-class citizens. We couldn't wait to leave "the Shit Factory," as we renamed it, and get out to LA, where we knew we would be treated like the metal gods we were.

What a difference eighteen months made! Whereas Twisted Sister were still a struggling band during the recording of *Stay Hungry*, now we were rock stars. Gone were the Oakwood Apartments in Burbank. Now the band stayed at nice hotels in the heart of West Hollywood. And me? Suzette, Jesse, and I moved into Marty Callner's house in Beverly Hills and lived large. Suzette and Marty's wife, Aleeza, had become great friends, and Jesse and Marty's (then) four children (Dax, Chad, Lynn, and Ariel) got along great. We lived there for almost two months, and the Callners made us feel completely at home.

The recording went pretty smoothly. Dieter Dierks was great to work with, and his engineer, Eddie Delana, was a great guy, too. The Record Plant did treat Twisted like gods, and their studios were filled with other giants of metal such as Judas Priest. Dieter brought the guys from Dokken in to do backing vocals on some of the tracks, and Alice Cooper and Clarence Clemons stopped by to do their parts on "Be Chrool to Your Scuel." It was very rock 'n' roll.

The one fly in the ointment on this record came not from the band, studio, producer, or other musicians, but from an actor. A second-rate, B-movie actor.

Another of my all-time favorite movies is *The Warriors*. This legendary, Walter Hill–directed gang movie is flat-out one of the coolest pictures of its type. The title of our fourth album came from the song I had written called "Come Out and Play," which was derived from a memorable moment in *The Warriors* when the bad guy, Luther, repeatedly taunts the Warriors with the chant "Warriors, come out to play." I decided that I wanted our album to start with that chant, slightly modified ("Twisted Sister, come out and play!"), and I wanted to hire the actor who played Luther, David Patrick Kelly, to do it.

When I spoke with David and told him of my plan, he *passed* on the offer, saying with an attitude, "I don't want to reprise the same character." Was he fucking kidding?! Since doing *The Warriors* he had been in three other movies, *Dreamscape*, *48 Hours*, and *Commando*, and portrayed essentially the same sniveling scumbag in each one. In *48 Hours* he was even called Luther! It's virtually the only part he's ever played.

The minute I hung up with *the thespian*, Joe Gerber and I worked out how to do it on our own. Joe clinked the three bottles together perfectly to create the rhythm, I did a fairly spot-on impression of David Patrick Kelly's sniveling voice, and it didn't cost us a penny.

THE *COME OUT AND PLAY* album, while filled with great songs (if I do say so myself), and while Dieter Dierks had great input on the arrangements, the sound suffered greatly from his overproduction and overprocessing of the sounds. *Sorry, Dieter.* You are a great, talented guy and I love you dearly, but ultimately, you weren't the right guy for the job.

One would think that adding more and more layers of music and technology to each track would make the record sound bigger. It has the opposite effect. It makes the songs sound smaller. I'm not saying the blame for the failings of *COAP* falls onto Dieter's shoulders—it doesn't—but the sound of that record, and how it came across on radio, certainly did not help. While the plan was to make Twisted Sister's *Come Out and Play* the album of the 1985 holiday season (all part of my megalomaniacal masterstroke!), due to the delay in locking in a producer there was no way we would make the mid-October release date. This meant we would not be able to lock in prime display space, promos, ad buys, etc., for our record. Undeterred (could anything stop me?), I relentlessly drove my team on toward a less than optimal release in late November. But I'm getting way ahead of myself.

Before we'd even finished recording the record, an unusual request came into Twisted Sister's management office. Little did I know, I was about to become an advocate in the national spotlight.

⚜ 42 ⚜

"mr. dee snider . . . the twisted sister"

In May of '85, Senator Al Gore's wife, Tipper, got a wild hair up her ass after realizing the words to Prince's "Darling Nikki" were about masturbation. Along with three other "Washington wives," she formed an organization called the Parents Music Resource Center (PMRC).

The PMRC's mission was to educate parents about "alarming trends" in popular music. They claimed that rock music encouraged/glorified violence, drug use, suicide, criminal activity, etc., and sought the censoring and/or rating of music. I remember thinking, who would possibly listen to the inane prattling of Washington busybodies with way too much spare time on their hands? A lot of people did.

This was the Reagan Era, and ultraconservatives were in control. That the PMRC and their coming witch trials—I mean, *Senate hearings*—were predominantly Democratic initiatives speaks volumes about the political and societal mentality of the day. The same environment that had fostered the Decade of Decadence was now trying to put an end to it.

As spring turned to summer, and the voice of the PMRC got louder and louder, I was still virtually unaware and completely unaffected by what was going on. I had bigger fish to fry. When my management office got the call for me to come to Washington and testify on September 19, at the (illegal, as you will soon discover)

Senate hearings on record labeling, I had to do some research to find out what was going on. Once I realized what was happening, I didn't hesitate to accept the invitation. I saw it as the metaphorical equivalent of carrying the flag into battle. I was sure the entire rock 'n' roll community would follow.

I had been asked to speak because not only was "We're Not Gonna Take It" on the PMRC's notorious Filthy 15, a list of the songs they found most objectionable, but at that time, thanks to my rampant overexposure, I was *the* most recognizable face in heavy metal. Who better to invite? I'm sure that looking at my photos and videos, and listening to my music, they were certain I would be the perfect heavy metal fool to make a very public example of.

Joe Gerber—a former Ivy leaguer and a very smart guy—and I went into immediate lockdown. With only a couple of weeks until the hearings, I needed to become educated on the subject at hand and well-informed about the PMRC, the senators I would be speaking in front of, and all of their cohorts. Joe gathered the research (this was the eighties—you couldn't just click a button) and even attended a PMRC rally/speech to find out everything he could about the enemy. He reported back to me daily and fed me the information he had gathered, which I absorbed like a sponge.

I was expected to make a statement of my position on this issue to the senators. Joe and I worked tirelessly on my speech, endlessly refining it until it was the ultimate weapon of the PMRC's destruction. We were positively diabolical! They had absolutely no idea whom they were dealing with. They really should have invited Vince Neil.

Another major part of prepping for the hearing was going over questions they were likely to ask and statements they were certain to make against me, and preparing my answers and rebuttals. Joe and I left nothing to chance. The one thing we knew I could not talk my way out of was Twisted Sister's rampant use of the initials SMF. But did I even want to?

The week before I was to appear, a request came in from the Senate committee for a copy of my speech. What? Apparently, everyone who testifies before the Senate is required to surrender their statement, in advance, to the committee, so they can read it and prepare their rebuttal. Were they kidding me?! This was a deal breaker. I was unwilling to show my hand, unless, of course, the senators were willing to share *their* statements with me. My manager notified the committee of my position, and they responded that it would not be necessary to see my speech in advance. They were probably all bent over in hysterics at my self-importance and chutzpah. What could a moron such as Dee Snider possibly have to say that would make any kind of difference to anything?

They were about to find out.

I ARRIVED IN WASHINGTON, DC, with my posse the night before the hearing. Joe Gerber, my right hand, was with me, as was Vic, my bodyguard. I asked my father—a Korean war veteran and a patriot—to accompany me, thinking he would enjoy a unique opportunity to see our nation's capital up close and personal. He jumped at the chance. My dear friend and rock-video god, Marty Callner, and his wife, Aleeza, flew in from the West Coast to support me as I did battle. Besides our great relationship, Marty felt a direct connection to what was going on. His video for "We're Not Gonna Take It" was on constant display whenever I, Twisted Sister, or the song was highlighted. I was glad to have him on my side.

The day of the hearings, I woke up in my hotel room feeling no trepidation whatsoever. I was fearless. Priding myself on never bowing to decorum, I donned my usual rock 'n' roll wear for the event: skintight jeans, tiger-head belt, snakeskin boots, sleeveless Twisted Sister T-shirt, and cutoff Twisted Sister denim vest. Finishing up with my tooth earring, aviator sunglasses, and a touch of mascara, I was ready to kick some PMRC ass.

Before heading out, I took the speech Joe and I had worked on so diligently and deliberately folded it up like a bad kid's homework and jammed it into my back pocket. This was my deceptive finishing touch. They weren't gonna know what hit 'em!

The drive to the Senate building was eye-opening. The streets were filled with protesters (for and against), spectators, and media. It was completely insane. The Senate hearing on record labeling was arguably one of the best-attended and media-covered hearings held before a Senate committee. To think that this unpopular kid from

Baldwin, Long Island, was right smack at the center of this controversy was mind-boggling. When I see footage today of me at that
event, I can't even fathom how cocksure I had to be, to walk into
that hostile environment with the attitude I had. Talk about being
full of yourself.

The hearing was held before the Senate Committee on Commerce, Science, and Transportation, and the truly infuriating thing
about it (besides the obvious) was that it was, essentially, an illegal
proceeding. The forum of a congressional hearing can only be used
to address issues for possible legislation, yet in his opening remarks,
the committee chair, Senator John Danforth, stressed, "The reason
for this hearing is not to promote any legislation ... but simply to
provide a forum for airing the issue itself, for ventilating the issue,
for bringing it out in the public domain." *WTF?!* Could it be that
the wives of committee members Albert Gore, John Danforth, and
Ernest Hollings—all three women affiliates of the PMRC—had used
their unfair influence and womanly ways with their husbands to
create a forum for their cause that no one else could possibly have?
Oh, hell yes!

Who knows how much taxpayer money was used to finance
this political circus and ultraconservative witch hunt? It's sickening
to think that our government officials can use their elected office,
irresponsibly, to satisfy their attention-needing wives. And we were
talking about the First Amendment! Not the Second, Third, or even
Fourth ... *the fucking First!* This wasn't an afterthought on the part
of our forefathers: "Oh, yeah, let's put something in this Constitution thingy about free speech." No! It was the first damn thing they
thought to put down!

To add insult to injury, before the hearing was even held, the
RIAA, the governing body of the recording industry, agreed to a
WARNING PARENTAL ADVISORY sticker. I was going to Washington
to fight a battle that had already been lost?! Again I say ... *WTF?!*

The hearing was exactly the media circus you might imagine.
Frank Zappa, John Denver, and I were brought in to represent the
musicians' point of view. As Frank and I stood "backstage" (in some
office) waiting to testify, we marveled at the insanity of the moment
and wondered what side John Denver would be on. We knew it
should be ours, but John was as American as mom and apple pie

and a beloved public figure. In fact he was testifying after meeting with NASA to discuss his possibly becoming the first musician in space! It doesn't get more American than that.

While Zappa and I waited, we shook our heads in disgust at Senator Paula Hawkins's inane speech. Holding a blowup of Def Leppard's *Pyromania* album cover, she shouted, "The message is clear: burn, baby, burn!" Burn what? The woman was clearly cracked and, I'm happy to say, not reelected to another term after her embarrassing rant.

There was a moment of elation when Senator Exon of Nebraska, during his remarks to Tipper Gore, said, "If we are not talking about federal regulation and we are not talking about federal legislation, what is the reason for these hearings in front of the Commerce Committee? Can anyone answer that?"

An actual cheer erupted from the gallery in the hearing room.

Of course, the next time Exon spoke—after being frantically bombarded by aides, explaining the political ramifications of his statement, I'm sure—he made a 180 and applauded the PMRC's efforts, indicating he would seek a way, if possible, to do away with the "outrageous filth" of "music interspersed with pornography." Way to stand up for your beliefs, Senator.

When it came time for Zappa to testify, he asked my father to watch his kids, Dweezil and Moon Unit, who were there with him, while he spoke. My father was honored. To this day he tells the story of the time "Frank Zipper had me watch Moon Weasel and Unit."

Frank was a brilliant man and tore those Washington morons a new one, but when he did mocking-voice characterizations of our opponents, he opened us up for criticism. Don't get me wrong, they deserved everything they got, but in an argument, the minute you start making fun of anything about your opponents, besides their position, you open yourself to rebuke. And that's just what happened.

Senator Gorton, of Washington State, pounced when it was his turn to speak: "I can only say that I found your statement to be boorish, incredibly and insensitively insulting to the people that were here previously; that you could manage to give the First Amendment of the Constitution of the United States a bad name, if I felt that you had the slightest understanding of it, which I do not."

Yikes! The press had a field day with that explosive statement, and some used video of *me* in connection with it because I was weirder looking than Frank. You can't give your enemies ammo like that to use against you. At least make them work for it.

When John Denver was called, you would not believe the fawning and ass-kissing that went on. The senators loved him! Frank and I watched on a television monitor, disgusted and nervous, waiting to hear what John would say . . . *and then JD let 'em have it!*

"May I be very clear that I am strongly opposed to censorship of any kind in our society or anywhere else in the world."

POW!

"Mr. Chairman, the suppression of the people of a society begins in my mind with the censorship of the written or spoken word. It was so in Nazi Germany."

BAM! You should have seen them scatter when John hit 'em with that.

During the cross-examination part of both Zappa's and Denver's testimonies, Al Gore made an absolute ass of himself, starting his questions to Frank with "I have been a fan of your music, believe it or not. I respect you as a true original and a tremendously talented musician." *Oh, please!* To John Denver, Gore had to say, "It is an honor to be able to ask some questions. I have been a fan for a long time, Mr. Denver." *Oh, brother!* What a sycophant!

It finally came time for me to speak, and I was formally introduced to the room: "Next we have Mr. Dee Snider . . . the Twisted Sister."

What the hell kind of intro was that!?

The doors to the room opened and I strode in, snakeskin, high-heeled boots clacking on the floor as I walked. The entire dais stared at me in shock, as the press armada went nuts filming and taking pictures. With every other person in the room dressed in suits and dresses for this important event—even Zappa and Denver had suits and ties on—my less-than-formal garb was a bit upsetting to the "straights." *My front teeth were filed to points, for Christ's sake!* Hey, they wanted a headbanger for their hearings . . . they got one.

I rolled up to the table, took off my "colors," exposing a T-shirt with my own screaming face full of makeup on it, pulled my speech out of my back pocket, sat down, and flattened it out on the table.

Joe Gerber was already sitting at the table (yes, that is the now legendary Joe Gerber on my right, in all the video footage you see from my testimony at the hearing), where he should have been, considering how hard he worked for the hearing and on the speech I was about to give. He was my right hand.

At that moment, just before I began to speak, the magnitude of what I was doing hit me. This was Washington, DC! These were important people. The world was watching! *What the fuck was I doing here!?*

As I started to read, my hand holding the paper began to subtly shake. I was nervous. I quickly reeled it in, and by the second paragraph or so, I had my swagger back. *I was Dee fucking Snider, dammit! That's what I was doing there!*

DEE SNIDER'S STATEMENT TO THE SENATE, SEPTEMBER 19, 1985

I do not know if it is morning or afternoon. I will say both. Good morning and good afternoon. My name is Dee Snider. That is S-N-I-D-E-R. I have been asked to come here to present my views on "the subject of the content of certain sound recordings and suggestions that recording packages be labeled to provide a warning to prospective purchasers of sexually explicit or other potentially offensive content."

Before I get into that, I would like to tell the committee a little bit about myself. I am thirty years old. I am married. I have a three-year-old son. I was born and raised a Christian and I still adhere to those principles. Believe it or not, I do not smoke, I do not drink, and I do not do drugs. I do play in and write the songs for a rock 'n' roll band named Twisted Sister that is classified as heavy metal, and I pride myself on writing songs that are consistent with my above-mentioned beliefs. Since I seem to be the only person addressing this committee today who has been a direct target of accusations from the presumably responsible PMRC, I would like to use this occasion to speak on a more personal note and show just how unfair the whole concept of lyrical interpretation and judgment can be and how many times this can amount to little more than character assassination. I have taken the liberty of distributing to you material and lyrics pertaining to these accusations. There were three attacks in particular which I would like to address.

ACCUSATION NO. 1

This attack was contained in an article written by Tipper Gore, which was given the forum of a full page in my hometown newspaper on Long Island. In this article Ms. Gore claimed that one of my songs, "Under the Blade," had lyrics encouraging sadomasochism, bondage, and rape. The lyrics she quoted have absolutely nothing to do with these topics. On the contrary, the words in question are about surgery and the fear that it instills in people. Furthermore, the reader of this article is led to believe that the three lines she quotes go together in the song when, as you can see, from reading the lyrics, the first two lines she cites are an edited phrase from the second verse and the third line is a misquote of a line from the chorus. That the writer could misquote me is curious, since we make it a point to print all our lyrics on the inner sleeve of every album. As the creator of "Under the Blade," I can say categorically that the . . . only sadomasochism, bondage, and rape in this song is in the mind of Ms. Gore.

ACCUSATION NO. 2

The PMRC has made public a list of fifteen of what they feel are some of the most blatant songs lyrically. On this list is our song "We're Not Gonna Take It," upon which has been bestowed a V rating, indicating violent lyrical content. You will note from the lyrics before you that there is absolutely no violence of any type either sung about or implied anywhere in the song. Now, it strikes me that the PMRC may have confused our video presentation for this song with the meaning of the lyrics. It is no secret that the videos often depict story lines completely unrelated to the lyrics of the song they accompany. The video We're Not Gonna Take It *was simply meant to be a cartoon with human actors playing variations on the Road Runner/Wile E. Coyote theme; each stunt was selected from my extensive personal collection of cartoons. You will note when you watch the entire video that after each catastrophe our villain suffers through, in the next sequence he reappears unharmed by any previous attack, no worse for the wear.*

By the way, I am very pleased to note that the United Way of America has been granted a request to use portions of our We're Not Gonna Take It *video in a program they are producing on the subject of the changing American family. They asked for it because of its "light-hearted way of talking about communicating with teenagers."*

ACCUSATION NO. 3

Last Tuesday a public forum regarding the lyric controversy was held in New York. Among the panelists was Ms. Gore. Trying to stem the virtual tidal wave of anti-ratings sentiment coming from the audience, Ms. Gore made the following statement: "I agree this is a small percentage of all music, thank goodness. But it is becoming more mainstream. You look at even the T-shirts that kids wear and you see Twisted Sister and a woman in handcuffs sort of spread-eagled." This is an outright lie. Not only have we never sold a shirt of this type, we have always taken great pains to steer clear of sexism in our merchandise, records, stage show, and personal lives. Furthermore, we have always promoted the belief that rock 'n' roll should not be sexist, but should cater to males and females equally. I feel that an accusation of this type is irresponsible, damaging to our reputation, and slanderous. I defy Ms. Gore to produce such a shirt to back up her claim. I am tired of running into kids on the street who tell me that they cannot play our records anymore because of the misinformation their parents are being fed by the PMRC on TV and in the newspapers.

These are the only three accusations I have come across. All three are totally unfounded. Who knows what other false and irresponsible things may have been said about my band or me. There happens to be one area where I am in complete agreement with the PMRC, as well as the National PTA and probably most of the parents on this committee. That is, it is my job as a parent to monitor what my children see, hear, and read during their preteen years. The full responsibility for this falls on the shoulders of my wife and I, because there is no one else capable of making these judgments for us. Parents can thank the PMRC for reminding them that there is no substitute for parental guidance. But that is where the PMRC's job ends.

The beauty of literature, poetry, and music is that they leave room for the audience to put its own imagination, experiences, and dreams into the words. The examples I cited earlier showed clear evidence of Twisted Sister's music being completely misinterpreted and unfairly judged by supposedly well-informed adults. We cannot allow this to continue. There is no authority that has the right or the necessary insight to make these judgments, not myself, not the federal government, not some recording industry committee, not the PTA, not the RIAA, and certainly not the PMRC. I would like to thank the committee for this time, and I hope my testimony will aid you in clearing up this issue.

My speech stunned everyone. Could what I was saying possibly be true? "We're Not Gonna Take It" wasn't about violence? "Under the Blade" wasn't about sadomasochism and bondage? No drugs? No alcohol? Married with a son? A Christian? *Who the hell was this freak?!*

The questions from the senators followed, and thanks to all my prep work with Joe, I handled them with aplomb. My favorite—and most telling—moment was when the chairman of the committee, Senator Danforth, said to me after my speech, "Mr. Snider, let us suppose that there is music which, say, glorifies incest; *not yours* . . ."

Victory!

Then, the moment I had waited for came. It was Senator Gore's turn at bat.

Before he could utter a word I fired a shot across his bow: "Excuse me. Are you going to tell me you are a big fan of my music as well?"

The entire gallery and *all* the senators laughed at my dig at the ass-kisser.

Gore was furious. "No, I am not a fan of your music." Without wasting a moment, Al went in for the kill. "Mr. Snider, what is the name of your fan club?"

Joe and I had rehearsed this one to death. "The fan club is called the SMF Friends of Twisted Sister."

Senator Gore was so excited. *He had me now.* "And what does *SMF* stand for when it is spelled out?"

Joe and I had discussed that there was no way around this question, so I took the opportunity to say the F-word, in a federal building, in front of the entire world. *Pretty cool when you think about it.*

"It stands for the Sick Mutha Fucking Friends of Twisted Sister."

"Is this also a Christian group?" Mr. High-and-Mighty retorted.

That really pissed me off. I hate people with a holier-than-thou attitude. *Like he doesn't curse?* In the immortal words of the late Redd Foxx, "If you say you don't curse, come outside with me and I'll slam your hand in a car door. You'll say *shit, cocksucker, and muthafucker*!"

Controlling my anger, I said to Gore, with a hair toss heard around the world, "I do not believe profanity has anything to do with Christianity. Thank you." *Asshole.*

We went back and forth for a while, with Gore trying to defend the honor of his wife. *Tipper needed to* get *some honor before he could defend it!* When the debate came to the apparently crazy idea I had offered up of parents taking responsibility for what their kids listen to, Al and I had this little exchange:

"Let us suppose the lyrics are not printed," asked Senator Gore. "Then what choice does a parent have? To sit down and listen to *every* song on the album?"

"Well, if they are really concerned about it, I think that they have to."

In utter disbelief at my suggestion, Gore responded, "Do you think it is *reasonable* to expect parents to do that?"

This was too easy. "Being a parent is *not* a reasonable thing," I answered, and the entire room gave a collective *Whoa!*

Schooled!

Next up at bat for the Washington, DC, Senators . . . Jay Rockefeller. Oh, a dirtbag was going to mix it up with an elitist snob! The piece of crap went right for my throat: "In the vehemence with which you attacked Senator Gore's wife, I detected a defensiveness somehow on your part, a lack of assuredness on where you stand on this."

Joe and I had wanted this issue to be brought up. The incestuousness of the whole PMRC/Senate hearing thing was almost too much to bear. We wanted to make a point of it, and ol' Fancy Pants set it up perfectly.

"First of all, I was not attacking Senator Gore's wife," I responded. "I was attacking *a member of the PMRC.*"

"You were attacking Senator Gore's wife by name," Rockefeller answered.

"Her name is Tipper Gore, is it not?" Apparently he'd forgotten. "I did *not* say *the senator's wife.* I said *Tipper Gore.*"

Game. Set. Match.

At the end of my testimony, I exited the room and a reporter stuck a microphone in my face. "Dee, how do you feel?"

Without even thinking I responded, "Dirty."

That was the truth. I was born in the fifties and grew up in the sixties and seventies. I was raised believing Washington, DC, was sort of like Oz; a beautiful, special place where great people watched out for our better interest and did great things. Sure I had lived through Watergate, the Iran-contra scandal, and the election of a B-movie actor and Joe McCarthy/House Un-American Activities Committee rat to the highest office in our country, but I still hung on to a childish belief that some good people were still working for us. Not anymore. Sitting face-to-face with those personal-agenda-driven opportunists, they beat the last bit of hope out of me.

Don't get me wrong. I'm not anti-American by any means. It's just that I now know politics is a dirty, ugly, selfish business and no place for a fair, honest, decent man. People have often asked me if I would ever consider going into politics. Not a chance. I'm too honorable to survive.

After a press conference—where I served pizza and soda—I flew back home that afternoon. It was Jesse's third birthday and I returned feeling I had set out to do something truly positive, for an important cause, and I had kicked ass. I had represented the music I love and fought successfully against unfair negativity toward it, and looking at the big picture, I'd stood up for the precious First

Amendment rights of every American. Me—a nobody from the suburbs of Long Island.

MY ELATION WAS SHORT-LIVED. The minute I got home and turned
on the television news, I was bombarded with misrepresentations
of what had happened at the hearing that day. While Frank Zappa,
John Denver, and I had kicked the collective ass of the PMRC and
their pussy-whipped husbands, the daily news shows and newspapers reported the outcome as at best a draw for us and at worst the
rockers had their asses handed to them. They were saying we had
lost the debate.

The *ABC Nightly News*, in a dazzling display of yellow jour-
nalism, took Senator Gorton's comments about Zappa's mocking
of the Washington wives and paired them with video of *me sitting
there as if I were being lectured by him!* Then they took my statement about "We're Not Gonna Take It"—"You will note from the
lyrics before you that there is absolutely no violence of any type
either sung about or implied anywhere in the song"—edited out
my words "you will note from the lyrics before you that," and put
it with the scene of the father being dragged down the stairs in the
WNGTI video. Misrepresentation upon misrepresentation.

What I realized too late is that the daily reporters' livelihoods
depend on their access to and relationships with the politicians and
their people in Washington, DC. They know them all on a first-name
basis; they can't afford to compromise those relationships. No way
was any daily reporter from our nation's capital going to say that
some dirtbag rocker came into town and outflanked seasoned politicians in their own backyard. Sure, the monthlies reported what
really happened, but remember they have a three-month lead time.
The truth didn't come out until December. By that time, the damage
was done and people's perceptions were locked. It wouldn't be until
years later that Frank, John, and I would finally get the recognition
and appreciation that we deserved for our efforts.

To add insult to injury, where I thought I was leading the heavy
metal community into battle on this important issue, I discovered
that *nobody* joined me in the fight. I was left standing alone with

my dick in my hand. For the most part, the other targeted bands lay low and went silent on the issue, waiting for the whole thing to blow over. Alice Cooper told me he thought I was crazy for even defending myself. He said, laughing, if it were him, he would have told the Senate committee it was all true and thrown himself on the mercy of the court. He's a wise man.

Ronnie Dio publicly berated me for having the gall to speak on behalf of the heavy metal community when I repeatedly stated that I could *not* speak for anyone but myself.* But the capper came when I found out that, after publicly embarrassing US officials, my phones were tapped and my mail and packages were being checked by the Feds. I had become a public enemy because I stood up for myself.

It didn't stop there.

Most rock fans were completely apathetic. They didn't understand what the big deal was. So what if there's a warning on the records? It would help them know which records were cool! They didn't understand that any infringement on our First Amendment rights could open the door to greater, future censorship. They didn't see how the warning label could (and would) be used to prevent them from knowing about and even having access to those "cool records." Stores would eventually use the warning label as a way of segregating "offensive" recordings from the others. Some wouldn't even put records with warning labels in the racks, others wouldn't carry "stickered" albums, and still others would use their buying power to force labels to produce edited and censored versions specifically for their chains of stores. *You heard me.*

This was serious shit, and the majority of the record-buying community just didn't get it.

As a result of the PMRC's bashing, my testifying, and the news media's rampant misrepresentation of what happened that day, Twisted Sister and I became the poster band/boy for everything that was wrong with heavy metal. When parents thought of the evils of the genre, they immediately flashed on my image. Twisted Sister became the band that parents used as their line in the sand with

---

* Ronnie later publicly apologized for this unfair accusation after my brother Mark Snider, who was then producing a national heavy metal radio show called *Metal Shop,* informed him of my position at the hearing. Thanks, Mark.

their kids. "Okay, son, you can have the Mötley Crüe record, but not that Twisted Sister one!" "Young lady, you can go see those Iron Maidens, but forget about seeing those Twisted Sisters!" The kids knew we were one of the least offensive of the metal bands—and our popularity was flagging—so they happily "sacrificed" us for the sake of the rest of their favorite bands.

I remember meeting a kid after one of our *Come Out and Play* shows, which Dokken opened, and he was absolutely gushing about how Twisted Sister was his favorite band of all time, all the while wearing a brand-new Dokken shirt he had just bought from the merchandise stand. When I asked him why he didn't buy a Twisted Shirt, he responded, "If my parents knew I was seeing you tonight, they'd kill me!" That's just great.

Even MTV used us as scapegoats to pacify "concerned parents." After the poor initial showing for the *Come Out and Play* record and the video for "Leader of the Pack," they decided to ban our "zombie rock" video for "Be Chrool to Your Scuel," complete with cameos from Bob Goldthwait, Lainie Kazan, horror master Tom Savini, and Alice Cooper. They told us that the zombie content was "too gross" for MTV and absolutely no amount of editing would fix it. What?! It was no worse than Michael Jackson's fourteen-minute, MTV Award–winning zombie opus for "Thriller," but ours was unairable? Like the fans, MTV discovered that they could throw concerned parents a bone with Twisted Sister that would have little effect on their viewership. Scumbags.

Click. Click. Click.

Before our *Come Out and Play* album was even finished, the videos shot, or the world tour begun, all of the pieces were falling into place for a career implosion of epic proportions . . . and we never saw it coming.

43

what do you mean "nobody showed up?"

In anticipation of the coming demand for Twisted Sister product, we decided to shoot our first two videos in advance and create a *Come Out and Play* home-video compilation that would include the "We're Not Gonna Take It" and "I Wanna Rock" videos, all connected by a loose story line. This was yet another thing the band would have to finance.

Once again teaming up with Marty Callner (why would we go anywhere else?), he and I set out to make more of the kind of videos the MTV audience had come to expect from Twisted Sister: laugh-filled, entertaining rock romps.

For the first time, Marty let me handle the writing chores completely myself. Since my amazing experiences making the first two videos (I had little to do with the "The Price" video), I had decided to become a screenplay writer. I had no idea how to do it, but that had never stopped me before. I would figure it out. Clearly I had ideas people found interesting; I just needed to learn the proper way to present them to production companies and film studios. That said, I was more than prepared to write the next Twisted Sister video masterpieces.

"Leader of the Pack" was going to be our first single and video. I was positive this was the track that would break down any barriers left for Twisted Sister and bring us to the level of Springsteen, Prince, and Madonna. No, I'm not kidding! I believed that I/we were the band that could bring metal to the mainstream.

It should be noted that El Presidente of Atlantic Records was one of the few people who (openly) questioned my choice of this song. In a long phone conversation in which I refused to listen to any opinion but my own, he said to me, "This track will either make Twisted Sister the biggest band in the world, or it will kill your career."

Click.

I assured my confused record company president there was nothing to worry about. Twisted Sister had been playing "Leader of the Pack" since our club days; it was on our earliest release, *Ruff Cutts*. Our core audience was guaranteed to love it. The original, Shangri-Las version was a bona fide, number one, worldwide megahit in 1964 and had stood the test of time. Virtually everyone was familiar with the Shangri-Las original. This was the track to lead with, I insisted. Just wait until he saw the video.

Continuing with the idea of including movie icons as video guest stars, Marty and I came upon comedian Bob Goldthwait. Bob had just become a breakout star with his role as Zed in *Police Academy 2* and was blowing up as a stand-up comic. An offer was made through his agents and he took the role. "Bobcat" and I quickly became close friends.

The opening scene for *Leader of the Pack* was shot in a storefront, Halloween night, on Santa Monica Boulevard in West Hollywood—smack-dab in the middle of the annual Halloween Parade. Like the same parade in the West Village of New York, it is dominated by the local gay community, who let it all—sometimes literally—hang out. It's a great time.

I remember sitting inside a commercial van on the street outside the video location hiding from the throng of celebrators, with the doors open so I could still see what was going on, when a drag queen walking by spotted me, spun around, and started singing, "You're gonna burn in hell!" Awesome! Wait . . . *what?*

The connecting footage for all four videos was shot in Los Angeles at a torn-down steel mill where the "future world" scenes from the *Terminator* movie had been shot. It called for the reuniting of the featured actors in all three of our "acted-out" videos and the one to come. Dax Callner (the boy who transformed into me in *We're Not Gonna Take It*), Bob Goldthwait (the shopkeeper in *Leader of the Pack* and soon-to-be teacher in *Be Chrool to Your Scuel*), and the fat kid (I wish I could remember his name!) from *I Wanna Rock* were all reunited.

Leader of the Pack includes a subtle—yet major—change from our past videos. One I didn't make consciously, but speaks volumes: Twisted Sister never performs as a band in the video. We never even got close to musical instruments. In all our previous videos, they ultimately came back to our doing what we did best: rocking out. Not in this one. I'm not even going to speculate what that meant, but I'm sure a psychiatrist would have a field day with the "psychological ramifications of this subconscious decision." It was definitely a creative mistake on my part. Twisted Sister should always have remained heavy metal rockers first and foremost. Period.

The second of our *Come Out and Play* videos, for "Be Chrool to Your Scuel," was expensive and incredibly involved. My idea was for a young teacher (Bobcat Goldthwait) to be struggling to connect with his class. Completely disrespected by the students (as so many young high school teachers are), the young teacher finds solace by listening to his favorite band, Twisted Sister, on his Walkman in the teachers' lounge. Yes, it did cross my mind that I had the teacher being mean to the kids in the "I Wanna Rock" video, and now I had the students being mean (sort of) to the teacher. To me, Twisted's music had mass appeal, and this was a way of communicating that. Doing that may have been yet another in a series I like to call Dee Snider's Greatest Mistakes.

Back to the video concept. While listening to our music, the teacher falls asleep and dreams that he's become Dee Snider, his coworkers become the other members of Twisted Sister and Alice Cooper, and the school has turned into a "zombie high." Great idea, right? Executing it was a whole other thing. Not only did we need a school that we could trash, paint up, and "cobweb" for our set, but we needed a school full of students to become zombies and fill our classroom, hallways, gymnasium, and cafeteria scenes.

Once again, I had to have the best. As a fan of the *Dawn of the Dead* and the horror genre in general, I knew there was only one man for the shoot's special effects makeup: Tom Savini. The man was (and still is) a horror-movie makeup legend, and he wrote the book on zombies. No one else would do. Tom agreed to do the video and to act as well (you've seen him in such movies as *From Dusk till Dawn* and *Grindhouse: Planet Terror*). He was cast as the teacher who turned into Alice Cooper, who was already locked in for the video shoot. Bonus.

Filling the school with students turned zombies wouldn't be a problem. We had so many fans turn out when we announced an open call for *I Wanna Rock*, we had to bring in the police to control the situation. Twisted Sister was a bigger band than ever; the turnout for this open call was going to be out of control. Because of my high profile and the expected large crowd, Marty Callner thought it best I sit this casting call out. Marty and his team, along with the security force hired to control the crowd, could handle it. I remember seeing Callner and his crew off that night; Marty was carrying a bullhorn so he could address the anticipated massive crowd.

When they returned a couple of hours later, the whole production crew seemed pretty dejected.

"How'd it go? What happened?" I asked.

"Nobody was there," Marty answered.

Click.

"What do you mean, nobody was there?" I asked, completely confused.

"Nobody showed up for the open casting call. Don't worry, we can hire a whole bunch of extras."

Nobody showed up? What was the deal with that? I had heard the radio announcements and saw the large ad in the local music paper. There was no way people didn't know about it. Why didn't they come? I had so many other production and recording issues to deal with that I stopped thinking about it immediately. It had to be a fluke.

With Bob Goldthwait, Alice Cooper, Tom Savini, and Lainie Kazan as the lunch lady, the *Be Chrool to Your Scuel* shoot was incredible. The transformation of the school and Tom Savini's zombifying of our extras* was world-class. It took so long to make them

---

* Years later, when watching the video with my kids, I would spot a then unknown Luke Perry (normal and zombie-fied) in the classroom.

all up, and filming the first day went so late, we asked our zombies if they would wear their makeup home, sleep in it, and come back "camera ready" the next day. Every one of them agreed and had a tale to tell the next morning.

Be Chrool to Your Scuel turned out to be one of our best videos. Too bad nobody got to see it.

THE *COME OUT AND PLAY* initiative was a huge undertaking and required a large injection of cash, far greater than the band could afford or the record company was willing to lay out. I would accept only the best for every aspect of the project. The money would roll in after the release of the *Come Out and Play* album and the tour commenced. As far as I was concerned, money was no object.

Emulating the specialty album covers of my heroes Alice Cooper, the *COAP* cover was a custom-ordered, one-of-a-kind, embossed pop-up cover. Besides all the obvious expenses of the design and the mechanics of the cover, the *COAP* record featured a TS manhole cover with me popping out of it when the manhole cover was lifted. No faux, miniature manhole covers for Twisted Sister. For the cover photo shoot I insisted on an actual cast-iron manhole cover be made with a twelve-by-twelve-foot piece of asphalt "street" poured for the manhole cover to sit in. Now that's heavy metal (and asphalt).

To give the graffiti art used on the front and back covers an authenic look, we hired a team of top New York graffiti artists. They worked on the album cover, designed our individual logos for the graffiti wall, did the graffiti art on our stage set, and even graffitied my stage outfits for the tour.

The back cover of the album was a project and a half. I wouldn't accept the band members' graffiti logos being drawn in on the photo after we were shot in front of the wall. I insisted it had to be authentic, and we rented an empty lot with a wall that our artists "tagged." The painting of the huge wall and the photo shoot took two days, but we didn't account for a major problem that arose.

Graffiti artists are territorial, and to have a group of artists from another part of New York City come in and start tagging up walls nearly caused a full-blown turf war. Security had to be hired round the clock to keep the art from being messed with and to protect everyone from potential attacks. The minute the photo shoot was done, the wall was painted over and everything calmed back down.

The worldwide *COAP* tour needed to be grandiose. My idea for the stage set was an inner-city street, complete with sidewalk. The design included a three-story brownstone apartment building with accessible upper windows for performances during the show, there was a candy-store front for Eddie to come out of, a junkyard for Mark the Animal to enter the stage from, and a burned-out car for Jay Jay to climb out of, all under an elevated train trestle. The "street" (performing area) even had a re-creation of the album-cover manhole (this one of wood so I could lift it without humiliating myself) for me to crawl out of and onto the stage. A.J.'s drums were painted and designed to look like garbage and paint cans that "emerged" through the front doors of the brownstone at the start of each show. It was fantastic!

I wanted the stage to look and be lit like a Broadway set and not a rock show. All lights, amplifiers, speaker cabinets, and other equipment were hidden so as to not ruin the theatrical look of the production. Bringing to life this vision was a massive undertaking.

Once again, Suzette designed and made all the stage costumes, and with no budgetary limits, she outdid herself. For the first time the band (other than me) got out of spandex and into tattered denim, which started a new trend in the hair metal world. Throughout the history of Twisted Sister, Suzette's designs were innovative and influenced a lot of the styles of the eighties, but she gets virtually no credit for it.

As you might imagine, it was incredibly expensive to design and then build and transport a show like this from city to city. It required a huge crew, an unprecedented amout of semitrucks and buses, and, of course, everything had to be the best of its kind. Read: a lot of money. I didn't care. We were Twisted fucking Sister, one of the biggest bands in the world (I thought), and this was going to be my ultimate creative statement and hopefully . . . *the end of my rock 'n' roll career.*

Those of you in the know are probably thinking, *He wanted the album and the tour to be a flop?* Of course not. As I wrote that statement, I actually chuckled, because it's the first time I realized I had been granted my wish, but not the way I wanted it. Thanks, Satan. *I'm kidding!*

I had always planned on retiring from rock 'n' roll by the age of thirty-five and living happily ever after. I'd often stated this in interviews and even proclaimed it in response to a question at the Senate hearings. Senator Rockefeller questioned my ability to monitor my then three-year-old son's music when he was twelve if I was always on the road. I replied, "To be perfectly honest, nine years from now I am going to be well retired." *Well retired.* At best I envisioned one more album and tour after this one, so I knew I needed to make this one count.

So where did we get the money to finance this? Not being a numbers guy I can't give you all of the specifics, but I do know the record company laid out their "normal" investment (advancing money for the recording budget and some video costs that we would have to repay) and the band put in what we could. We also got some money from the distributors of the coming home video, but the big influx of cash came in the form of the largest advance ever given to a band by a merchandising company.

Winterland Productions of San Francisco was the biggest rock 'n' roll merchandising company at that time. They—like pretty much everybody else—knew Twisted Sister's follow-up record and tour to the *Stay Hungry* album was going to be huge. They wanted to handle our merchandising and agreed to give us a million-dollar advance on future sales to secure it. This was just what we needed to make the whole initiative happen, and *everyone* agreed to put the entire advance into the production. The band did not take one dollar for ourselves. We should have been committed—I mean, we were *that* committed.

Our deal with Winterland had one caveat. Their lawyers insisted we each sign the contract personally and not as a corporation, making us individually liable for the total advance. I'm not sure I understood this fully at the time, but even if I did, I would have signed anyway. There was no way in a zillion years it was going to fail. But fail I did.

I don't think any manager or attorney worth his salt should ever let his client sign personally for something like this, no matter how much the artist insists he wants to. I was then a charging rhino on a mission, and nobody could have changed my mind about anything, but someone should have got the most powerful tranquilizer gun available and brought me down before I signed on that dotted line. But in fairness to them, I guess they (our manager and lawyer) may have "drank the Kool-Aid," too. They all believed Dee Snider and Twisted Sister could not fail.

But I did. *Big-time*.

COME OUT AND PLAY was to be released just before Thanksgiving, and the preorders from record stores were huge. Whereas they had initially bought five, six, or maybe a dozen copies of *Stay Hungry* before its release, this time out they were buying thirty, forty, fifty, or even a hundred copies in anticipation of high seasonal demand. This was the first of our albums to be available in the brand-new compact-disc format—the ultimate stocking stuffer—so stores were ordering LPs, cassettes, *and* CDs. Everyone was sure *COAP* would be the holiday gift for the rocker in your house.

Upon its release, the "Leader of the Pack" single got a great reception at radio and MTV, with hundreds of stations adding it to their playlist and MTV making the video the Hip Clip of the Week, immediately putting it into heavy rotation. I remember watching the world premiere of the video on MTV, and the VJ, Mark Goodman, introducing it, saying, "Here it is, for the first time anywhere, another Twisted Sister *cartoon* video."

Click.

Cartoon? Twisted Sister wasn't a cartoon. Were we? That certainly wasn't what I was going for.

The day "Leader of the Pack" was released to radio, I did an all-day tour of every rock station in Twisted Sister's power base, the tristate area, to launch the single. In a limo accompanied by my bodyguard, Vic, and an Atlantic Records rep, we started at the crack of dawn and drove from station to station all day long. I expected fans to be lined up at the stations to meet me when I arrived. No such luck. The lack of fans shocked me. What the hell was going on?

Click.

Then came the day I heard "Leader of the Pack" on the radio for the first time. As the music went straight from another popular rock track into our song, "LOTP" sounded terrible. Not only did it not pop, but the song sounded as if it had fallen into a hole. No way would it ever catch the ear of the casual radio listener.

Click.

The actual demand for the *Come Out and Play* album was anything but impressive. It was selling, but it certainly wasn't flying out of the stores. But everything is relative, isn't it? When we were starting out, we were lucky if a record store carried three or four copies of our album. Before SoundScan (computerized tracking of sales) started being used in the '90s, record company reps would call the stores each week to see how the product was selling, if the three of four copies were gone, and the store had been asked by a few more people for the album, the record-store salesclerk would say something like "We can't keep it on the shelves!"

Impressive words to hear about a band.

Now, cut to our fourth album, with thirty or forty albums on the shelves. The same store might have sold twenty copies in the first week, but when that call came from the record company and the clerk looked and saw twenty copies still on the shelves, he probably said something like "We still got a pile of 'em." It gives quite a different impression, doesn't it? And yet we had sold five times as many albums as before!

I remember when AC/DC's *For Those About to Rock* album came out, it was the follow-up to their 10-million-plus-selling *Back in Black* (it's now at 45 million copies worldwide). Expectations were so high that when it sold *only* 3.5 million copies, the record industry called it a failure. *Three and a half million copies!? For Those About to Rock* a flop!? Twisted Sister was suffering from this same industry mind-set (though certainly not on the same level).

No doubt I am making excuses for the record's sluggish sales, but I'm just trying to show how much this record had going against it.

And it got worse.

As we headed into the holidays, having just finished a week of full rehearsals on our massive new stage set for our upcoming tour,

I was filled with uncertainty. Advanced ticket sales for our coming shows were soft. Yet, I was still sure that once we got on the road and got to do what we do best—performing live—everything would fall into place and the *Come Out and Play* master plan would ultimately be the massive success it was destined to be.

If only.

❧ 44 ❧

and then the other shoe dropped

Despite growing concern about the future of the *Come Out and Play* album and tour, I still headed into the holidays feeling like a rock star. *If anything, I'm adaptable.* I can always find a way to rationalize my situation or position myself to continue to move forward. Hell, that's how I got Suzette. The same out-of-control ego that got you (meaning any struggling musician) to the top won't allow you to believe or acknowledge that you might be losing your star. I was a rich, famous rock 'n' roll star and nothing could or would ever change that. So I thought.

Christmas was upon us, and Suzette, Jesse, and I went to see the Rockefeller Center tree like a true rock star and his family; we took a limo. While Jesse and Suzette got out to visit the tree, I peered at it through a slightly lowered window, so nobody would see me. I could almost smell it. As I peered, my driver (childhood friend Russ DiBenadetto) said to me, "Howard Stern was talking about you today."

"Who's Howard Stern?" I honestly didn't know. I'd been a rock 'n' roll vampire since 1974. I never listened to the radio in the daytime.

Howard was doing afternoon drive (2:00 to 6:00 p.m.) on K-Rock, and though he was rapidly creating quite a name for himself, he wasn't nearly the juggernaut he would become a few years later.

"He was talking about how ugly he thinks you are," Russ continued.

"Oh, yeah?" I chuckled. My skin had become so thick over the years that nothing like that could affect me. There's an old saying, "Any press is good press." As long as they get my name close to right (the mispronunciation *Schneider* does get a bit annoying), they can say whatever the fuck they want . . . as long as they don't try and say it to my face.

"Yeah," Russ went on, "he's gonna be on the David Letterman show tonight."

"Really." I turned to look out the window on the opposite side of the limo. We were parked right in front of 30 Rockefeller Center *— where *Late Night with David Letterman* was shot each day. "What time is it?" An idea was formulating in my head.

"Five o'clock—why?"

I had been on Letterman's show earlier that year and knew their filming schedule. The nightly show was shot around five each afternoon.

"I'm gonna give Howard Stern a little taste of reality." With that, I bolted from the car and headed into 30 Rock.

Besides that I was one of the most recognizable faces in rock (and this was New York, my power base), the staff knew me from my appearance. This being a very different time securitywise, I was immediately welcomed by the NBC staff and escorted up to Letterman's studio. I got off the elevator and was again received with open arms by everyone who worked on the show.

"Where's Howard Stern?" I asked.

Assuming I was a friend, they directed me to his dressing room. I angrily pounded on the door, shouted, "Howard Stern!" then threw it open.

Inside were an attractive black woman (Robin Quivers), a fairly normal-looking, semi-long-haired guy (Fred Norris), and a tall, glasses-wearing, small-Afroed, mustached geek (nothing like he looks today) with a look of terror on his face. It had to be Howard Stern.

"What the fuck did you say about me, you muthafucker!?" I screamed as I charged like the Zuni Fetish Doll in Karen Black's *Trilogy of Terror.* The others looked on in shock as I grabbed How-

---

* You can't park in front of 30 Rockefeller Center anymore; they've closed the street for security reasons.

ard and slammed him against the wall. Howard cowered in terror, as he should—I'm a big, scary guy.

Then I started to laugh.

"You're not mad?" Howard asked, not trusting my change of attitude.

"Of course not. I don't give a shit what you say. [As long as it's not to my face.] I was just fucking with you."

With that, we started talking. Howard was a year older than me, grew up in the town next to mine, was best friends with a guy from my neighborhood (Dr. Lou), and had even hung out in the same park I did (Coes Neck Park). In an effort to impress the man with the hugest mane in rock, Howard produced a photo of himself from his high school days, with extremely long hair. *I remembered him!* He was the tall white guy with crazy long hair who played basketball with all the black guys. When I told Howard how I used to look (big, frizzy-brown, parted-in-the-middle Afro, with a mustache), he remembered me as the guy with the crazy hair he used to see playing paddleball next to the basketball courts.

As we continued to talk, it became clear we were kindred spirits. We had both been with our women for years, didn't drink or do drugs, lived pretty near each other on the North Shore, and he had a daughter (Emily) the same age as Jesse.

Having no real friends of equal stature, I thought Howard and I might be able to hang. He was a geek, but seemed like a pretty cool guy. I was a cool guy—who used to be a geek. I suggested we get together with our wives and kids sometime, and we exchanged phone numbers. Howard and I didn't meet again until a few months later, but I heard he—true to what I would discover was his form—went off the next day on how he always wanted a rock-star friend, and whom does he get? *Dee Snider.* As it turned out, he could have done a lot worse.

WHEN WE REHEARSED THE *Come Out and Play* world tour with the full stage production for the first time, it was positively stunning. The New York street-scene set, the dramatic lighting, the insanely powerful opening with each band member emerging from a different set piece, was something to behold. Twisted Sister had reinvented the wheel of a dramatic metal stage show. Too bad we never thought to film its short run for posterity.

Every other element of my elaborate, layered concept was perfect, too. From the album packaging to the costumes, the merchandising, the tour program, and the home video, each aspect of it was executed perfectly.

On January 8, we launched the tour in Binghamton, New York, to half a house. Even with a strong opener in up-and-comers Dokken, the numbers weren't good. Ticket sales were light across the board for our upcoming shows, too. We were headlining arenas and not coming close to selling out. I kept telling myself that we were just having a soft start, and once word of our amazing show spread and we got closer to the actual show dates, ticket sales would pick up. They had to.

Before a show, I always got into my attack mind-set. I was preparing for battle. Metal audiences can be notoriously tough, and I believe you need to show them who's the boss from the get-go, or you can be eaten alive. When I hit the stage that first tour date in Binghamton, ready for a war, I was greeted with squeals of delight from the young pop-rock fans who had come to see us. They liked us, they really liked us.

To make matters worse, the set list I had designed for the tour was our typical metallic assault—light on the pop metal, heavy on the real metal. It was the totally wrong set for this crowd. They were completely confused by such songs as "The Fire Still Burns" and "Tear It Loose." They wanted to hear the fun, funny songs.

Twisted Sister's core metal audience was gone.

Clunk!

The final tumbler in the combination lock of the undoing of our career fell into place, and the sound was deafening. The true SMFs, our original fans, the diehards who had been with us from the very beginning . . . had abandoned us. I know they felt we had abandoned them.

The next show, I completely scrapped the set list I had written (and staged) for the tour and made it much "happier." We needed to cater to the audience we had, not the one we wished we had.

A confusing thing about the tour was the media fanfare before each show. It didn't jibe with the weak ticket sales. In every city, the press demanded I hold a press conference (I never did them with the band). With all this interest from the mainstream press, I couldn't understand why our ticket sales weren't stronger. Around the fourth or fifth show it hit me.

After answering the usual barrage of questions about the Senate/ PMRC hearings, I stopped the proceedings and asked a question of the media. "Does anyone have a question about Twisted Sister, our album, or the tour?"

Silence.

It dawned on me that none of the press or media seemed to care about my band. Frank Zappa and Tipper Gore were making the talk-show circuit, continuing the debate about censorship and keeping the subject very much alive, but I had no interest in doing that. I was a rock star, not a politician.

That was the last press conference I did as we continued to perform night after night to lightly attended shows. Starting in the Northeast, we were performing in our strongest region, so we had some glimmers of hope. Two sold-out shows at Radio City Music Hall and a nearly sold-out arena in Philadelphia, but as we moved farther out of the Northeast, our numbers began to plummet.

We had so much working against us. As I said before, being the poster boys for everything that was wrong with rock, we became the band parents forbid their kids to see. And most of our new audience needed Mommy and Daddy's permission (and sometimes their escort) to attend our shows. Perfect.

Then there was the city in Texas that had actually passed a law specifically to keep Twisted Sister out. Banning any concert performance that promoted the occult, drugs and alcohol, bestiality, deviant sex, or violence, the town's fathers were sure they'd covered all the bases needed to keep my band and me out. When—knowing that our music and philosophy had nothing to do with those things—we booked a date anyway, the concerned parents of the community came to our show and sat right in the front row, ready to file complaints and have us shut down and arrested the minute we broke the new law. By the end of the show those front-row parents were *literally* onstage rocking with us.

The day after we left, the local politicians adjusted the law to limit the decibel level at concerts. It was so limiting we could never return. Twisted Sister could not get a break.

One month into our planned "never-ending" US tour, we were bleeding money. We couldn't admit that the tour was a complete flop, so I faked a throat polyp and we canceled the remaining dates. Deep in debt, and knowing we had no way to raise the kind of money we needed to repay Winterland (the merchandise company that gave us our million-dollar advance), we still had no choice but to cut our losses. We *said* we would regroup and finish the tour once spring and summer came—a much better time for rock tours in the States—but we were fooling ourselves. It would never happen.

I WENT HOME IN defeat. No doubt I had been knocked down hard, but I still refused to accept the reality of what was happening to the band and me. We were done. We had struggled for so long to make it, and now—less than two years from the time we broke through— we were on our way out. Apparently we had been for some time. Therein lies the problem. Every aspiring performer—of any type— dreams of making it, viewing it like some sort of finish or goal line. We see ourselves taking that victory lap or spiking the ball, then living happily ever after. No one tells us "making it" is just another point on the journey. *Sustaining it* is a whole other thing. But that's just not in the cards for most of us.

The life span for the success of most bands back then was three to five years; these days it's more like one to three. The Ozzy Osbournes, Eric Claptons, and U2s of the world are the exceptions, not the rule. They are the .000001 percenters. The rest of us? We're gone before we really get anything.

When you don't break until your third or fourth album, you are in debt to your record company for all the recording budgets, videos, tour support, and whatever other bullshit they're allowed to charge against your account that has accumulated over the years, you are deep in debt, baby. One big-selling record only serves to pay it back. You need to sustain your career to make any real money.

My songwriting royalties were sacrosanct—with the exception of some creative bookkeeping and royalty adjusting by the record company. But I still made a lot of money from record sales. The rest of the band were just arriving at the plateau where the real money starts to come in, but there was no plateau for Twisted Sister—just a sheer drop off the other side.

So why didn't I throw on the brakes, reduce my spending, and save all the money I had made? Are you kidding? I was a rock star, this was my dream, and the ego that had kept me going through all the disappointments of my career—the ego that had convinced me I was going to make it—would not allow me to accept or believe that the band's current circumstances were definitive. I could have given you a dozen reasons why things were going to turn around and get better. No one could talk any sense into me.

I went home, laid low, and continued to live large. The rock and mainstream press had run with our tour cancellation due to my "throat operation," and to be caught in a bald-faced lie would only add significantly to the problems the band was having. Already some asshole manager of other bands was out there—who some say is a real mensch—calling up industry people saying we were lying about the reason for our canceling the tour and that it and the album were a total failure.

With "Leader of the Pack" tanking at radio and on MTV, we needed to unleash our secret weapon, *Be Chrool to Your Scuel*, sooner than originally planned. To our shock and surprise, not only did MTV ban the video, but our record company pulled the plug on the *Come Out and Play* album entirely.

The president of the label—the guy who had never wanted to sign Twisted Sister in the first place—decided not to release a follow-up single to the failed "Leader of the Pack"! This was insanity. We had sold 5 million records worldwide on *Stay Hungry*, and he wasn't going to give our new album a second shot?!

It seemed that El Presidente used MTV's "banning" of our video to justify his position. No MTV, no "Be Chrool to Your Scuel" single release. No single, no continued support for *Come Out and Play*.

As we desperately tried to figure out a way around MTV's edict, we made a mind-blowing discovery. While on the surface, MTV's rationale for the banning of *BCTYS* was its "horrific content," the truth was far more horrific. One of the new top dogs at MTV was a former Atlantic Records junior executive. We were told that he had received word from Atlantic Records, his old employer, telling him to make sure Twisted Sister's *Be Chrool to Your Scuel* video never saw the light of day. To me, that was the final nail in the coffin of our career.

⇥ 45 ⇤

"we all fall down"

The cancellation of the North American *Come Out and Play* tour was like a death nobody wanted to acknowledge or mourn. We all just went home and waited for the European leg of the tour. Twisted Sister's *Come Out and Play* tour of Europe was long over-due, and a huge success, but it was too little too late.

If we had spent more time overseas on the *Stay Hungry* tour, we might have avoided the massive overexposure in the States and built our draw even more in Europe. All of our shows were selling out there, and the *Come Out and Play* record was doing well—better than *Stay Hungry* in some countries.

Even in the UK, where that WEA exec had hamstrung the *Stay Hungry* record by cheaping out on postage, Twisted Sister was experiencing a surge in popularity. While attending one of two sold-out nights at the legendary Hammersmith Odeon, and hearing the ovation for "We're Not Gonna Take It," said exec was overheard saying, "Maybe I should have got behind that record." Asshole.

The success of the European tour gave Twisted Sister a glimpse of what might have been, and a brief reprieve from the reality of failing in our largest territory and homeland.

I now know, I not only miscalled and mishandled the success of the band in North America and around the world, but I continued to do all the wrong things careerwise for years to come. I don't want to make excuses, and I certainly won't point fingers at anyone but myself, but success definitely clouded my judgment. Not until I hit rock bottom six years later did my sight finally begin to clear. But I still had a lot of long, hard falling to do.

Twisted Sister's final shows of the *Come Out and Play* tour were in Italy. Now earlier that year, in April, under the command of President Ronald Reagan, the United States had run retaliatory air strikes against Libya for its bombing earlier that same month of a Berlin disco frequented by US soldiers. While from afar Americans applauded this show of strength, Twisted Sister discovered Europeans weren't so crazy about the idea of US jets dropping bombs in their backyard, so to speak. When you are only hundreds of miles away from things like that, you feel the effects a lot more than when you're thousands of miles away. Some Europeans were outwardly unhappy with their feelings toward Americans at that time—in particular, the Italians.

We received word that in Italy some American bands were being spit on, and one band had their tour bus set on fire (no one was injured). Upon hearing this, we wanted to cancel our shows there. I knew if confronted like that by some Italian assholes (in this instance), I would not be able to just turn the other cheek and walk away. It's my nature to "return fire," so to speak, and I could see where, in this current political climate, that could lead to no good (possibly incarceration far from home). Pulling out of the two Italian shows seemed to make the most sense.

Instead, our management opted to have us met at the airport by a phalanx of bodyguards, who surrounded us (à la Prince and the Revolution at the Grammys) and escorted us everywhere we went, making sure there were no problems. That worked for me.

Twisted Sister's final show of the *COAP* tour was on June 2, 1986, with Motörhead, in Bologna, Italy. It would be the last time the "real" Twisted Sister played together for fourteen years. Sure, Jay Jay French loves to tout the fact that there have been three singers, four guitar players, two bass players, and seven drummers (and four corpulent porpoises) in Twisted Sister since its inception—*and that he is the only original member!*—but that's just his attempt to minimize the importance of any other member of the band and maximize his significance. It's all bullshit.

Only *five* members of Twisted Sister will ever matter: Dee Snider,

Eddie "Fingers" Ojeda, Mark "the Animal" Mendoza, A. J. Pero . . . and Jay Jay French. Not one fan gives a shit about the other eleven former members—other than for band historical purposes—and out of the five who count, only one is being paid to write about his life . . . and it ain't Jay Jay. I'm just sayin' . . .

As we flew home from Europe, it signaled the official end of the entire *Come Out and Play* initiative. To the band (other than me), the album and everything that went with it would come to symbolize the culmination of everything that went wrong with Twisted Sister and be the focus of our fall from dizzying heights. Despite the album's being our second-biggest-selling and second-best-known record in North America and being successful throughout Europe and most of the rest of the world, to this day we play little if any music from *COAP* live, and "Leader of the Pack" is absolutely never mentioned. It is that ugly and painful a memory to my band members.

As in denial as I was about the seriousness of the situation, deep down inside I knew *the real pain was only beginning.*

THE MAGNITUDE OF MY failure took a while to set in. Even the news that the album's CD—a new medium in 1985—was officially the first in history to be "cut out" * (clearly one more bit of retribution from Atlantic Records) didn't openly shake me. The same ego that had got me to the top and into this mess would not allow me to accept or believe just how huge a fall Twisted Sister had taken. We were Twisted "fucking" Sister, for God's sake!

On the surface, I was still convinced this was just a mere setback that could and would be fixed, but subconsciously I began to come apart. I knew that *I* had blown it, and I took the full responsibility for the band's failure. I know I just went through at length all the things and people who were working against us/me, but I blamed

---

* Records are "cut out" when the label discontinues production and sells off remaining stock at a drastically reduced price.

myself for *allowing* those things to happen. I should have known better. *It was all my fault.*

With the acceptance of responsibility came shame. I was embarrassed by my failings and disgusted with myself. And if *I* couldn't stand me, whom could I possibly expect to? As I emotionally began to break down, I pushed away everyone around me. *Why would they want anything to do with me?* I thought. So before any of them could abandon me, I saved them the trouble and began to get rid of them. I remember Alice Cooper wanted me to "return the favor" and sing on his new record. I didn't return his calls because I couldn't believe he *really* wanted me on his album. He had to be asking me out of obligation.

My band, my friends, my family—one by one I pushed them away for things they did to me, but in reality I was pushing them away before they had a chance to reject me. I knew I had to be an embarrassment to them all.

The saddest and most catastrophic thing I did was to slowly alienate the one person who had always been there for me: Suzette, my wife—and as a result my young son, Jesse, as well. Over the years, I had grown more and more insufferable. I was (and guess I still am) a textbook narcissist and had grown to believe the sun rose and set around me. Starting in the clubs and bars, and building steadily with the rise of Twisted Sister, I acted as if I knew it all, and my needs and concerns came before all others. The one thing I had going for me, that got Suzette to give me a chance, was that she thought I was a nice guy. Over the years I chipped away at that niceness and became anything but. And that was when things were going well.

When things came apart, rather than pull together with the one person who had been unfailingly supportive of me for my entire career, I built a wall between us and drove her away. *Why would Suzette want to be with a loser like me?* As my career spiraled downward, I became convinced it would be better for Suzette—and Jesse—if I went on alone.

I truly believe Suzette and I are one of the great love stories of our generation. We were destined to be together, and clearly our lives joined for reasons known . . . and not yet known (who knows what our children or children's children will achieve?). Now at more than thirty-five years together, I am more convinced of that than ever. Yet I nearly threw it all away—including my son and the subsequent birth of our other three children—because I was too proud to accept, or admit, I needed help. And Suzette was the one person who had been helping me all along.

I BECAME CONVINCED THAT everything would be set right with the release of my next record. But what should that record be? Since Twisted Sister had become more of a mainstream act and the metal community had essentially turned its back on us, I believed my next move should be an even more mainstream album. And I was sure my next release should be a solo album. I didn't have any intentions of quitting Twisted Sister, I just thought taking a break from the band and doing my own record was the smart move to make. It would give Twisted a break publicly and—I believed—allow us to mount a comeback in a couple of years after the dust settled.

I planned on calling my side project *Me and the Boys*, and it was going to be very different from Twisted Sister. For starters, I planned on having a keyboard player and a saxophone player (my experience with Clarence Clemons had a great effect on me), and the songs I was writing were much more pop-influenced. I was listening to and studying a lot of Bryan Adams, feeling his mix of rock and pop would be the right balance for me. I even envisioned a radical image change, seeing this band as a bunch of guys you'd find hanging around the local 7-Eleven wearing ripped jeans, Converse All Stars, T-shirts, and jackets—almost an early punk look. That's the photo I wanted for the album cover.

While I worked on the songs for the record, I continued to film episodes of *Heavy Metal Mania* for MTV, worked on my book, *Dee Snider's Teenage Survival Guide*, and my first screenplay,* and spent a lot of time hanging out on *The Howard Stern Show*.

---

* This long self-teaching process eventually led to my writing and selling screenplays, sitcoms, and reality-show ideas, and writing, coproducing, and starring in *StrangeLand*.

❖   ❖   ❖

HOWARD AND I, ALONG with Suzette and his wife, Alison, started socializing and became friends. Not only did our relationship grow, but
our involvement in the show as well. I say *our* because while I was
having my influence on the *Howard Stern Show* content, Suzette
was helping Howard develop his image.

From the time I first met and then *heard* Howard on the radio,
I couldn't understand why he looked the way he looked. I'd say to
him, "You're a pirate on the radio; why the hell do you look like an
accountant?" Howard asked how he *should* look, and Suzette and I
showed him. In the beginning, I would give him some of my clothes
to wear. Suzette became his stylist, taking him out shopping, picking
his clothes, and cutting his hair. I convinced him to start wearing
sunglasses instead of plain glasses.

"Why?" asked Howard.

"Because it will make your nose look smaller," I said. Hey, it
works for me.

In his movie *Private Parts*, by the eighties Howard already had his
"brunette Dee Snider" look happening.* That was creative license
taken by the writer of the screenplay, necessary for the story arc of
the movie. In reality, Howard's full-blown, eighties hair-metal look
didn't peak until much later. Thanks to Suzette.

A major influence I had on the *Stern Show* was the introduction
of comedians to the regular show mix. My buddy Bob Goldthwait
was on tour and coming to New York City to do a show. I told him
about the *Stern Show* and how I thought it would be a great place
for him to promote his appearance. Bobcat said he was in. When I
called Howard and suggested he have Bob on, he told me he didn't
have comedians on the show because "all they do is shtick." I told
Howard a whole new school of comedians were out there, like Bobcat and Sam Kinison, who were sharp and improvisational. Howard
wasn't convinced, but agreed to give Goldthwait a try. Bobcat killed
on *The Howard Stern Show*, and as a result of his repeat appearances and success, it led to Howard's bringing on Kinison, Andrew

---

* Frustratingly, as Howard's star rose and mine sank, people started telling me
I looked like Howard Stern!

Dice Clay, Gilbert Gottfried, Pat Cooper, and more. Great comedians became a staple on the show (and still are) and are responsible for some of Howard's most legendary broadcasts.

With the band unexpectedly off the road, and time on my hands, I began to appear regularly on Stern's show and had some pretty legendary appearances myself. Howard's show had moved back to mornings, so since I lived fairly near him, I would go to his house at 5:00 a.m., and we would limo (driven by Ronnie, his legendary driver, of course) into the city. Howard would meditate for the half-hour ride, while I sat fairly comatose—*it was five in the damn morning!* Starting at 6:00 a.m. I would sit in as a show member for the entire five-hour broadcast, then Howard and I would limo back home. Some weeks I did this multiple times. I loved the original team of Howard, Robin Quivers, Fred Norris, Jackie Martling, and Gary Dell'Abate and couldn't get enough of just hanging out and joking around with them for hours on end. I felt like a member of the team, and I was honored to be treated like one by all who were involved. It was an incredible experience. This camaraderie was what had been missing for so many years for me in my band.

Howard Stern was the first person to recognize my value beyond singing with Twisted Sister. As my music career began to backslide and the entertainment industry backed further and further away from me, the *Stern Show* continued to have me on. One day I asked Howard why, and he said, "Dee, it doesn't matter to me *who* you are, *it's what you are.* I've had huge stars offered up to me for interviews and I have passed because they are boring on the air. You're great on the radio. The listeners love you."

Not only did I really need to hear something like that at a dark time, but appearing on Howard's show eventually led to my doing voice-over work, my own radio shows, television shows, making movies, and more. Howard not only championed me with agents and producers, but by my being on the show, people started to realize I had more to offer than "We're Not Gonna Take It." *Thanks, Howard. I love you, man.*

⚜ 46 ⚜

how do you say "holy shit!" in russian?

My first book, *Dee Snider's Teenage Survival Guide*, wasn't my idea. I was approached by Doubleday Publishing to write a sequel to a popular book from the fifties called *'Twixt Twelve and Twenty* by a singer named Pat Boone. Being a popular artist of the time whom—apparently—young people related to, his book on growing up was a bestseller. The editors at Doubleday saw me as a modern-day (Pat Boone?) pop figure whom kids would listen to. I'd never thought about doing a book like that, but accepted the challenge . . . and the check. Since at that time I wasn't up to the task of writing the book myself, I was assigned a rock journalist named Philip Bashe to work with.

Phil did extensive interviews with me on a wide range of teen-related subjects, from cliques in school, to masturbation, to coping with death, and I gave him my insights and opinions at length on all of them. His job was to translate the interview tapes and put them into book form along with any pertinent facts and information (such as Suicide Prevention hotline numbers or how to contact Planned Parenthood) that would be useful to my readers. I wanted the book to read as if a big brother or cool uncle were talking to you, not be overintellectualized—*like this book*—just straight talk, in terms a teen could understand.

When *Dee Snider's Teenage Survival Guide* was released, with the exception of the *Christian Science Monitor* (which denounced the book because it was pro-choice), everyone from *Psychology Today* to *Circus* magazine said it was the best book ever written on growing up. It was head and shoulders above everything else out there, and a godsend for teens. Every other book was written by a teacher, psychologist, doctor, parent, or minister.

Several years later, the brother of Twisted Sister's incredible assistant manager (and future Widowmaker manager), Pam Rousakis, came back from a summer college-exchange program in the then Soviet Union.

"They're using your book as a textbook," he said.

"The *Teenage Survival Guide*?" I asked. It was the only book I had written, but I must have heard him wrong.

"Yes. It's being used as a textbook."

"In a Soviet college? No way."

"I'm not kidding you. I couldn't believe it either."

Tommy was not the kind of guy to mess around with something like that, but still . . .

A few years after that, I received word my book was being released in installments in the only Soviet teen magazine. Was that even possible?! In the mideighties the only Soviet television channel had held up a photo of me, with all of my makeup on, saying, "This is Daniel Dee Snider, from Baldwin, New York. He is a typical example of American decadence. You can't tell if he is a man or a woman." Maybe in the Soviet Union you couldn't. I could just picture some massive, steroided-out Soviet shot-putter gazing lovingly at my photo in his gym locker: "Look at Dee Snider. Isn't she beautiful?"

I still could not believe they were reading my book behind the Iron Curtain . . . until I met a Russian fan who brought me *all* of the issues of the Soviet teen magazine my book was in.

After the Berlin Wall came down and the Soviet Union came apart at the seams, my agents received a call from a Russian publisher who wanted to release my book in hardcover. A deal was cut and the book was released. The original picture of me on the cover with my mass of long, blond, curly hair had been removed and replaced with a "jazzy" drawing of some "happening" teens. Not long after that, I got a call for an interview with the *Moscow Times*. They wanted to know how it felt to know that every Russian child had to read my *Teenage Survival Guide*. My book was mandatory reading!?

To this day, I hear from people (American and Russian) who tell me how my book helped them when they were growing up and changed their lives. Copies, if you can find them, can go for hundreds of dollars. Go figure. My own kids have read the book on their own and say it is great but gives them a bit too much information about their dad. Nobody needs to know about the first time their father masturbated. Back then, I just tried to be as honest and as frank as I could be with my readers. Now with four kids and grandchildren, I don't know if I could still be that honest about my teen years, but I'm glad I was.

WITH MY MUSICAL CAREER in a tailspin, having quit *Heavy Metal Mania* because I was overexposed (and MTV didn't want to pay me), and with my marriage crashing and burning, somehow both my management and record companies convinced me to make the next bad move in my career: turn my solo album into a Twisted Sister record.

I don't remember how they convinced me, but in the depths of a deepening functional depression, I was becoming less and less sure of myself. Not even a year after Twisted Sister's and my fall from grace, we went back into the studio and started to work on a new album, this time with legendary Ratt producer Beau Hill. Guaranteed by Atlantic Records' president that the label was going to get totally behind Twisted's new album and reestablish the band, Hill signed on to a sinking ship.

During the band's relative hiatus of several months, A. J. Pero had quit Twisted Sister to do a solo album with a band called Cities. While I always knew he was unhappy about "playing like a monkey" (read: simple, straight drumbeats) as he called it, I could never understand why he quit. Twisted Sister wasn't doing anything at that time, why not just do the Cities record as a side project? We were getting weekly salaries the entire time we were on break, he could have collected his check while working on the Cities album, which paid nothing.

Years later, when I finally got to ask him that question, A.J.

explained to me that when he told Jay Jay he wanted to do a side project, Jay Jay told him he couldn't stay in Twisted Sister and play with Cities; he would have to make a choice. With things in Twisted Sister being so uncertain, and A.J. wanting to play and show people his range as a drummer (believe me when I tell you, A. J. Pero can play absolutely *any style*), he resigned. Twisted Sister's next drummer, Joe Franco, is an incredible journeyman drummer (he wrote *the* book on double bass drumming, the standard in the industry, used at the Berklee College of Music) and a longtime friend to us all. He had been in the band the Good Rats during our club days, but had moved on to work with a ton of other recording bands, including Canada's Chilliwack and Atlantic recording artist Fiona, Beau Hill's then love.* He was a perfect fit.

Love Is for Suckers musically reflects the more commercial direction I wanted to take my solo record in, while lyrically reflecting my dour mental state. I was mad at the world and saw no future in my relationship with Suzette. By the time we started recording the album in New York City, I was ensconced in a hotel and never went home.

In a last-ditch effort to save our marriage, Suzette and I agreed to see a counselor. With over ten years in the relationship and an amazing son together, a lot was riding on a potential divorce. The minute the therapist started talking to me, it became woefully apparent where—or should I say, *with whom*—the problem lay.

Surprise, surprise! I was the one with the total career crash-and-burn. Instead of clinging to my relationship with my always-supportive wife and partner, I was lashing out at her, along with everybody else in my world. The doctor said I needed to spend time working with him one-on-one before he could address any problems Suzette and I were having as a couple. I accepted his diagnosis, but I told him no way was I starting down a lifetime path of weekly therapy sessions so I could slowly sort things out. I arranged to see him every day for two or three hours straight, until we figured it out, and sure enough, the doctor and I made it through the muck and

---

* Joe would go on to work with me on many more projects and play drums on some of the biggest records by Mariah Carey, Celine Dion, and other pop divas.

mire of a lifetime of personal issues.* By the end of recording in the spring of 1987, Suzette and I were back together and on our way to being stronger than ever . . . and she was pregnant shortly thereafter. Too bad I can't say the same thing about Twisted Sister. Being back together and stronger . . . *not pregnant.*

THE MISGUIDED RECORDING OF *Love Is for Suckers* as a Twisted Sister album did absolutely nothing to improve my situation with the band. It only made things worse. Maybe the whole group should have gone into therapy.

While the album was technically a Twisted Sister record, I didn't do anything differently recording it than if it were my solo album. I made a more commercial-sounding record, brought in outside musicians for various parts, and used what I wanted from the Twisted Sister arsenal of talent. I'm not saying it was all as simple as that—I still had to play all sorts of games politically—but ultimately that was the result.

To make it even less of a Twisted Sister record than it already was, I/we decided to take off our war-paint makeup and tone down our costumes to fit in with every other hair band out there at that time. Brilliant! The band that had essentially created the hair metal genre was abandoning their look to fit in with the bands that came after them. Idiot. I was even doing photo sessions in pastel colors and acid-washed jeans, wearing Converse All Stars. How not Twisted Sister was that!?

Love Is for Suckers, while a great record with hit potential, was *not* a Twisted Sister album. Sure, there are definitely some "twisted" moments ("Wake Up the Sleeping Giant" for one), but with the songwriter of Twisted Sister (me) writing the songs after only writing Twisted songs before that, and Twisted Sister playing the songs, the TS sound and attitude was going to come through somehow.

The album was released in August, and—prepare yourself—

---

* For the record, this is an amazing way to address your issues, and if you can afford it and dedicate the time to it, I highly recommend it. Doing it in this way, you can actually see improvement and change happening.

Atlantic Records didn't pull out all the stops! What a shocker. The label did go through all the motions of a record release. We shot a typical hair-metal video for our single "Hot Love" with former Billy Joel and the Hassles/Attila drummer turned video maker Jon Small (best known for his video work with Billy Joel). Upon release, the video was immediately put into "nonexistent rotation" on MTV. Sure, Twisted Sister helped establish and define MTV as a network, and I cocreated and hosted what would become the hugely successful *Headbangers Ball*, but what had we done for them lately? *Pricks*.

The album's promotion was limited, as was any kind of real record-company push. To quote Beau Hill, "I went looking for the record in the stores and found one copy under a half-eaten hamburger in the stockroom." Not quite the full-court press he'd been promised by El Presidente.

To be fair to all guilty parties involved, in the summer of '87, Twisted Sister was still suffering from the drubbing we had taken in 1986. Not nearly enough time had passed for the dust to have settled and the metal community to be ready and open to the return of Twisted Sister. This is why I wanted to do a solo album. I believed it would have been a success—which it more than likely would *not* have been—but more important than that, it would have given the band and the fans a chance to catch our breath, regroup, and come back much stronger in, say, 1988 or '89. I believe if we had followed my plan, Twisted Sister would not have broken up. Sure, we would have been crucified, had the flesh ripped from our still-quivering carcasses and our bones stomped to dust by grunge in the early nineties . . . but we wouldn't have broken up!

The *Love Is for Suckers* tour didn't last long and was depressingly disappointing. Touring with the then rising Great White and TNT, I was reminded of our first tour with the band Blackfoot, who were then at the end of their career. I looked at them as has-beens, and here we were in the same position. After the glory of the *Stay Hungry* tour and the—albeit failed—magnitude of the *Come Out and Play* world tour, traveling now from city to city, a shell of our former, powerful selves (using Stryper's leftover stage ramps because they were cheap!), was pathetic and sad. To make matters worse, our friend and soundman, Charlie "Sixth Sister" Barreca, and the band's longtime road/tour/co-manager and friend, Joe Gerber, were no longer working with the band.

Joe Gerber had quit after being denied a long-promised "piece of the action." He had always been assured by the band that his years of dedication and service would be rewarded; Joe trusted us to do the right thing. When the band finally sat down before the release of *Come Out and Play* to decide what to give him, the majority voted (not me) to give Joe an insulting bonus structure with a cap that gave him an ice cube's chance in hell of making any real money. Joe's then girlfriend, Stacey Sher (former Creamcheese Productions' production assistant, now a big-time Hollywood producer), called the failure of the *COAP* album and tour "the curse of the cap." Hurt by the band's vote of no confidence, Joe, being the professional he is, stayed through the *COAP* tour, then left.

Our soundman, Charlie Barreca, was another story. Having been a member of Twisted Sister since Jay Jay resurrected the band in the fall of 1975, Charlie's sound-mixing style eventually became a point of contention for some of us. He was a huge Grateful Dead fan and believed in a dry, straight-ahead live sound. Some of the band members (especially Mark Mendoza and I) wanted a more "treated" live sound (using echo and such) to make the concerts more reflect our albums. Charlie and I often went head-to-head on this, but with love. Charlie Barreca was the most dedicated and loyal friend and member of our team—*he would have done anything for the band*.

With the even more polished sound of the *Love Is for Suckers* album, the band knew our live sound requirements were going to be that much greater (we even had Billy Squier's keyboard player and longtime friend Alan St. Jon offstage on the tour, to implement some of the sound elements of the record). The band had a meeting and unanimously decided it was time to part company with Charlie. Fair enough. When the discussion turned to how we were going to let him go, I assumed he would be given the dignity of a band meeting. After all, he was a member of the band. The others didn't see it that way. After more than a dozen years of struggle—standing shoulder to shoulder with us in the trenches—they wanted to dismiss Charlie with an *official letter from management*! I couldn't believe it. When I told them I was going to call Charlie personally and let him know he was being let go, my band members actually had a vote to prevent me from calling! Unbelievable.

The *LIFS* tour ended, unceremoniously, on October 10, 1987, in Minneapolis, due to lack of fan interest and disappointing album sales.

Two days later, I announced my official resignation from the band.

Sometimes the end of any relationship is brought about by a major event or moment that changes everything. Most times it's the cumulative effect of a series of smaller issues that build to a boiling point. Sure, there is often some straw that breaks the camel's back, but this is just another symptom, not the affiliation-ending disease.

As you have read, my band and I had problems from day one that slowly grew, multiplied, and festered. "Untreated," what were once minor annoyances became unbearable conditions to function under. Rather than address these situations as we went along, our management (Jay Jay included) opted to put Band-Aids on wounds that festered and eventually became untreatable cancers. In all fairness, as I've documented, at times attempts were made to address some of these issues, but even then, people refused to speak openly. The result: the demise of a truly great rock 'n' roll band. Twisted Sister really did kick ass.

The worst part for me is the way it ended . . . *with a whimper.* From the day I joined Twisted Sister, we had been a force to be reckoned with. We were the Demolition Squad. We were *always* the band to beat. To go out as quietly as we did was an insult to everything we had fought so hard for and achieved. Most of the public didn't even know we had broken up . . . *but had we?*

The band never officially dissolved. To the best of my knowledge, two of the remaining three partners, Mark and Jay Jay (at that point brothers-in-law, through Jay Jay's marrying Mark's sister, Jody), used their majority to vote Eddie out of the band, officially making the two of them Twisted Sister. After that bold move (did Eddie even know?), they proceeded . . . *to do virtually nothing until I returned in 2002.* Clearly I had been holding them back.

Oh, yeah. In 1992 they released their personal statement, *Big Hits and Nasty Cuts,* which included no music from *Come Out and Play* or *Love Is for Suckers* (albums they both despised), but it did have photos of every incarnation of the band prior to when Eddie, Mark, A.J., and I joined. *Who fucking cared!?* With the exception of Jay Jay, not one of those other Twisted Sister members played on even one song on the *Big Hits and Nasty Cuts* CD.

After more than eleven years and thousands of live shows with the band, I was on my own. Good thing I didn't get that Twisted Sister–logo tattoo I had been considering.

ARRIVING HOME AFTER THE demise of Twisted Sister, I was filled with a wide range of emotions. My home has always been my oasis, and with things back on the right track with Suzette, I couldn't have been happier. But leaving Twisted Sister, while a great relief after the months and years of intraband issues, was heartbreaking. I not only thought Twisted would be the band to take me to the top, but that I would be in it forever. *I loved being in Twisted Sister.* I had never seriously considered starting over.

Then there were my finances. I'd been terrible with money my whole life, always living on my next paycheck (and sometimes more) before I'd even done the work for it. I could not remember a time where I didn't owe somebody or some company money. No matter how much money I made, I was always using money I didn't yet have. I was painfully irresponsible.

Up until the *Come Out and Play* record, I was getting away with it. Things were always getting better, so there was no problem getting advances (no-interest money on future earnings), Even after *Come Out and Play* (which sold about a million copies worldwide), I wasn't completely down for the count. Dee Snider was considered a wild card. There was always a chance I might resurrect myself.

But after the absolute lack of interest in *Love Is for Suckers*, my proverbial goose was cooked. Not only had I run out of avenues to get legitimate advances (as opposed to actual loans or loan sharks), but Winterland, the merchandise company that had advanced Twisted Sister a million dollars, had been waiting in the wings to pounce.

We still owed Winterland almost all of that groundbreaking advance, and once the *LIFS* tour was canceled and I left the band, their lawyers put me on notice. They wanted their money and they wanted it *all* from me. Each band member had signed the contract with them *personally*, not as a corporation or a band, making us each responsible for the full debt if we defaulted. Since I was the one with the most money and assets, they wanted the entire amount repaid by yours truly. No pressure.

My people explained to their people that I was more than willing to pay back one-fifth of the total amount due, as I was only one of five members in the band. If they insisted that I pay the entire million-dollar debt, I would file for bankruptcy and they would get nothing. To this Winterland responded, they wanted it *all* from me, and they didn't care if I went bankrupt and they got nothing . . . *they wanted to make an example of Twisted Sister.* Nice bunch of guys, huh?

With that hanging over my head, I headed into what would turn out to be my ultimate demise and my longest period of inactivity. Of course, I had no idea of this at the time. Like any long, dark tunnel, I optimistically thought it had to end soon. *I was wrong.*

47

"putting the 'desperate' in desperado"

In rock 'n' roll, the lead singer/lead guitarist pairing is iconic: Robert Plant and Jimmy Page, Steven Tyler and Joe Perry, Mick Jagger and Keith Richards. In just about every great rock band with a lead singer, there has been that guitar-hero "foil," onstage and in photos, beside him, defining the band and providing the fans with a musical equal to the front man's bombast. Not in Twisted Sister.

Twisted Sister had two solid guitar players, but neither connected with the audience in that way. Eddie Ojeda is a great guitar player, but I think he lacks the flashiness to command the audience's true adoration. When I first joined Twisted Sister, I thought Jay Jay French would be that guy, and initially the audience connected with him. The Twin Towers of Rock 'n' Roll they used to call us.

The '60s and '70s guitar virtuosos stood flat-footed with their guitars up around their necks. The showmen ran around the stage, their guitars practically dragging on the floor, playing "dog doody" guitar riffs that wowed the crowd but were technically vacuous. Snake-oil salesmen. Of course there are exceptions, but for the most part this held true; you were either/or. Jay Jay was the latter, and people used to be impressed by his onstage antics (much to Eddie Ojeda's chagrin).

Then Eddie Van Halen changed everything.

The day Eddie Van Halen hit the scene, the game changed. He showed the audience, and a world of aspiring guitar players, you could have it all: be flashy and active onstage, technically stunning . . . and have a damn good time doing both. By the time Randy Rhoads showed up two years later, the fate of the old-school, all-flash/no-substance guitar player was sealed: nobody was buying their snake oil anymore.

So Twisted Sister climbed the road to international fame and fortune with that one important piece to the puzzle missing. *We didn't have a guitar god.*

While I'm pointing fingers, I need to direct one at myself. I wasn't willing to recognize this back then, but in all those legendary guitar/vocal duos, the front man provided one other thing besides a distinctive voice and performing ability: *sex appeal.* Every one of those legendary front men had the girls/women falling over themselves to get at them. Each and every one of them are what is known in the trade as cock rockers. *I am anything but.* I've never had much female appeal. If anything, I scared the girls away. Sure, some find my scary antics and attitude appealing, but not the masses. So, even if I'd had a Jimmy Page or Eddie Van Halen by my side in Twisted Sister, I didn't bring what was needed to the party. I'm quite the snake-oil salesman myself.

However, as I headed into my post–Twisted Sister world, I believed I could make the transition to cock rocker and knew the cornerstone of my new band had to be the singer/guitar-player duo. I needed to have substance as well as flash. I had to find my guitar god. I had achieved fame and fortune and become a rock star, but I wanted to be recognized as one of the greats. It pissed me off to be dismissed as a flash in the pan and a one-hit wonder. The musical and performing style of my choosing had bitten me in the ass and limited the rock audience's respect and appreciation for me. A large part of the rock world viewed me as "lucky." *Lucky?!* Struggling for eight and a half years, playing thousands of live shows, and being rejected by every record label—some multiple times—until you finally make it is not luck. Stupidity maybe, but definitely not luck. I had to do it again to prove my detractors wrong. My success was no accident: I had set out to do something, and against all odds I achieved it. Doing it again—and better than the first time—would shut all of their fucking mouths!

Part of my physical-training regimen was a regular five-mile run in a nearby nature preserve. On those runs—always with anger in my heart, my great motivator—I would listen to both new bands (Guns N' Roses' *Appetite for Destruction* not only did it for me, but gave me some of my best running times—7.6-minute miles!) and tapes of potential guitarists for my new project.

One day I was listening to a new band out of England called Mammoth and stumbled upon the perfect guitar player, assuming it was *one* guitar player and he would leave his band. Upon further investigation, I discovered that the guys in the band had brought in an Irish guitar player named Bernie Tormé to record the tracks. I knew about Bernie from both his egocentric solo efforts (Bernie Tormé's Electric Gypsies—he saw himself as the white Jimi Hendrix) and his stunning, yet short, run with Ozzy Osbourne, after Randy Rhoads's death.

Bernie received the call to take over for Randy shortly after Randy died. Apparently Bernie was one of the few guitar players *not* insensitive enough to ask for the gig while Randy's body was still warm. One guitarist I know, who shall remain nameless, actually woke Ozzy up in his hotel room hours after Randy Rhoads had died to ask for the gig. Ozzy wasn't pleased. Bernie Tormé not only had to learn all the songs, but to play the "hammer-on" style (tapping the strings on the fret board with your picking hand) Randy was known for. In two weeks Bernie was onstage at Madison Square Garden, shredding. Amazing. Ozzy asked Bernie to join the band permanently, and—"in the biggest mistake of my career" (Bernie's words)—he said no. Bernie was just out of Gillan (Deep Purple singer Ian Gillan's post-Purple band. Bernie was the guitarist in the band before Janick Gers) and riding high in Europe. He had a pretty major offer for a solo project (that whole "white Hendrix" thing) and was sure he would be a bigger star without Ozzy. Oops.

Bernie and I bonded over thoughts for a new group. I didn't want to be a solo artist. I never wanted to be a solo artist. Rock 'n' roll is meant to be played by a band, and with Bernie I now had the cornerstone of a new band that would not only take me back to the top, but show the world I was anything but a lucky, flash-in-the-pan one-trick pony who had stumbled upon his success.

Within a few weeks, Bernie Tormé came over to the States to begin the long, overly drawn-out process of songwriting, putting together the band, and recording our first album.

But I still had to deal with that pesky little bankruptcy thing.

BANKRUPTCY IS A SCARY word, but I quickly learned there are two different kinds: *rich people's* and *poor people's*. I was in the former category at that point—I would learn about the latter soon enough.

People with money and resources lose virtually nothing in this ridiculous process. By hiring the best bankruptcy law firm in the business, I was carefully guided through the—totally legal—process of protecting the majority of my assets and turning nothing of significance over to my creditors. Besides a missing Jeep and Cadillac hearse from my driveway, I wouldn't even have known anything had happened. My house, the vast majority of my possessions, my song catalog/rights—pretty much everything was secured and untouched by the proceedings.

My current economic condition (cash poor) was perfect for what I was about to go through. The bankruptcy allowed me to negate pretty much all of the contracts I was tied to—including the Winterland licensing deal—and start completely over with a clean slate. You would think that a bankruptcy would make potential business partners wary of getting involved with me, but it was just the opposite. Businesses viewed my being postbankruptcy as a positive. As far as they were concerned, I was unencumbered by past relationships and financial responsibilities ... *and I couldn't go bankrupt again for ten years.*

The bankruptcy was long and drawn-out, but once it was finalized, I was free to make new record and publishing deals. Despite the ultimate failure of Twisted Sister, I found quite a bit of interest in my new project and a small bidding war between labels. Ultimately, I signed a pretty handsome deal with Elektra Records, courtesy of A&R man Brian Koppelman.

Brian Koppelman was a hard-core, original SMFF of TS and son of music-publishing magnate Charles Koppelman. While still in college working on his law degree, Brian had discovered Tracy

Chapman. The success of Tracy's record got Brian a top A&R gig with Elektra and made him a young voice to be listened to by the completely disconnected upper-level execs. The timing couldn't have been better for me to connect with Brian.

Having grown up on Long Island, Brian had seen Twisted Sister forty-five times in the clubs before we ever even had a record deal. This was my first opportunity to pick the brain of one of these original Twisted SMFs, and I asked Brian why he had come to see my band so often.

"Because I believed you believed," he said with idiot-savant clarity.

What the hell did that mean? I pushed for an explanation.

"When I saw you on that stage, singing and raging about how you guys were going to make it—and with such conviction—I had no choice but to believe in you and follow."

Wow. Talk about the power of positive screaming.

His belief in me now spilled over to my new project, and Brian landed Desperado (my new band's name) a major deal.

I JUST SUMMED UP a year and a half of my life in a handful of pages. If only it were that easy. From the time I left Twisted Sister to the time I signed a new recording contract was a long, frustrating, snail's-paced period with the singular bright spot being the birth of my second son, Shane Royal Snider, on February 29, 1988.

Nineteen eighty-eight was a leap year, and seeing how Suzette was due around that time, I told her how cool it would be to have a leap-year baby. Suzette said she would see what she could do and—always the accommodating wife—delivered our second child on the day.

Suzette had gone back to school to get her hairdressing license to enhance her value as a professional makeup artist, prior to Shane's birth. She returned to finish the required thousand hours of training shortly after having the baby. Being off the road and home for a prolonged period for the first time, I got to take care of Shane while Suzette was in school (with the help of our nanny) and experience so many of the things I hadn't been there for with Jesse. While I loved the opportunity to bond with my newborn, it did emphasize just how much I had missed with my first. A mixed blessing.

THE ROAD TO PUTTING my new band together wasn't nearly as rewarding. Bernie and I wrote more than a hundred songs together while waiting for all my financial problems to resolve. Cowriting with someone for the first time, I discovered how having an actual musician creating the musical parts took my songs to a whole new level. It added an entire dimension previously lacking in my music.

I'd like to apologize to the guys in Twisted Sister for not making them a part of the songwriting while I was in the band. Unfortunately, the way our relationships evolved over the years precluded me from working with anybody. It would take massive success and leaving the band to finally free me of all the emotional baggage we developed and allow someone else into my process. And trust me, it didn't happen overnight.

On the upside, writing all of those songs and working together for many months allowed Bernie and me to focus our vision for what the band should be. It went from an extension of my *Me and the Boys* concept with keyboard and saxophone, to a power trio with vocals, à la Led Zeppelin.

The Desperado band was finally fleshed out with a young English bass player Bernie had worked with named Marc Russel, and former Iron Maiden basher Clive Burr on the drums.

I had always been a fan of Clive Burr's creative playing style. Say what you will about his replacement in Maiden, Nicko McBrain (a great guy and a great drummer), but Clive Burr helped define the Iron Maiden sound that has been the template for everything they've done since. Those first three albums he played on are still the core of Iron Maiden's legacy. They owe Clive a lot and, to their credit, do show their appreciation. Clive has become ill in recent years, stricken with multiple sclerosis, and Iron Maiden have been incredibly supportive and generous. They are a good bunch of guys.

With still no record deal in hand, and floating an entire band's weekly salaries, I headed to the UK to rehearse, demo songs, do a photo session (true to our name, the band had taken to dressing like

Wild West outlaws, complete with spurs), and whatever else needed to be done with the new band toward the end of 1988. During the two-month stay, Desperado would perform what would turn out to be its only show ever, at a club in Birmingham under the pseudonym The Clinky Bits, referring to all the "jingling" our spurs and jewelry did.

With my new band musically tight and ready to rock, I returned home for the holidays, waited for the Elektra deal to be locked in, and the contracts drawn up. This took months and months. It was maddening. All the while, my financial situation—which had been cleared up less than a year earlier—was quickly eroding.

By the time the deal was done and signed, it was too late. I'd been supporting first Bernie Tormé, then the rest of Desperado, and all the ancillary expenses (housing, equipment, plane flights, per diems, etc.) since the end of 1987. As we prepared to head into the studio to record, almost two years later, I was already back in debt. The huge advance and budget from Elektra for the first album wasn't enough to save me.

On top of everything else, Suzette and I had an unplanned, wonderful surprise: she was pregnant with our third child.

Just before preproduction was to start on the new album, I finally made a decision I should have made long before. We had to sell our house and downscale. I say *I* made the decision because I tried to keep the severity of our economic troubles from Suzette, partly because I didn't want her to worry, but mostly because I didn't want to hear her tell me the obvious: we needed to do something drastic to fix it.

In my defense, I thought about selling the house (which had doubled in value since we had bought it) a number of times, but my manager kept persuading me to hang on to it. "Real estate is gold," he would say, and it was. But he was thinking in terms of how he, an average guy, would handle things: hang on to your home at all costs and cut back on every other aspect of your spending. I couldn't do that . . . I was a rock 'n' roll star. I had a public image to keep. Seriously. Perception is reality, and if people still perceive you as a rock star, you are one. If the public sees you as a broken-down valise, that's what you are. Plus, I had no doubt, as soon as I got the Desperado record out, everything would be fixed, I would be back on the top of the charts, and all of my monetary problems would be solved.

As I headed up to Woodstock with the band and our producer, Peter Coleman, in October, to begin recording, even though I had come to terms with the need to sell our house, in my heart of hearts I was sure that it wouldn't be necessary. Suzette, on the other hand, now knew full well the seriousness of our situation and set to work preparing the house to be sold. Being the dollar-conscious woman she is, Suzette wouldn't spend more money we didn't have to hire people to do the work. Five and a half months pregnant, she did everything herself, no matter how big the job.

FOR SOME SCHEDULING REASON, we had a couple of days off in the beginning of December. Suzette had been killing herself preparing our house to be sold. I was constantly telling her to take it easy, I would hire people to do these strenuous jobs, but Suzette's not one for waiting. She continued to work and push way too hard. Suzette was on a mission to get the house ready for sale right after the winter holidays. Each month that passed we were falling deeper into a financial hole. Just before I came home that week, I called to find out she had literally been on all fours, scrubbing the kitchen floors. She was more than seven months pregnant!

I was heading back up to Woodstock the afternoon of December 7, but first I went with Suzette to her ob-gyn appointment for her routine monthly checkup on her pregnancy. Suzette lay on the table, her feet in the dehumanizing stirrups, and her longtime gynecologist, Dr. Deborah Zitner, began her examination.

Suddenly the doctor's face went white. "You need to get to the hospital immediately."

We were stunned by this pronouncement, the full reality of what this could mean not even beginning to hit us.

"Okay," I replied calmly, "we'll just stop off at our house and pick up Suzette's things." We lived only fifteen minutes from the doctor's office.

Still white as a sheet, Dr. Zitner said, "No. Don't stop off for anything. You've got to go directly to Schneider Children's Hospital.

They have specialists that can help you. You're going to have this baby today."

Completely confused, and now more than a little freaked out, we got in our car and headed to SCH instead of our local hospital, which was down the block. We were familiar with the hospital. It was almost an hour away. Jesse had been born at Long Island Jewish Medical Center, and Schneider Children's Hospital was their specialized wing for premature births and babies with birth issues. Having to go there was not a good thing.

When we arrived at the hospital, they were expecting us and rushed Suzette into a room. A doctor came in shortly after and proceeded to scare the living shit out of both of us.

He explained that not only was Suzette partially dilated (meaning the beginning process of childbirth had begun), but the placenta (the sac holding our unborn child) had broken loose and descended down the birth canal. Normally, after a forty-week, *full-term* (fully developed) pregnancy, the mother-to-be's water breaks (the placenta breaks), and the baby descends through the birth canal, free of the sac. Our baby was still in the sac, not full-term, and already beginning to exit my wife's vagina. That's why Dr. Zitner was so unnerved. She saw the baby, in the placenta, beginning to birth in her office!

As if that weren't already enough, in a now standard practice for doctors to protect themselves from any potential malpractice litigation, our obstetrician (he actually was a cool guy) told us the litany of things that might possibly be wrong with our about-to-be-prematurely-born baby . . . *including death.*

One of the great things about a normal, full-term pregnancy is that by the time a woman gets to that last month of carrying her child, she is so tired of it, and all its indignities (shortness of breath, low-back pain, swollen feet, heartburn, headaches, sweats, frequent urination, difficulty sleeping . . . do I need to keep going?), she is more than ready to go through whatever it takes to give birth. Hell, give her a scalpel and she'll take the baby out herself. Obviously I'm grossly exaggerating, but it's to make a point. Mentally, emotionally, and physically, by the end, most women are ready to give birth.

Unfortunately, at under thirty-three weeks into her pregnancy— a full seven and a half weeks early—Suzette was not nearly at that point. Given that, along with the panicked look on Dr. Zitner's face and the grocery list of nightmarish things that could be wrong presented by our new doctor, she was—understandably—freaked-out. I wasn't having the baby and I was freaking. We would not know the health or condition of our child until it was delivered, and that was positively terrifying. We were completely blindsided by this premature birth.

They induced labor (gave my wife drugs) so Suzette would be fully dilated for the birth. The minute they took Suzette out of the room to prep her for delivery, I got on a phone to my manager.

Calling him every kind of muthafucker, I unleashed all my frustration, fear, and anger on him. I irrationally blamed him for our baby's prematurity, believing that Suzette's Herculean effort while pregnant to prepare the house for sale had caused this. If he hadn't kept telling me not to sell the house (when I would have been available to help), this would never have happened. God help him if something was wrong with our baby!

Our third son, Cody Blue Snider, was born on December 7, 1989. Weighing only four pounds seven ounces, and looking like a scrawny chicken, he was otherwise totally healthy. Still, he was premature and would have to be monitored in the neonatal unit until he fattened up a bit and they were sure he was all right. Even healthy premature babies face potential problems. For example, Cody stopped breathing one night. Why? Because that's what premature babies sometimes do. They aren't developed enough to *remember* to breathe all the time.

Luckily, today's NICUs monitor babies for things like that and have alarms that go off so nurses can gently nudge the baby to get him or her breathing again. Freakin' scary, right? You bet it is. Fortunately, Cody experienced no further health issues and put on enough weight for us to take him home for the holidays. What a joyous Christmas gift!

REGRETTABLY CODY WOULD NOT be our last scare with premature birth. In 1996 Suzette would get pregnant for a fourth time, this time with our daughter, Cheyenne, and after only a few months of pregnancy, began to dilate and was in danger of miscarrying.

To prevent further cervical dilation and the baby's descending into the birth canal, Suzette was admitted to Schneider Children's Hospital, where she was committed to bed rest on a *decline,* and a variety of medications (some potentially lethal), for as long as she and they could keep the baby from being born. The hope was to build our daughter's birth weight and accelerate her physical development so she would survive.

When Cheyenne Jean Snider was finally born on Halloween night 1996 (I was in the delivery room wearing a Leatherface mask, of course), Suzette was thirty-three weeks pregnant and Cheyenne's birth weight was five pounds eight ounces. For a premature baby, she was a heavyweight. Like her brother before her, she had to spend time in the neonatal unit for observation.

While we were lucky not to have any of the major health issues of premature birth befall us, as you sit day after day in the NICU, you can't help but notice all the babies and families around you who are less fortunate. Some babies are born weighing less than a can of soda! Many preemies and their families have to endure a lifetime of health issues and hardships.

A few years later, I would discover (actually they found me) that the March of Dimes research and efforts helps those less fortunate families dealing with premature births and birth defects. Through being a grand marshal, chairing my own ride, and eventually becoming a national spokesperson for their Bikers for Babies Ride initiatives, I found a way to give back and show my appreciation for how lucky my family had been with our two preemies.

⚜ 48 ⚜

"whadaya mean you didn't listen to the record?"

We finally finished recording and mixing Desperado's *Ace* album by the end of that winter, then started the long process of readying the record for release. With my personal finances continuing to worsen, things seemed to take even longer and go that much slower. It was hell.

I found it positively painful to watch MTV. Hair metal was a massive force to be reckoned with at that time, and to have to witness bands that had opened for Twisted Sister on tour or, even worse, watched us in the clubs (hello, Bon Jovi and Poison) taking the spotlight was killing me. Twisted Sister—the band who had created the "hair metal" genre, helped to bring it to the mainstream, and whose videos changed the medium completely—had been utterly forgotten by MTV. Even my show *Heavy Metal Mania* had been changed to *Headbangers Ball* and was being hosted by someone I *knew* was being paid. Not much I'm sure, but I know Riki Rachtman got something!

In the spring, Suzette and I finally sold our house. While its value had doubled by the late eighties, the housing market was quickly softening in the winter of 1989/90 (perfect timing, eh?). But finally, the day of Cody's baptism and party, a couple came to see the place and were taken by the magic of a beautiful spring day and the family love pouring from us all at that important event. Though the market value of our home had dropped considerably from its peak, we still made a nice profit, solving our financial problems for the time being.

The plan was to buy a new house in Florida, near where the majority of Suzette's family lived. With my career and current "international" band, I no longer needed to live in New York as in my days with Twisted Sister. With the impending absences sure to result from my readying a major record release and hitting the road again in a big way to establish a brand-new band, it made all the sense in the world to move to Florida, where Suzette and our children would have the support of her loving family.

While I dealt with pre-record-release issues in New York, Suzette headed down to Florida and homed in on the perfect house. It was amazing how much further our money went down there. As the summer began, the date for our big move and my album release approached. Everything was finally falling back into place.

There's that word again . . . *falling*.

IN AUGUST, DESPERADO WAS set to shoot the video for our first single off the new record: "There's No Angels Here." This single and the rest of the songs on the record were the culmination of more than two years of creative struggle, during which I had put a lot of time into achieving artistic growth. By heavily studying the singing of Paul Rodgers, I'd reworked my vocal style considerably. Digging deeper into my more blues-based musical influences such as Led Zeppelin, Humble Pie, and Bad Company, and cowriting with Bernie Tormé, had improved my songwriting as well. The *Ace* album had—and still has—some of the best songs I ever wrote, recorded, or sang.* I couldn't wait to unleash it on what I saw as a doubting public.

I was literally packing to leave for England to shoot our video when I received a devastating call from my manager, Mark Puma. Elektra Records had dropped Desperado and shelved our album.

---

* Desperado's *Ace* CD was finally released on indie labels in 2006.

The news hit me as if I'd been told a family member died. I collapsed in a chair and listened to an explanation of how my record—which already had a catalog number and was in the Elektra database and slated for release in just weeks—had come to an end. Brian Koppelman—the fan who had signed us—had left the label for a better offer at a new record company called Giant Records. Insulted by Brian's move, Elektra got even with him by "shelving" *all* the projects he was working on. As if we were inanimate objects, Elektra Records shut down our careers. I couldn't believe it.

When I asked on what legal grounds they could do this, it turned out that one little phrase—actually one *word* in our contract did us in. "*Commercially* viable recording" instead of "*technically* viable recording" made all the difference in the world. *Technically viable* means you put the record in/on the player and it plays. *Commercially viable* means the album you deliver has to be salable, *which is completely subjective.* What is *salable* is so variable, the phrase leaves it up to the personal opinion of the individual. That phraseology is deliberately put in contracts as an out for the record label. A good lawyer will catch it, dispute its place in the contract, and have it changed. Unfortunately, I did not have the best lawyer, or manager, for that matter.

I had heard a story about Elektra president Bob Krasnow—not a fan of heavy metal—trying to do the same thing to Mötley Crüe on their second album, *Shout at the Devil.* Mötley's managers, McGhee/Thaler, stormed into Krasnow's office and threatened to do everything in the book to Elektra Records if they didn't release the record. Krasnow—disgusted not only to have to talk to these people, but to even have a band such as Mötley Crüe on his eclectic label—caved to their demands, promising to do nothing for the record and saying he would let it "die on the vine." This story was told to an associate of mine as they watched Bob Krasnow—wearing a Mötley Crüe headband—standing on his chair singing "Shout at the Devil" with the Crüe at Madison Square Garden after the album had sold over 2 million copies. So much for commitment to your beliefs.

That's how great managers handle the situation. My manager couldn't even get Bob Krasnow to return his calls.

When I finally spoke to Krasnow (whom I had never met—another mistake of my management's), and asked him how he could do this, the asshole replied, "Dee, it's nothing personal; it's just business."

Not personal!? It couldn't be any more personal.

"I'm sure your group is very good," he continued.

What?! He hadn't even *listened* to our record?!

"Hey," I recall him saying, "if it was up to me, I would get rid of all the heavy metal bands we already have on our label."

The audacity of this piece of shit! Those "heavy metal bands" he was talking about getting rid of included Metallica, Mötley Crüe, and the Cult. This was 1990; Metallica's *Black Album,* Crüe's *Dr. Feelgood,* and the Cult's *Sonic Temple* were selling millions upon millions of copies! Include the heavily metal-influenced Elektra band Queen, and those heavy metal bands were paying this arrogant fuck's salary and keeping the label afloat!

For the next year, my lawyer tried to get my band and me out of the recording contract, the rights to our songs returned, and the right to license the record to another label for a fair price. Elektra Records would not let me out of the deal or allow me to rerecord the songs, and the only thing they would accept in payment for the use of the actual masters was full reimbursement of the money they'd laid out for the deal—$500,000, or $50,000 per song.

This created problems for me on so many levels. The half a million dollars Elektra spent was an exorbitant amount, pushed up by the interest of other labels, a signing bonus, and money spent developing the project. The actual album-recording cost wasn't anywhere near that. Also, with Elektra shelving the record after spending so much money, even if other labels liked what they heard—*especially* if they liked what they heard—they wondered what was wrong with Dee Snider and Desperado that we had been dropped. The actual explanation just didn't make sense: Elektra ate half a million dollars to get even with an A&R guy who quit?

When we did get some interest from smaller labels to put out the record, Elektra held steadfast to their demand of full reimbursement. They would rather have nothing than something. I just couldn't understand the position they were taking. Finally, after months of struggle with the company, someone gave me the answer, off the record. They told me that Dee Snider's career seemed dead, but he might resurrect himself. The company view was, it's better to write off a half-million-dollar loss than to take a chance, let the record go, and have it be a hit for another label. That would be career suicide for whoever released me.

That I could understand. They were right. I don't do dead well.

While I struggled to salvage something from the now nearly three years of effort and hundreds of thousands of dollars of my own money spent (on top of Elektra's half million), Suzette and I were forced to reevaluate our housing situation. Buying another house was now out of the question. All Suzette's efforts in this area were for naught. It was August and we had to move out by September. Our only choice was to rent a house in Florida until I figured out what the hell I was going to do. I was at the end of my rope . . . when Ric Wake stepped in.

IN THE EARLY AND mid-eighties Twisted Sister recorded our demos at a studio in Merrick, Long Island, called Bolognese. Owned and run by an accordion-playing limo driver named Lou Bolognese, it did the trick for our pre-album recording.

Upon returning to Bolognese Studios to demo the songs for our *Come Out and Play* record, there I met a young English house engineer named Ric Wake. A nice kid, he was an aspiring producer and had signed a draconian employment contract with Lou Bolognese to both "assist" in the studio (read: do whatever work needed to be done, from engineering to cleaning the bathroom) and mix twelve-inch dance records for the local club scene. In exchange, Ric got to live in the boiler room with his hopeful future manager, Dave Barrat, practice his craft during studio downtime, and make something like $100 a week. Ric and Dave were so broke they used to share a chow mein dinner "special" at the local Chinese takeout each night, grabbing as many free bags of noodles and packets of duck sauce as they could. That was their meal for the day.

One day during a quiet moment in recording, Ric asked if I would listen to a song he had recorded. He had written it, sung all the vocals, played every instrument (except the drums), recorded the tracks (with the help of engineer Bob Cadway), and mixed it, all during downtime and overnights at the studio.

I was blown away with the kid's work.

A week or so later, I arrived at the studio to find Ric extremely shaken. When I asked him what was wrong, nearly in tears he told me how he had asked Lou Bolognese to release him from his indentured servitude—I mean, *employment contract*—and Lou had threatened to break his legs. Ric was terrified.

Now, to young English Ric and his pal Dave, any Italian American with a Brooklyn accent had to be in the mob. When Lou threatened them, they took it dead seriously. Not only did I know real mobsters—which Lou was not—but I also knew Lou was in discussions with Island Records, a subsidiary of Atlantic, to distribute his dance records. Lou was hoping to make the giant leap from accordion player to record mogul. I'll bet that would have been a first.

I walked into Lou's office and sat down. Lou was happy to have the attention of an actual rock star.

"Did you threaten to break Ric's legs?" I said. Why pussyfoot around?

Lou was taken aback. "Dee . . . when I told Ric I'll 'break your legs,' I didn't mean *literally*, I meant *figuratively*." Pretty eloquent for a "mob guy."

"So, Ric can leave if he wants to?"

"Of course. He can leave whenever he likes," replied Lou, from the corner I had put him in.

I moved to lock the deal. "That's good, Lou, 'cause I don't think Island Records would like to hear someone they're considering doing business with uses threats of violence to get what he wants."

"Believe me," Lou said, panicking, "the kid misunderstood my intentions. He can go anytime."

I left Lou's office and told Ric the good news. He couldn't believe it.

"Believe it," I said, "but leave as soon as you can, before he changes his mind. You did sign a contract."

Ric and Dave packed up their stuff as quickly as they could and were out that night.

A week or so later, I brought Ric to Cove City Sound Studios, a major Long Island recording studio, owned by Billy Joel's sax player, Richie Cannata. I recorded there from time to time. I introduced Richie and his partner, Clay Hutchinson, to Ric, telling them what an amazing talent he was and how they should give him a shot. On my word (and hearing his great-sounding tracks), they let Ric work in the studio for free during the overnights (usually three or four in the morning until 10:00 or 11:00 a.m.).

Ric immediately began secretly working with another artist signed to a terrible Lou Bolognese contract, Leslie Wunderman, aka Little Leslie Wonder. Within the year, Ric had recorded a full album with her, Leslie had got out of her deal with Lou, and Ric got record mogul Clive Davis to sign her to Arista Records. Leslie's new stage name (which she gives me undeserved credit for) was Taylor Dayne. Her first Ric Wake–produced album, *Tell It to My Heart*, had four Top 10 songs and went double platinum in the United States (plus worldwide acclaim). Ric Wake's producing career was shot out of a cannon.

Ric Wake was/is one of those loyal people who never forgets what you do for them. This is rare and amazing, but not the reason I helped him. So few people ever gave me or Twisted Sister a hand, I vowed to help other struggling artists whenever I could. I do not want others to go through the hell I did. It beats the joy out of you.

I WAS SO DEVASTATED by the destruction of my career and personal finances by Elektra Records, I was practically catatonic. Ric Wake now lived in a huge, custom-built home only a few miles away from me. Since first meeting at Bolognese Studios, we had become close friends (and still are).

Ric came over to my house to have a talk with me. "You are going right back into the studio and starting work on a new band and album."

I stated the obvious: "But I don't have any money or a record deal."

"Don't worry about that. You can record in my studio for free while we put together a new band and get you a deal."

Ric was now the *co-owner* of Cove City Sound Studios, and a powerful and influential person in the music business. Since his success with Taylor Dayne, he'd produced multiplatinum records for Mariah Carey, Celine Dion, and Jennifer Lopez, and he still always credits me with giving him his start. Now he was returning the favor.

Still, I was defeated and packing up the house with Suzette for our move to Florida in weeks. "Ric, I appreciate your offer, but I really don't feel like recording."

"I don't give a shit what you feel like doing. You're going back into the studio. *You are not giving up!*" Ric was not taking no for an answer. He could see how beaten I was and was forcing me back onto the proverbial horse.

So, shortly after moving out of our house on Long Island and getting situated in a nice rental house Suzette had found in Coral Springs, Florida, I flew back up to New York and began work on new music for a new band and a new label. Of which I had none. It was heading into 1991 and I was starting completely over.

The first order of business was to get me free from my deal with Elektra Records. They didn't actually drop Desperado; they shelved the record and *suspended* my contract, preventing me from recording for anyone else. My lawyer, who represented me when I signed personally for the Winterland deal and my Elektra contract with the words "commercially viable," had been working for months trying to get me cut loose from Neglect-tra (a name Joe Lynn Turner of Rainbow—another Elektra Records victim—came up with), but to no avail.

Twisted Sister's longtime entertainment lawyer, and now mine, was Clay Knowles, a former guitarist from a band with Twisted's first bass player, Kenny Neill. He had been representing the band since their earliest club days, and Clay proudly displayed on his office wall the double-platinum *Stay Hungry* album we presented him. It shone alone.

Ric Wake was connected with the most influential shakers and movers in the music industry and insisted I finally meet his attorney, Bobby Flax of Grubman, Indursky & Schindler, the most powerful law firm in the entertainment industry.

"This guy will be able to help you," Ric promised.

I couldn't see how, since Clay Knowles had exhausted every possible avenue (at great expense to me) trying to get my situation with Elektra straightened out.

When Ric and I walked into the law offices of Grubman, Indursky & Schindler for our meeting with Bobby Flax, I was nearly blinded by the wall-to-wall platinum and gold albums of virtually every major artist in the music business. At their peak the firm represented a large percentage of the top recording artists in the world. Amazing. My lawyer's only success was Twisted Sister.

Ric was warmly welcomed. Why shouldn't he be? Ric had produced some of Grubman, Indursky & Schindler's biggest clients, and they represented Ric as well. Notoriously, Grubman, Indursky & Schindler (along with most of the other major entertainment law firms) were also on retainer by every major record label. That meant they were negotiating for both sides on most deals, playing each against the other, but ultimately beholden to whoever paid them the most. It was as incestuous as it could possibly get!

Bobby Flax asked me to explain my situation to him—which took me all of about three minutes—then he picked up the phone and dialed from memory.

"Steve? It's Bobby."

He listened for a second, then replied, "She's good. How's Mindy?"

Who the hell was he talking to? And on my dime?!

"Sure, sure. We'll do dinner with the girls next week," Bobby continued his casual conversation. "Listen, I'm sitting here with Dee Snider and I need to get him out of his deal." Bobby listened again. "Sounds fair. Have your secretary write something up and fax it over for signature. I'll see you Thursday on the links."

With that, Bobby hung up and nonchalantly turned to me. "You're free to record for whoever you want, and you can use the original Desperado masters or rerecord the songs at a rate of five thousand dollars per track, with a two-point override."

What?! I was out of my deal and could use the original tracks at an affordable rate? *Was he kidding me?!*

He wasn't. With one short call to "a friend" he had solved all my problems—as a favor to Ric!

I was stunned. I had wasted almost a year and spent thousands of dollars trying to get loose from Elektra's stranglehold and blown the only interest in Desperado there was from a couple of indie metal labels. They both fell by the wayside because they couldn't come close to paying Elektra's demand for half a million dollars for me and my band. They sure as hell could have afforded $50,000, but now those ships had sailed.

Free of the Elektra albatross from around my neck, I started over. I hoped to use the guys from Desperado as my new band—they, too, had gotten killed by the whole mess—and both Bernie Tormé and Marc Russel signed on immediately. Unfortunately, Clive Burr wouldn't be involved if there was no paycheck. In fairness to Clive, not everyone is willing or can afford to work for free.

With drummer Joe Franco taking Clive's place, we began writing and demoing songs in hopes of landing a new deal and getting our musical careers back on track. Bernié Torme and I worked on songs transcontinentally, while Marc Russel moved to the States and took up residence in Ric Wake's house. Yet another generous gesture on Ric's part. I was back in business.

AS THE WEEKS AND months dragged on, with absolutely no money coming in, I had to draw on the profit we had made on the sale of the house to keep the family afloat. The money we had hoped would be used to buy a new home for the five of us was slowly being eaten away. The lifestyle change and the move to Florida had certainly reduced our monthly nut, but not enough. Yet I still firmly believed I was a rock star and what I was experiencing was just another temporary setback, soon to be rectified. I really needed to get a clue.

Suzette and I didn't take to life in Florida immediately. After the first month we wanted to run back to New York screaming. The second month, we seriously considered taking our own lives. By the third month, we were starting to adapt, and a full six months in, our blood thinned, and we were full-blown Floridians.

Our home life was amazing. While I was spending a lot of time in New York, whenever I came back to Florida, it was like going on vacation. Suzette and the kids would pick me up at the airport in her hot-pink Jeep (rock stars gots ta have their cars) and whisk me home for day after day of retirement-like living. Suzette and my relationship just kept getting stronger, despite continuously growing financial concerns.

The need to batten down the hatches and find ways to live more economically seemed to be bringing us closer. Even my loss of popularity and recognition had an upside: I was able to relax and we started acting like a normal family for the first time. I know that may sound humdrum to most of you, but believe me, a degree of normalcy in an abnormal life has advantages. It was a screaming bright lining to a steadily darkening cloud.

TRY AS RIC WAKE might—and using all of his considerable influence— he could not find a taker in 1991 for a new Dee Snider project. Despite that hair bands and heavy metal could not have been more popular, to the industry my career couldn't have been deader or my value less. Ric—a huge believer in his ability to judge talent and songs, and in Dee Snider—refused to give up. In a last-ditch effort to get me a deal, Ric started his *own* record company, Esquire Records, to put out my album.

I could not have been more blown away by this insane gesture. The idea of someone raising the capital, opening facilities, hiring staff, and setting up distribution just for me still has me shaking my head in disbelief to this day. But that's what Ric did.

When I was finally ready to begin recording a new album, the project had another huge setback when Bernie Tormé was admitted to the hospital because a black spot was discovered on his lung during a routine chest X-ray. When Bernie awoke—in an oxygen tent—from his biopsy, through the tent he heard his doctor say, "I've got good news and bad news." *Uh-oh.* Those are words you never want to hear in a hospital.

The good news was the spot on Bernie's lung wasn't cancer, it was just a spot. The bad news? They had punctured Bernie's lung during the biopsy. As a result, Bernie had a long hospital stay ahead of him, followed by more recuperation and an extended period of being unable to fly. The pressurized cabins of airplanes might cause his lung to collapse again. Bernie Tormé could not be a part of my new band. Were we living under a black cloud or what?!

Upon the high recommendations of a number of people I respected, guitarist Al Pitrelli was enlisted to replace Bernie. Al had

worked with quite a number of major and minor artists, most nota-
bly Alice Cooper during the *Trash* album and tour (and since with
Megadeth and the Trans Siberian Orchestra), and had everything we
needed for the type of band we were putting together, except one:
his personality. I found Al to be an arrogant, self-important SOB,
and I predicted to Marc Russel and Joe Franco that he wouldn't last
six months with me. I was wrong. Al Pitrelli lasted for two records
and tours, would later help create and record the Van Helsing's
Curse project with Joe and me, and remains a good friend to this
day. Sorry, Al; I misjudged you.

The music of my new band consisted of Desperado-era Tormé/
Snider outtakes, some rerecorded Desperado *Ace* album tracks,
a cover of a classic Howlin' Wolf song ("Evil"), and a couple of
Pitrelli/Snider originals, including what would become our first single and video, "The Widowmaker."

The song title was taken from an ill-fated Luther Grosvenor aka
Ariel Bender (Spooky Tooth, Mott the Hoople) and Bob Daisley
(Rainbow, Ozzy Osbourne) band of the same name. Oddly, the
father of my bass player, Marc Russel, had been the tour manager
for the original Widowmaker.

When wrestling with a name for the new band, Ric Wake said,
"Why don't you use the name of your song and call the band Widowmaker?"

We explained that there had already been a band called Widowmaker.

"I never heard of them," said Ric. "Were they popular?"

"No," I replied.

"When were they around?"

"In the mid-seventies."

"That's like twenty years ago!" Ric exclaimed. "Who gives a
shit?!"

In fact, virtually nobody cared but Marc Russel, who was taught
to play by the Widowmaker bassist, Bob Daisley.

"My dad will 'take the piss out of me'* if I'm in a band called
Widowmaker," Marc complained. "I can't do it."

---

* "Make fun of" in English slang.

I thought for a minute, then responded, "What if I get Bob Daisley's blessing?"

Marc said that would make him feel a bit more comfortable, so I got Daisley on the phone.

"Hey, Bob, this is Dee Snider. How would you feel about me using the name Widowmaker for my new band?"

"I don't give a shit," Daisley replied. "We did fuck all with it!"

Blessing received.

We weren't the first to recycle a band name. Irish guitar god Gary Moore had a band called Skid Row long before the American band of the same name, and there was a Trixter before the New Jersey band of the same name started singing "Give It to Me Good." We weren't the first and sure as hell wouldn't be last.

Widowmaker was born.

With the album-cover artwork would come the next indignity. I was informed that due to the lyrical content of the CD, the complex cover design (better in concept than execution) that I had worked so hard on with Esquire Records' art department would need to have a PARENTAL ADVISORY label on it. I couldn't believe it.

"I thought stickering your record was optional?" I said.

"It is, and our distributors label their records," Ric Wake told me. "Some stores won't carry an explicit record without a sticker."

One of my fears about these warning labels was coming true. Labeling your record wasn't exactly optional if stores wouldn't carry your record if you didn't. Even worse, some stores were using the label to segregate records or, even worse, not rack or even carry the record. And in a real catch-22 with some stores, if you *didn't* label your explicit record they wouldn't carry it, and if you *did* label it, they wouldn't carry it. *That's not much of a fucking option, if you ask me!*

Just when I thought it couldn't get any worse, it did.

"Oh, yeah," Ric added, "it's not a sticker, its part of the artwork."

What!? Was he fucking kidding me!? Indignity heaped upon indignity. They took the art on the cover and made the warning label a physical part of it, something that could not be removed after purchase. *The idea boggles the mind!* These conservative assholes were taking it upon themselves to mutilate an artist's vision. Don't get me wrong, I'm not saying the *Blood and Bullets* cover art was a work of genius, but the very thought of doing something like this was an insult to artists everywhere.

"You either do it or they won't distribute your CD," Ric finished after listening to a long, expletive-laced tirade from me in need of its own PARENTAL ADVISORY sticker.

If I had known about this in advance, I would have made the PARENTAL ADVISORY sticker the album cover and put a sticker-size square of the album art on the sticker.

That's what's known as irony.

⚜ 49 ⚜

pissin' against the wind

In the spring of 1992, Widowmaker's *Blood and Bullets* was unleashed on a literally unsuspecting public by fledgling indie label Esquire Records. After a four-and-a-half-year absence from the music scene, Dee Snider—sort of—had a new band and album out. Say muthafuckin' hallelujah!

By the summer, the CD had made enough inroads on the scene that the band was ready to tour. In August, after a week of rehearsals, *Windowmaker* (the first radio ad for the band mispronounced our name) made our premiere performance at the Live Wire nightclub in Stanfordville, New York. It was essentially my first time back onstage in almost five years. I never thought I would be away for so long.

Widowmaker toured through the end of 1992, slowly building awareness of my new project and album sales. We had crossed a major indie-record plateau of fifty thousand CD sales and were starting to show signs of life, when the *final* final nail was driven into the coffin of my creative career and financial stability. Esquire Records closed its doors. Actually, they didn't close their doors as much as the Canadian government seized all their property and chained their doors shut. Esquire Records' Canadian financiers had raised their money in a *questionable* manner, and the Canadian authorities weren't happy about it.

With the death of Widowmaker's label came the end of the

record's availability, the end of the tour, and the end of the band. Just like that, I was finished and out of options. No more record-company or publishing-company advances (I was deep in the red), no more credit-card cash advances or charging (the cards were all maxed out), no more lines of credit or loans (I was a bad credit risk). I was 100 percent, absolutely, without a doubt, totally done. *Check and fucking mate.*

I RETURNED TO MY wonderful family—my oasis—for the holidays and, in 1993, began desperately trying to figure out my next moves... of which I had none. I was further delving into screenplay writing (something I had started after my experiences with making rock videos) and was working on my third screenplay, *The Junk Squad*. A family film, based on my kids and their friends in our Coral Springs neighborhood, I would eventually sell it (a couple of times to different studios, but it was never produced), but that wouldn't happen for years.

The last of our house-sale money was running out, and I began to make desperate financial moves such as selling our possessions, cashing out retirement-plan money, and selling the valuable Disney stock my father had given me for the kids.

When I met Suzette, I knew if I could win her heart, I would have someone who loved me for me and be with me through thick and thin. Well, things had gotten *paper-thin*, but there was never the slightest doubt that she would stay by my side through these darkest of times. We started out with nothing, got everything, and now, even though we'd/I'd lost it all, Suzette still stood shoulder to shoulder with me. I had written the Desperado song "Ride Through the Storm" * about her, and since Bernie Tormé and I had created it in 1988, things had gone from bad to way worse.

The storm had turned into a Category 5 hurricane.

Obviously, we could no longer afford our beautiful rental house

---

* It was later recorded and released on my Koch Records solo album, *Never Let the Bastards Wear You Down*, as "Ride Through the Storm (Suzette's Song Part 2)."

in Florida, so in the summer of '93, Suzette and I went up to New York and searched for a much more economical rental to move our family into. I couldn't foresee any work for me in Florida (I didn't even know what kind of job I could get) and thought my chances for some kind of employment were better back North.

The rental houses we went to see were terrifying. Impoverished living conditions in downscale neighborhoods were all we could afford. I couldn't imagine living in them and having people sooner or later figure out it was *the* Dee Snider, lead singer of the multiplatinum band Twisted Sister, living there. That my poor family had to suffer as well for my failings made me feel even worse. The true humiliation of this next massive step down began to set in.

Having run out of time and options, and about to lock in one of the awful choices Suzette and I had found, a brand-new real estate ad appeared in the paper. In the realm of what we were dealing with, it seemed too good to be true: a suitable house for rent in a good school district, for the right price. We rushed to see it immediately and snapped it up. All things considered, it was perfect. Well, at least it wasn't horrible.

Whereas professional movers had moved us down to Florida in August of 1990, in the last week of August 1993, we packed up all of our belongings, loaded up a couple of rental trucks, and with the help of Suzette's brother Billy, moved our stuff back to Long Island ourselves. Our family and friends met us at the other end and helped us stuff thirty-five hundred square feet of furniture and possessions into a nineteen-hundred-square-foot house. We had sold off all but one of our cars—the pink Jeep—and downsized what we could, but still we had a basement filled with stuff we hoped would one day furnish our *own* house again.

WITHIN ONE WEEK OF cramming my family and what was left of our belongings into our run-down Long Island rental house, my dog was run over by a car and killed. *Are you fucking kidding me?!* It was like living some terrible country song: "I lost everything, then my dawg dieeeed!" What a freakin' nightmare! This was how things continued to spiral downward, yet I still wasn't defeated. Why?

Because my wife and children were all fine, and I was healthy and strong enough to get up each day and try again. This was and still is my sole criterion for staying positive and continuing to fight.

Picture the reverse: I had all the money, fame, and success in the world, but my family life was a mess. To me, that is the definition of true tragedy. Sure, we all want and hope to have it all, but it doesn't always work like that—especially not for me . . . *then*.

With no income to support our family, Suzette immediately stepped up and got a part-time job at a local hair salon. Though loath to do it, she did because it needed to be done. Imagine you're working in a beauty parlor, washing someone's hair, and through conversation (or gossip) they find out you're Dee Snider the rock star's wife. You can predict the question that followed every time: "Why are you working here?" The mainstream views rock 'n' roll stardom the same way aspiring rock stars view it . . . as a finish line. Most think that once they've heard people on the radio or seen them on television, they must be set for life. If only.

The money Suzette brought in working part-time at a salon surely helped, but it wasn't enough to pay all the bills, and I certainly wasn't going to put the weight of the family's well-being on her shoulders alone. But if I couldn't record or perform music, what else was I qualified to do? As my mind raced through the terrible few job choices a former rock star with no other talents, training, or abilities could do, an opportunity was presented to me. Albeit a humbling one.

My brother Matt and his wife, Joyce, had a few businesses going and needed an office assistant to answer phones, do some light bookkeeping, and make calls. This menial labor paid just $5 an hour. Matt knew I was looking for some kind of work, but was hesitant to even mention it to me, for fear he might insult his rock star older brother. *When he did, I jumped at the offer.*

Though the job paid terribly, it had two valuable aspects: my brother's office wasn't in a public area, and since this was the early nineties and computers were not as ubiquitous as they are today, Matt said I could tell people I was there using his office computer to work on my new screenplay. I'd be an employee undercover!

With only one car in the family, I couldn't leave my wife and children without transportation. Fortunately, my brother's office wasn't too far away. Every morning, I would get on my bicycle and ride the four miles to work, passing through a cemetery on the way. This brought me back to the perspective Marty Callner had made me aware of that day almost ten years earlier in LA: *at least I was still aboveground!*

BETWEEN THE COUPLE OF hundred bucks I was making each week and the money Suzette was bringing home, we were barely squeaking by—and we still had debts. Looking at our second bankruptcy in less than five years (only I had gone bankrupt the first time; now we would have to bankrupt Suzette), I wanted to make every effort to work something out before reneging on what we owed and completely destroying what was left of our credit.

I contacted the Better Business Bureau's debt-consolidation arm to discuss their helping me somehow get our creditors to ease up on us. The only way the BBB would take a look at my situation was for me to bring my "books" to their Manhattan offices and meet them face-to-face. *This was my worst nightmare!* I could not imagine a more embarrassing situation, but I had to do it. I had no one to blame for the financial mess we were in but me. I almost wished I'd drank and got high, because then I could at least blame my screwing up on the alcohol and drugs.

I gathered up all the financial records, tax returns, and bank statements showing my economic demise, got on the Long Island Rail Road, and rode into the city. At the BBB, I sat with all the others suffering from overwhelming debt and waited my turn. Even with my hair pulled back and wearing a baseball cap, I was sure everyone there recognized me, though no one said anything. Why would they? Would any of them in their wildest dreams—would I, in my wildest dreams, for that matter—imagine that Dee Snider from the multimillion-record-selling rock band Twisted Sister would be sitting next to them on the Better Business Bureau's debt-consolidation bench?

When my turn came, I entered the office and laid out my case. I danced around the issue of exactly what I had done as an entertainer to make a living.

Finally the examiner asked, "What kind of entertainer were you?"

"A singer."

"What kind of singing do you do?"

"Rock." I wasn't giving away any more than I had to.

"In a band?"

"Yes," I said, fighting the tide.

I could see she was clearly getting tired of playing Twenty Questions. "Mr. Snider, what band did you sing with?"

"Twisted Sister," I mumbled.

Thankfully, my caseworker was unimpressed. That was probably the only time I was happy someone didn't care.

After going over all the numbers and my situation, she concluded the BBB could do nothing to help me. My only recourse was to file for bankruptcy . . . *again*. This time it would not be some luxurious, high-end, everything-handled-by-the-best-lawyers, lose-nothing-and-come-out-smelling-like-a-rose bankruptcy. This was going to be a DIY, down-and-dirty, starting-over-from-the-bottom bankruptcy. The only upside was we had already bottomed out and had nothing left to lose.

Starting over again is every bit as ugly as you might imagine. Thrift shops become your friends (and thank God for 'em), and cutting coupons is a must. You can't do anything unless you find a deal or a sale—everything is done on the cheap—and what a treat all-you-can-eat buffets are. The kids love 'em.

Don't get me wrong; there's no shame in doing these things. It was some of the smartest money-handling we ever did. It's just that after having struggled so long, and having finally made it to the top, to have lost it all and fallen so far . . . living this way was a constant reminder of my epic failure.

The toughest part for us was the impact it would have on the kids. All parents want their children to have the best of everything; especially the things they never had. To have to say no to our kids was terrible. It made us feel like bad parents. We wouldn't even let them come into a convenience store with us because we didn't have the money to spare to get them a piece of candy. We were that fucking broke!

Both a blessing and a curse when you are doing poorly is the outpouring from family and friends. While you welcome the help and appreciate their "donations," you feel even worse about yourself and loathe their pity. One of those donations was from my brother Doug. He had a 1984 Toyota minivan (oddly the year of my greatest success) he had bought from our brother Matt (and still owed two payments on) he used for his hardware/lawn-mower store as a service vehicle. Doug and his employees had run the odometer up past 135,000 miles and put huge holes in the floor. The car still ran great, but looked and smelled like shit, so Doug was going to get rid of it. He asked me if I would like to have it. I jumped at the offer.

With a little elbow grease, some pieces of sheet metal for the holes in the floor, and a hand-cut carpet, Galileo (the nickname I gave it because it looked so much like the space shuttle on the original *Star Trek* television series) was ready to transport our tribe wherever we needed to go. We were grateful to have it.

ONE DAY SUZETTE CAME to me with another idea for how she could make some extra money. Brides-to-be and their wedding parties often paid to have their makeup and hair done for the big day; she had seen many of them come into the beauty parlor where she worked. Suzette thought she could make money going to brides' homes the day of their wedding, and doing them up for a fee. Other than the fact that I would be sending my wife and mother of my children into total strangers' houses, it sounded like a good idea. We were desperate. All she needed were customers, so I printed up flyers to put on windshields of parked cars at the same local catering hall we had had our wedding reception at eleven years before. *I had officially hit rock bottom.*

As I headed out that night, I didn't allow myself to feel bad. I still had "it." That feeling of completion I had discovered driving with my young family all those years ago. With the exception of Suzette's and my near breakup several years earlier, I had never lost "it," and through all the ups and downs, "it" had been the one constant that kept me going. As long as I had Suzette and the kids—and they were happy, safe, and healthy—I had it all. And as long as I could get up each day and continue to fight the good fight—providing for them the best that I could—I had nothing to gripe about. Whining and complaining creates negative energy, and I am all about staying positive. With Suzette, Jesse, Shane, and Cody in my life, a roof over our heads, and food in our bellies—while there was plenty more to achieve and want—I had everything I needed.

I still had "it."

Unbelievably, things *did* get worse. By the mid-nineties my sole *obvious* talent became obsolete. With the advent of grunge, it was as if I had spent my entire life studying and working in a field of medicine where the disease had been cured. The record-buying public no longer had any interest in the way I sang, performed, looked, or wrote songs. Heavy metal—especially my brand—could not have been deader.

I released a second Widowmaker record, this time on the fledgling CMC Records (thanks again to Ric Wake, Pam Rousakis Praetorius, and company), *Stand By for Pain*. This great record tried to embrace the changing times, but as one MTV executive put it, "Kids want their own rock 'n' roll heroes, not their brothers'." Maybe not true in Ozzy Osbourne's case, but certainly in mine.

Since I needed to do other things to pay the bills, I couldn't commit the time Widowmaker needed to make it happen. I did allot a couple of months to tour and help promote the CD, but we were cut short when our drummer, Joe Franco, got his hand slammed in a van door on our way into a show. This was just the straw that broke the camel's back. Things hadn't been going well, and I was tired of pulling into towns for a show* only to find no CDs in the stores.

---

* During my post–Twisted Sister days, I always insisted on driving the van that would transport my band from town to town. Not that I wanted to drive, but I viewed it as self-flagellation for my failure. I was punishing myself.

The record company support was pitiful. My brother Mark, who had gone from radio production to record promotion, observed that my even being aware of how much product was in the stores meant I was getting too old for a young man's game. He said the same conditions most certainly existed in the early days of Twisted Sister, but I was too naive to know any better and just continued to smash my heavy metal head against the wall until the band's fans and the record stores *demanded* our album. Young Dee Snider didn't "allot" time for a tour and call local record stores to find out how many pieces of "product" were in the bins. Young Dee Snider put his head down, dug in his five-inch heels, and charged.

Mark was right.

Yet another of my brothers, Matt, when I related my maddening need to prove that I wasn't a one-hit-wonder, uttered these life-changing words: "Does it have to be music?"

"What?"

"Well, if you are a success in another field, won't that prove it wasn't an accident? Wouldn't that prove it wasn't luck?"

He was right. All this time I had been fighting the tide to prove my value when I could just as effectively have made my point by succeeding at something else.

But what? What else could I do?

OVER THE NEXT ALMOST two decades, I would do, and succeed at, a lot of different things. My long climb back to the top was filled with a lot of struggle, strife, love, and plenty more "Dee Life Lessons." But you'll have to wait for *Shut Up and Give Me the Mic Part 2* to read about that. (Sorry.) In a nutshell, I started out studio-managing a stable of writers for Ric Wake's publishing company (it was hard for them to act egotistical with someone who had sold more records than they had), then moved on to worked in creative development for a toy company (thank you, Don Spector and Balzac). From there, my careers in both voice-over and radio blossomed. Besides all the commercials and documentaries I've voiced, in 2000 I was the voice of MSNBC ("*Hardball with Chris Matthews.* Tonight at eight on MSNBC!"). My radio career took me from a late-night metal show on Long Island (Thanks, WRCN!) to successfully doing morning talk radio in Hartford, Connecticut (WMRQ), and Richmond, Virginia (WRXL), to evenings in Philadelphia (WMMR). As of this writing, my weekly syndicated radio show *The House of Hair* is entering its fifteenth year and can be heard on more than two hundred stations in North America.

The advent of *The House of Hair* in 1996—a show dedicated to *my* era of heavy metal—reflected a change in the musical climate. While hair metal certainly wasn't returning, people were looking back at it fondly. The minimalist stage-production values and "life sucks and I wanna die" messages of the grunge era made some rock fans yearn for the Decade of Decadence and the middle-finger attitude of eighties rockers. Suddenly my music was no longer an embarrassment, and I had the publishing statements* to prove it. I eventually paid back all the money I had been advanced over the years, and I've never gone back in the red again. Fool me thirty-seven times, shame on me!

The nostalgic interest in eighties rock led to the reunion of Twisted Sister. Originally instigated for *Eddie Trunk's New York Steel,* a concert event staged to help the families of the police, firefighters, and EMTs who lost their lives on 9/11, we have been doing sold-out shows, for massive crowds, the world over, for more than a decade.

My writing career has done pretty well, too, as I've sold a couple of television-show ideas and a few screenplays. The one film I wrote that's been produced, *StrangeLand*, I also starred in. It led me to acting and television work.

I've done quite a bit of television (hosting, reality, and as an actor) and some other films as well, since my bottoming out in the early nineties, including *Growing Up Twisted*, *Gone Country*, *Howard Stern's Private Parts*, and VH1's *Warning Parental Advisory*. And somehow I've become one of the voices of my generation. As Alice Cooper said, I guess they just got used to me.

---

* Publishing statements are documents reflecting music sales, airplay, and licensing (commercials, television, movies, etc.). When there is a lot of activity, they are always accompanied by a nice big check.

• • •

IN 2010, I WAS asked to star in the hit Broadway show *Rock of Ages,* one of the 100 longest-running shows on Broadway, centering around the club scene of the Los Angeles Sunset Strip in the 1980s. Featuring the greatest music of that time—*including two of my songs!*—it shines a light on a musical era that rock 'n' roll critics and historians look down their noses at, but audiences loved . . . and still do.

But it didn't stop there.

As of this writing, I'm part of the 2012 *Celebrity Apprentice* cast (and did well) and have recorded a star-studded album called *Dee Does Broadway*. My career is headed in a whole new direction and I'm becoming a bigger star then I ever was in the '80s. Hell, I've even had my memoirs published!

IT WAS STANDING ON the stage of the Brooks Atkinson Theatre opening night, taking my curtain call, that the full realization of how far I'd come washed over me. Suzette and my now-grown children—including my granddaughter, Logan Lane—were in the house, and the crowd was on its feet, cheering, while behind me the cast sang the refrain of Journey's "Don't Stop Believin' " over and over. The lyrics hit me like a ton of bricks:

"Don't stop believin'. Hold on to that feelin'!"

In the years since that terrible night putting flyers on cars, I had fought, clawed, and struggled my way back to the top. Now I was taking my bow on Broadway? How the mighty had fallen . . . *and risen again!*

Through it all, my wife and children had stood by me, but there was one word—one poem—that had also inspired me to never give up. Written by William Ernest Henley—a man who suffered from lifelong tubercular disease—it's entitled "Invictus":

Out of the night that covers me,
Black as the pit from pole to pole,

I thank whatever gods may be
For my unconquerable soul.

In the fell clutch of circumstance
I have not winced nor cried aloud.
Under the bludgeonings of chance
My head is bloody, but unbowed.

Beyond this place of wrath and tears
Looms but the Horror of the shade,
And yet the menace of the years
Finds and shall find me unafraid.

It matters not how strait the gate,
How charged with punishments the scroll,
I am the master of my fate:
I am the captain of my soul.

Don't ever stop believin'. . . . *Invictus!*

Thank-Yous

Ron Starrantino
Mick Foley
Joe Gerber
Dave Marfield
Randy Jackson
Jesse Blaze Snider
John French
Adam Green
Eddie Ojeda
Mark Mendoza
Anthony Pero
Alfred "Ralph" Allen
Savage Steve Holland
Lisa Marber-Rich
David Katz
Traci Ching
Don Specter
Eric Hermann
Larry Meistrich
Cooch Luchese
Danny Stanton
Sheryl Buckridge
Terri Baker
Mitchel H. Perkiel

Matt Mangus
Kevin McPartland
Pam Edwards
Steve Lehman
Jay Beau Jones
Eric Sherman
Eric Luftglass
Ric Krim
Chuck LaBella
Greg Bavaro
Michael Caputo
Ed Schlesinger

And most of all to my wife and children for their constant support and encouragement through it all and during this entire writing process. I love you all more than you will ever know. . . .

Page 9:
Photo 1: Courtesy of the author's personal collection
Photo 2: © Mark Weiss

Page 10:
Photos 1–3: Courtesy of the author's personal collection

Page 11:
Photos 1 and 2: Courtesy of the author's personal collection

Page 12:
Photo 1: Courtesy of the author's personal collection
Photo 2: © Mark Weiss

Photo 13:
Photo 1 and 2: Courtesy of the author's personal collection

Page 14:
Photo 1: © Mark Weiss
Photo 2 and 3: Courtesy of the author's personal collection

Page 15:
Photos 1 and 2: Courtesy of the author's personal collection
Photo 3: © Bruce Dworkin

Page 16:
Photos 1 and 2: Courtesy of the author's personal collection
Photo 3: © Jeff Katz, Los Angeles Studio

Photo Credits

Page 1:
Photos 1–4: Courtesy of the author's personal collection

Page 2:
Photo 1: © Sal Di Bennetto
Photo 2: Courtesy of the author's personal collection.
   Photo credit: Laurie Palahnek

Page 3:
Photos 1–3: Courtesy of the author's personal collection

Page 4:
Photos 1 and 2: Courtesy of the author's personal collection
Photo 3: © Sal Di Bennetto

Page 5:
Photo 1: © Sal Di Bennetto
Photo 3: © Chip Rock

Page 6:
Photos 1–4: Courtesy of the author's personal collection

Page 7:
Photos 1–3: Courtesy of the author's personal collection

Page 8:
Photos 1–3: Courtesy of the author's personal collection